KOYOHARU GOTOUGE

Hi! I'm Gotouge. Volume 18 is out. Thank you very much to everyone who supports the series. Thanks to the wonderful anime they made, it seems more people have been picking up the graphic novels, for which I'm incredibly grateful. I had no idea this would happen, so I'm trembling for many reasons. I took my comforter to the cleaner's at a poor time, so I'm cold every day. But until the day I get it back, I'll wear multiple layers and work hard.

DEMON SLAYER:
KIMETSU NO YAIBA
VOLUME 18
Shonen Jump Edition

Story and Art by
KOYOHARU GOTOUGE

KIMETSU NO YAIBA
© 2016 by Koyoharu Gotouge
All rights reserved. First published in Japan
in 2016 by SHUEISHA Inc., Tokyo. English
translation rights arranged by SHUEISHA Inc.

TRANSLATION John Werry
TOUCH-UP ART & LETTERING John Hunt
DESIGN Jimmy Presler
EDITOR Mike Montesa

Printed in Italy

Published by VIZ Media, LLC
P.O. Box 77010
San Francisco, CA 94107

10 9 8 7 6
First printing, November 2020
Sixth printing, October 2021

viz.com

KIMETSU NO YAIBA

ASSAULTED
BY MEMORIES

KOYOHARU
GOTOUGE

CHARACTERS

TANJIRO KAMADO

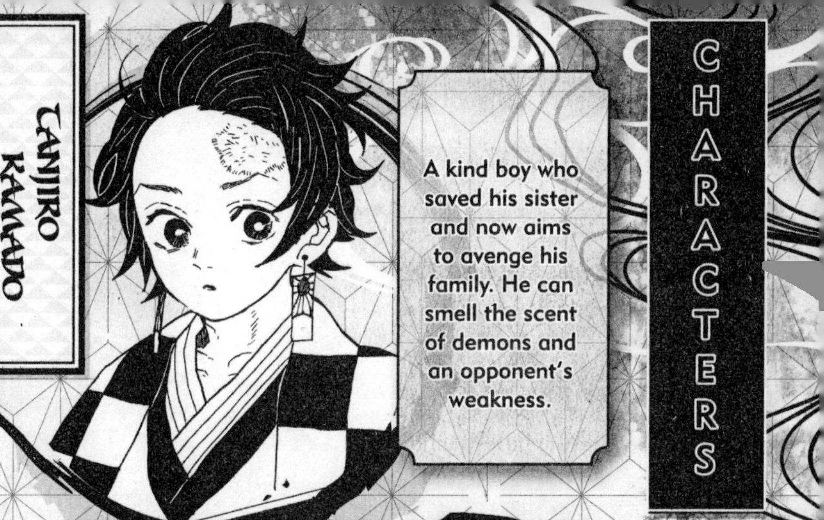

A kind boy who saved his sister and now aims to avenge his family. He can smell the scent of demons and an opponent's weakness.

NEZUKO KAMADO

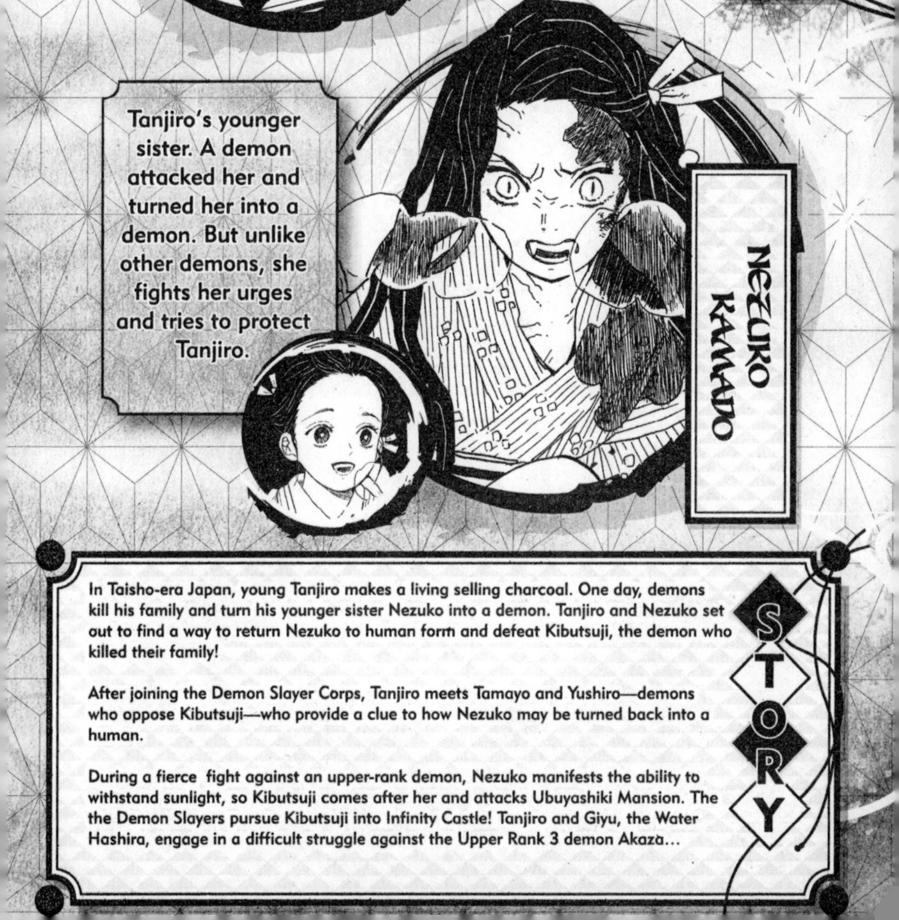

Tanjiro's younger sister. A demon attacked her and turned her into a demon. But unlike other demons, she fights her urges and tries to protect Tanjiro.

STORY

In Taisho-era Japan, young Tanjiro makes a living selling charcoal. One day, demons kill his family and turn his younger sister Nezuko into a demon. Tanjiro and Nezuko set out to find a way to return Nezuko to human form and defeat Kibutsuji, the demon who killed their family!

After joining the Demon Slayer Corps, Tanjiro meets Tamayo and Yushiro—demons who oppose Kibutsuji—who provide a clue to how Nezuko may be turned back into a human.

During a fierce fight against an upper-rank demon, Nezuko manifests the ability to withstand sunlight, so Kibutsuji comes after her and attacks Ubuyashiki Mansion. The the Demon Slayers pursue Kibutsuji into Infinity Castle! Tanjiro and Giyu, the Water Hashira, engage in a difficult struggle against the Upper Rank 3 demon Akaza…

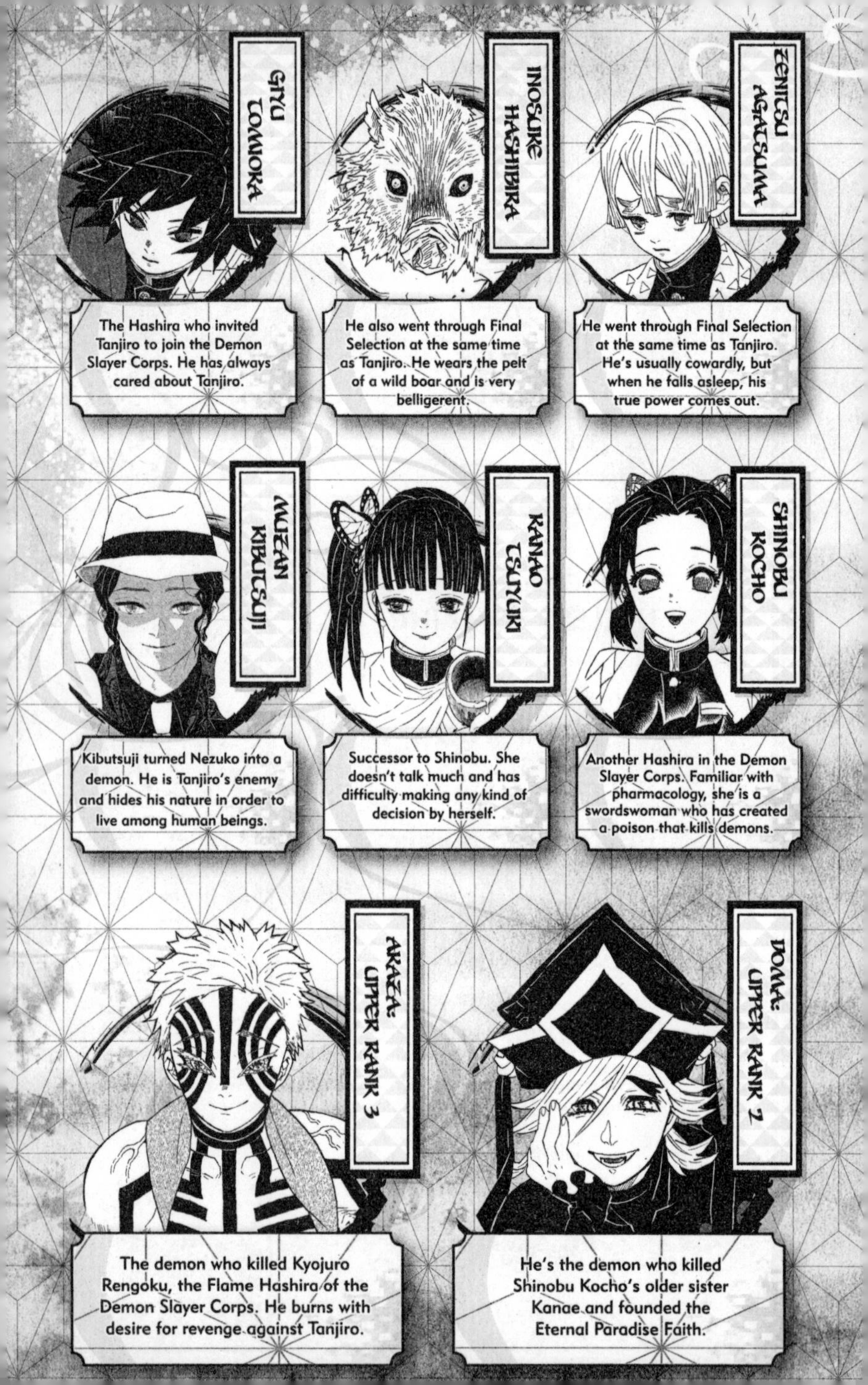

ZENITSU AGATSUMA
He went through Final Selection at the same time as Tanjiro. He's usually cowardly, but when he falls asleep, his true power comes out.
INOSUKE HASHIBIRA
He also went through Final Selection at the same time as Tanjiro. He wears the pelt of a wild boar and is very belligerent.
GIYU TOMIOKA
The Hashira who invited Tanjiro to join the Demon Slayer Corps. He has always cared about Tanjiro.
SHINOBU KOCHO
Another Hashira in the Demon Slayer Corps. Familiar with pharmacology, she is a swordswoman who has created a poison that kills demons.
KANAO TSUYURI
Successor to Shinobu. She doesn't talk much and has difficulty making any kind of decision by herself.
MUZAN KIBUTSUJI
Kibutsuji turned Nezuko into a demon. He is Tanjiro's enemy and hides his nature in order to live among human beings.
DOMA: UPPER RANK 2
He's the demon who killed Shinobu Kocho's older sister Kanae and founded the Eternal Paradise Faith.
AKAZA: UPPER RANK 3
The demon who killed Kyojuro Rengoku, the Flame Hashira of the Demon Slayer Corps. He burns with desire for revenge against Tanjiro.

CONTENTS

DEMON SLAYER

KIMETSU NO YAIBA

18

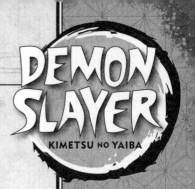

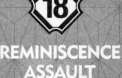

REMINISCENCE ASSAULT

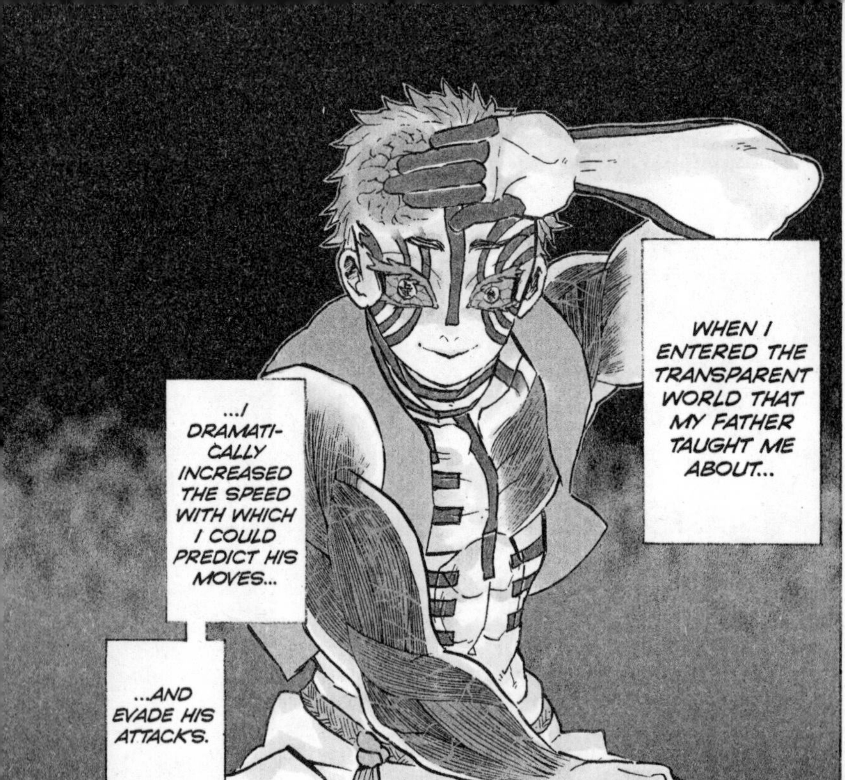
WHEN I ENTERED THE TRANSPARENT WORLD THAT MY FATHER TAUGHT ME ABOUT...
...I DRAMATICALLY INCREASED THE SPEED WITH WHICH I COULD PREDICT HIS MOVES...
...AND EVADE HIS ATTACKS.
CHAPTER 152: THE TRANSPARENT WORLD

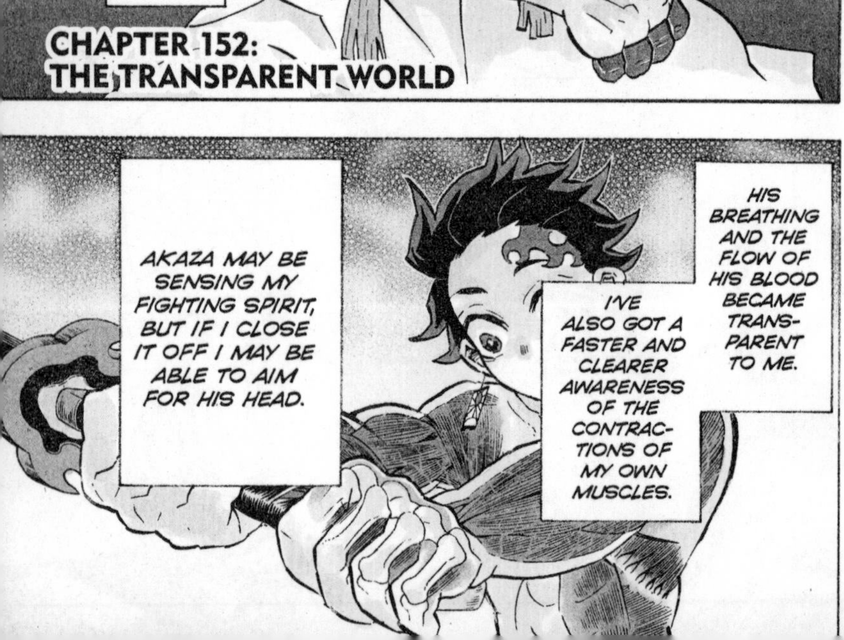
HIS BREATHING AND THE FLOW OF HIS BLOOD BECAME TRANSPARENT TO ME.
I'VE ALSO GOT A FASTER AND CLEARER AWARENESS OF THE CONTRACTIONS OF MY OWN MUSCLES.
AKAZA MAY BE SENSING MY FIGHTING SPIRIT, BUT IF I CLOSE IT OFF I MAY BE ABLE TO AIM FOR HIS HEAD.

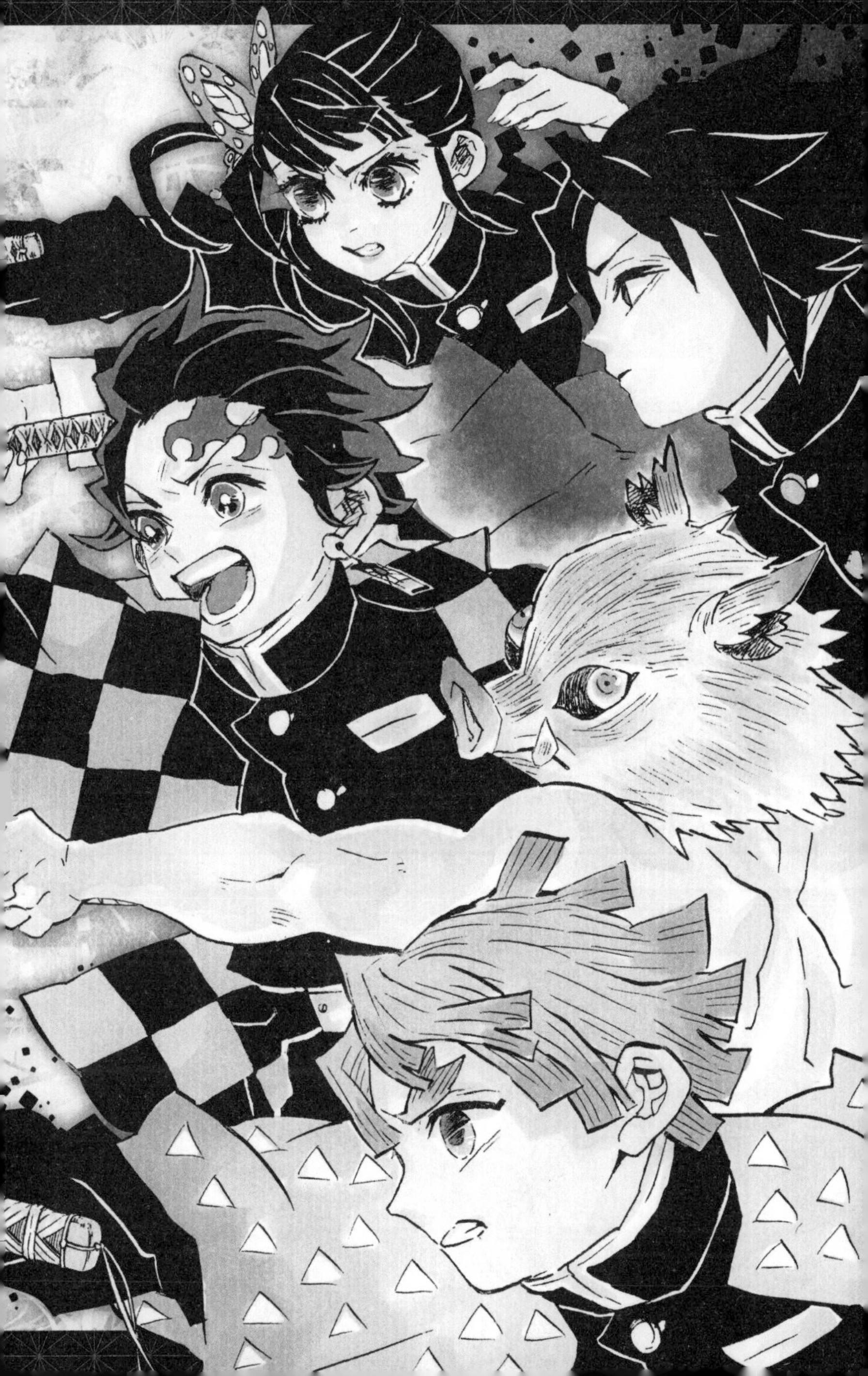

CHAPTER 152:
THE TRANSPARENT WORLD

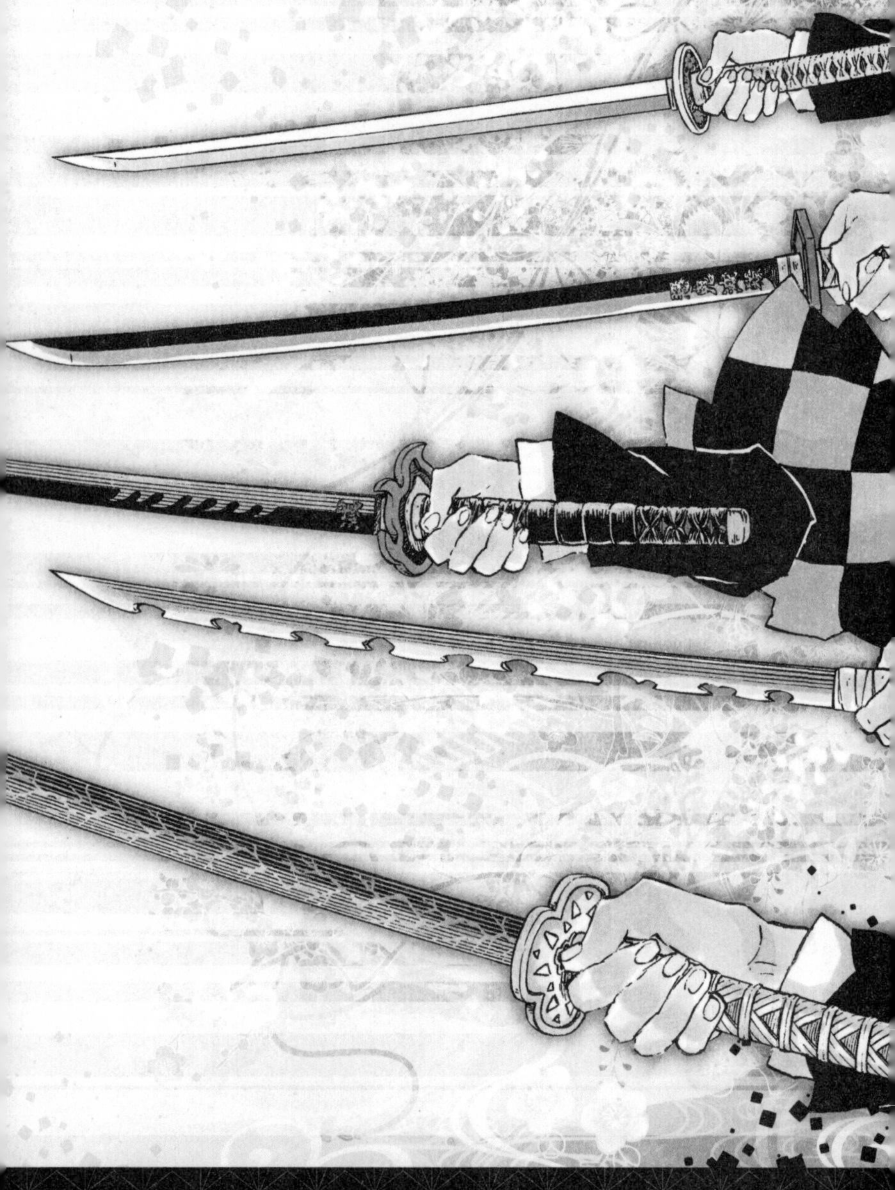

Inosuke before the previous two-page spread.

No, Inosuke! Everyone is facing the other way!

THRUST THRUST

HOP HOP

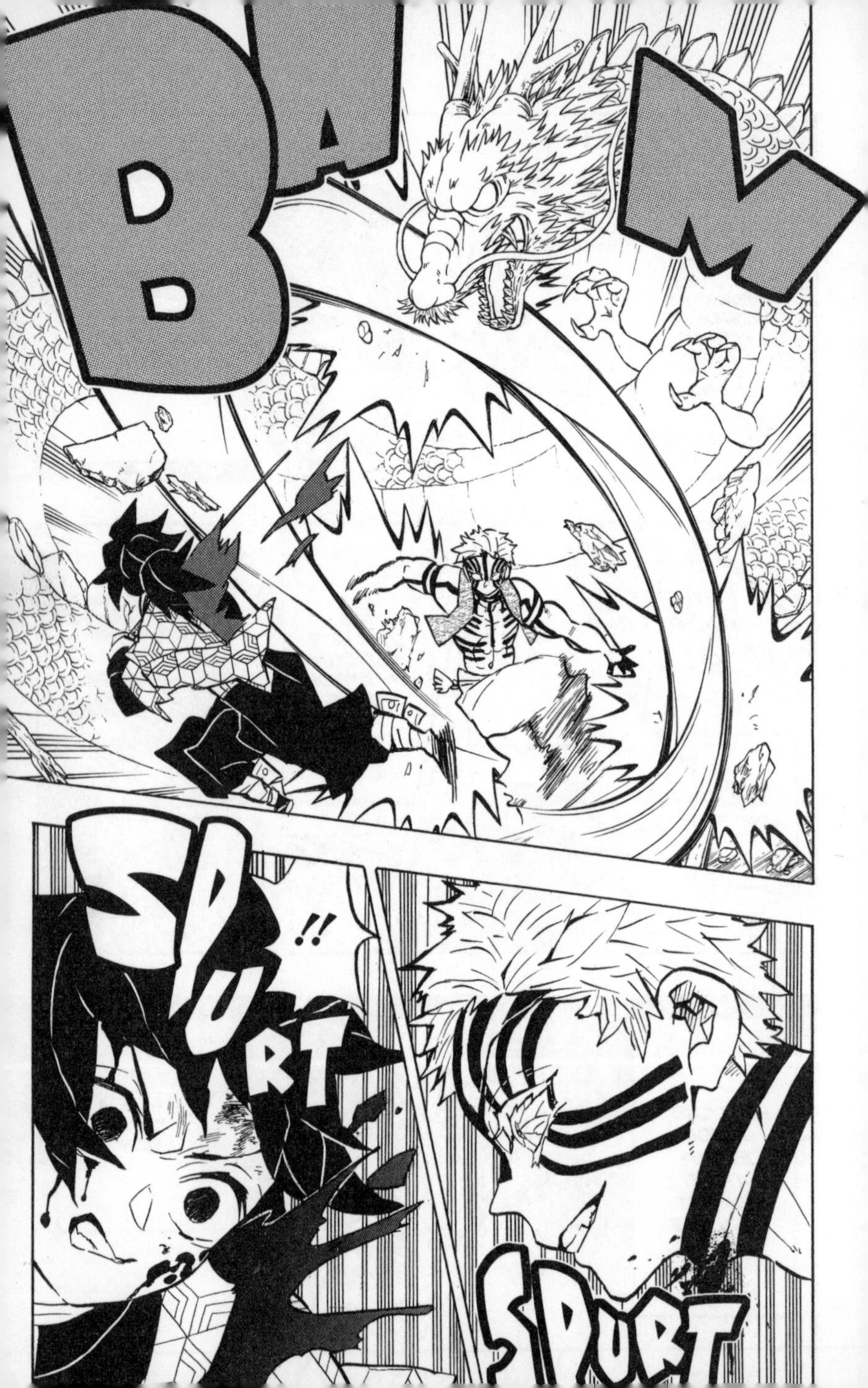
BAM
SPURT
SPURT
!!

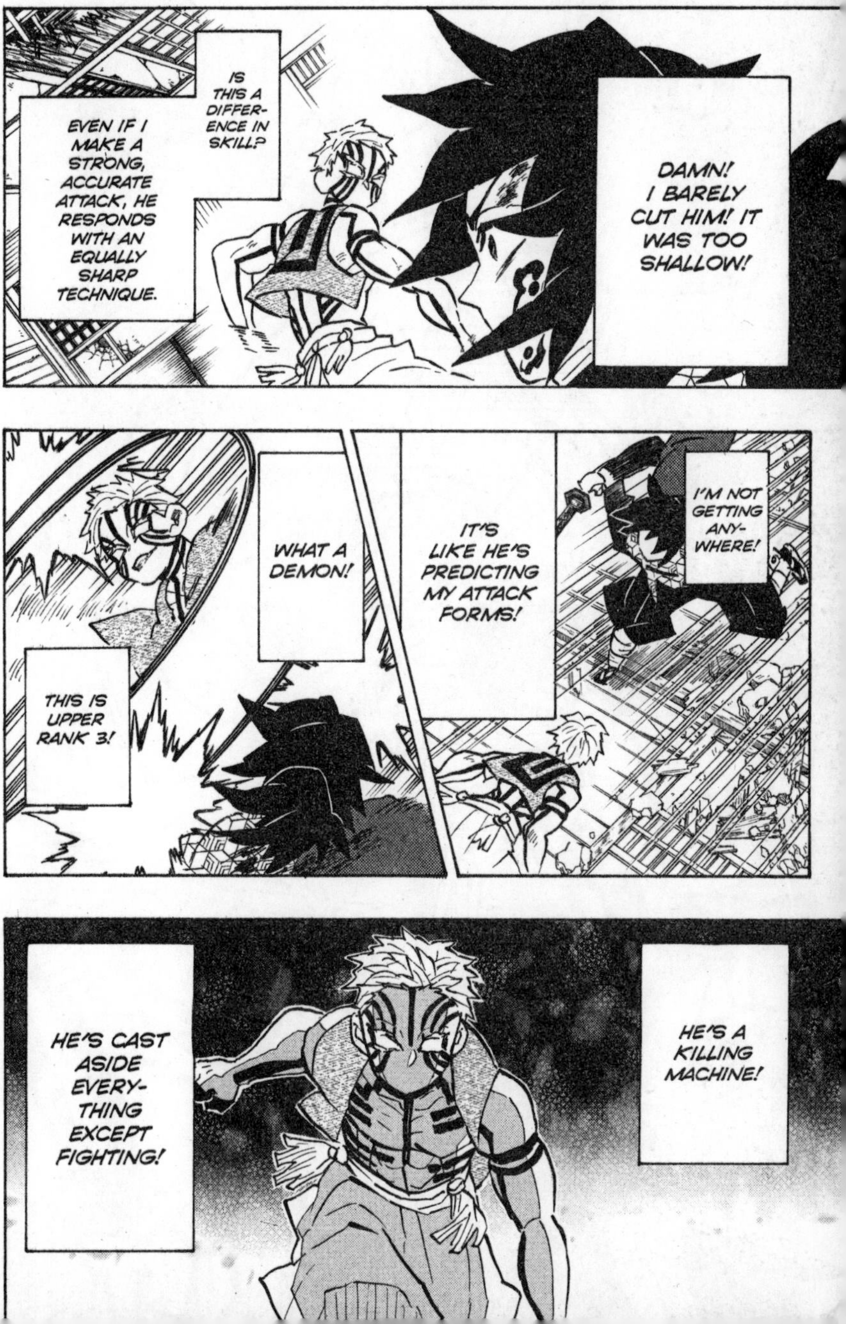
DAMN! I BARELY CUT HIM! IT WAS TOO SHALLOW!
IS THIS A DIFFERENCE IN SKILL?
EVEN IF I MAKE A STRONG, ACCURATE ATTACK, HE RESPONDS WITH AN EQUALLY SHARP TECHNIQUE.
I'M NOT GETTING ANYWHERE!
IT'S LIKE HE'S PREDICTING MY ATTACK FORMS!
WHAT A DEMON!
THIS IS UPPER RANK 3!
HE'S A KILLING MACHINE!
HE'S CAST ASIDE EVERYTHING EXCEPT FIGHTING!

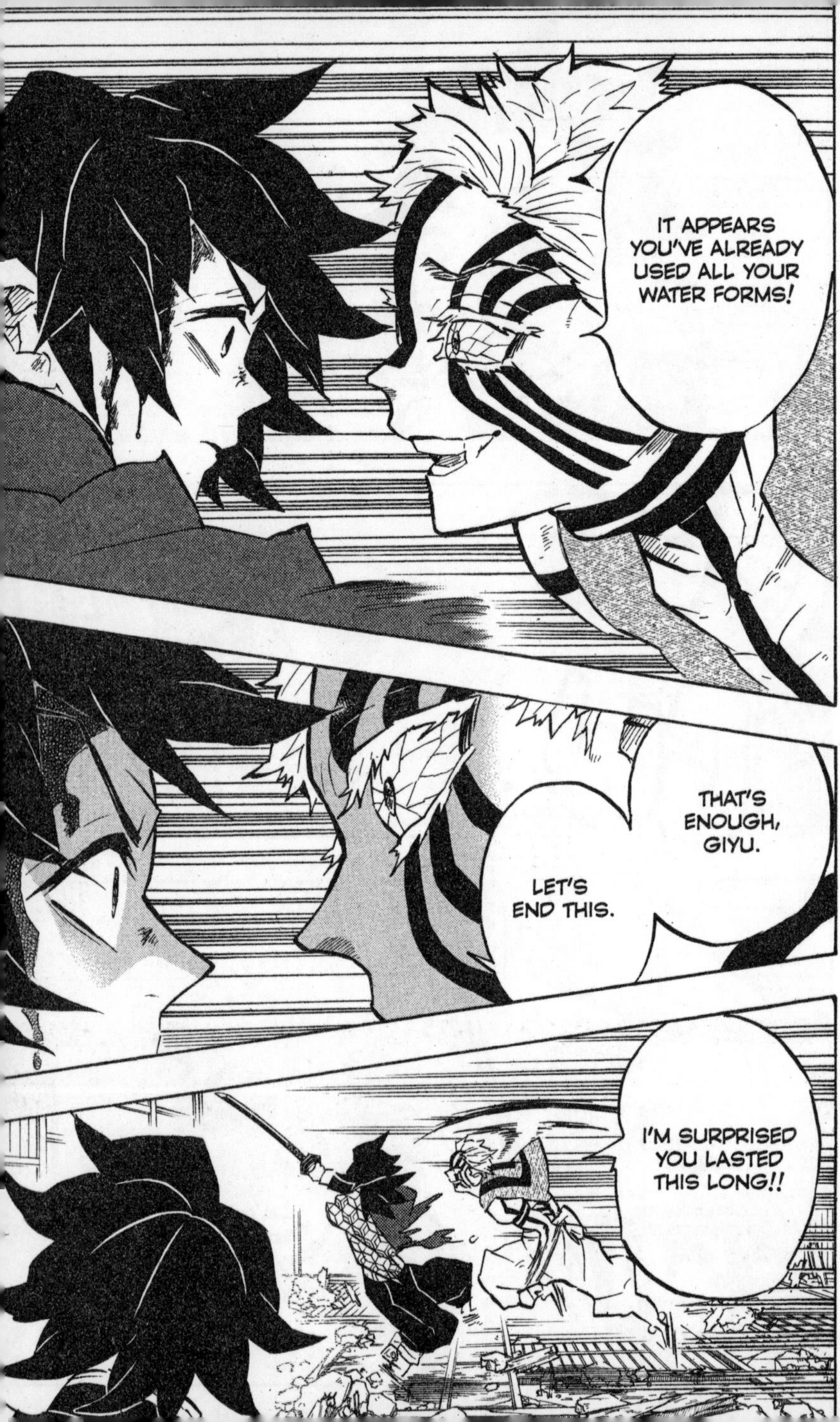
IT APPEARS YOU'VE ALREADY USED ALL YOUR WATER FORMS!
THAT'S ENOUGH, GIYU.
LET'S END THIS.
I'M SURPRISED YOU LASTED THIS LONG!!

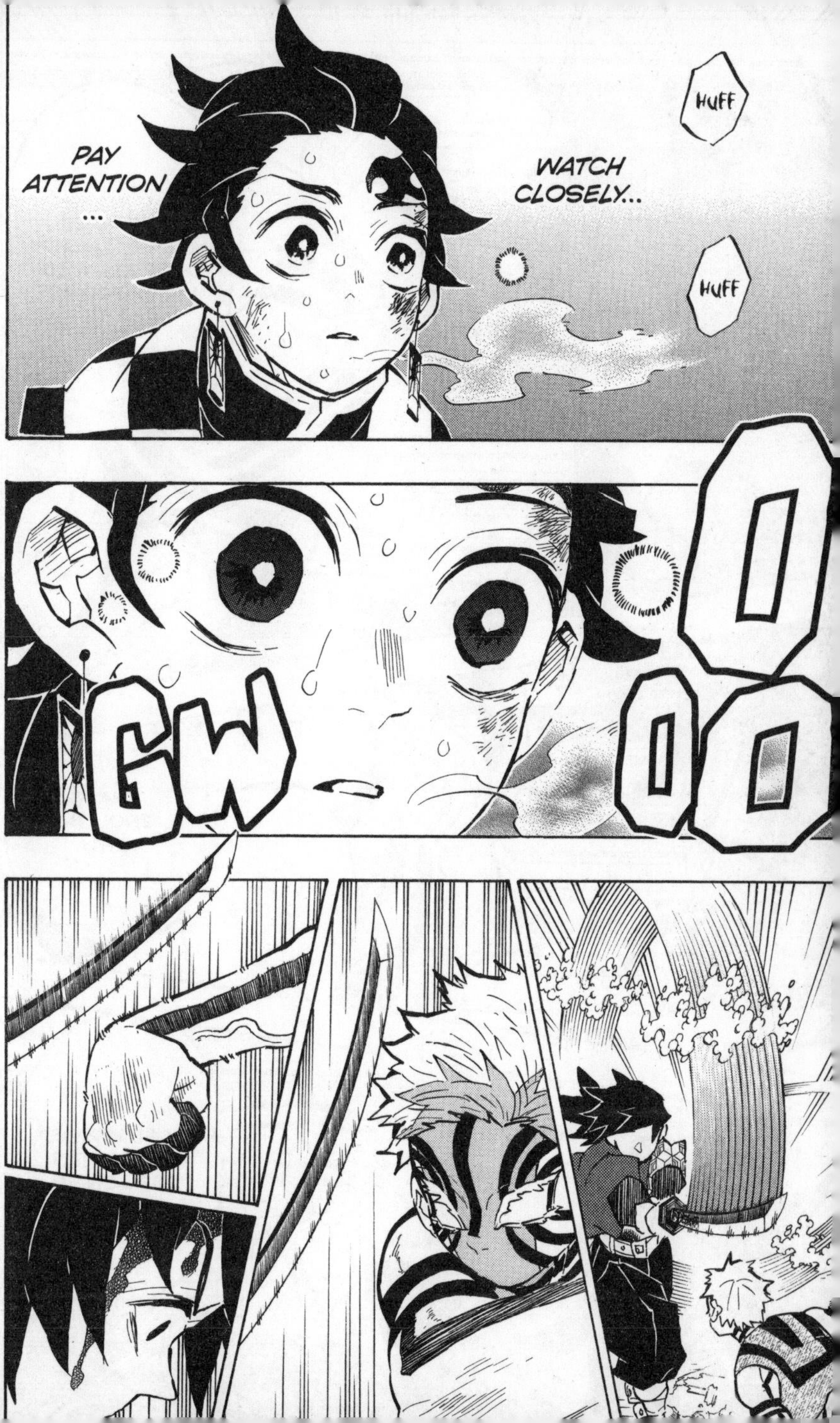
HUFF
HUFF
WATCH CLOSELY...
PAY ATTENTION ...
GWOOOO

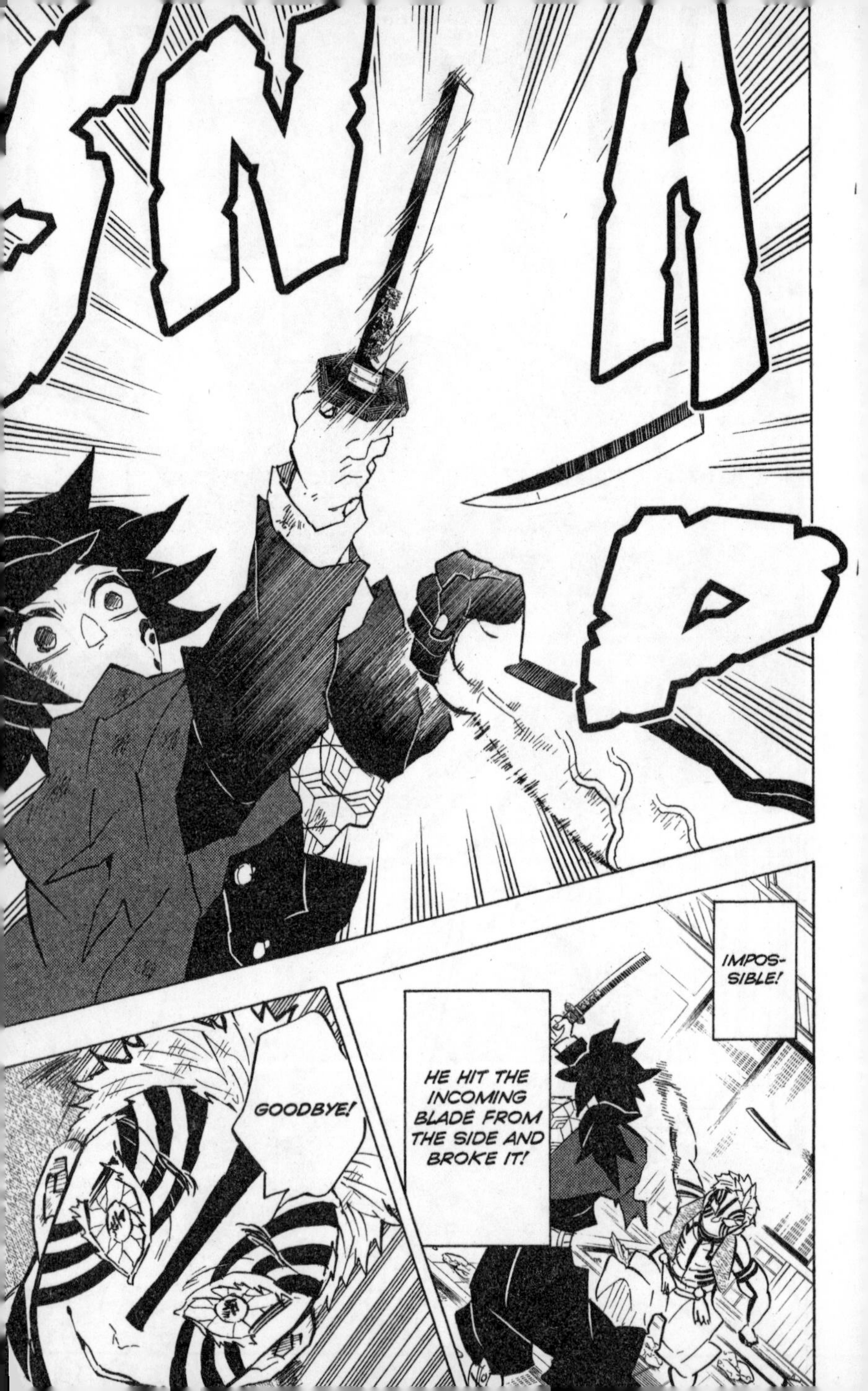
SNAP
IMPOS-SIBLE!
HE HIT THE INCOMING BLADE FROM THE SIDE AND BROKE IT!
GOODBYE!

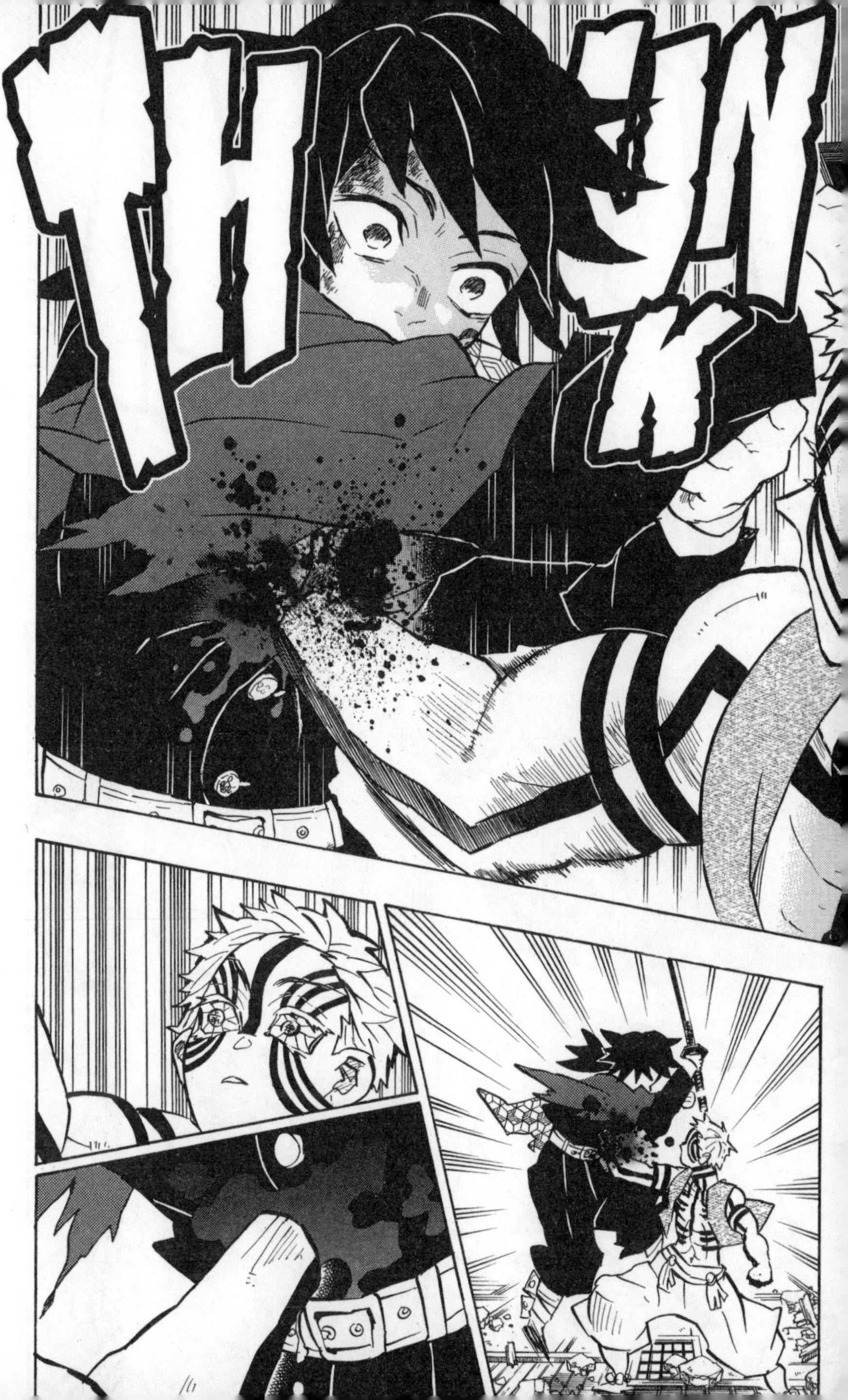
THUNK

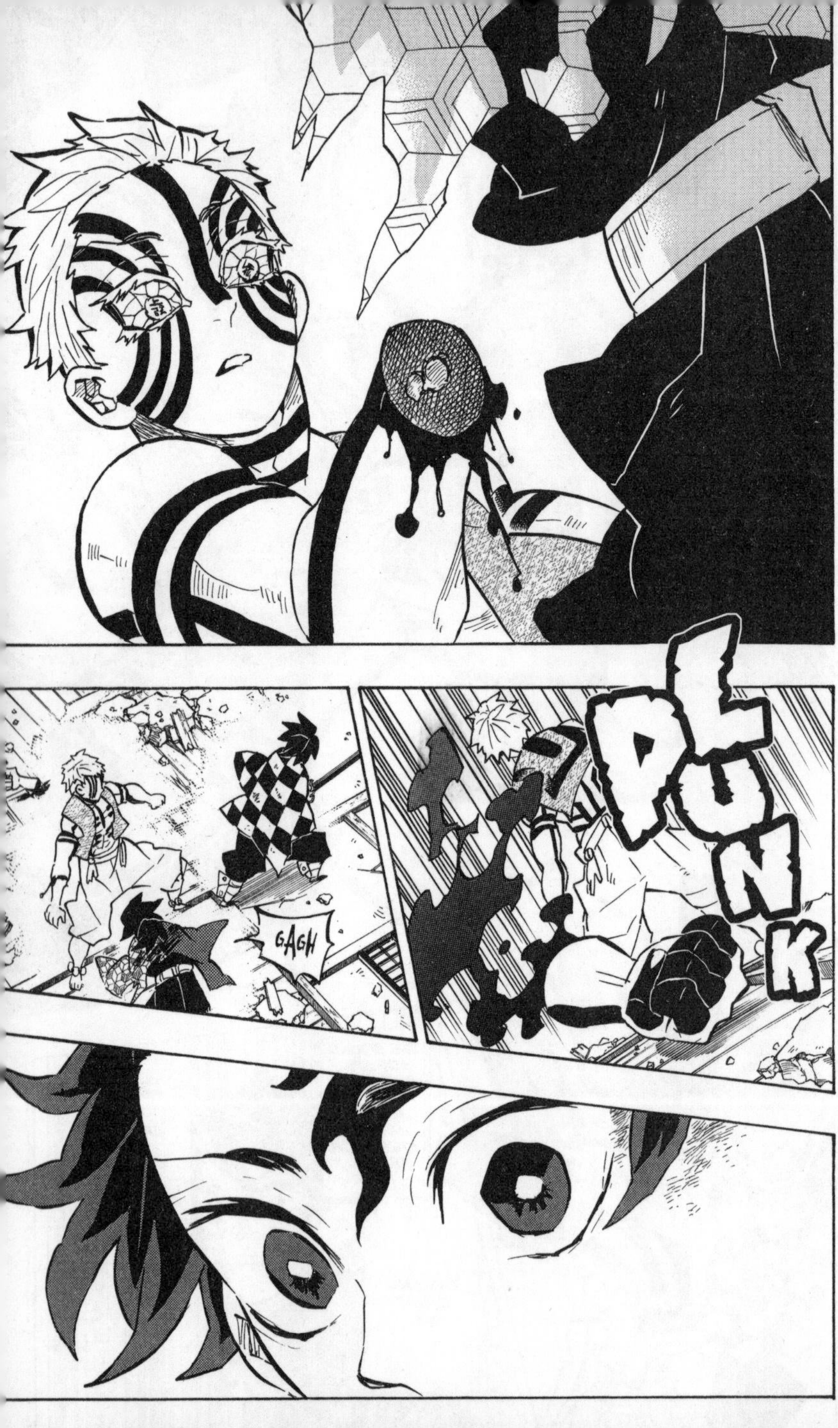
PLUNK
GAGH

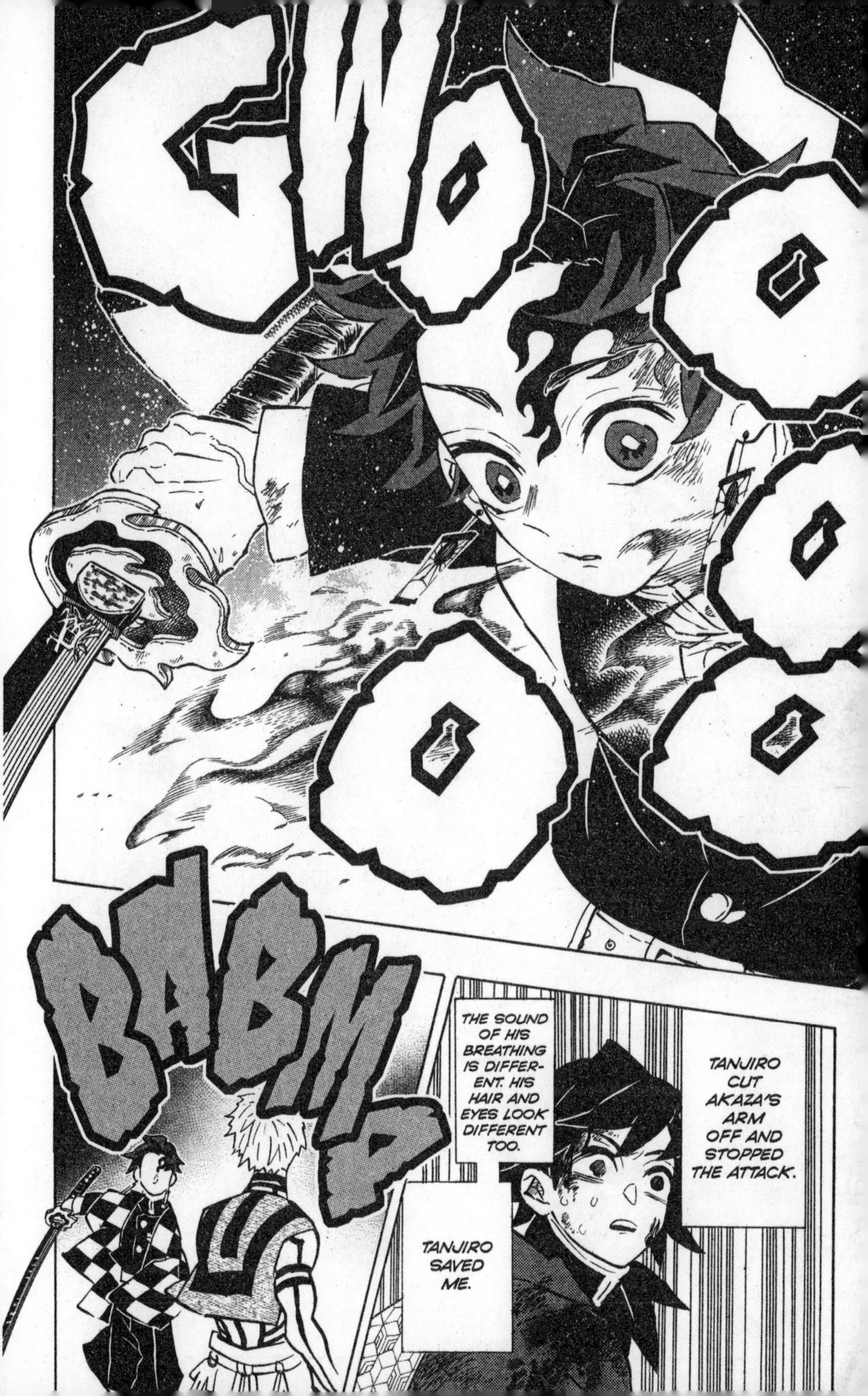
GWOOOOO
TANJIRO CUT AKAZA'S ARM OFF AND STOPPED THE ATTACK.
THE SOUND OF HIS BREATHING IS DIFFERENT. HIS HAIR AND EYES LOOK DIFFERENT TOO.
TANJIRO SAVED ME.

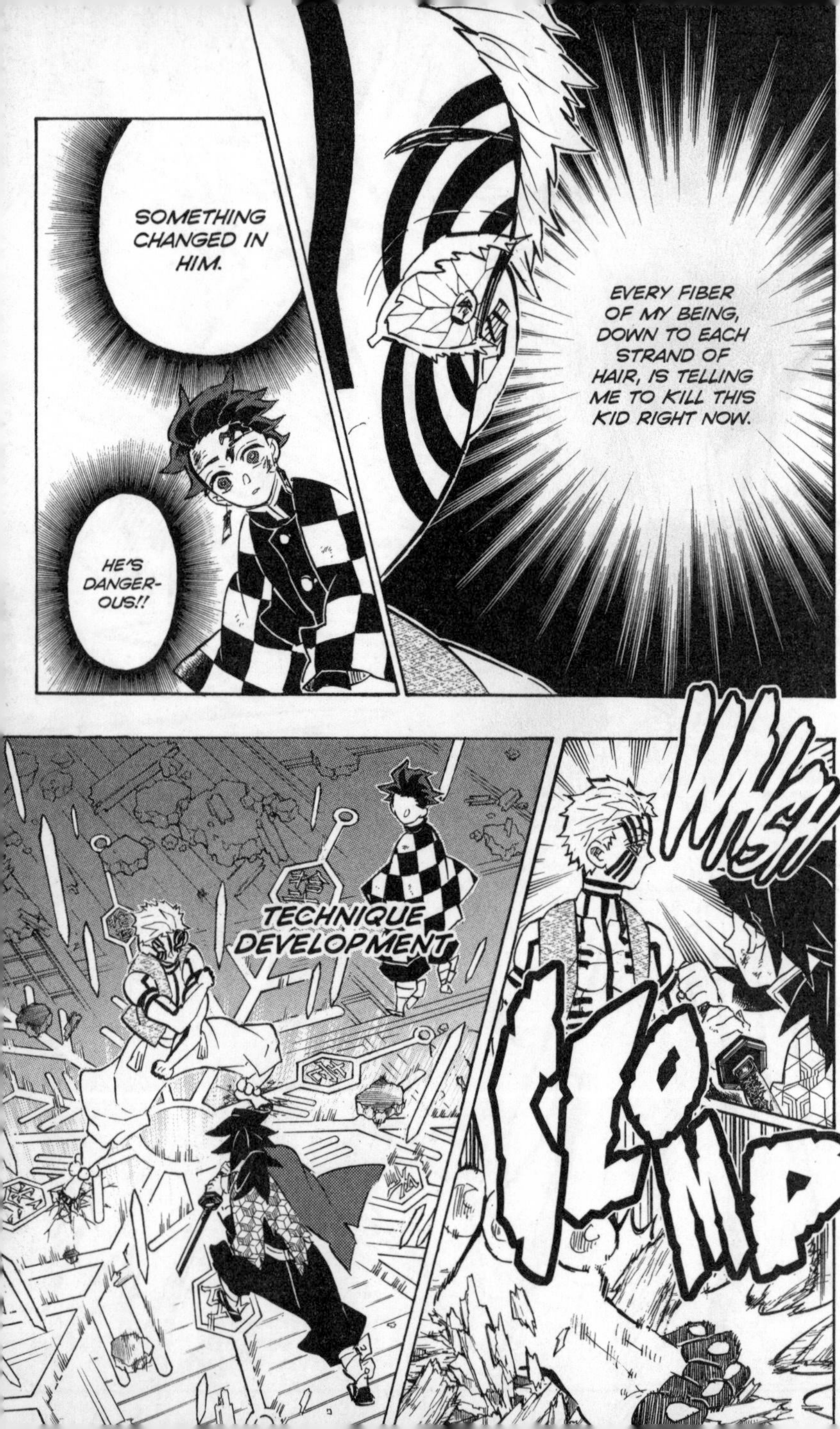
EVERY FIBER OF MY BEING, DOWN TO EACH STRAND OF HAIR, IS TELLING ME TO KILL THIS KID RIGHT NOW.
SOMETHING CHANGED IN HIM.
HE'S DANGER-OUS!!
WHSH
CLOMP
TECHNIQUE DEVELOPMENT

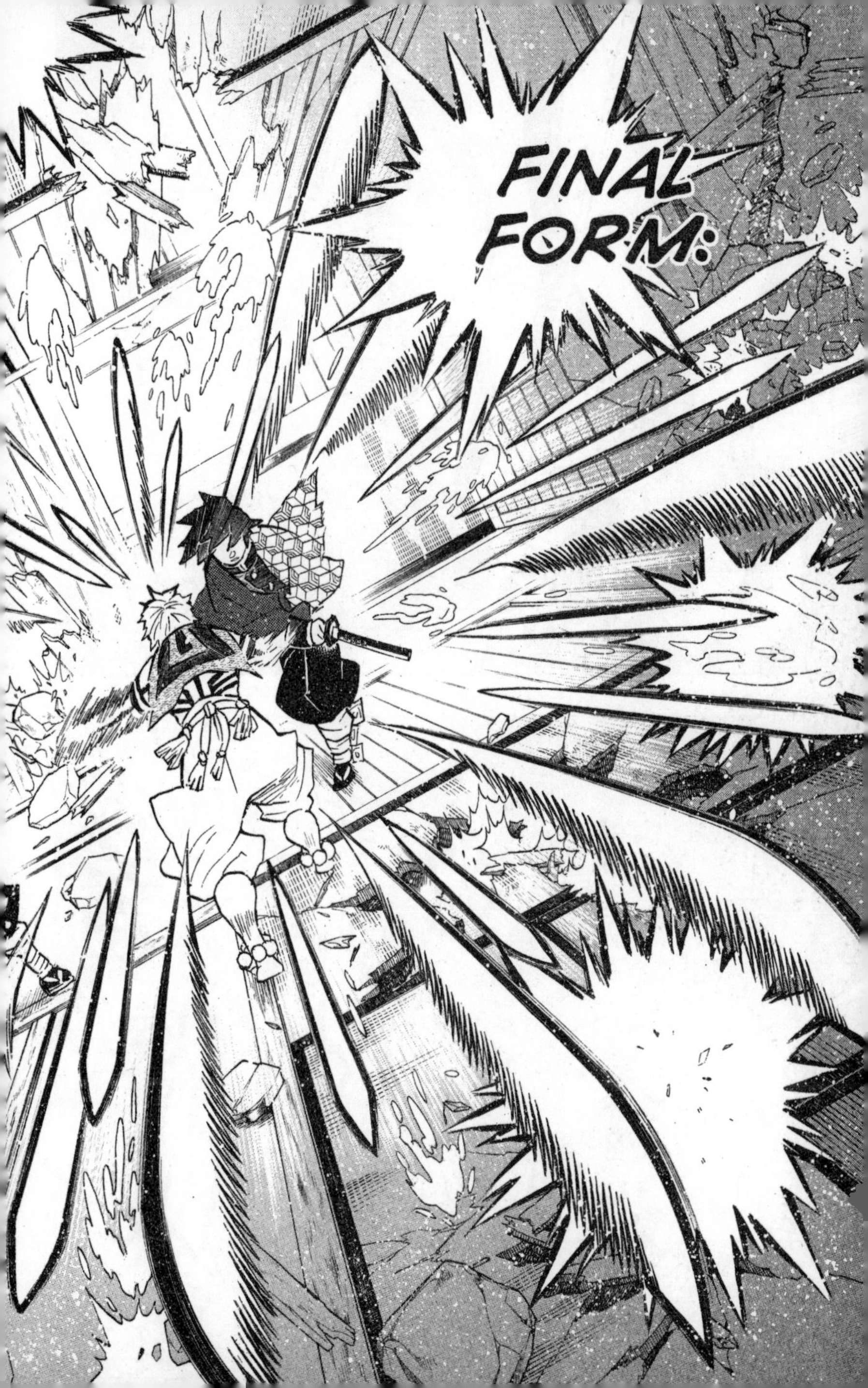
FINAL FORM:

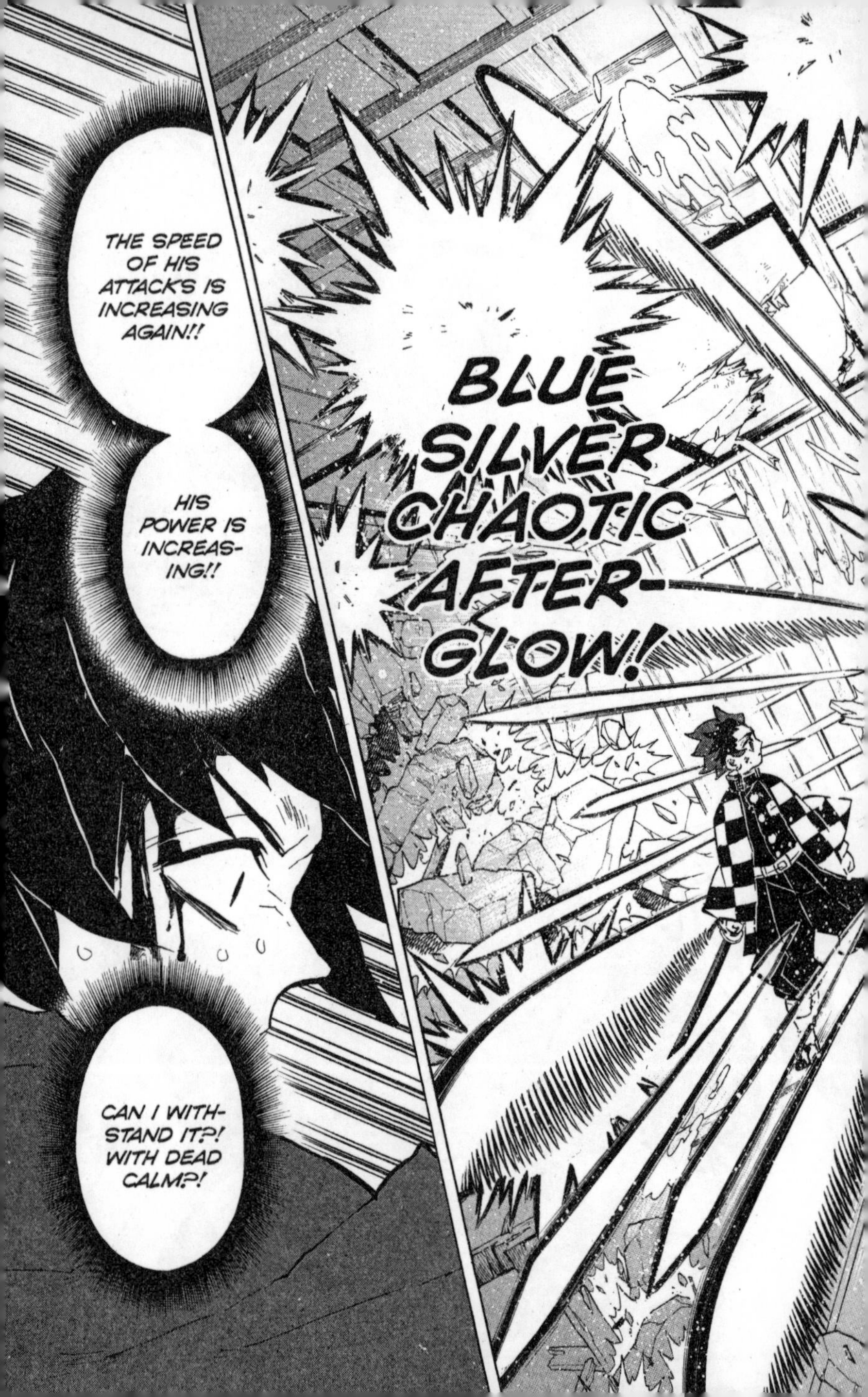
BLUE SILVER CHAOTIC AFTER-GLOW!
THE SPEED OF HIS ATTACKS IS INCREASING AGAIN!!
HIS POWER IS INCREAS-ING!!
CAN I WITH-STAND IT?! WITH DEAD CALM?!

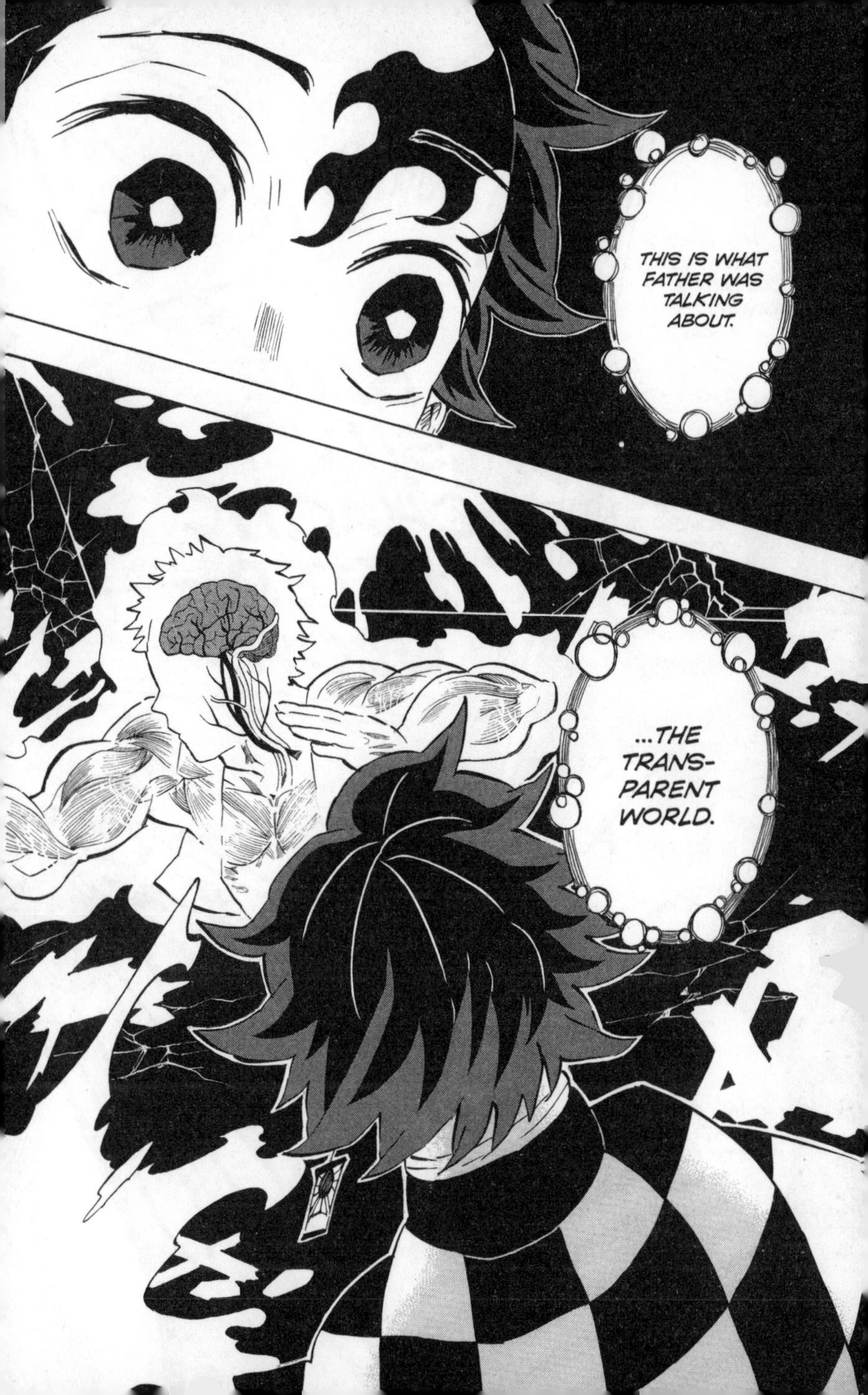
THIS IS WHAT FATHER WAS TALKING ABOUT.
...THE TRANS-PARENT WORLD.

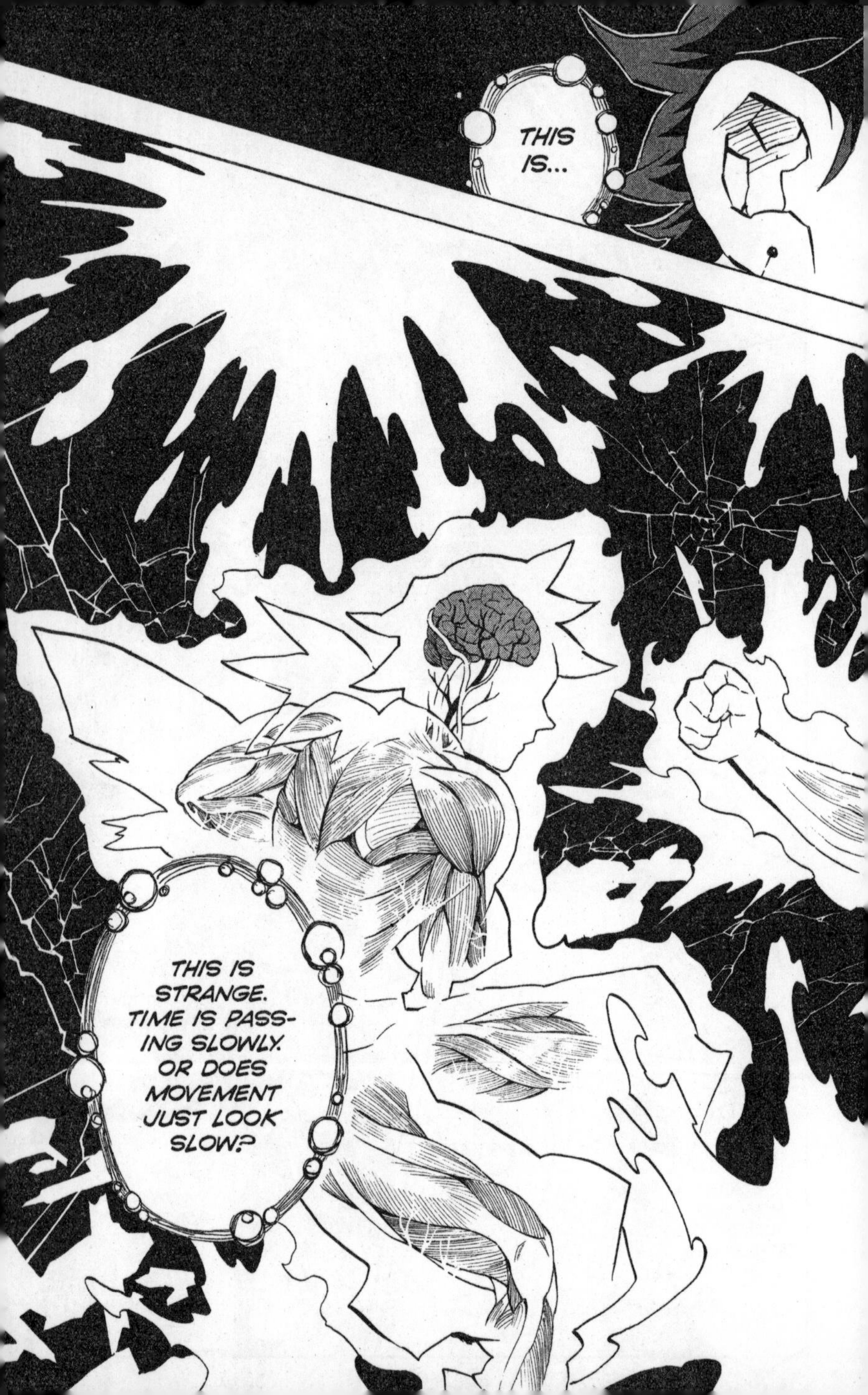
THIS IS...
THIS IS STRANGE. TIME IS PASS-ING SLOWLY. OR DOES MOVEMENT JUST LOOK SLOW?

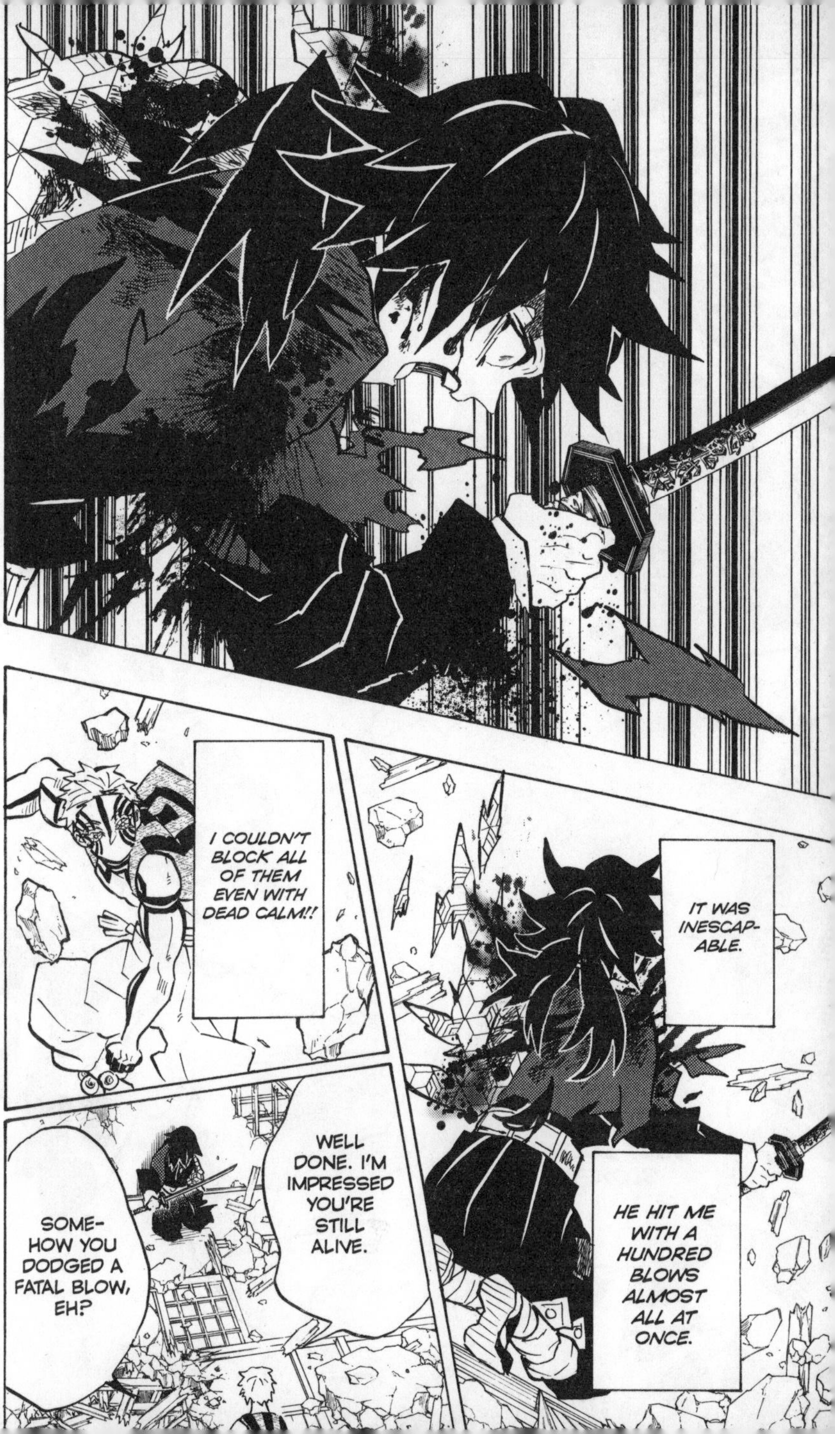
IT WAS INESCAPABLE.
HE HIT ME WITH A HUNDRED BLOWS ALMOST ALL AT ONCE.
I COULDN'T BLOCK ALL OF THEM EVEN WITH DEAD CALM!!
WELL DONE. I'M IMPRESSED YOU'RE STILL ALIVE.
SOMEHOW YOU DODGED A FATAL BLOW, EH?

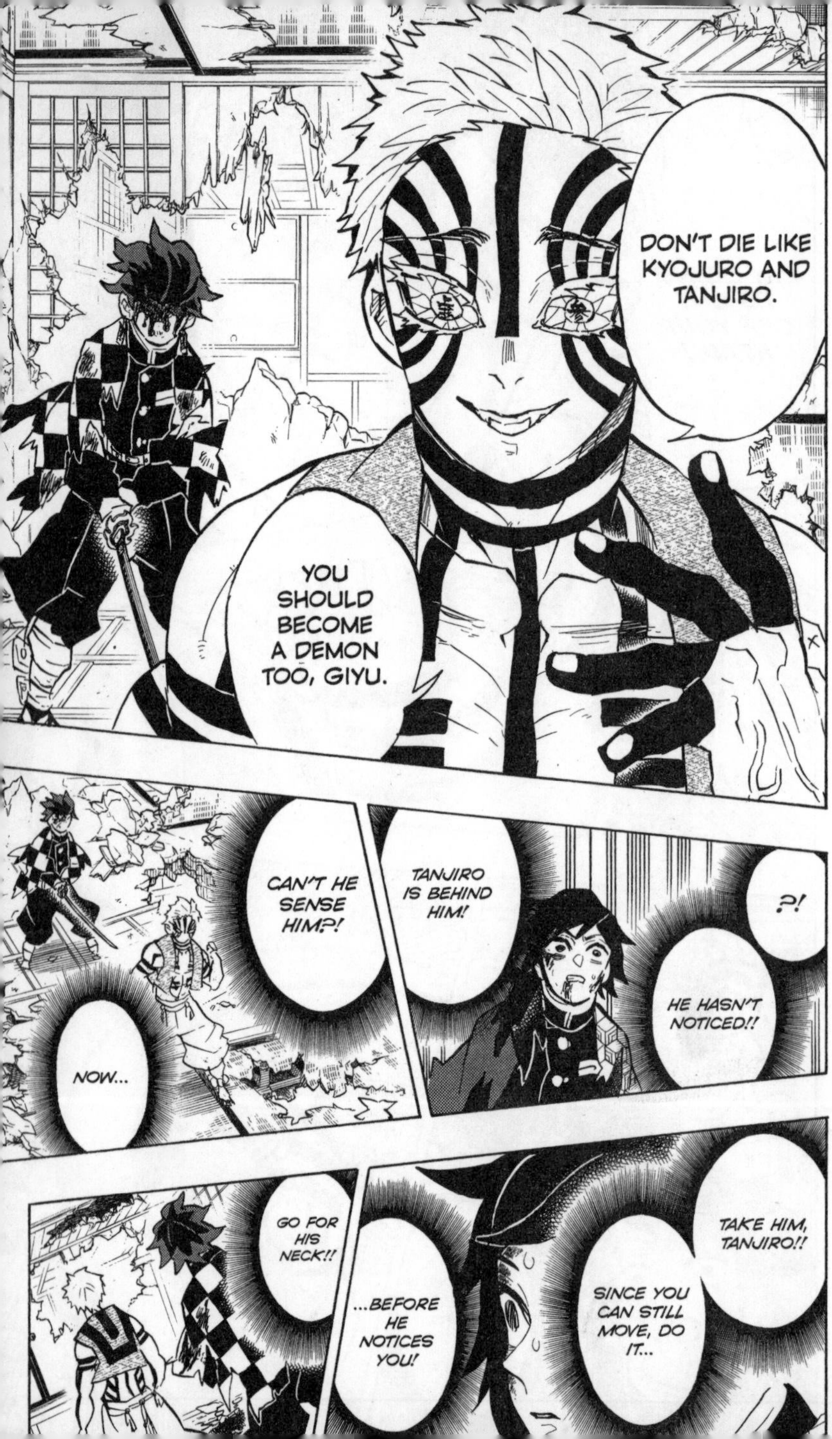
DON'T DIE LIKE KYOJURO AND TANJIRO.
YOU SHOULD BECOME A DEMON TOO, GIYU.
?!
HE HASN'T NOTICED!!
TANJIRO IS BEHIND HIM!
CAN'T HE SENSE HIM?!
NOW...
TAKE HIM, TANJIRO!!
SINCE YOU CAN STILL MOVE, DO IT...
...BEFORE HE NOTICES YOU!
GO FOR HIS NECK!!

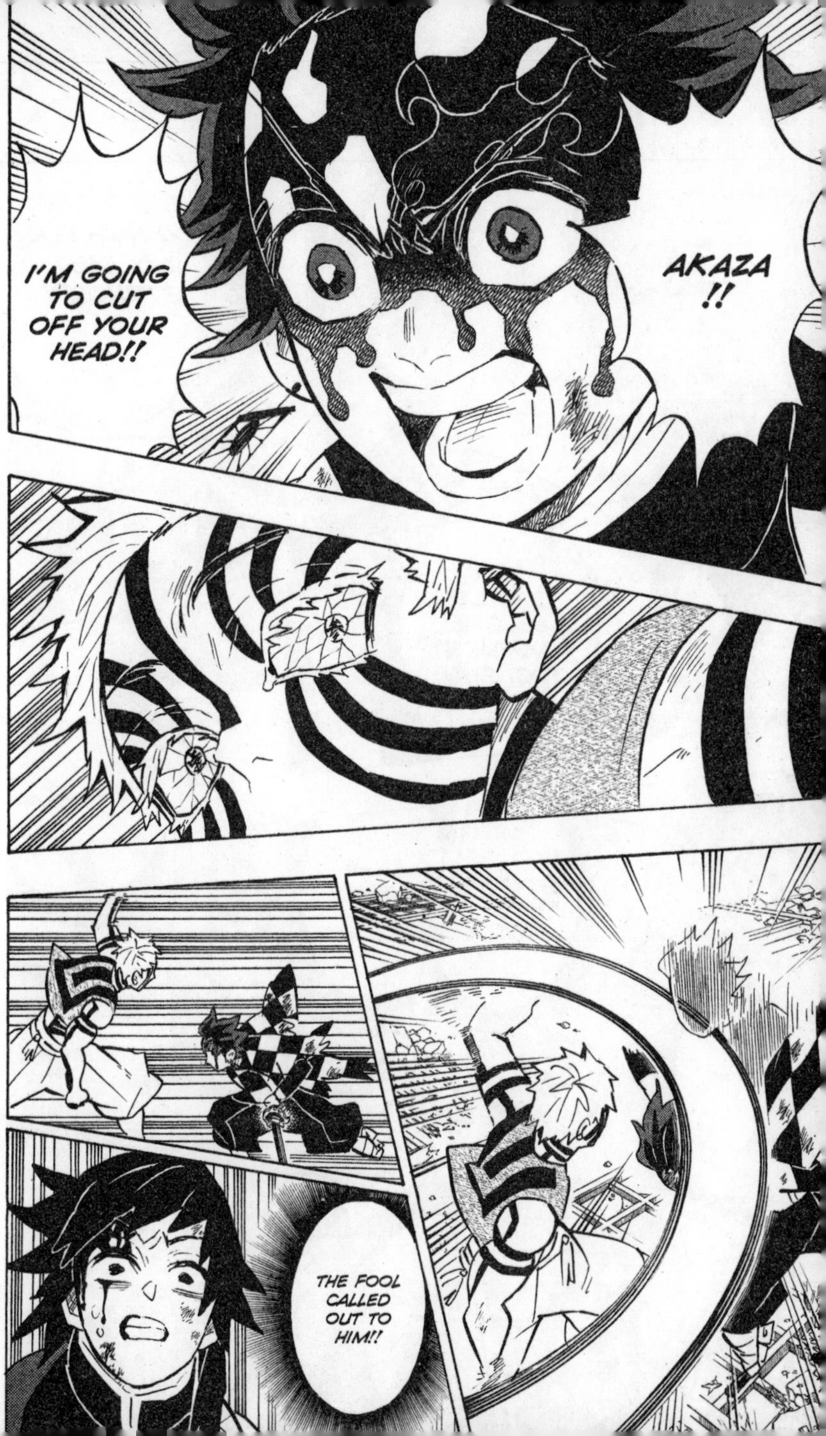
AKAZA !!
I'M GOING TO CUT OFF YOUR HEAD!!
THE FOOL CALLED OUT TO HIM!!

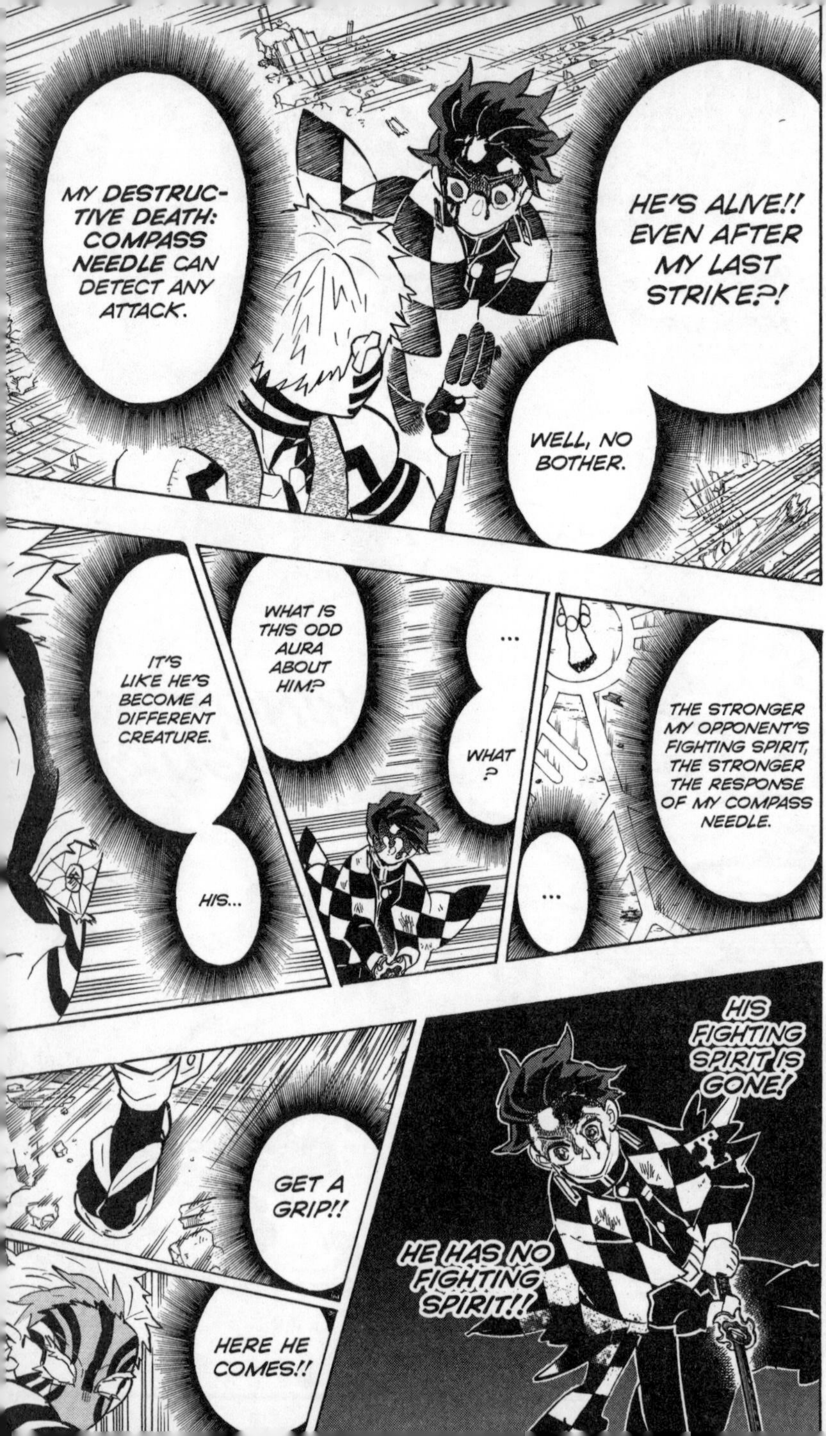
HE'S ALIVE!! EVEN AFTER MY LAST STRIKE?!
WELL, NO BOTHER.
MY DESTRUCTIVE DEATH: COMPASS NEEDLE CAN DETECT ANY ATTACK.
THE STRONGER MY OPPONENT'S FIGHTING SPIRIT, THE STRONGER THE RESPONSE OF MY COMPASS NEEDLE.
...
...
WHAT ?
WHAT IS THIS ODD AURA ABOUT HIM?
IT'S LIKE HE'S BECOME A DIFFERENT CREATURE.
HIS...
HIS FIGHTING SPIRIT IS GONE!
HE HAS NO FIGHTING SPIRIT!!
GET A GRIP!!
HERE HE COMES!!

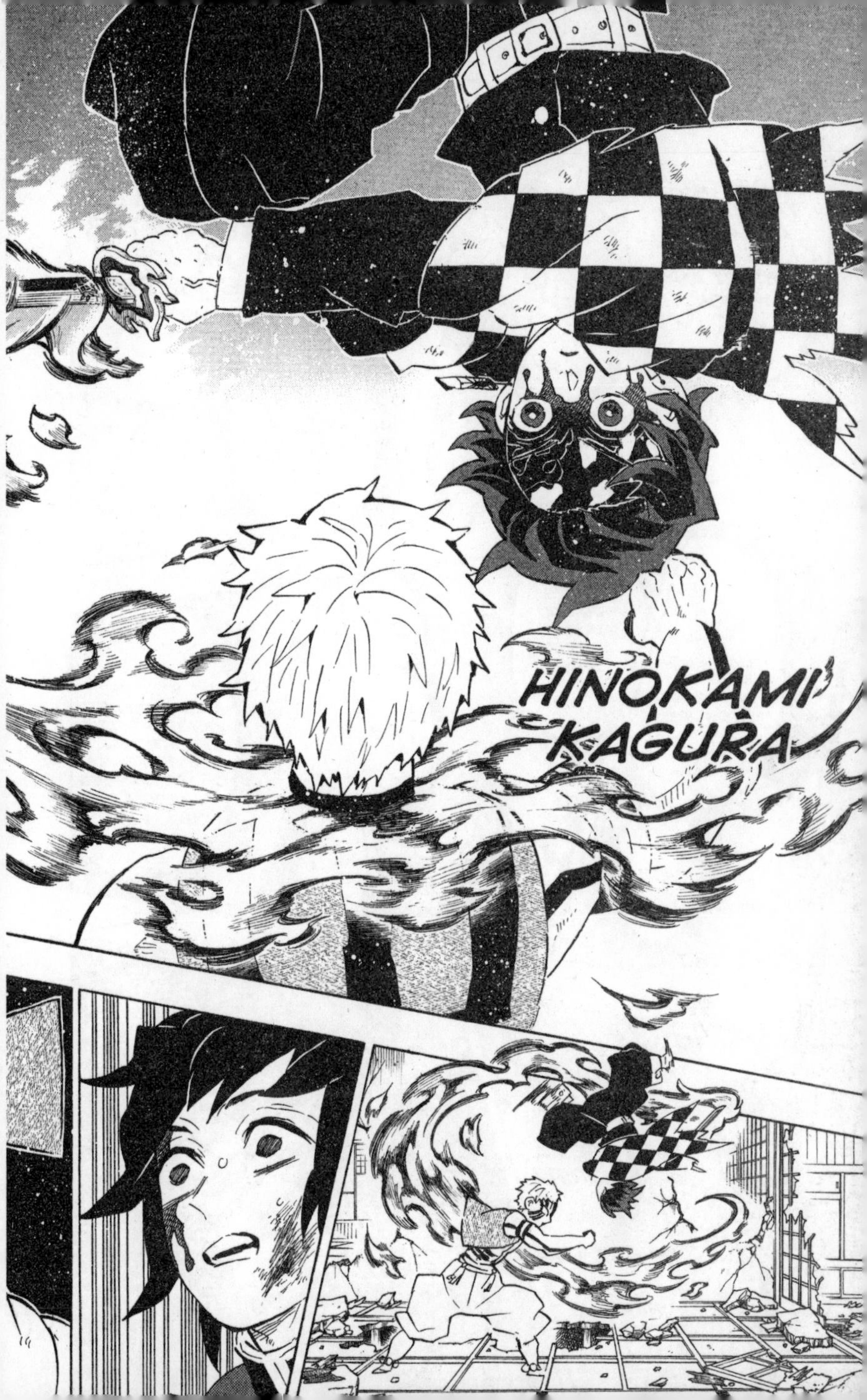
HINOKAMI KAGURA

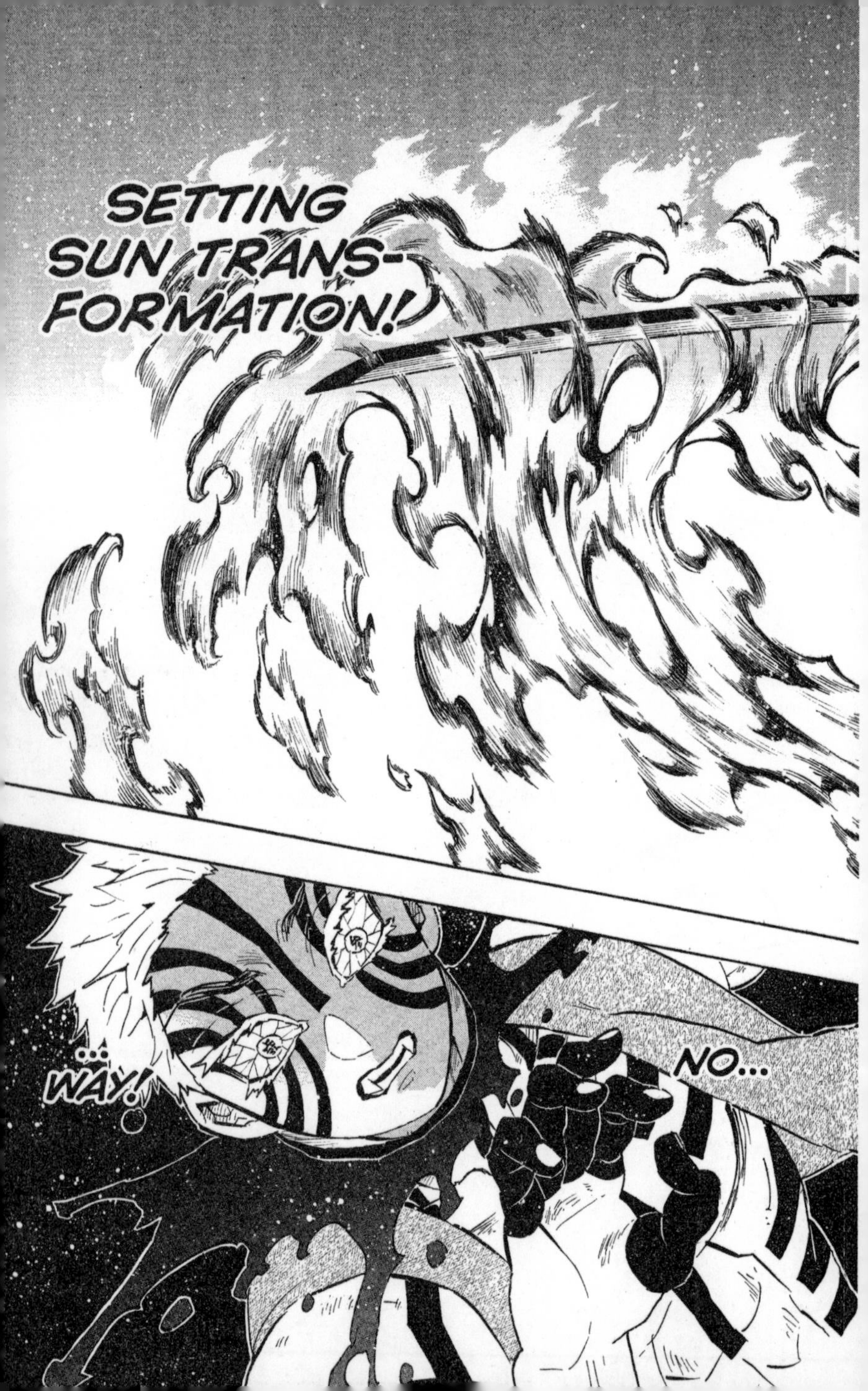
SETTING SUN TRANS-FORMATION!
NO...
...WAY!

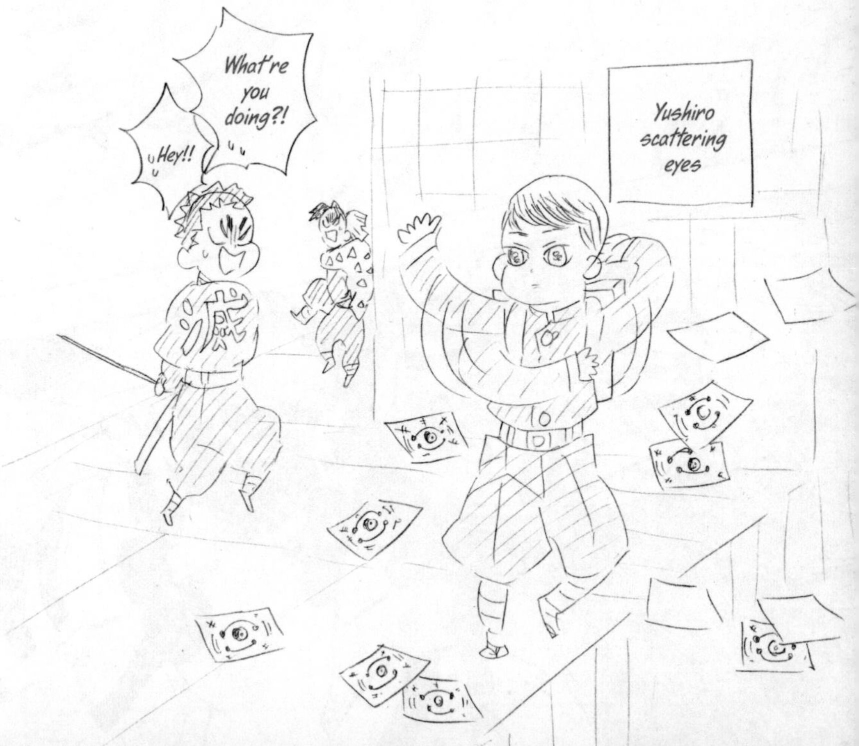
Yushiro scattering eyes
What're you doing?!
Hey!!

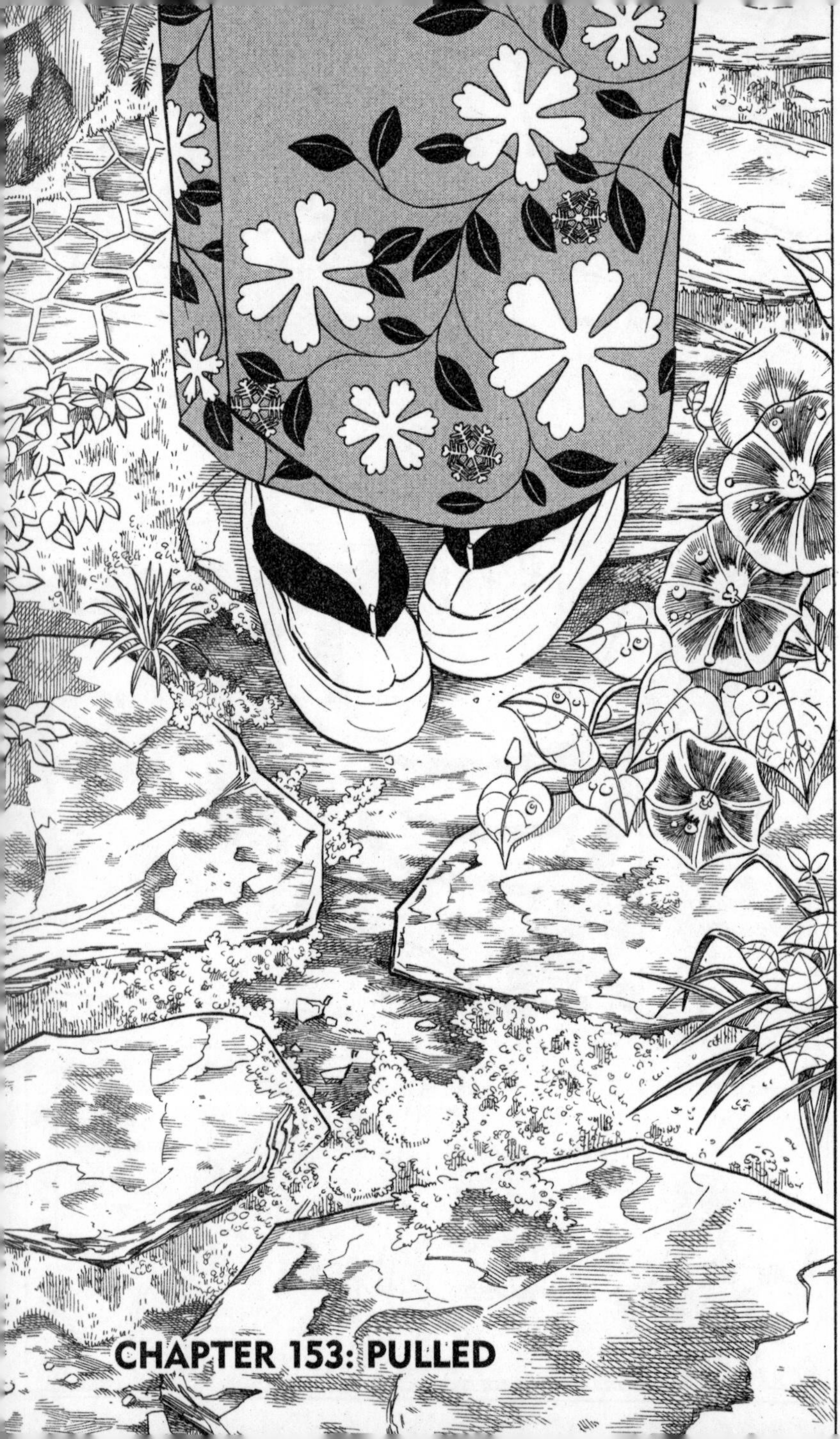
CHAPTER 153: PULLED

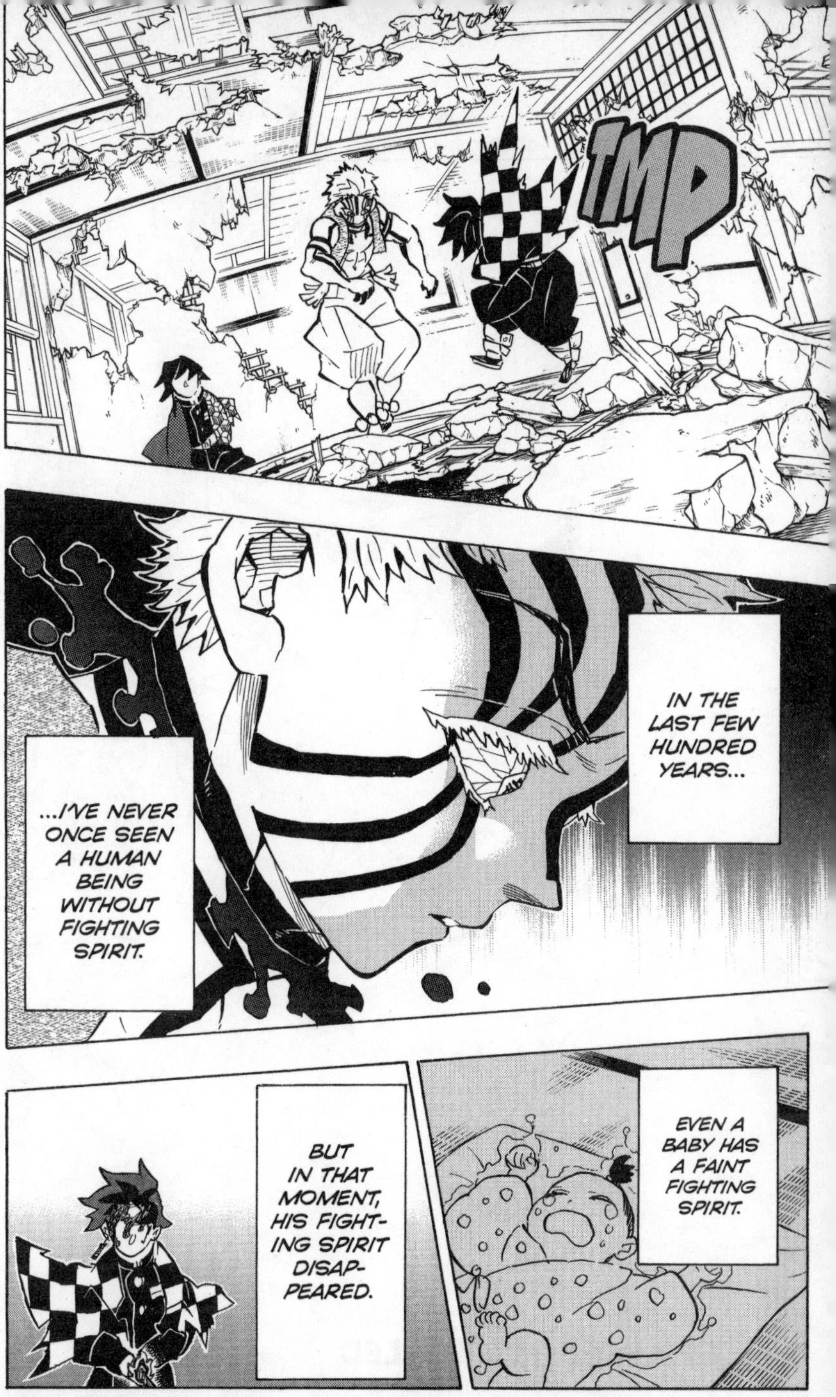
TMP
IN THE LAST FEW HUNDRED YEARS...
...I'VE NEVER ONCE SEEN A HUMAN BEING WITHOUT FIGHTING SPIRIT.
EVEN A BABY HAS A FAINT FIGHTING SPIRIT.
BUT IN THAT MOMENT, HIS FIGHTING SPIRIT DISAPPEARED.

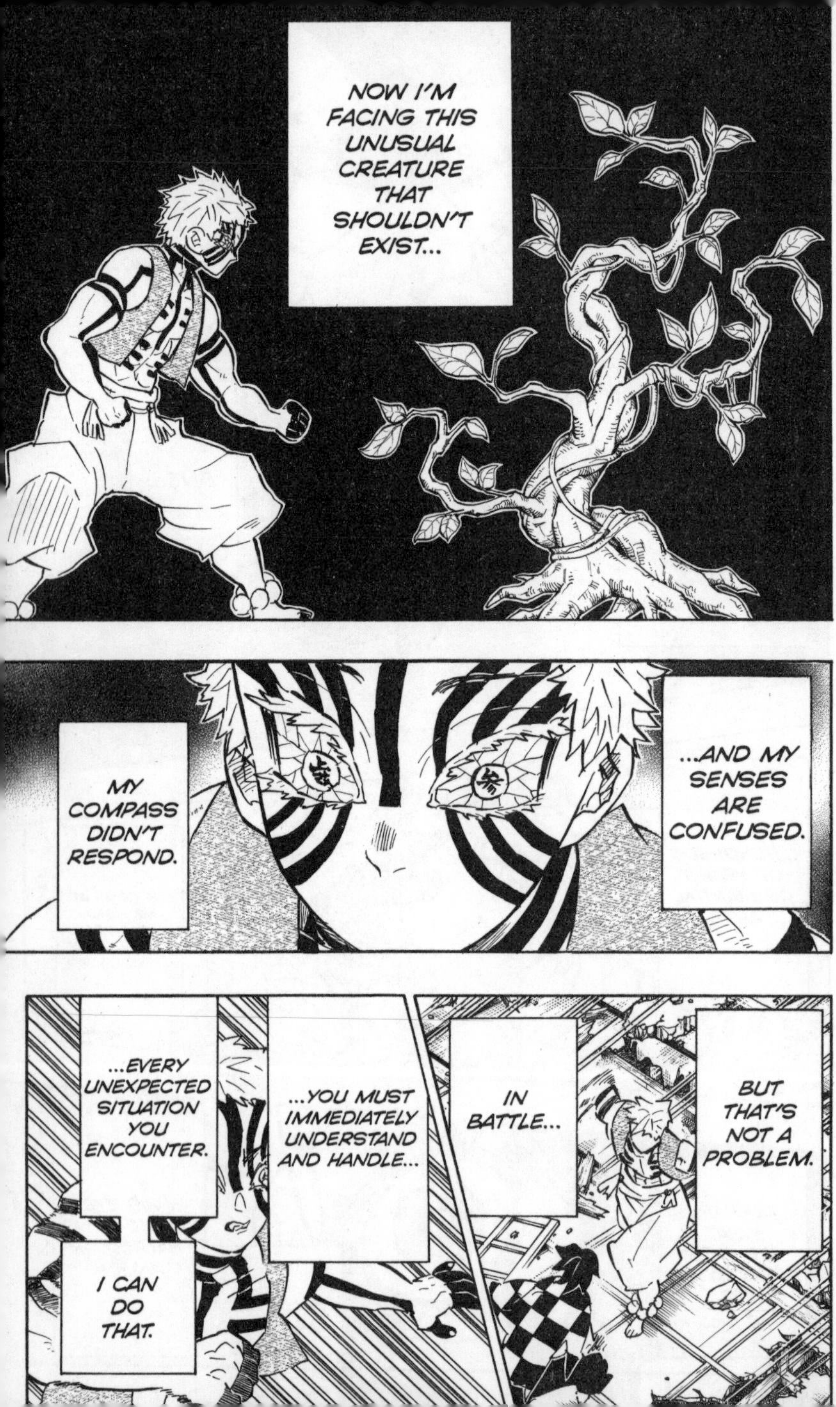
NOW I'M FACING THIS UNUSUAL CREATURE THAT SHOULDN'T EXIST...
...AND MY SENSES ARE CONFUSED.
MY COMPASS DIDN'T RESPOND.
BUT THAT'S NOT A PROBLEM.
IN BATTLE...
...YOU MUST IMMEDIATELY UNDERSTAND AND HANDLE...
...EVERY UNEXPECTED SITUATION YOU ENCOUNTER.
I CAN DO THAT.

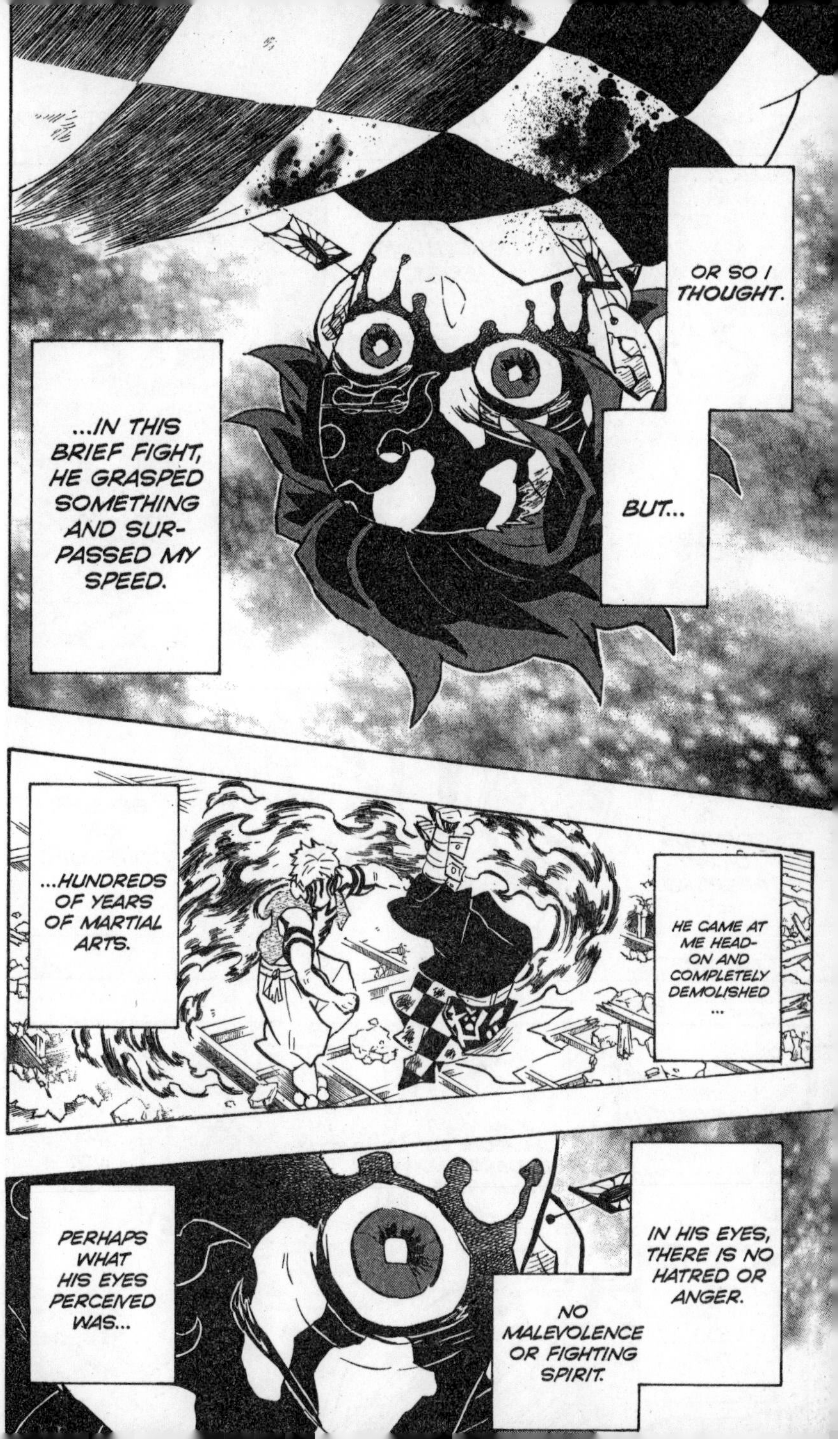
OR SO I THOUGHT.
BUT...
...IN THIS BRIEF FIGHT, HE GRASPED SOMETHING AND SURPASSED MY SPEED.
HE CAME AT ME HEAD-ON AND COMPLETELY DEMOLISHED ...
...HUNDREDS OF YEARS OF MARTIAL ARTS.
IN HIS EYES, THERE IS NO HATRED OR ANGER.
NO MALEVOLENCE OR FIGHTING SPIRIT.
PERHAPS WHAT HIS EYES PERCEIVED WAS...

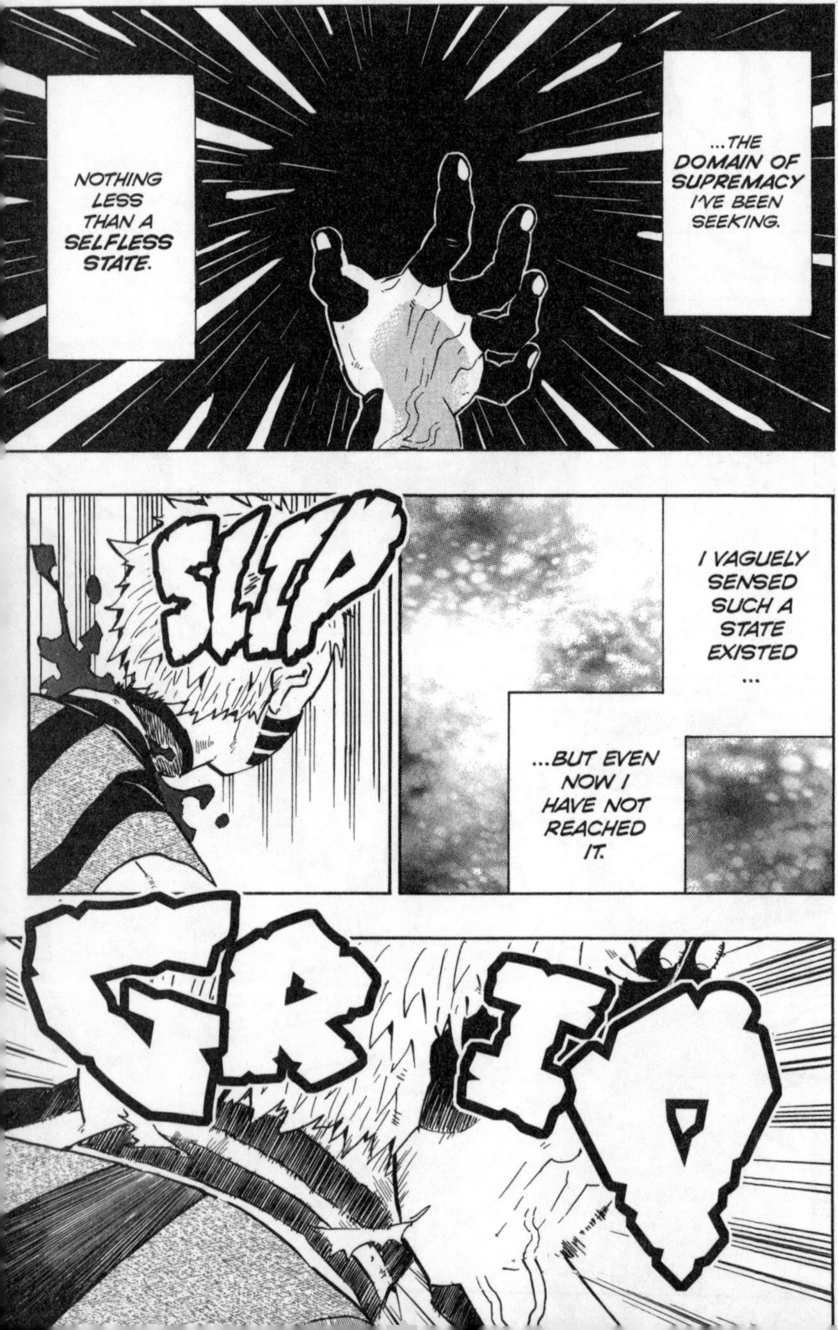
...THE DOMAIN OF SUPREMACY I'VE BEEN SEEKING.
NOTHING LESS THAN A SELFLESS STATE.
I VAGUELY SENSED SUCH A STATE EXISTED ...
...BUT EVEN NOW I HAVE NOT REACHED IT.
SLIP
GRIP

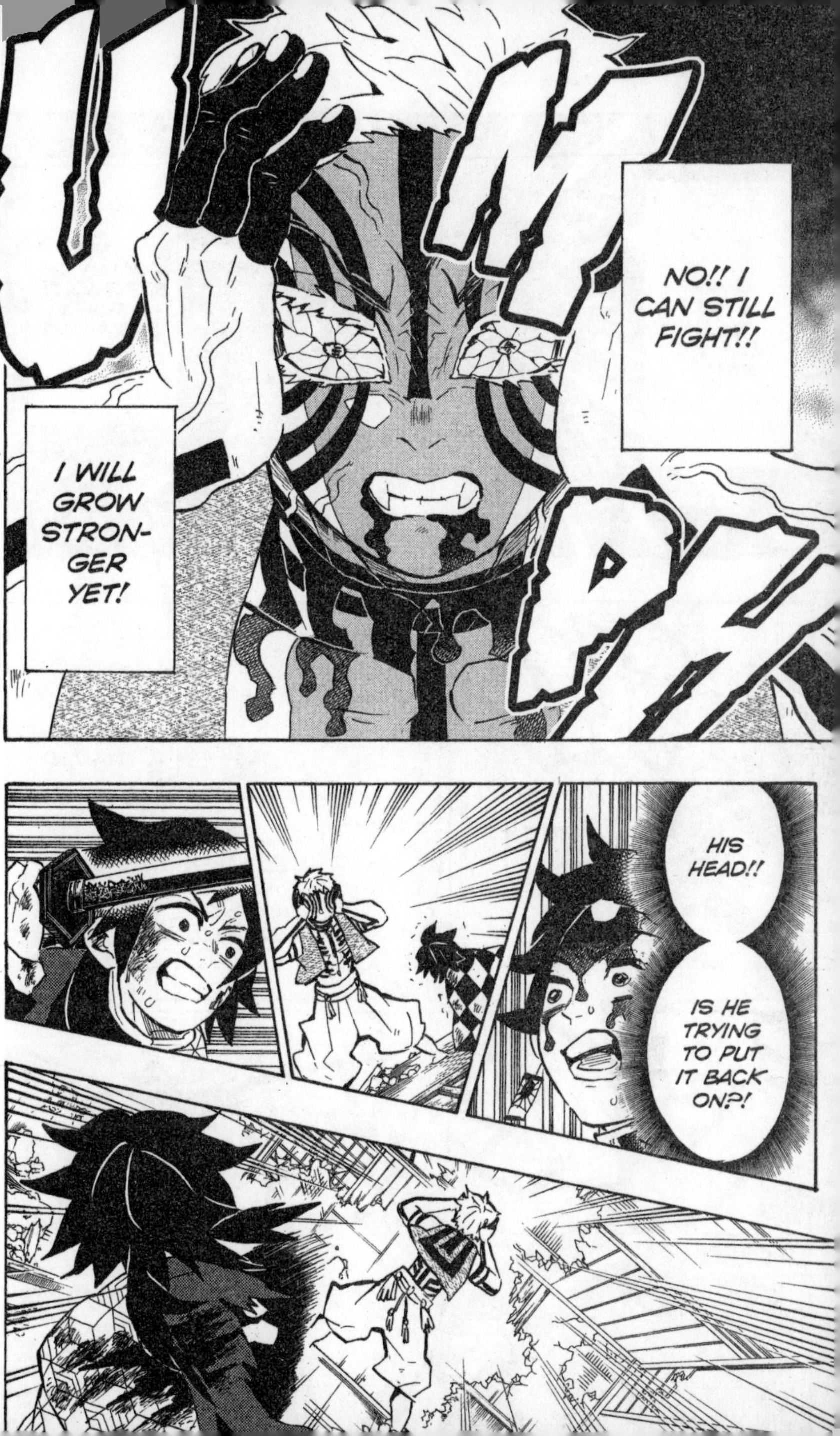
NO!! I CAN STILL FIGHT!!
I WILL GROW STRON-GER YET!
HIS HEAD!!
IS HE TRYING TO PUT IT BACK ON?!

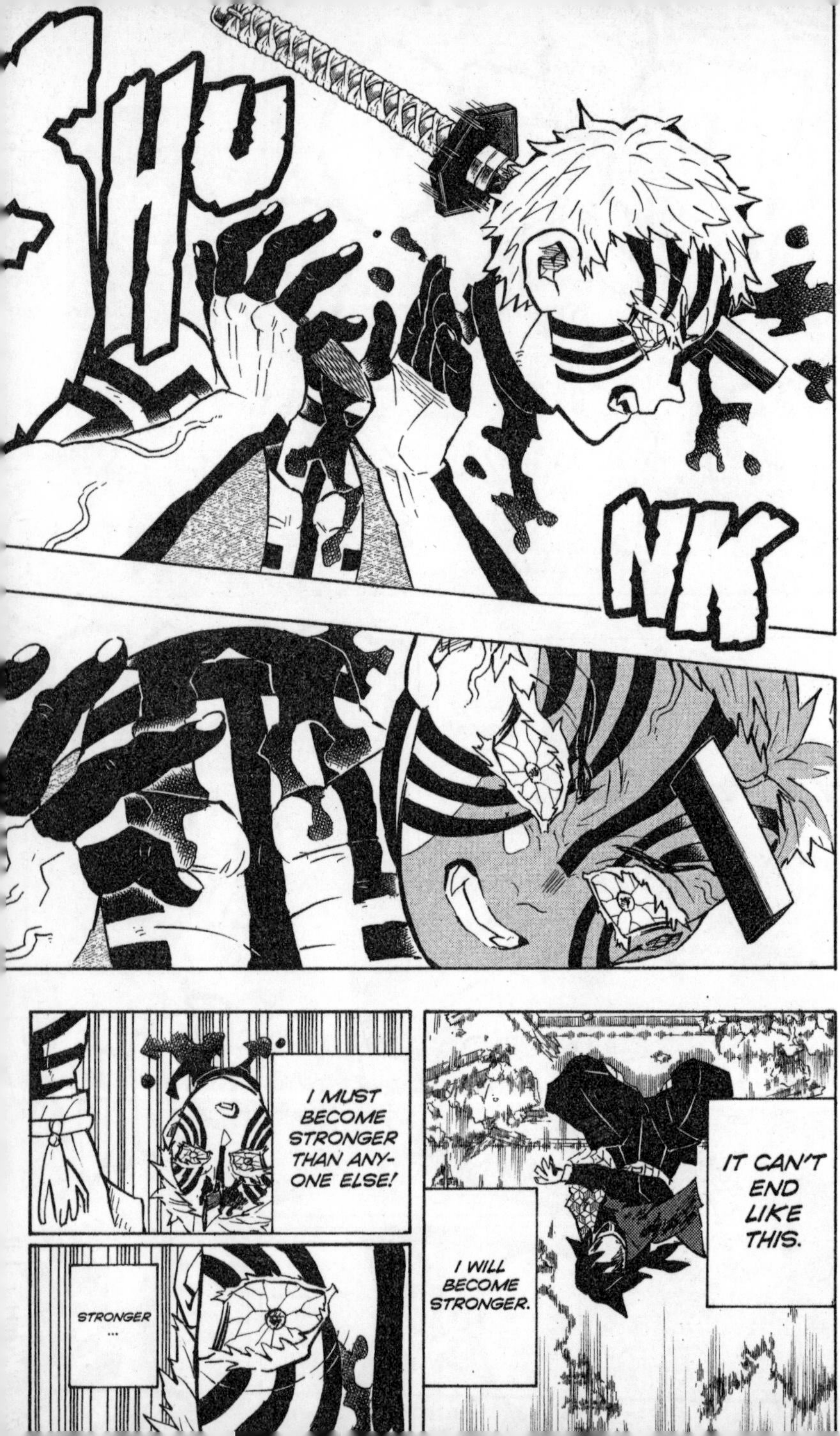
SHU
NK
IT CAN'T END LIKE THIS.
I WILL BECOME STRONGER.
I MUST BECOME STRONGER THAN ANY-ONE ELSE!
STRONGER ...

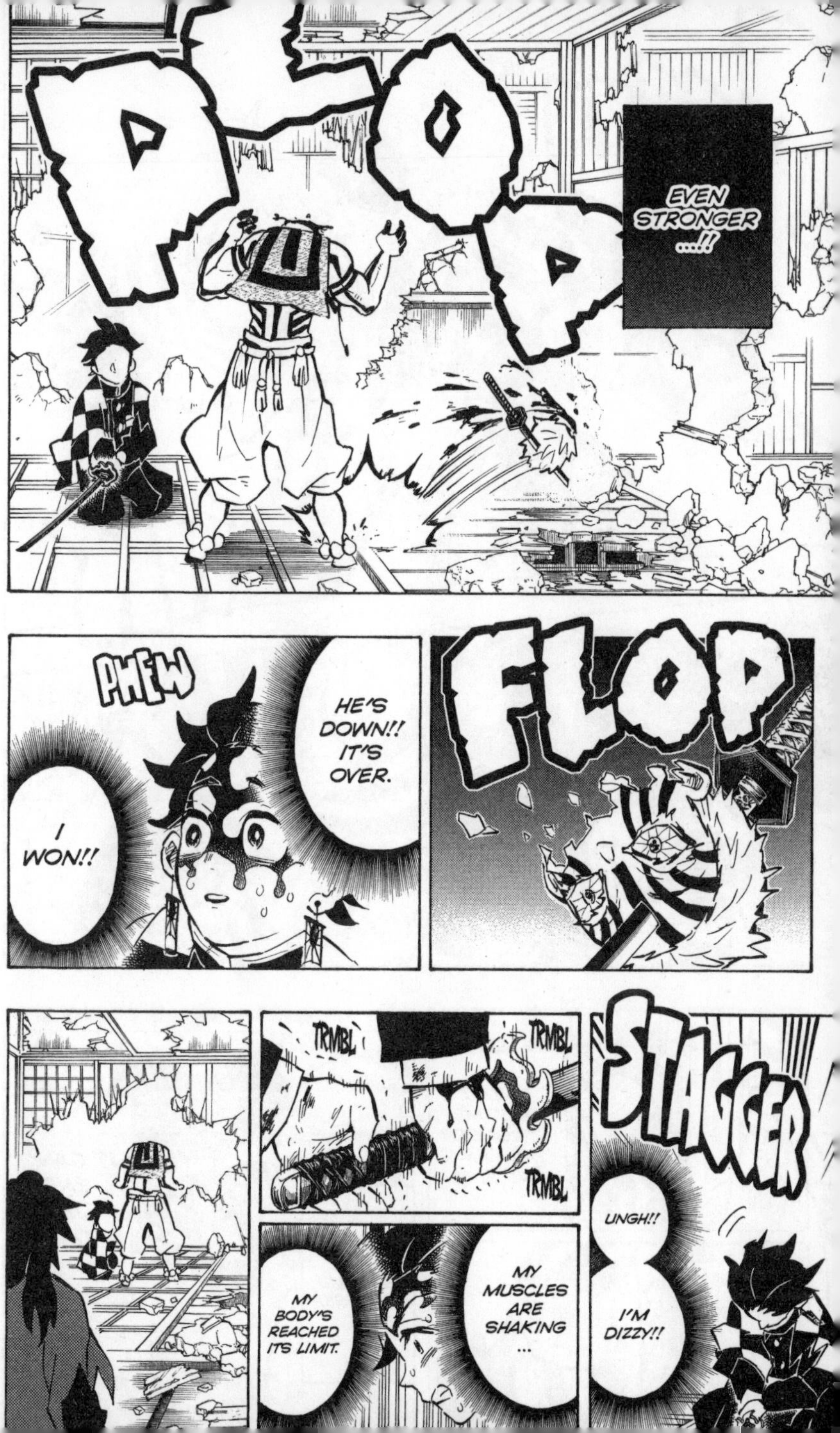
PLOP
EVEN STRONGER ...!!
FLOP
HE'S DOWN!! IT'S OVER.
PHEW
I WON!!
STAGGER
UNGH!!
I'M DIZZY!!
TRMBL
TRMBL
TRMBL
MY MUSCLES ARE SHAKING ...
MY BODY'S REACHED ITS LIMIT.

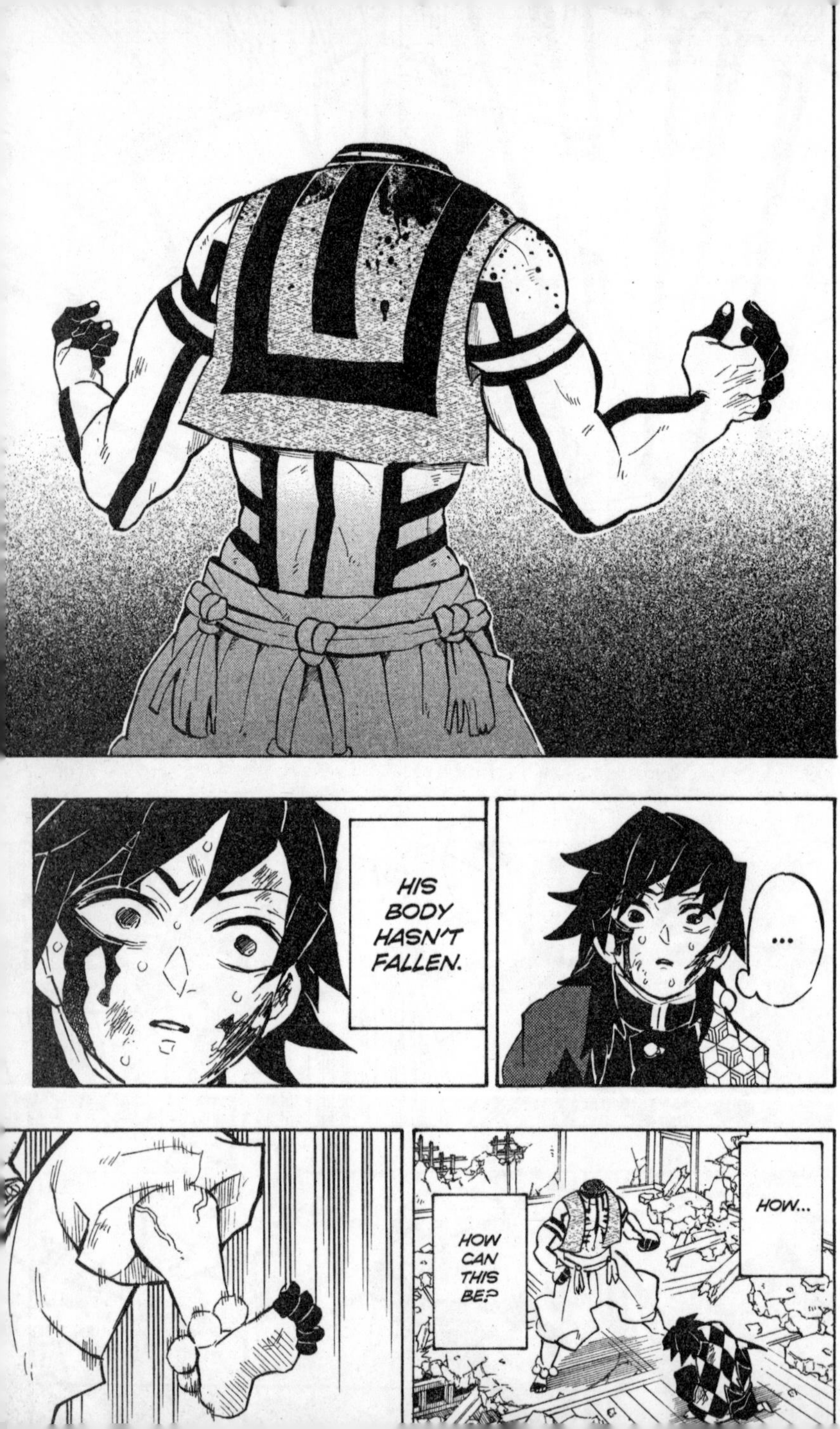
...
HIS BODY HASN'T FALLEN.
HOW...
HOW CAN THIS BE?

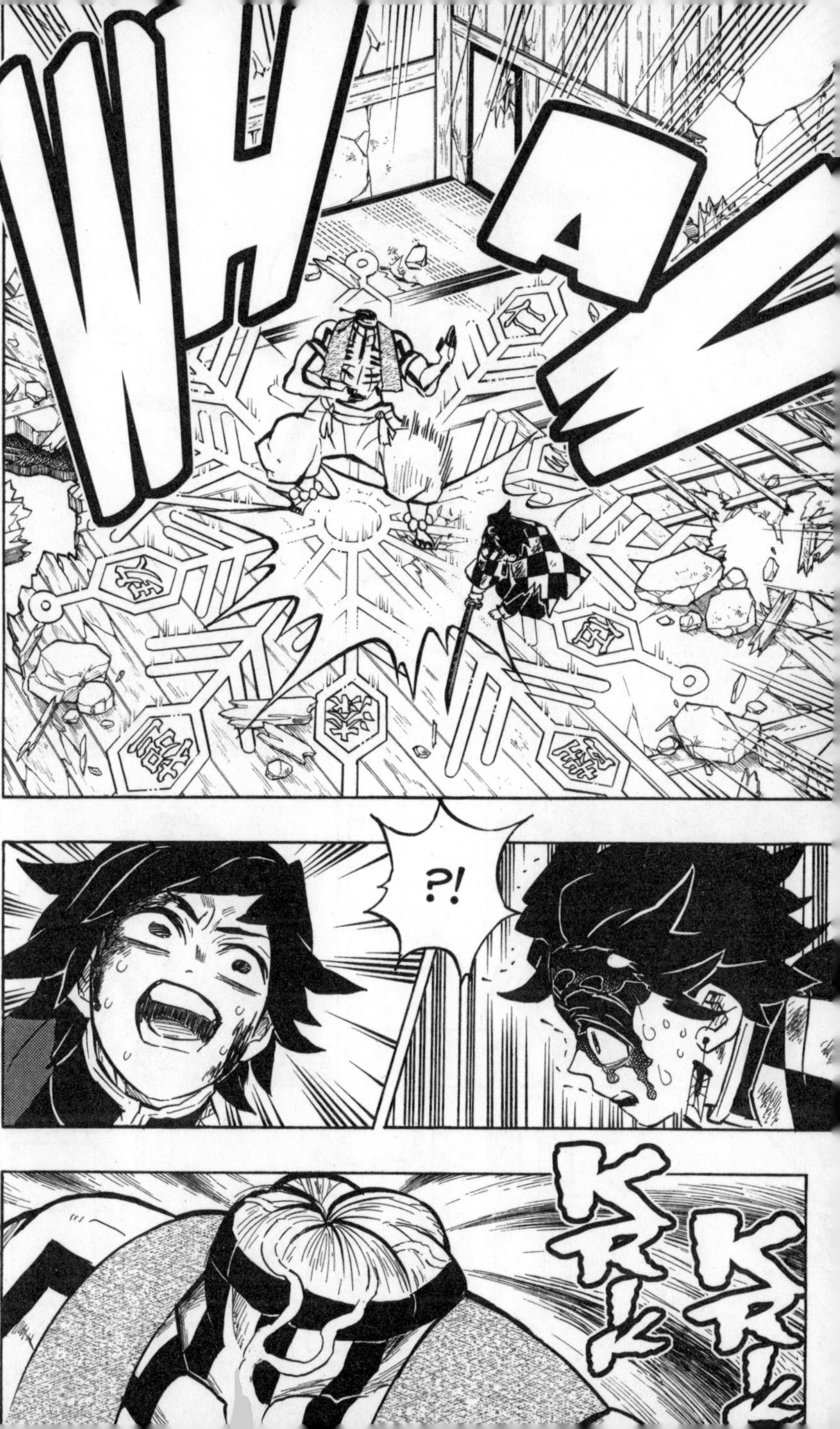
WHAM
?!

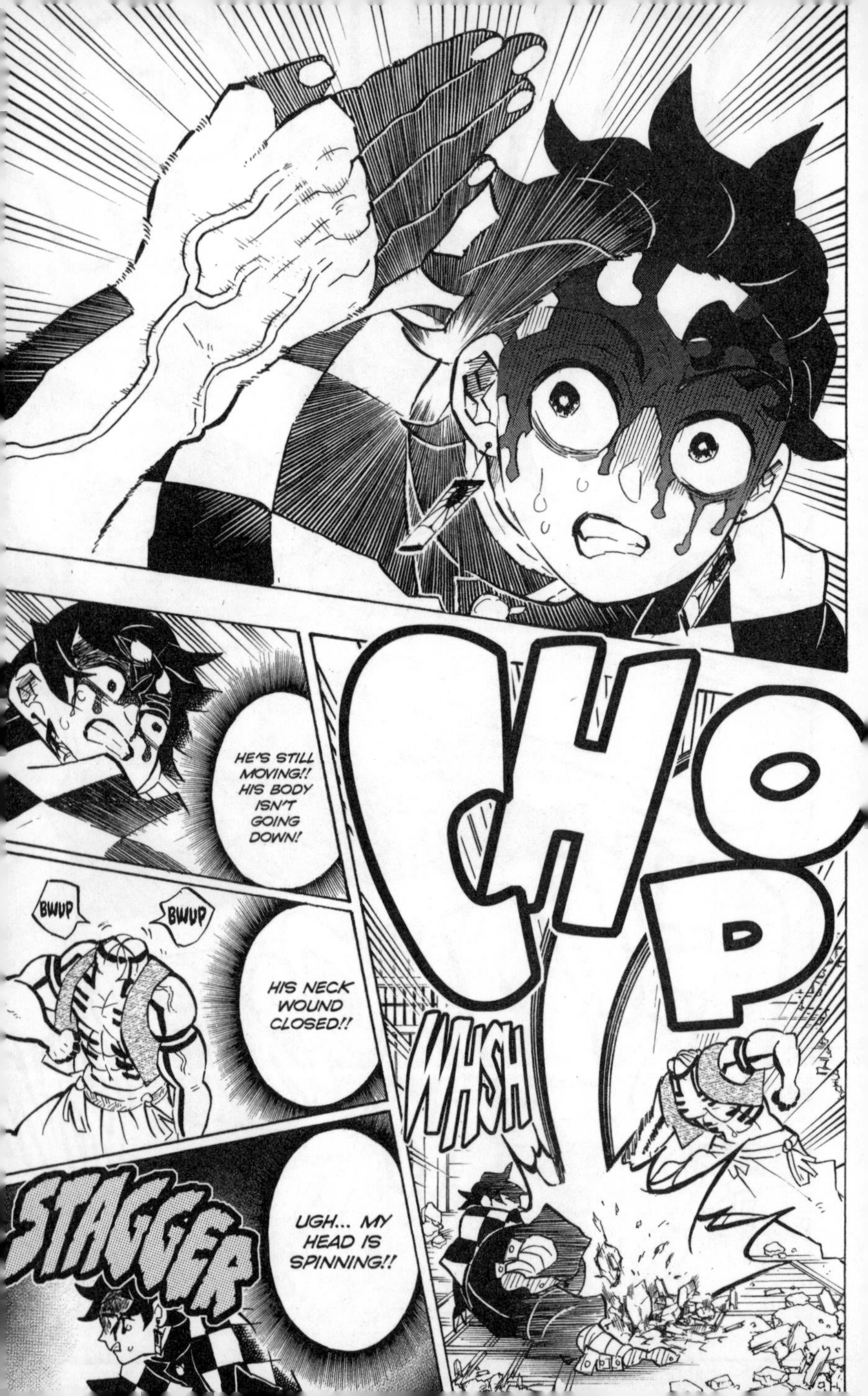
CHOP
WHSH
HE'S STILL MOVING!! HIS BODY ISN'T GOING DOWN!
BWUP
BWUP
HIS NECK WOUND CLOSED!!
UGH... MY HEAD IS SPINNING!!
STAGGER

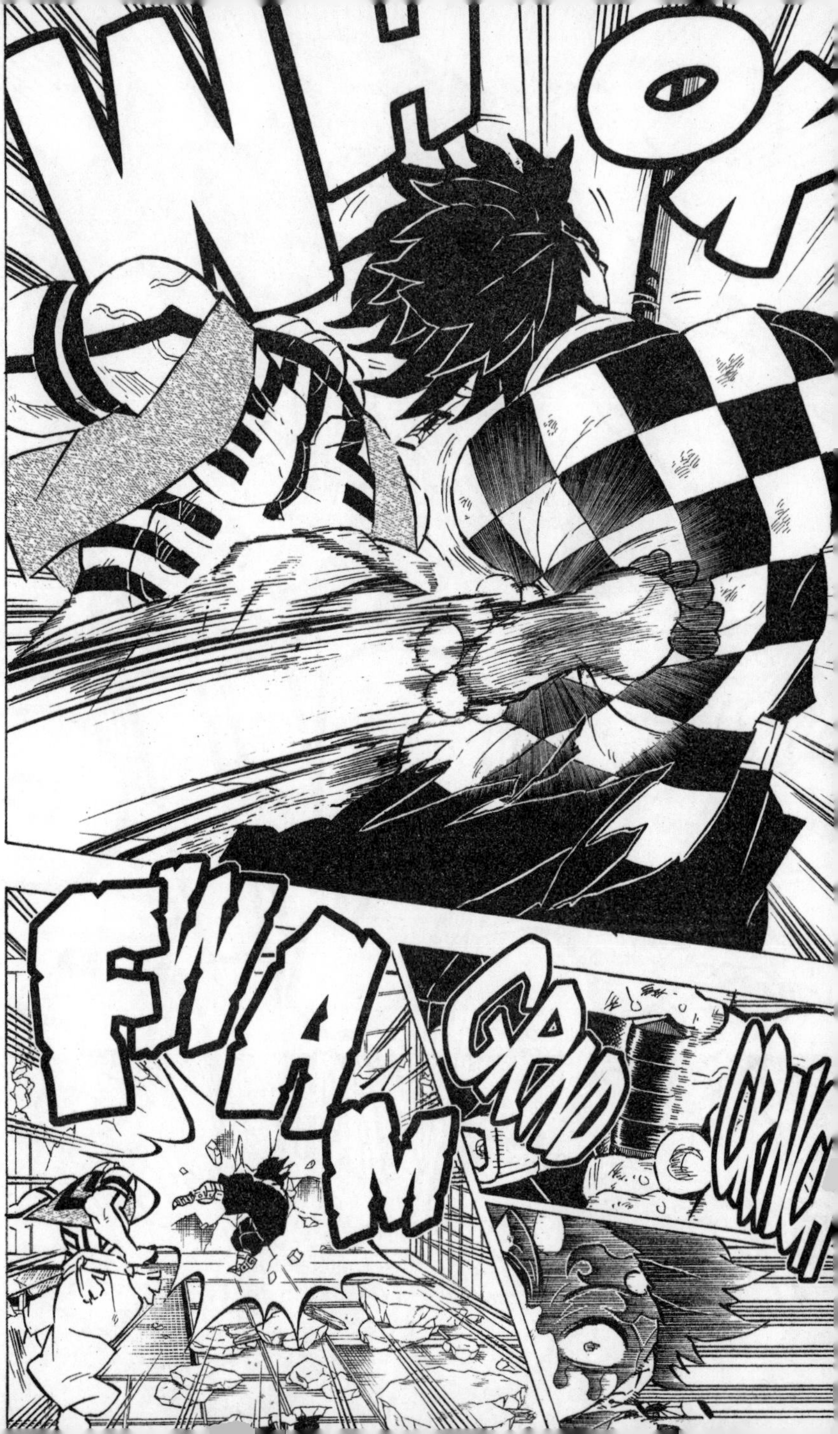
WHOK
F'WAM
GRIND
CRNCH

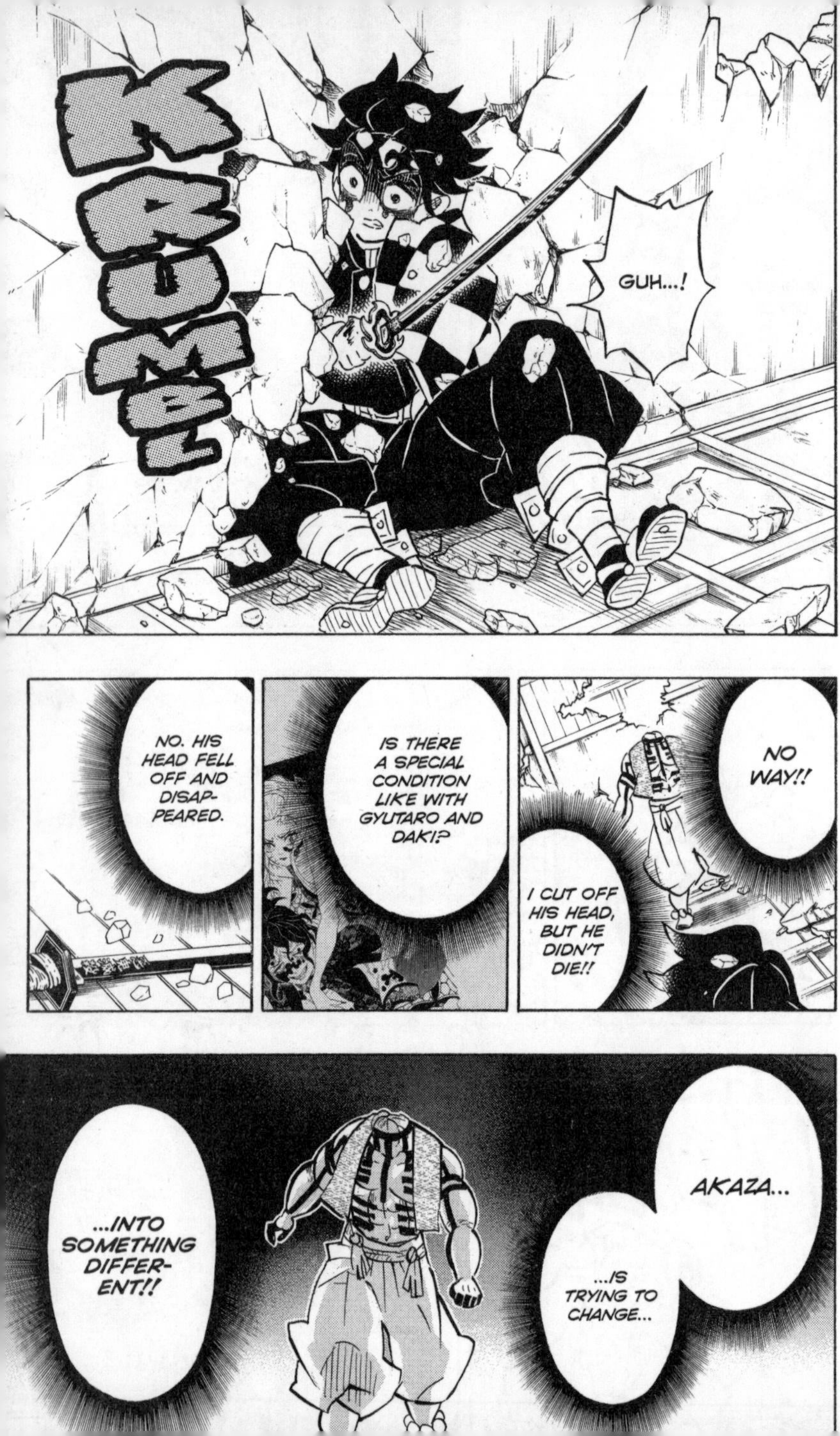
GUH...!
KRUMBL
NO WAY!!
I CUT OFF HIS HEAD, BUT HE DIDN'T DIE!!
IS THERE A SPECIAL CONDITION LIKE WITH GYUTARO AND DAKI!?
NO. HIS HEAD FELL OFF AND DISAP-PEARED.
AKAZA...
...IS TRYING TO CHANGE...
...INTO SOMETHING DIFFER-ENT!!

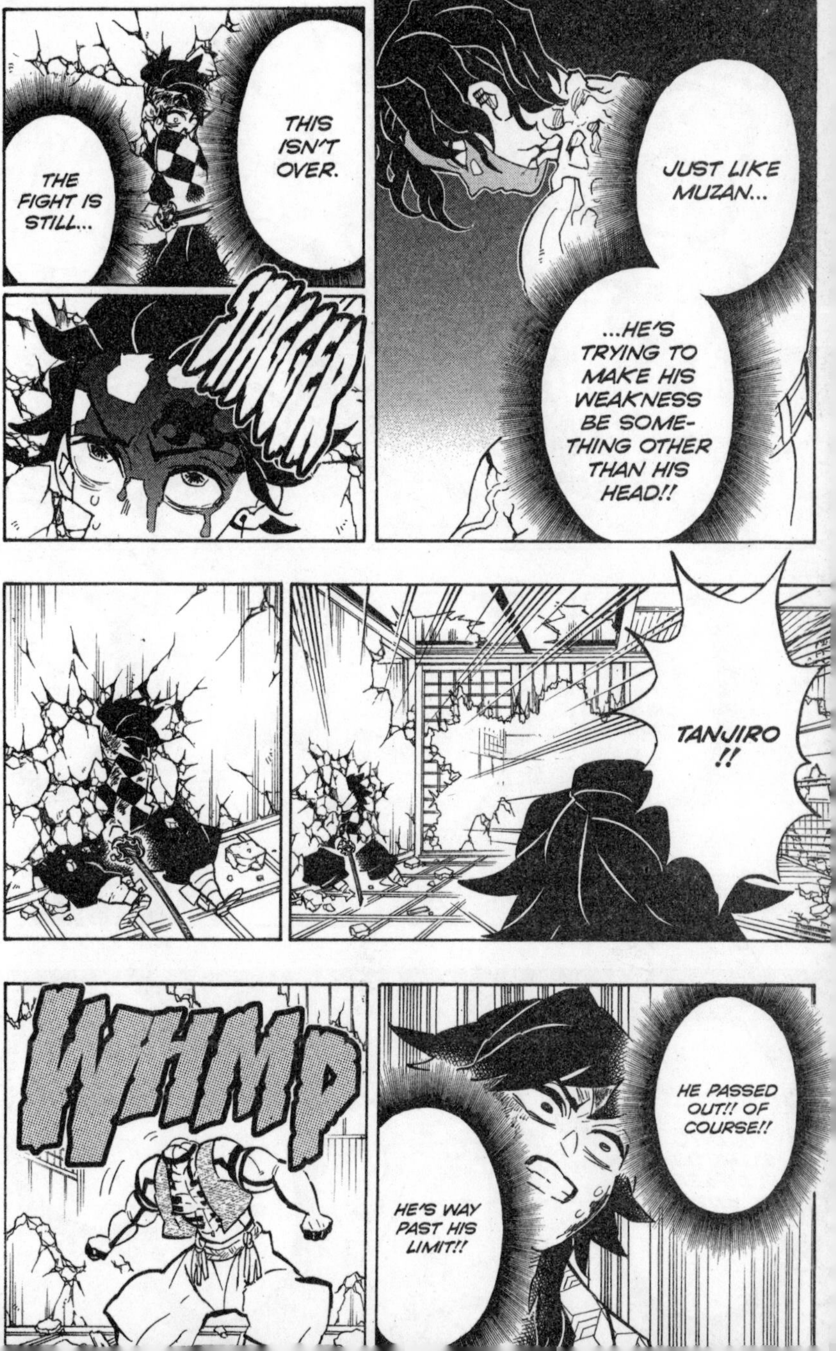
JUST LIKE MUZAN...
...HE'S TRYING TO MAKE HIS WEAKNESS BE SOME-THING OTHER THAN HIS HEAD!!
THIS ISN'T OVER.
THE FIGHT IS STILL...
TANJIRO !!
HE PASSED OUT!! OF COURSE!!
HE'S WAY PAST HIS LIMIT!!
WHMP

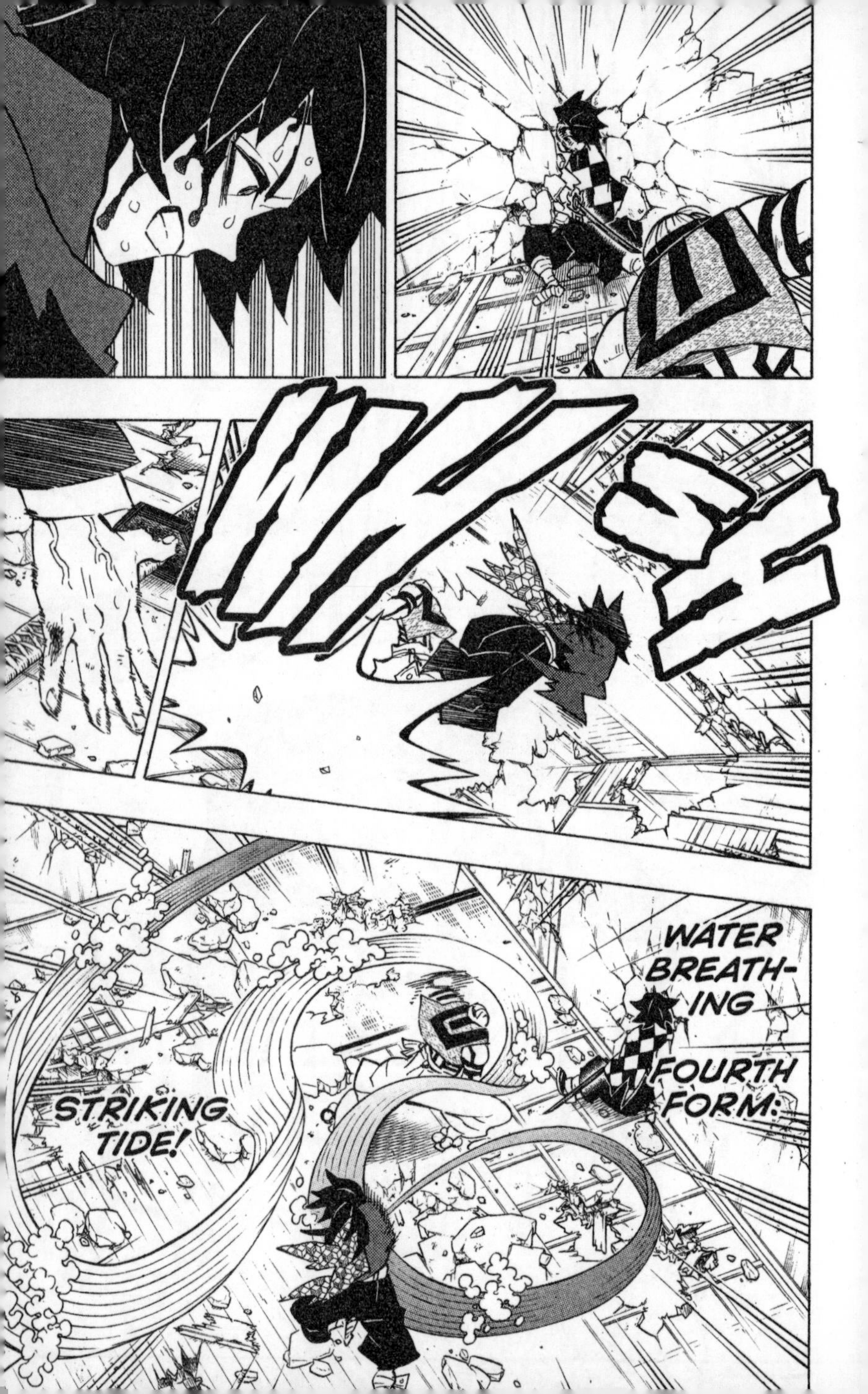
WHAM!
WATER BREATH-ING
FOURTH FORM:
STRIKING TIDE!

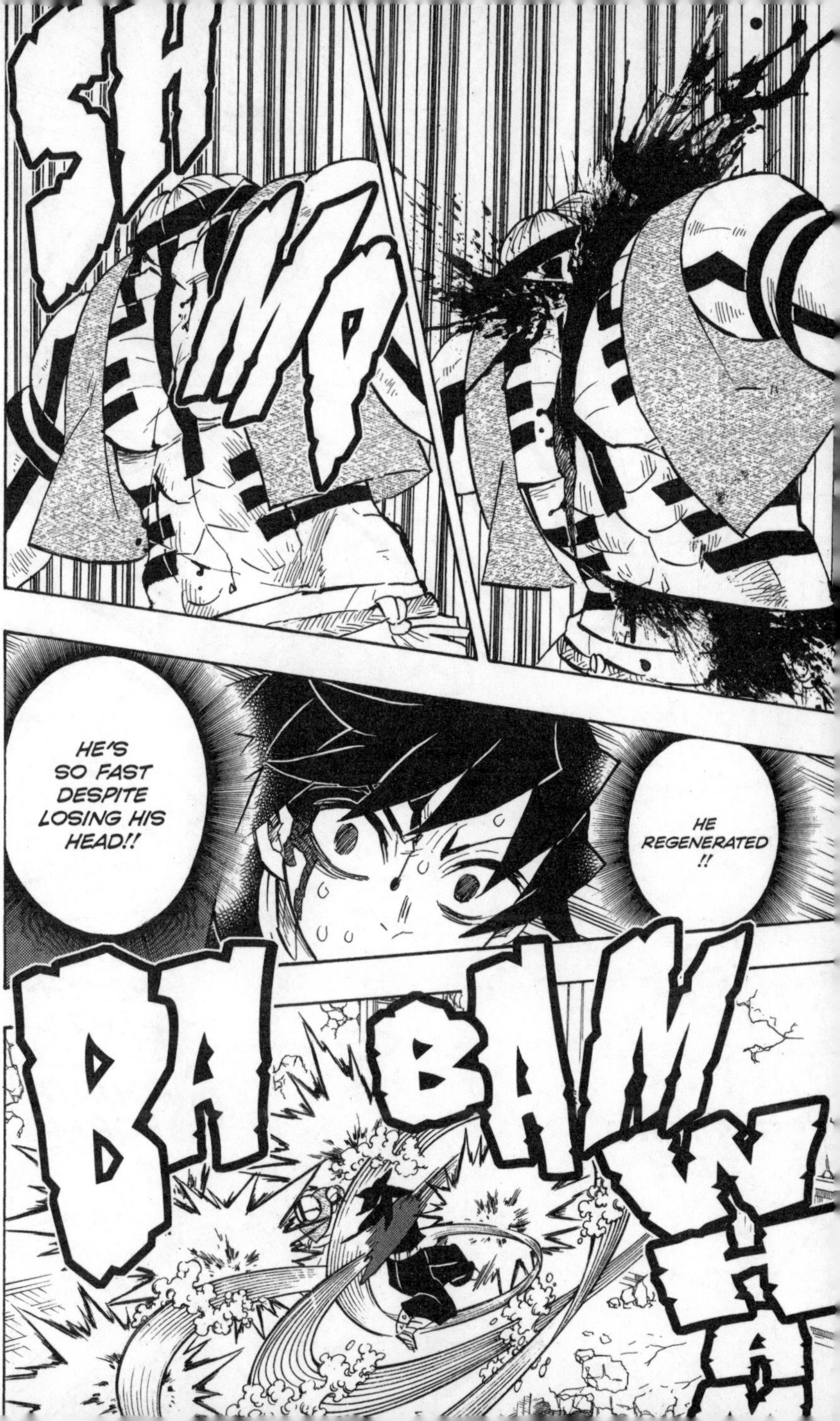
SHMP
HE REGENERATED!!
HE'S SO FAST DESPITE LOSING HIS HEAD!!
BA BAM

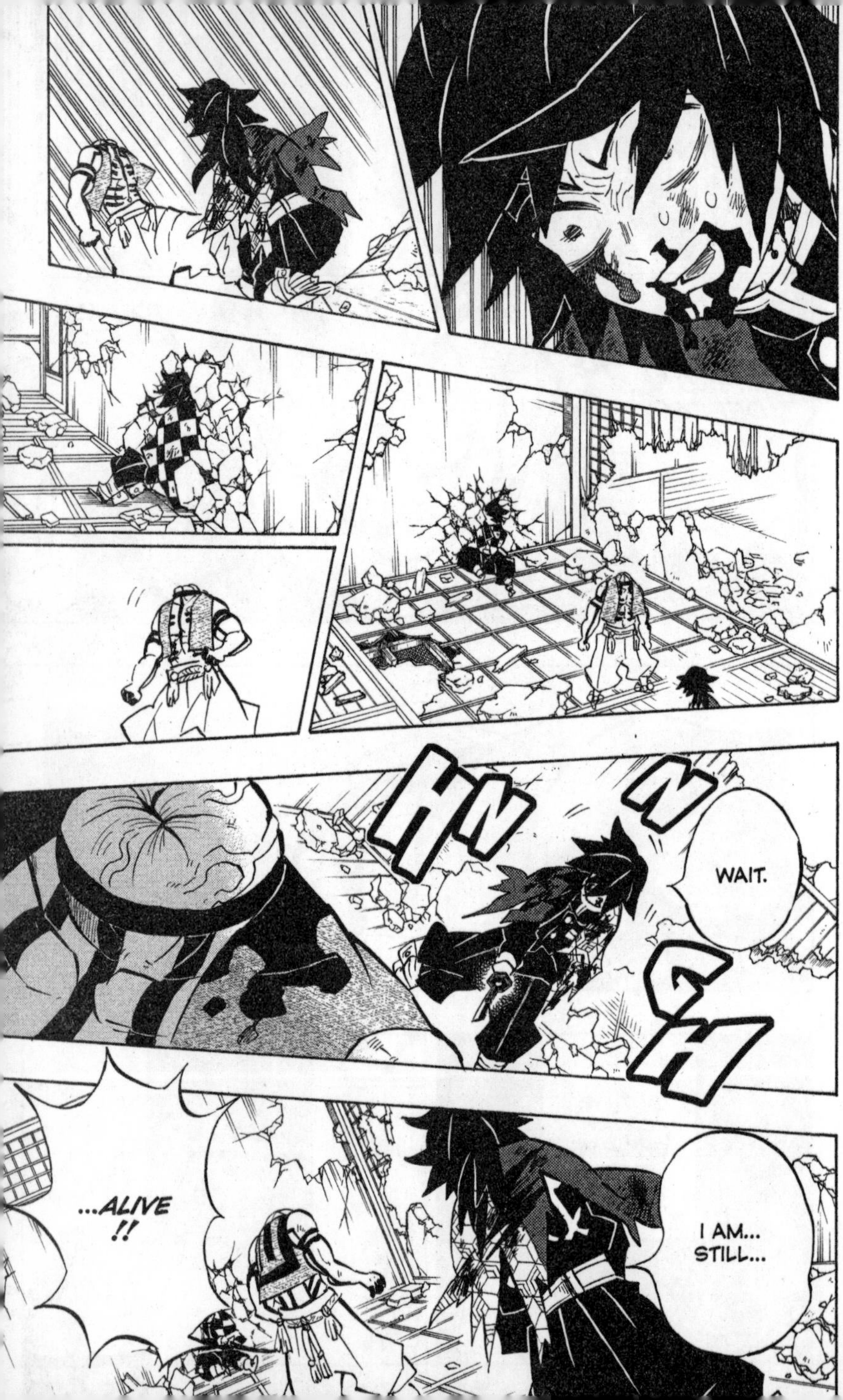
WAIT.
HNNGH
I AM... STILL...
...ALIVE !!

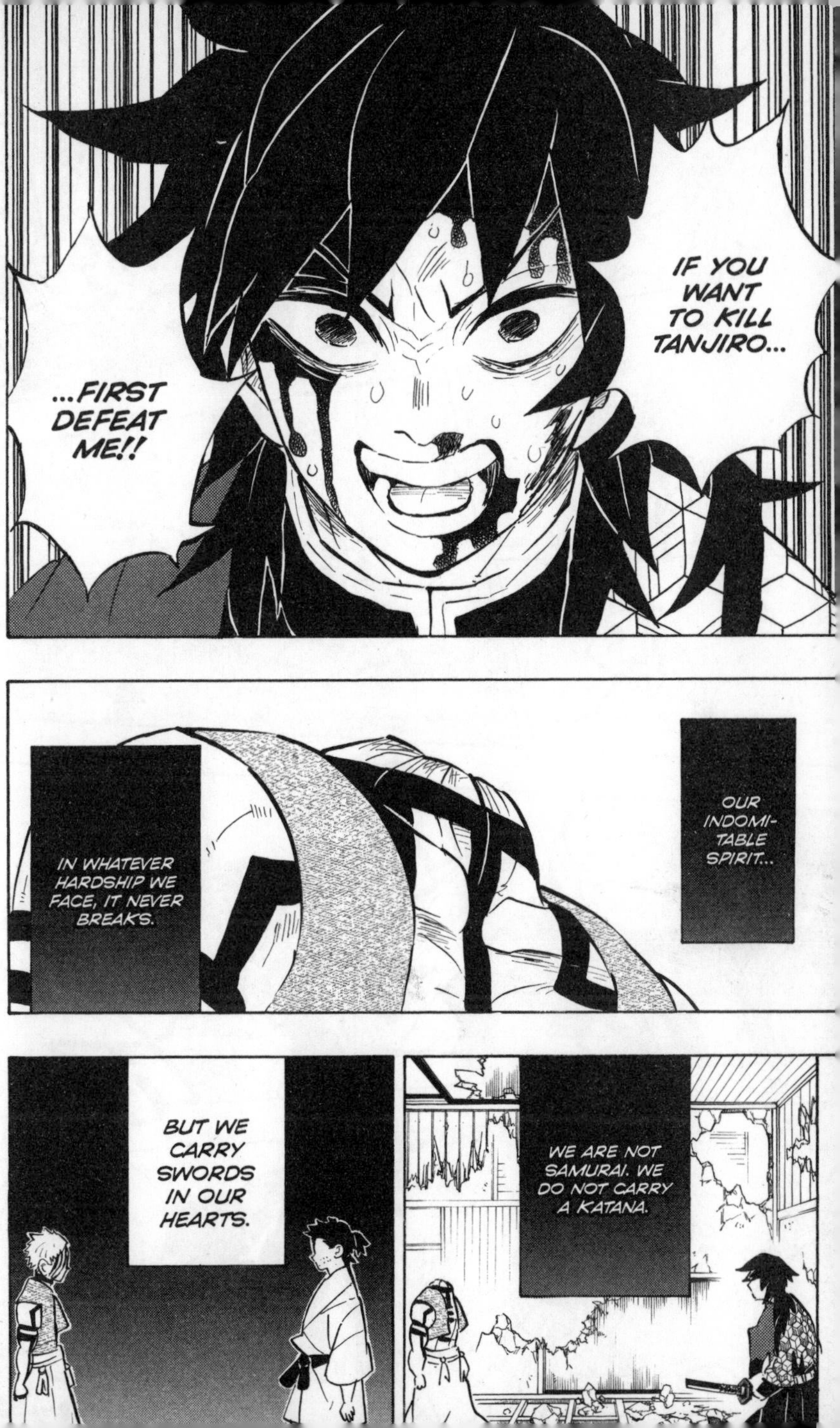
IF YOU WANT TO KILL TANJIRO...
...FIRST DEFEAT ME!!
OUR INDOMI-TABLE SPIRIT...
IN WHATEVER HARDSHIP WE FACE, IT NEVER BREAKS.
WE ARE NOT SAMURAI. WE DO NOT CARRY A KATANA.
BUT WE CARRY SWORDS IN OUR HEARTS.

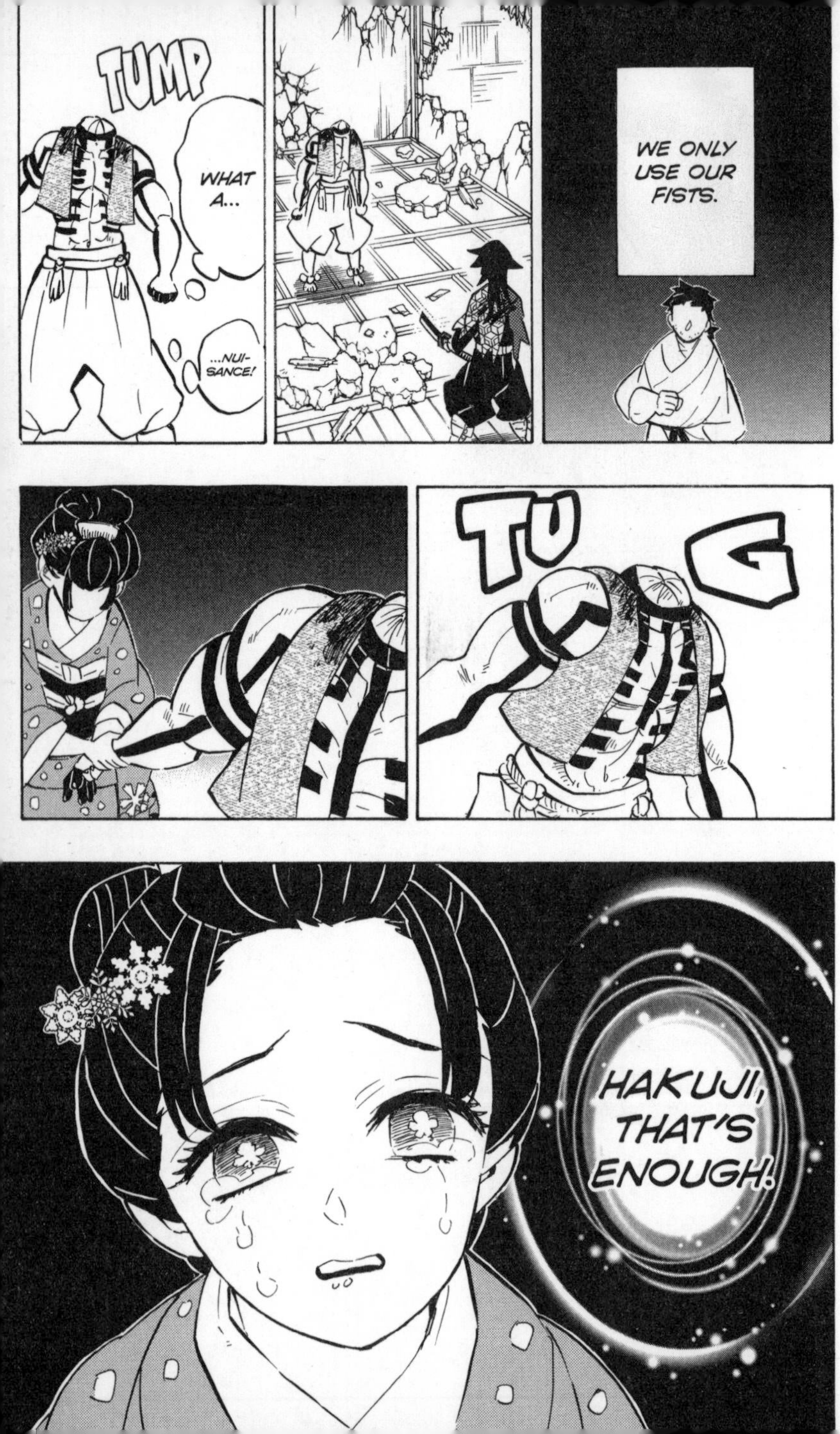
WE ONLY USE OUR FISTS.
TUMP
WHAT A...
...NUI-SANCE!
TU G
HAKUJI, THAT'S ENOUGH!

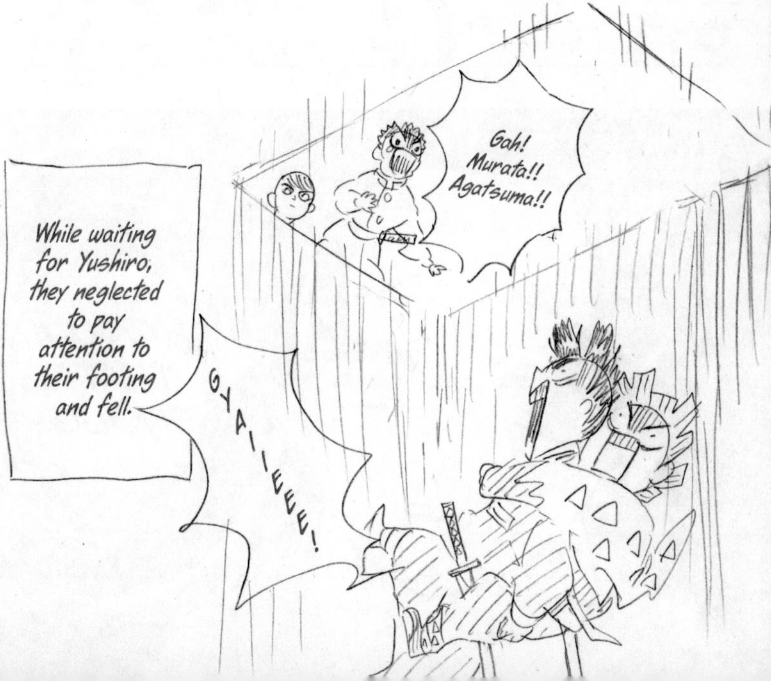
Gah! Murata!! Agatsuma!!
While waiting for Yushiro, they neglected to pay attention to their footing and fell.
GYAIIEEE!

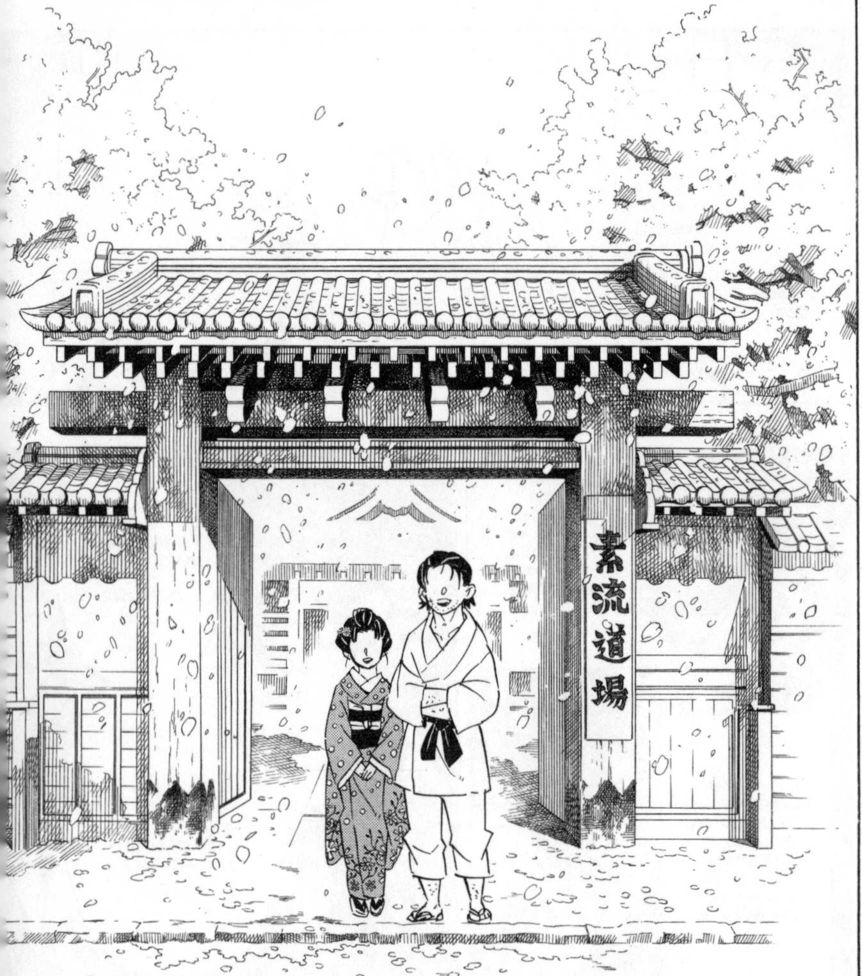
素流道場

CHAPTER 154: ASSAULTED BY MEMORIES

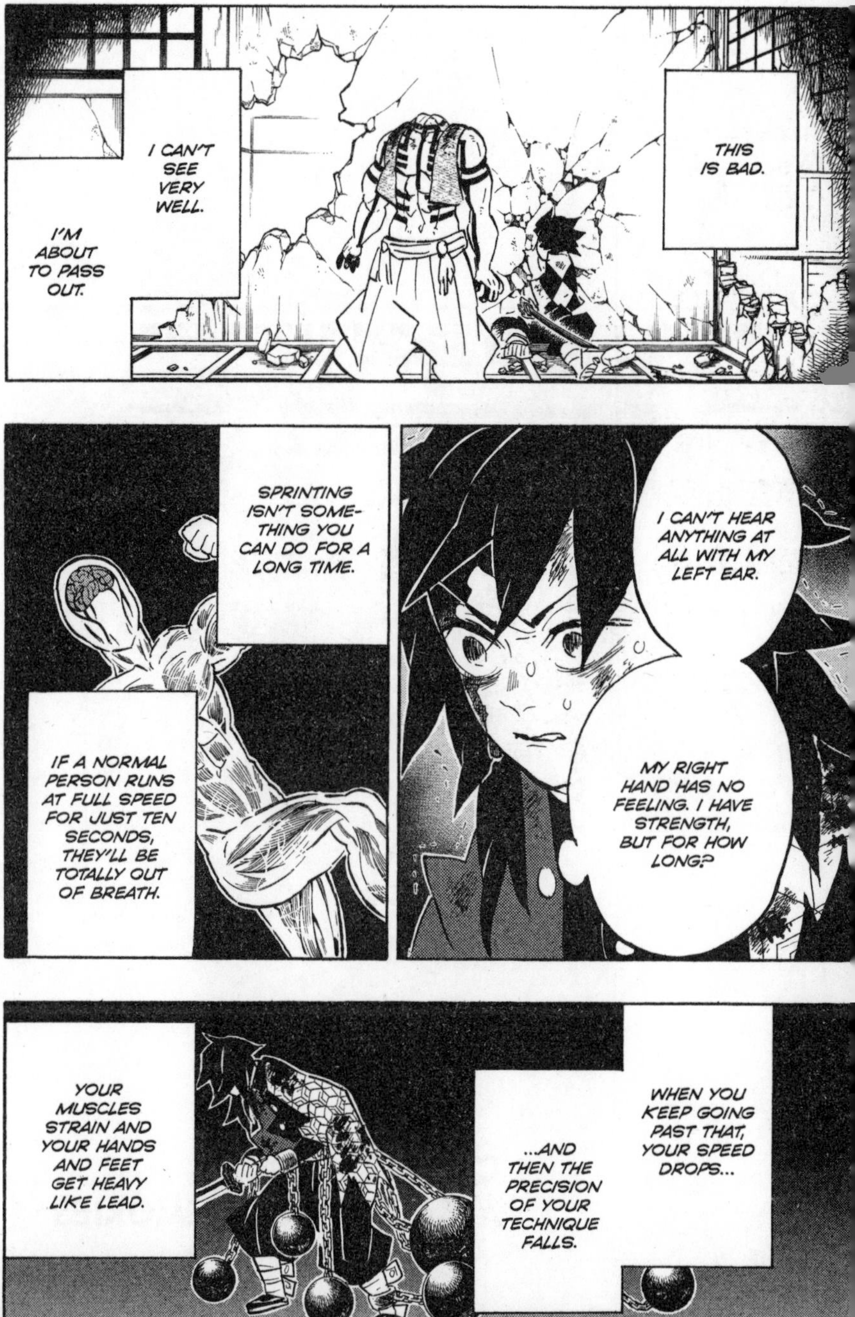
THIS IS BAD.
I CAN'T SEE VERY WELL.
I'M ABOUT TO PASS OUT.
I CAN'T HEAR ANYTHING AT ALL WITH MY LEFT EAR.
MY RIGHT HAND HAS NO FEELING. I HAVE STRENGTH, BUT FOR HOW LONG?
SPRINTING ISN'T SOME-THING YOU CAN DO FOR A LONG TIME.
IF A NORMAL PERSON RUNS AT FULL SPEED FOR JUST TEN SECONDS, THEY'LL BE TOTALLY OUT OF BREATH.
WHEN YOU KEEP GOING PAST THAT, YOUR SPEED DROPS...
...AND THEN THE PRECISION OF YOUR TECHNIQUE FALLS.
YOUR MUSCLES STRAIN AND YOUR HANDS AND FEET GET HEAVY LIKE LEAD.

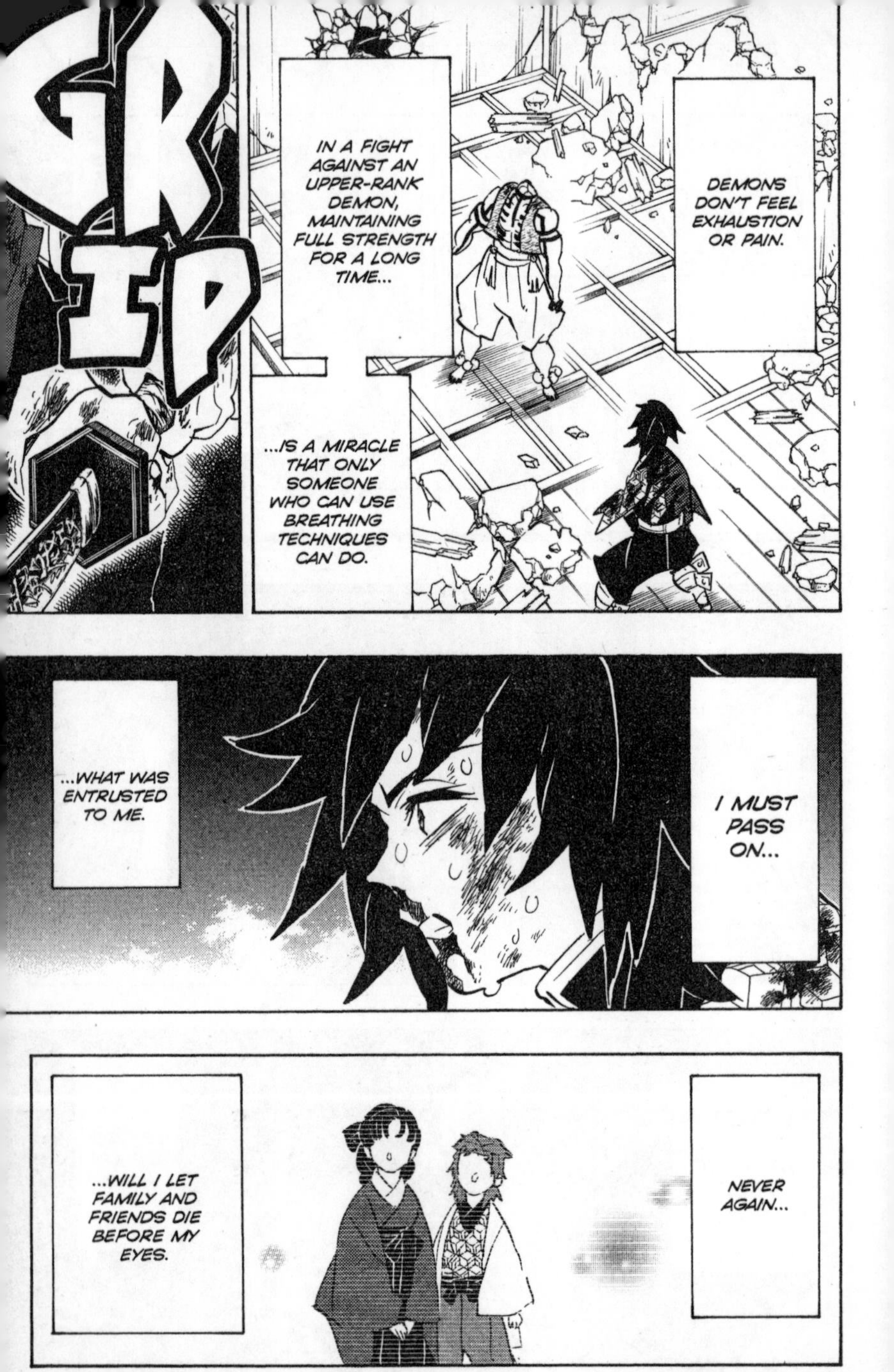
DEMONS DON'T FEEL EXHAUSTION OR PAIN.
IN A FIGHT AGAINST AN UPPER-RANK DEMON, MAINTAINING FULL STRENGTH FOR A LONG TIME...
...IS A MIRACLE THAT ONLY SOMEONE WHO CAN USE BREATHING TECHNIQUES CAN DO.
GRIP
I MUST PASS ON...
...WHAT WAS ENTRUSTED TO ME.
NEVER AGAIN...
...WILL I LET FAMILY AND FRIENDS DIE BEFORE MY EYES.

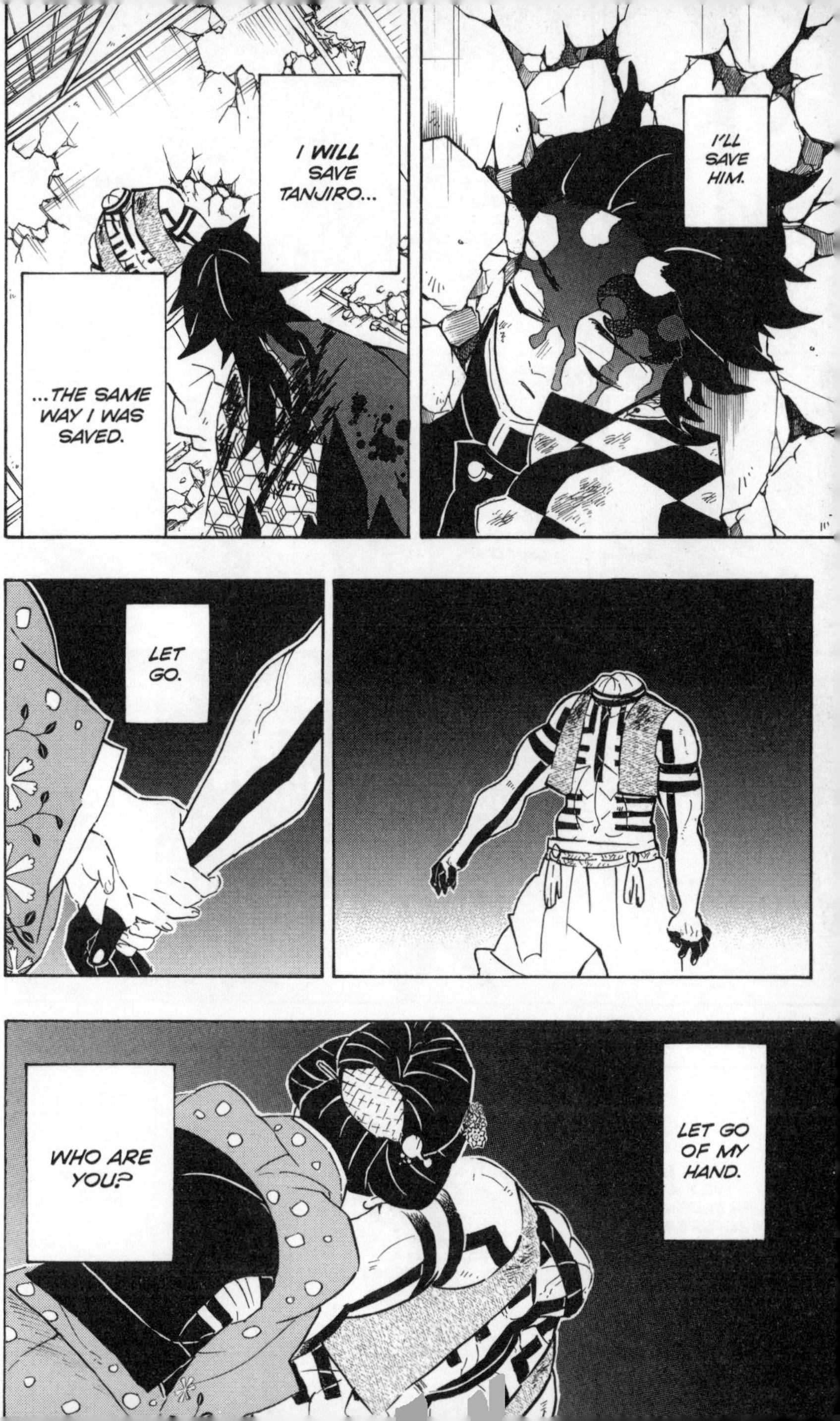
I'LL SAVE HIM.
I WILL SAVE TANJIRO...
...THE SAME WAY I WAS SAVED.
LET GO.
LET GO OF MY HAND.
WHO ARE YOU?

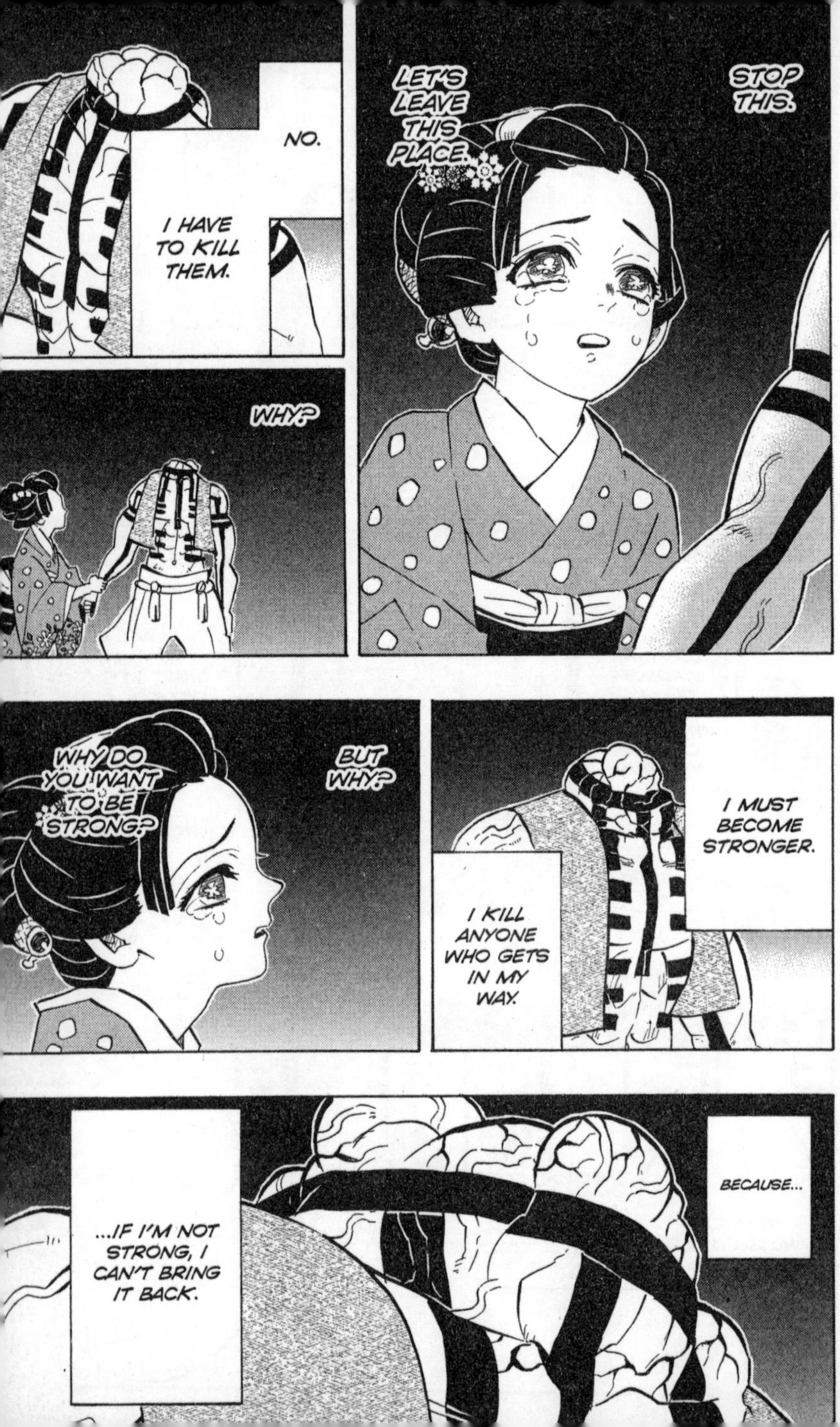
STOP THIS.
LET'S LEAVE THIS PLACE.
NO.
I HAVE TO KILL THEM.
WHY?
I MUST BECOME STRONGER.
I KILL ANYONE WHO GETS IN MY WAY.
BUT WHY?
WHY DO YOU WANT TO BE STRONG?
BECAUSE...
...IF I'M NOT STRONG, I CAN'T BRING IT BACK.

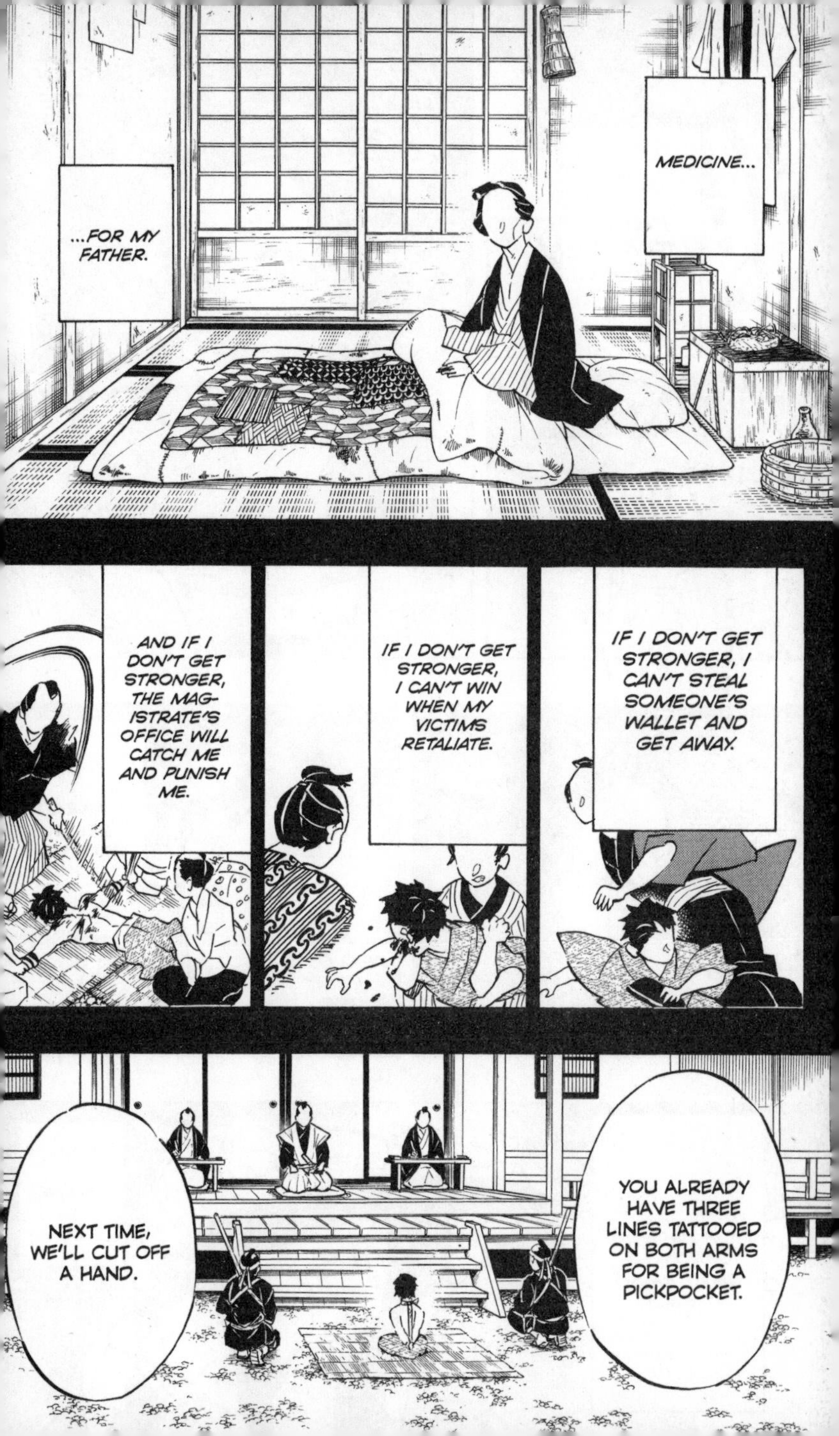
MEDICINE...
...FOR MY FATHER.
IF I DON'T GET STRONGER, I CAN'T STEAL SOMEONE'S WALLET AND GET AWAY.
IF I DON'T GET STRONGER, I CAN'T WIN WHEN MY VICTIMS RETALIATE.
AND IF I DON'T GET STRONGER, THE MAGISTRATE'S OFFICE WILL CATCH ME AND PUNISH ME.
YOU ALREADY HAVE THREE LINES TATTOOED ON BOTH ARMS FOR BEING A PICKPOCKET.
NEXT TIME, WE'LL CUT OFF A HAND.

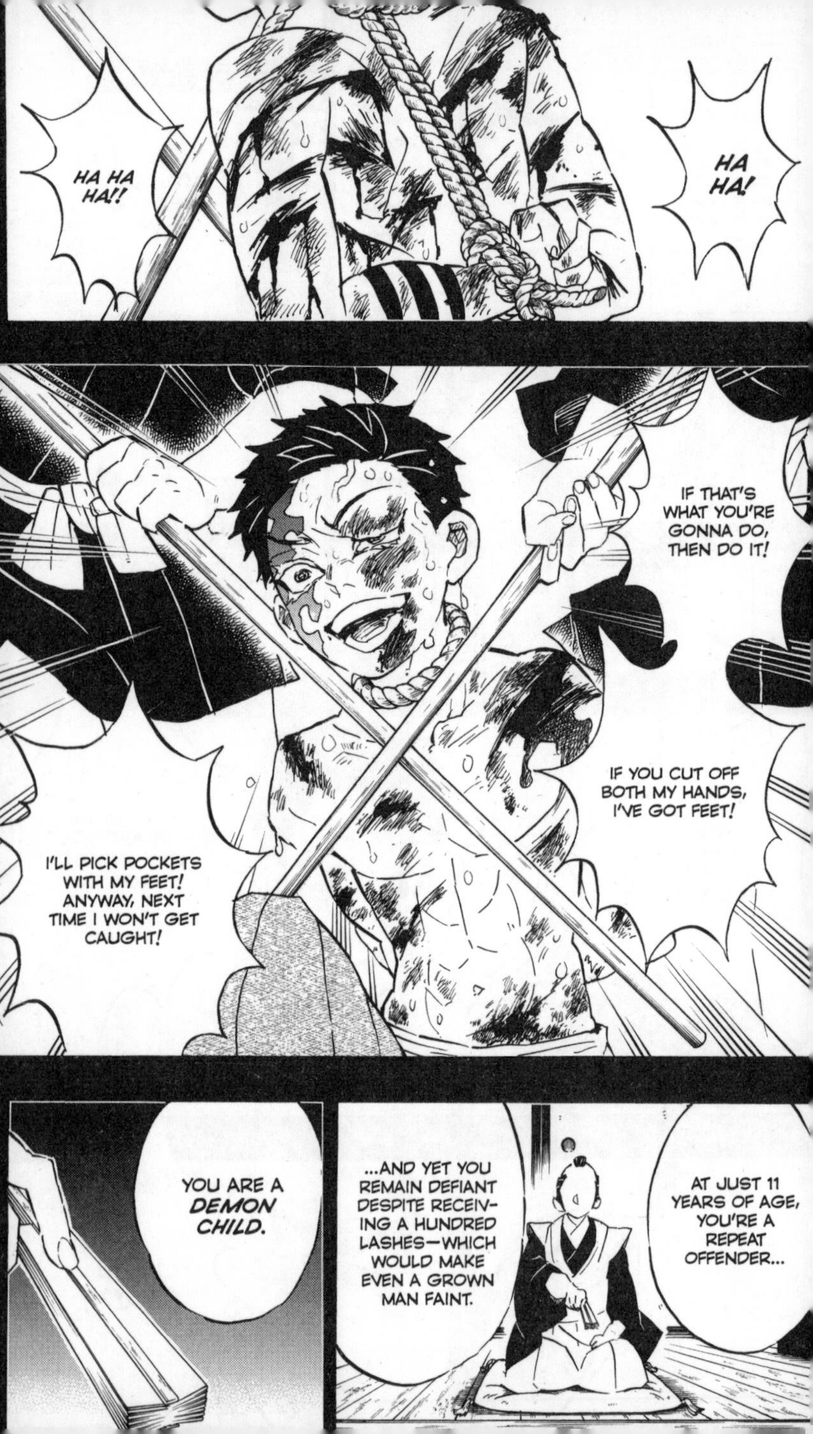
HA HA!
HA HA HA!!
IF THAT'S WHAT YOU'RE GONNA DO, THEN DO IT!
IF YOU CUT OFF BOTH MY HANDS, I'VE GOT FEET!
I'LL PICK POCKETS WITH MY FEET! ANYWAY, NEXT TIME I WON'T GET CAUGHT!
AT JUST 11 YEARS OF AGE, YOU'RE A REPEAT OFFENDER...
...AND YET YOU REMAIN DEFIANT DESPITE RECEIV-ING A HUNDRED LASHES—WHICH WOULD MAKE EVEN A GROWN MAN FAINT.
YOU ARE A *DEMON CHILD.*

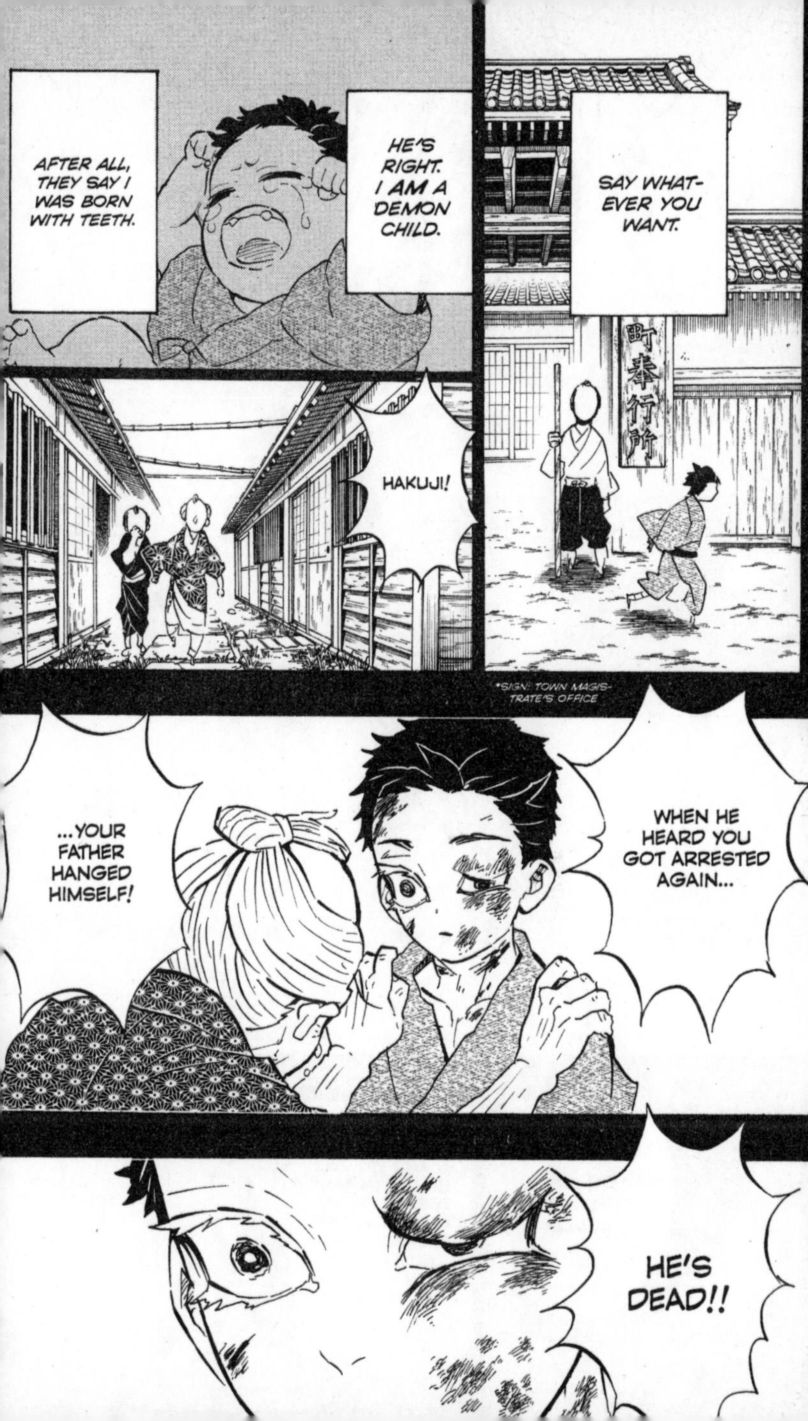
SAY WHAT-EVER YOU WANT.
町奉行所
*SIGN: TOWN MAGIS-TRATE'S OFFICE
HE'S RIGHT. I AM A DEMON CHILD.
AFTER ALL, THEY SAY I WAS BORN WITH TEETH.
HAKUJI!
WHEN HE HEARD YOU GOT ARRESTED AGAIN...
...YOUR FATHER HANGED HIMSELF!
HE'S DEAD!!

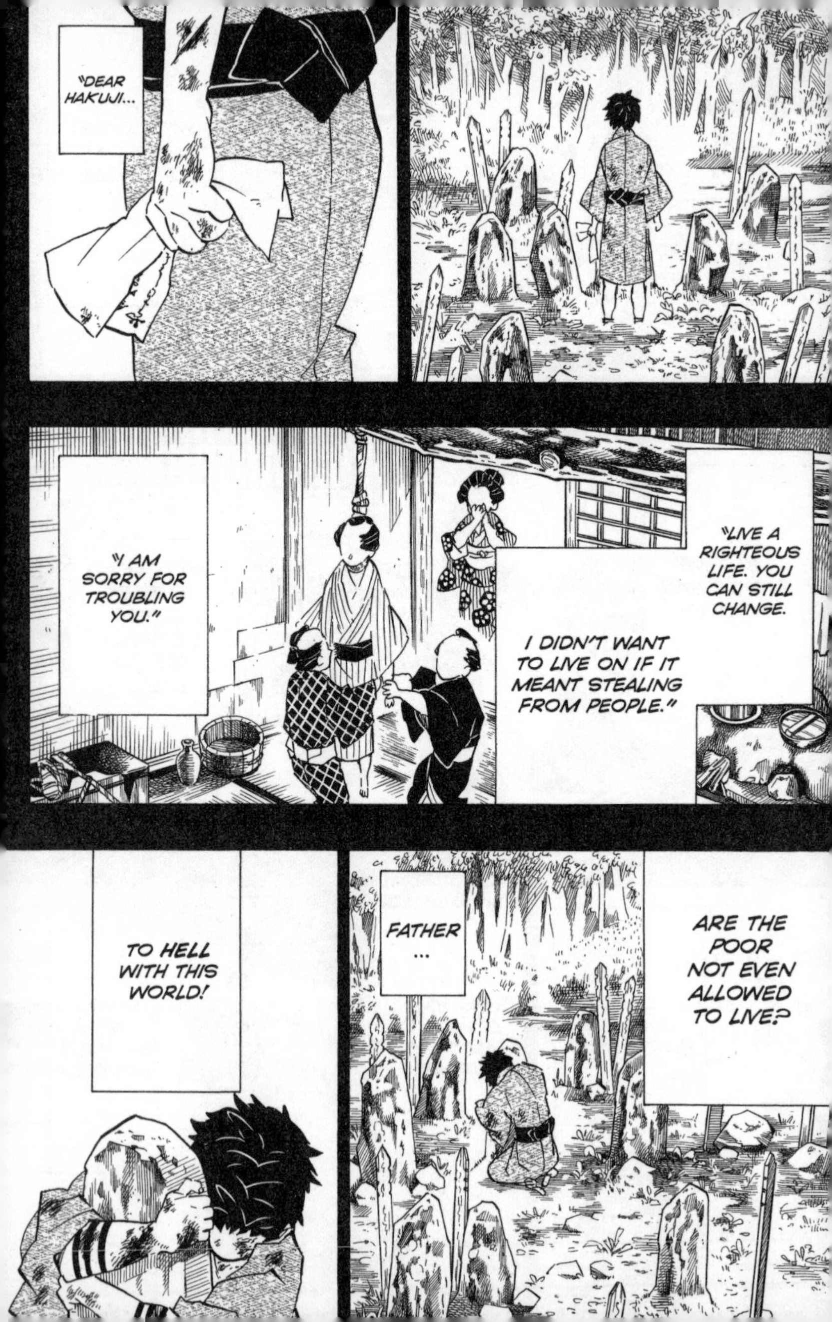
"DEAR HAKUJI...
"LIVE A RIGHTEOUS LIFE. YOU CAN STILL CHANGE.
I DIDN'T WANT TO LIVE ON IF IT MEANT STEALING FROM PEOPLE."
"I AM SORRY FOR TROUBLING YOU."
ARE THE POOR NOT EVEN ALLOWED TO LIVE?
FATHER ...
TO HELL WITH THIS WORLD!

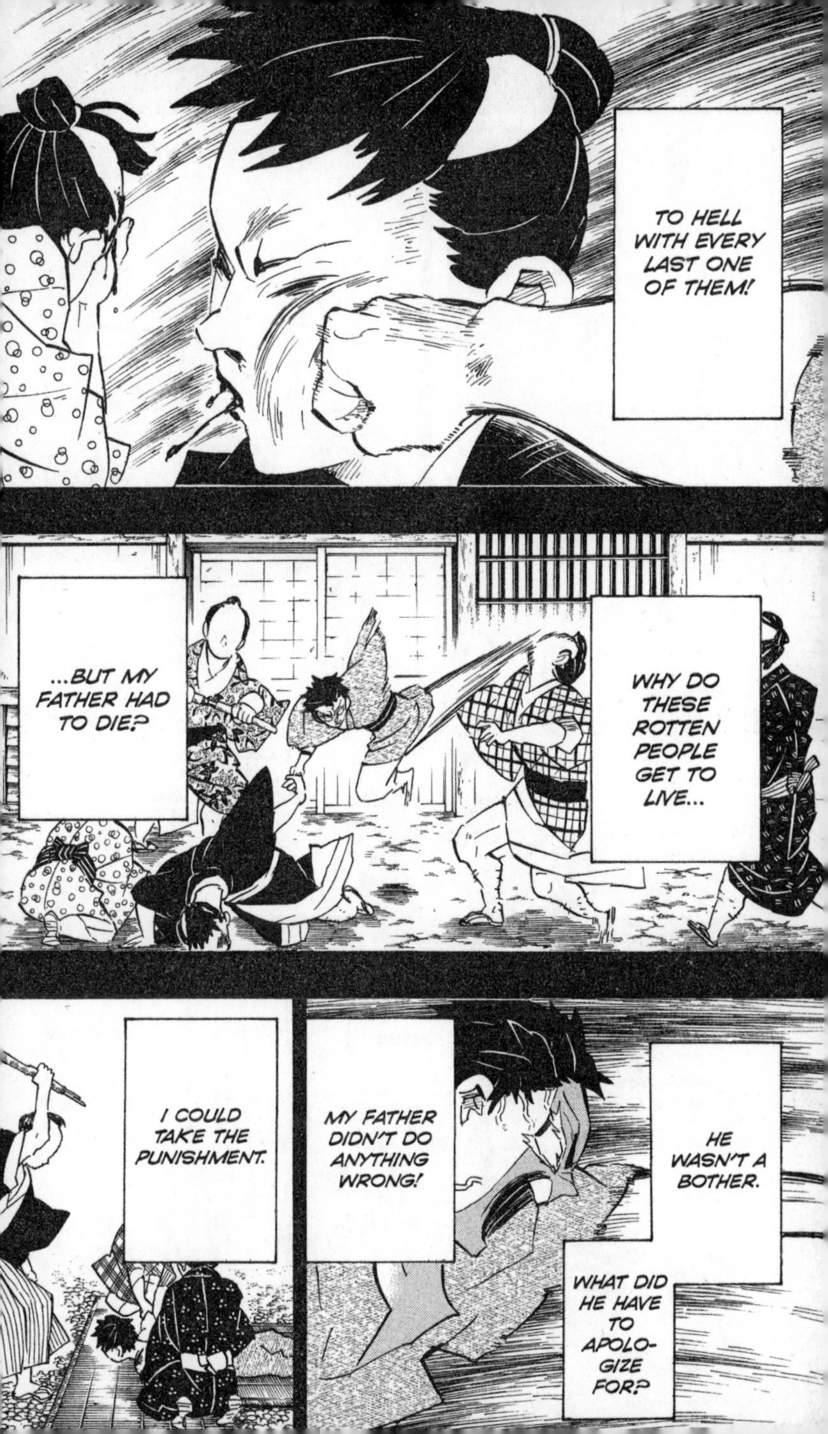
TO HELL WITH EVERY LAST ONE OF THEM!
WHY DO THESE ROTTEN PEOPLE GET TO LIVE...
...BUT MY FATHER HAD TO DIE?
HE WASN'T A BOTHER.
MY FATHER DIDN'T DO ANYTHING WRONG!
WHAT DID HE HAVE TO APOLO-GIZE FOR?
I COULD TAKE THE PUNISHMENT.

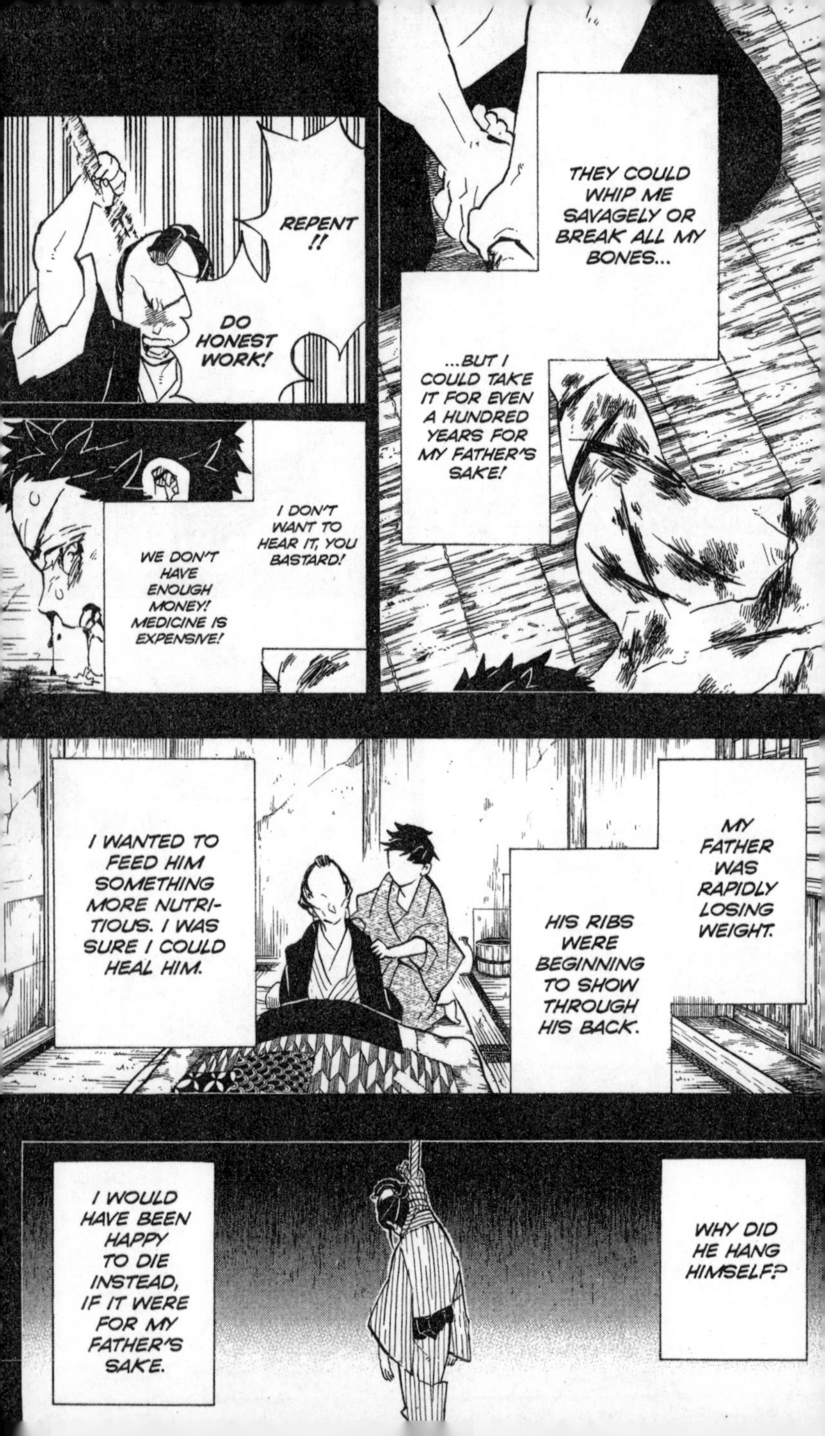
THEY COULD WHIP ME SAVAGELY OR BREAK ALL MY BONES...
...BUT I COULD TAKE IT FOR EVEN A HUNDRED YEARS FOR MY FATHER'S SAKE!
REPENT!!
DO HONEST WORK!
I DON'T WANT TO HEAR IT, YOU BASTARD!
WE DON'T HAVE ENOUGH MONEY! MEDICINE IS EXPENSIVE!
MY FATHER WAS RAPIDLY LOSING WEIGHT.
HIS RIBS WERE BEGINNING TO SHOW THROUGH HIS BACK.
I WANTED TO FEED HIM SOMETHING MORE NUTRI-TIOUS. I WAS SURE I COULD HEAL HIM.
WHY DID HE HANG HIMSELF?
I WOULD HAVE BEEN HAPPY TO DIE INSTEAD, IF IT WERE FOR MY FATHER'S SAKE.

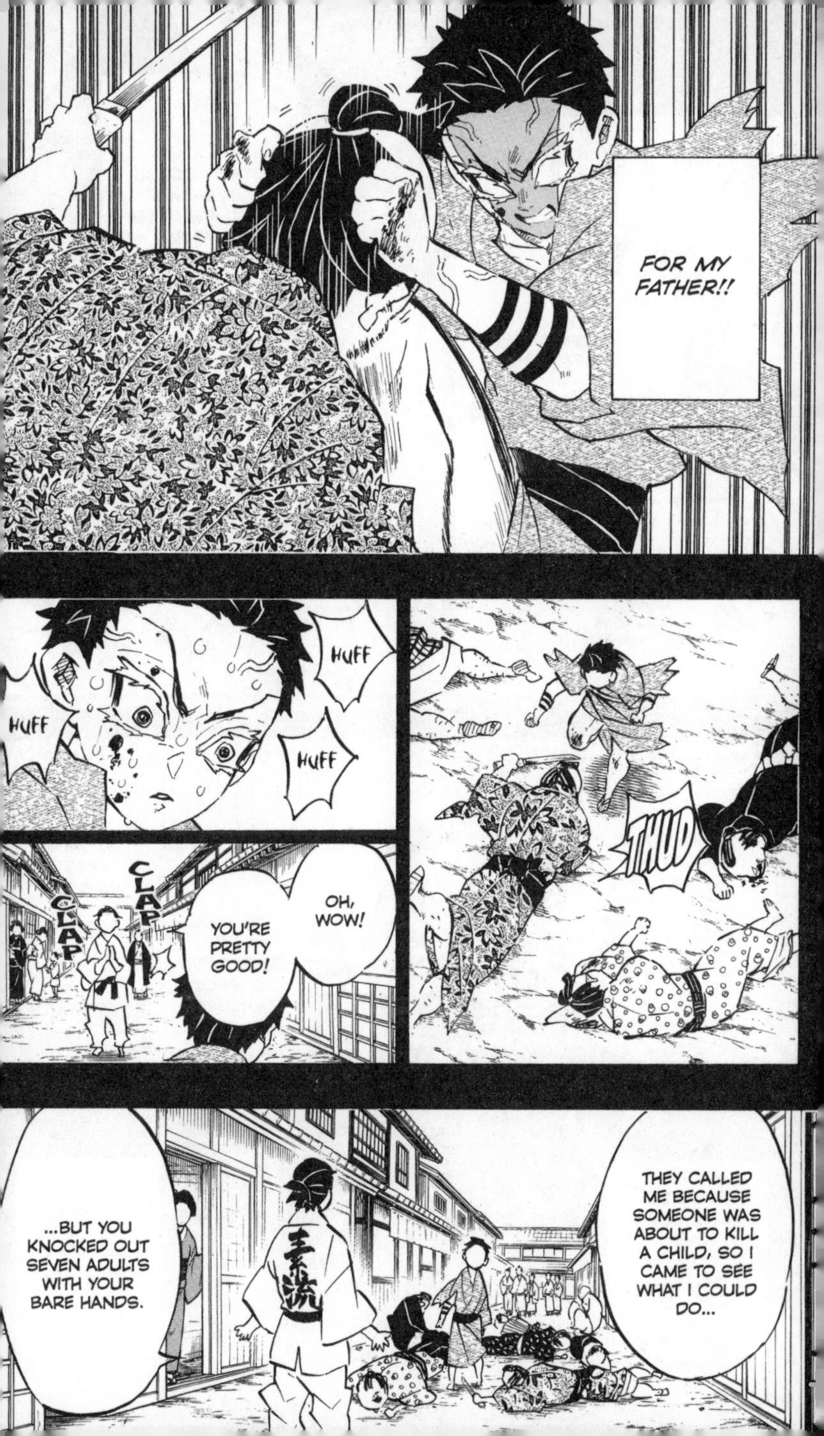
FOR MY FATHER!!
THUD
HUFF
HUFF
HUFF
OH, WOW!
YOU'RE PRETTY GOOD!
CLAP
CLAP
THEY CALLED ME BECAUSE SOMEONE WAS ABOUT TO KILL A CHILD, SO I CAME TO SEE WHAT I COULD DO...
...BUT YOU KNOCKED OUT SEVEN ADULTS WITH YOUR BARE HANDS.

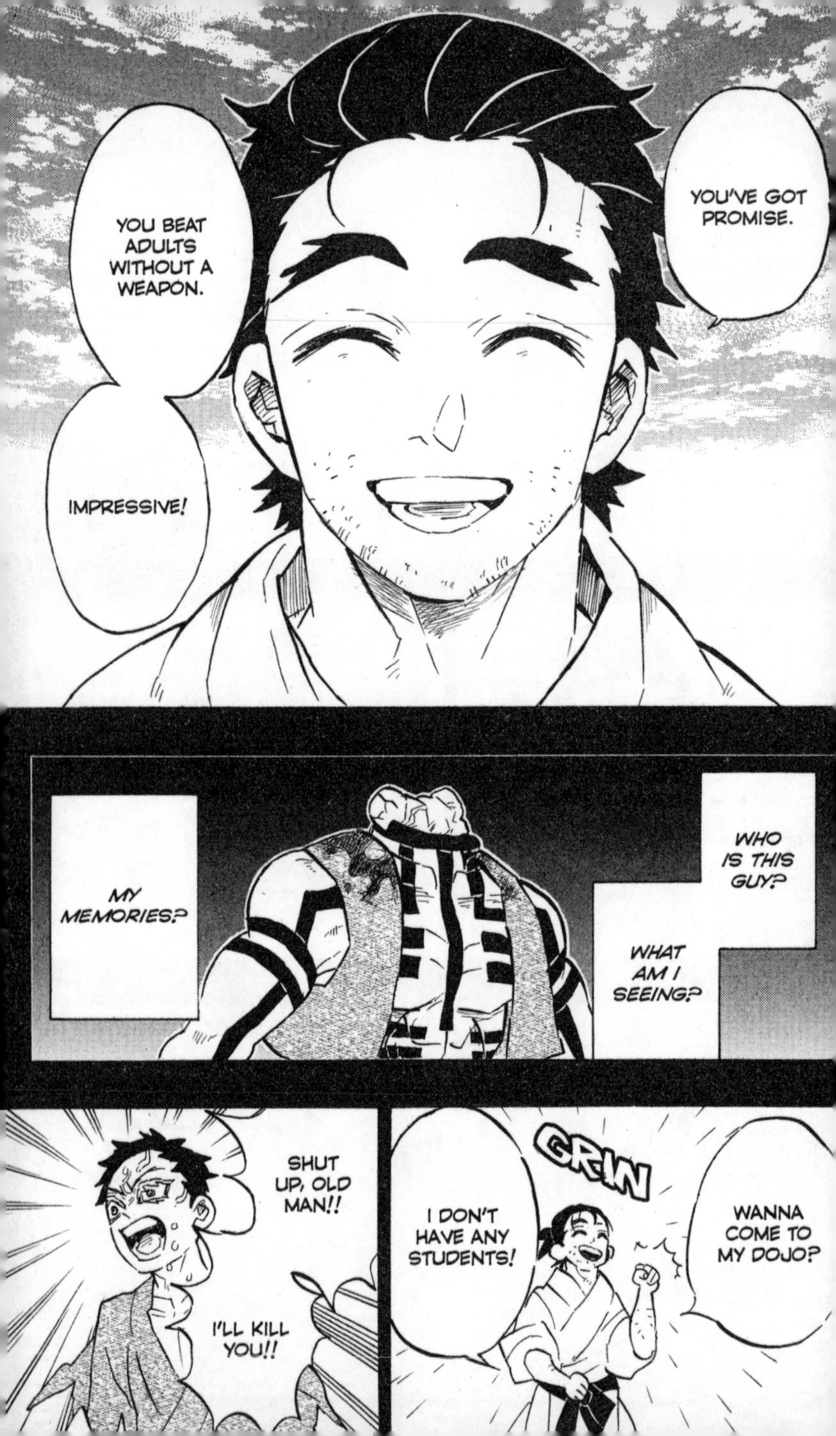
YOU'VE GOT PROMISE.
YOU BEAT ADULTS WITHOUT A WEAPON.
IMPRESSIVE!
WHO IS THIS GUY?
WHAT AM I SEEING?
MY MEMORIES?
WANNA COME TO MY DOJO?
GRIN
I DON'T HAVE ANY STUDENTS!
SHUT UP, OLD MAN!!
I'LL KILL YOU!!

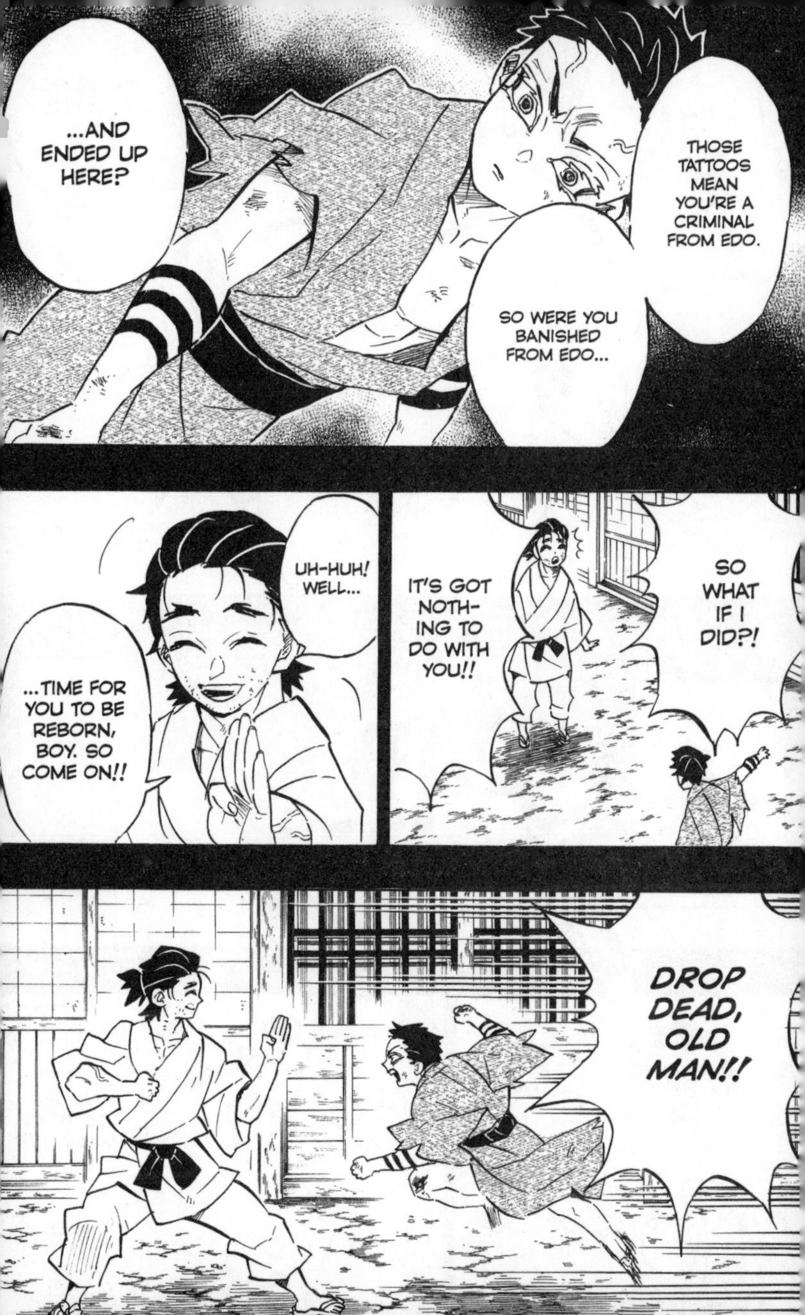
THOSE TATTOOS MEAN YOU'RE A CRIMINAL FROM EDO.
SO WERE YOU BANISHED FROM EDO...
...AND ENDED UP HERE?
SO WHAT IF I DID?!
IT'S GOT NOTHING TO DO WITH YOU!!
UH-HUH! WELL...
...TIME FOR YOU TO BE REBORN, BOY. SO COME ON!!
DROP DEAD, OLD MAN!!

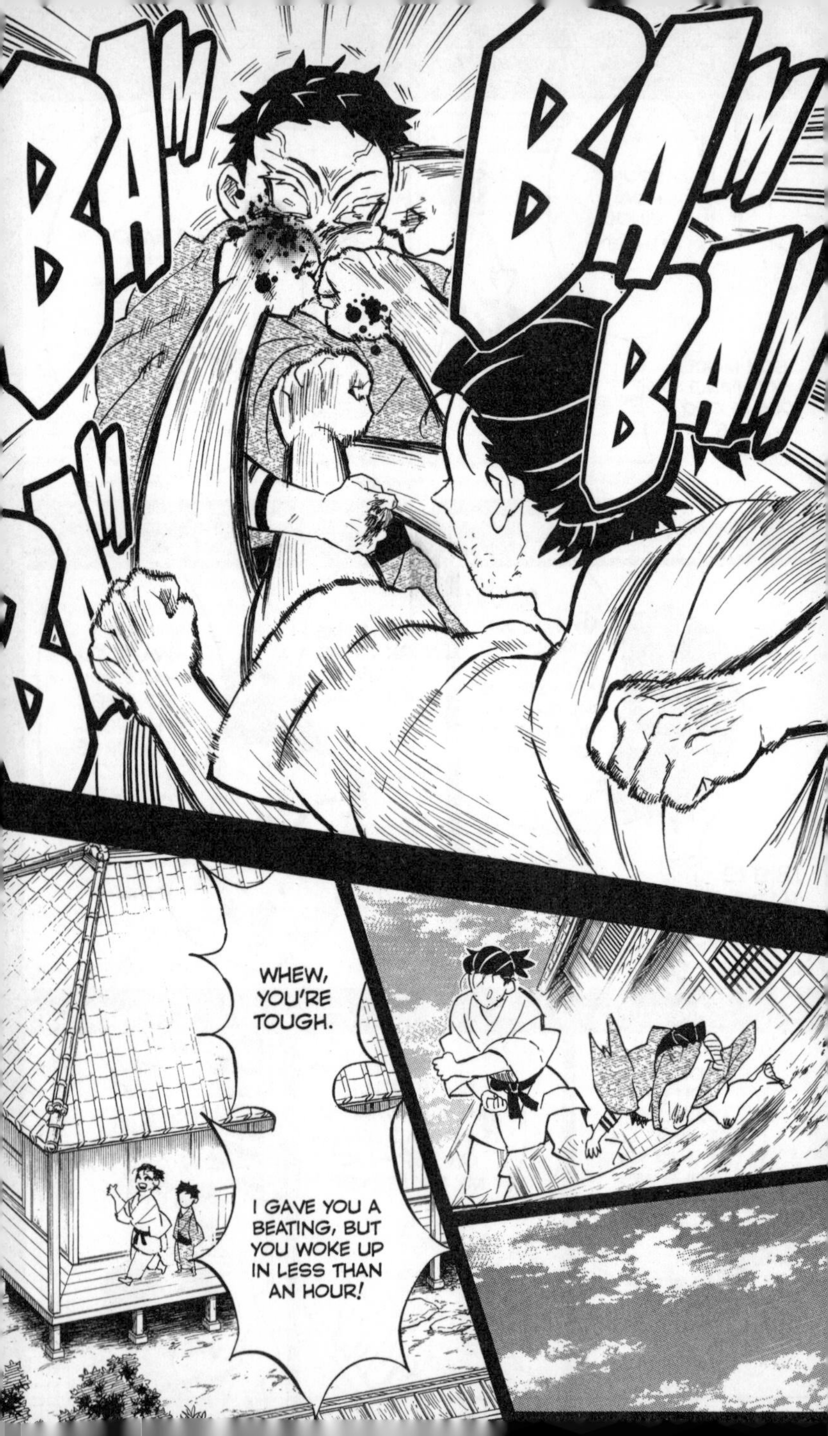
BAM
BAM
BAM
BAM
WHEW, YOU'RE TOUGH.
I GAVE YOU A BEATING, BUT YOU WOKE UP IN LESS THAN AN HOUR!

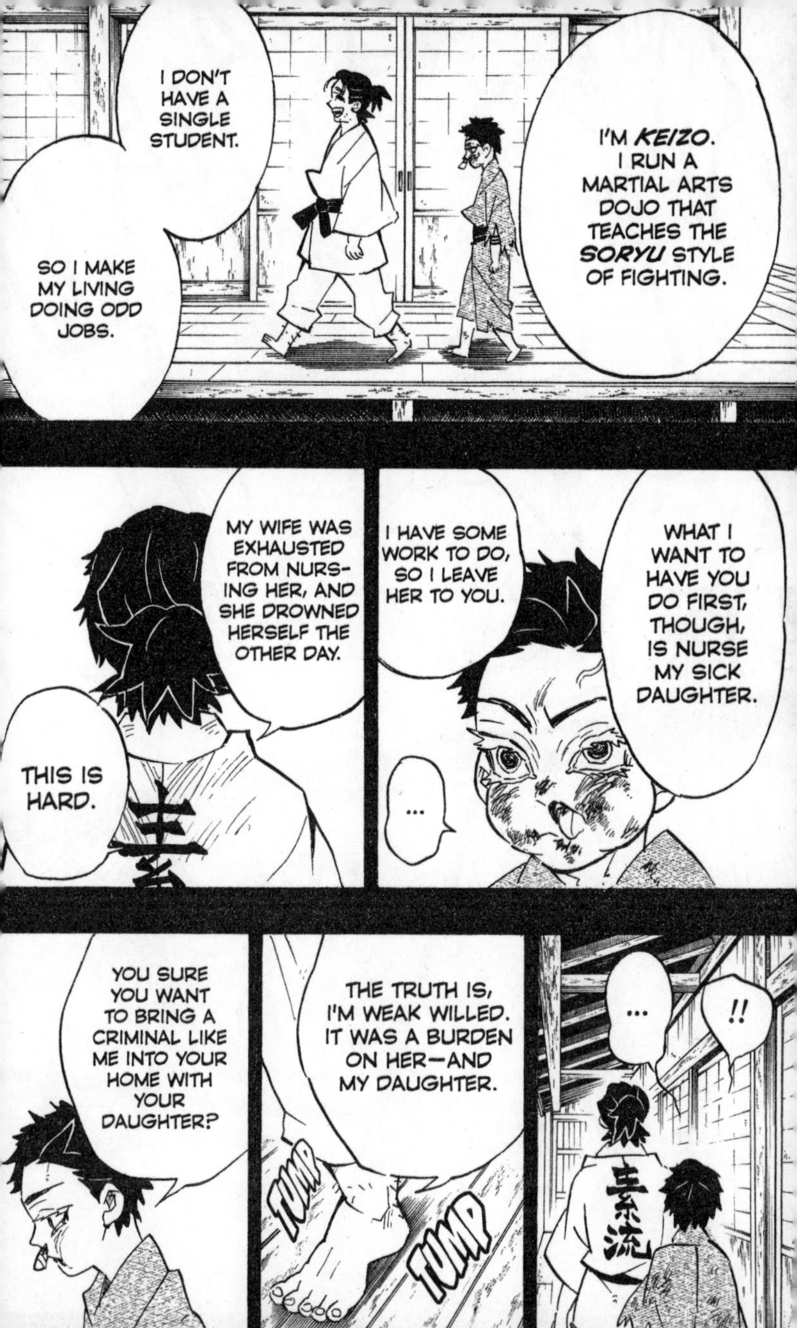
I'M KEIZO. I RUN A MARTIAL ARTS DOJO THAT TEACHES THE SORYU STYLE OF FIGHTING.
I DON'T HAVE A SINGLE STUDENT.
SO I MAKE MY LIVING DOING ODD JOBS.
WHAT I WANT TO HAVE YOU DO FIRST, THOUGH, IS NURSE MY SICK DAUGHTER.
I HAVE SOME WORK TO DO, SO I LEAVE HER TO YOU.
...
MY WIFE WAS EXHAUSTED FROM NURSING HER, AND SHE DROWNED HERSELF THE OTHER DAY.
THIS IS HARD.
!!
...
THE TRUTH IS, I'M WEAK WILLED. IT WAS A BURDEN ON HER—AND MY DAUGHTER.
TUMP
TUMP
YOU SURE YOU WANT TO BRING A CRIMINAL LIKE ME INTO YOUR HOME WITH YOUR DAUGHTER?

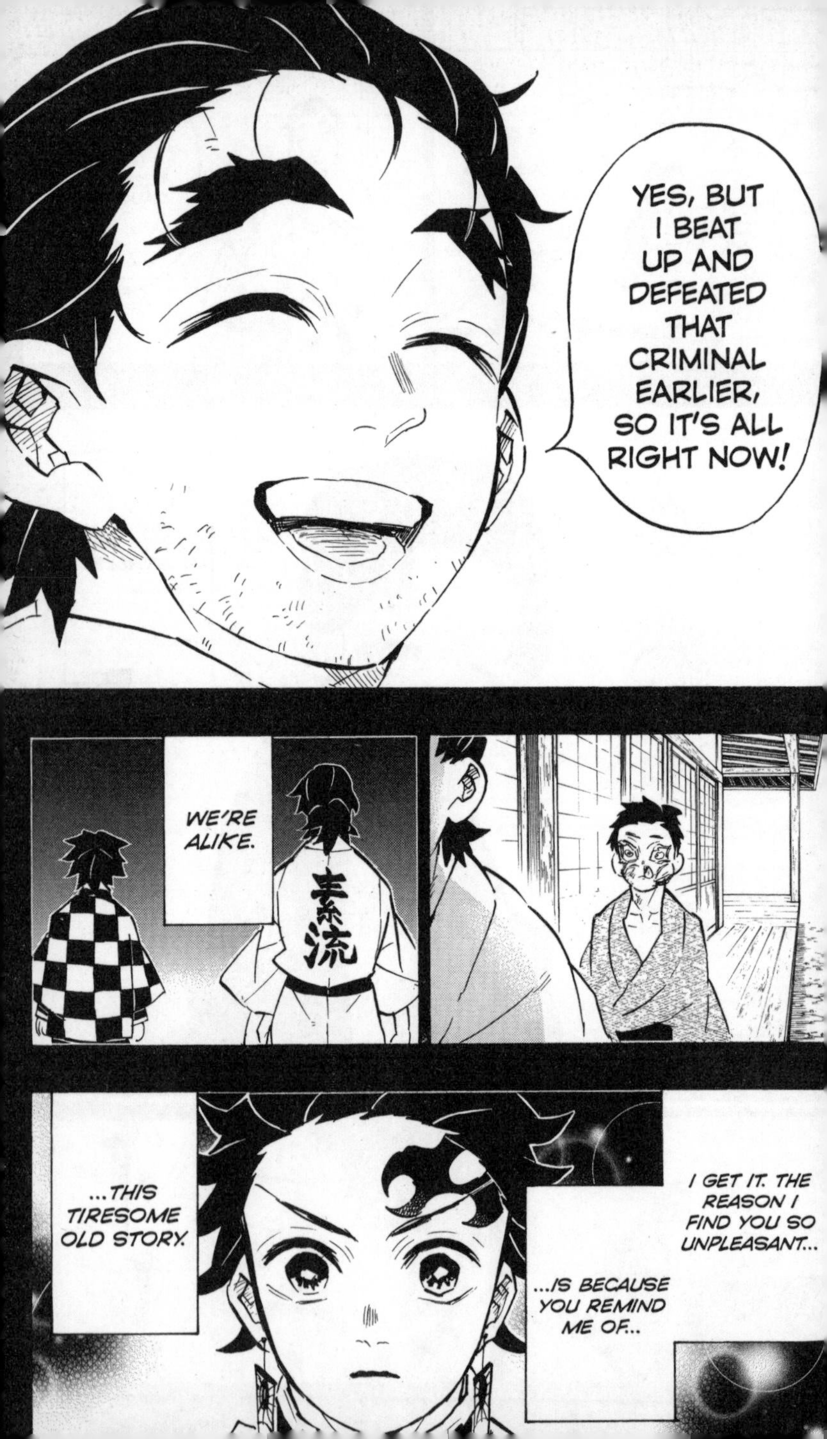
YES, BUT I BEAT UP AND DEFEATED THAT CRIMINAL EARLIER, SO IT'S ALL RIGHT NOW!
素流
WE'RE ALIKE.
I GET IT. THE REASON I FIND YOU SO UNPLEASANT...
...IS BECAUSE YOU REMIND ME OF...
...THIS TIRESOME OLD STORY.

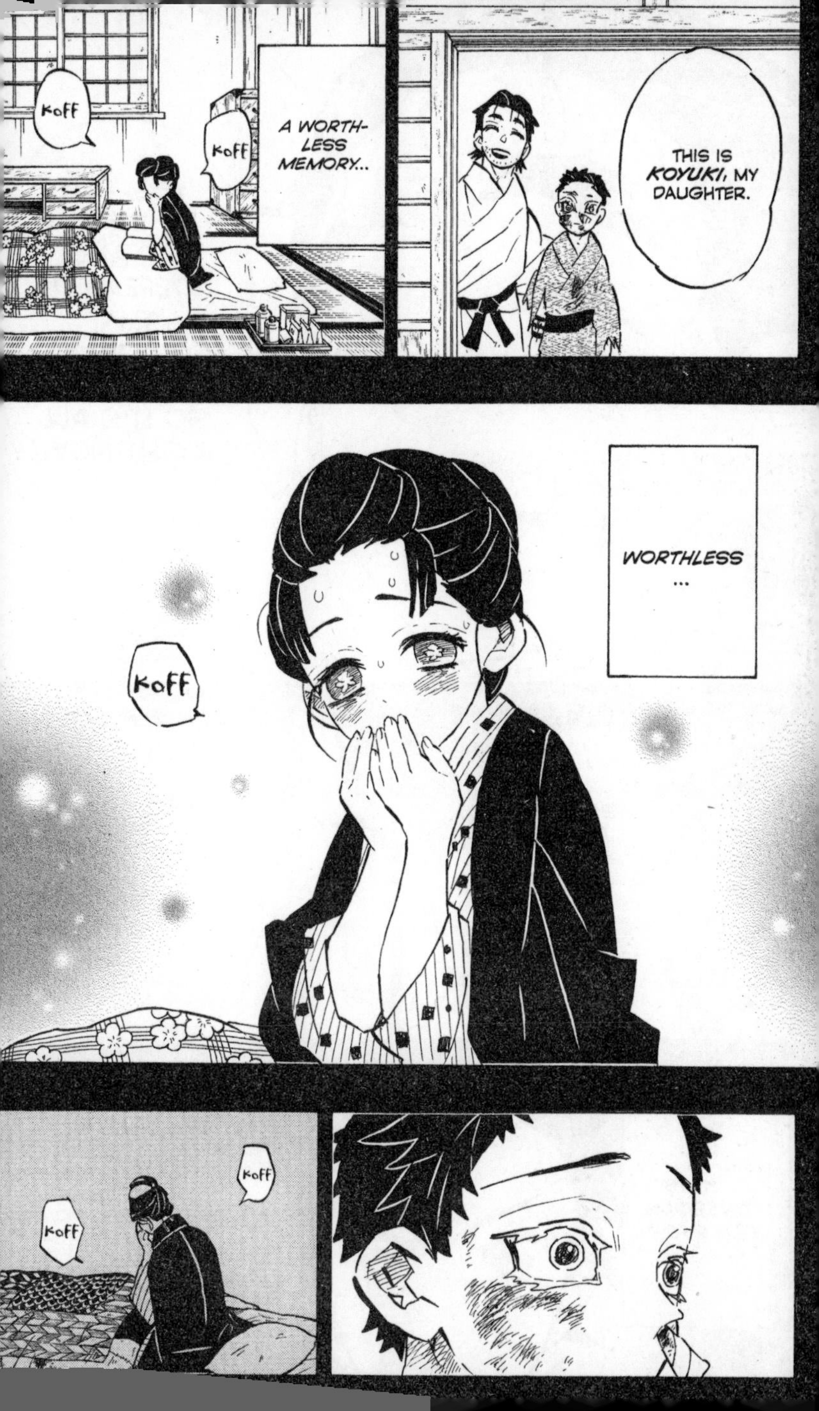
THIS IS KOYUKI, MY DAUGHTER.
A WORTH-LESS MEMORY...
Koff
Koff
WORTHLESS ...
Koff
Koff
Koff

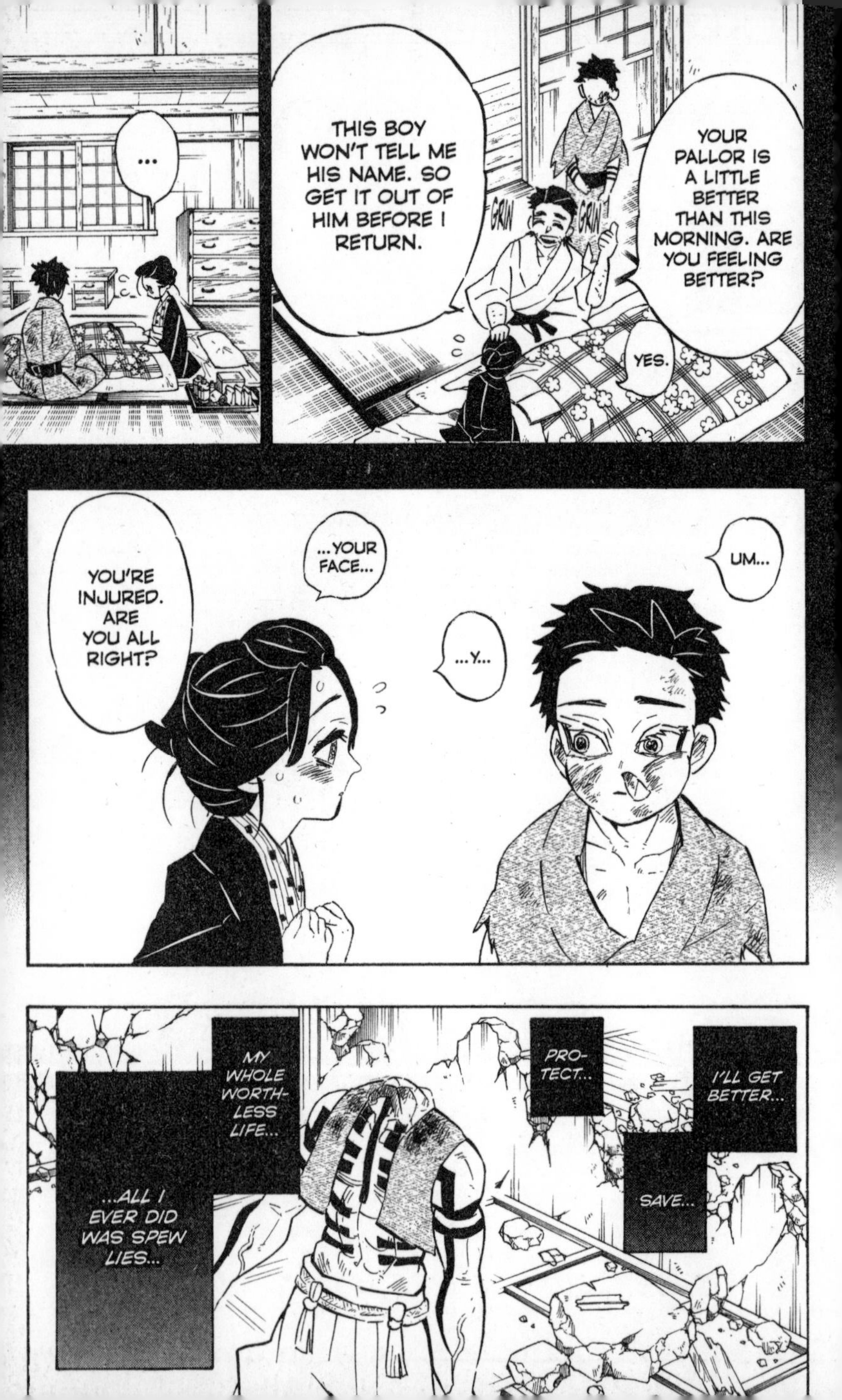
YOUR PALLOR IS A LITTLE BETTER THAN THIS MORNING. ARE YOU FEELING BETTER?
GRIN
GRIN
YES.
THIS BOY WON'T TELL ME HIS NAME. SO GET IT OUT OF HIM BEFORE I RETURN.
...
UM...
...Y...
...YOUR FACE...
YOU'RE INJURED. ARE YOU ALL RIGHT?
I'LL GET BETTER...
SAVE...
PRO-TECT...
MY WHOLE WORTH-LESS LIFE...
...ALL I EVER DID WAS SPEW LIES...

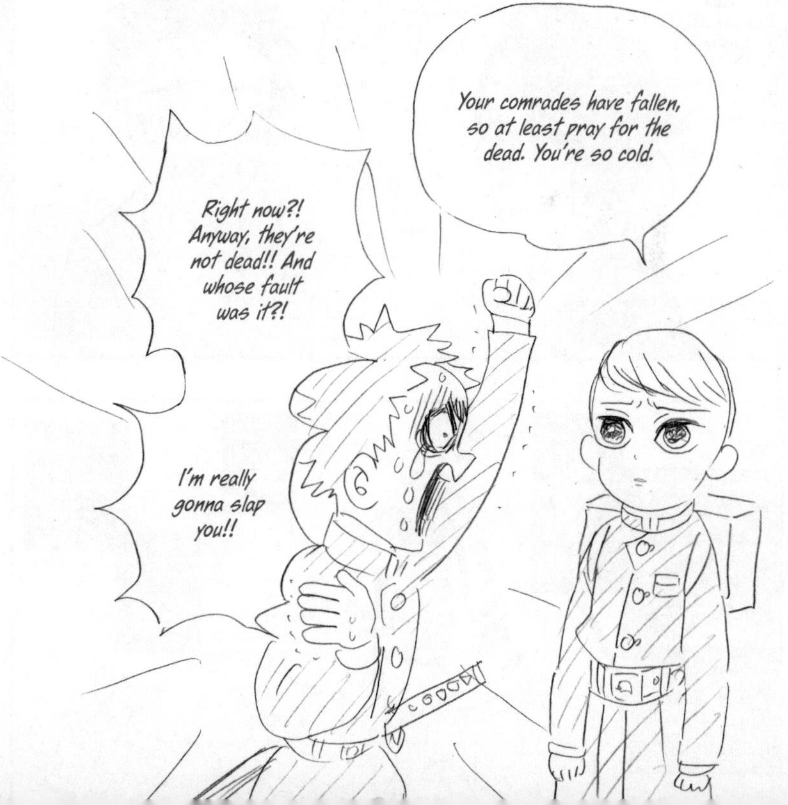
Your comrades have fallen, so at least pray for the dead. You're so cold.
Right now?! Anyway, they're not dead!! And whose fault was it?!
I'm really gonna slap you!!

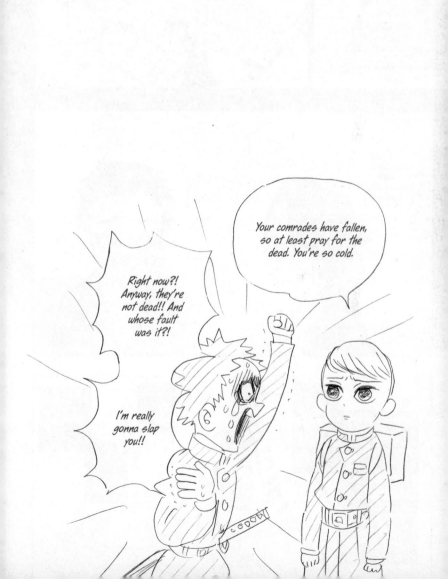

CHAPTER 155: USELESS KOMAINU

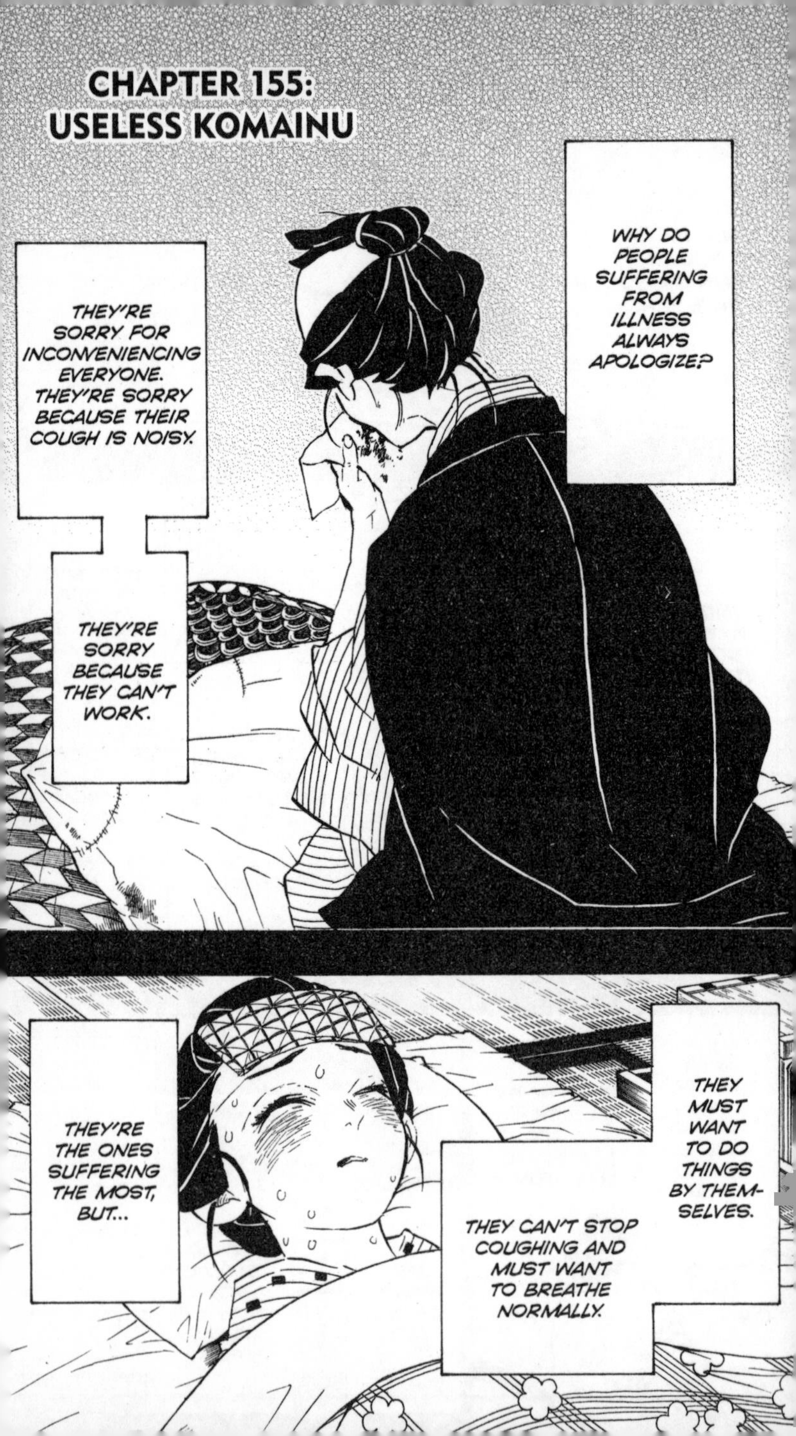
WHY DO PEOPLE SUFFERING FROM ILLNESS ALWAYS APOLOGIZE?
THEY'RE SORRY FOR INCONVENIENCING EVERYONE. THEY'RE SORRY BECAUSE THEIR COUGH IS NOISY.
THEY'RE SORRY BECAUSE THEY CAN'T WORK.
THEY MUST WANT TO DO THINGS BY THEMSELVES.
THEY CAN'T STOP COUGHING AND MUST WANT TO BREATHE NORMALLY.
THEY'RE THE ONES SUFFERING THE MOST, BUT...

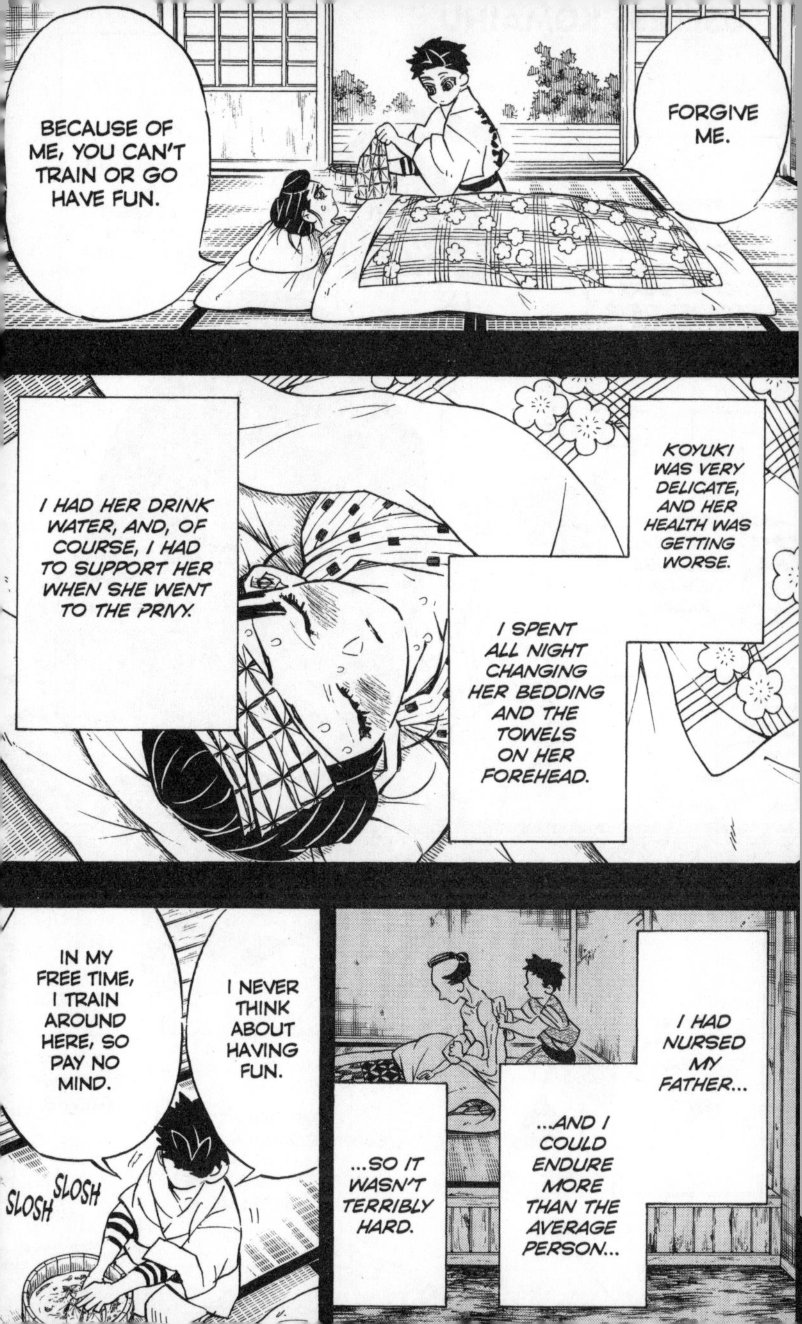
FORGIVE ME.
BECAUSE OF ME, YOU CAN'T TRAIN OR GO HAVE FUN.
KOYUKI WAS VERY DELICATE, AND HER HEALTH WAS GETTING WORSE.
I SPENT ALL NIGHT CHANGING HER BEDDING AND THE TOWELS ON HER FOREHEAD.
I HAD HER DRINK WATER, AND, OF COURSE, I HAD TO SUPPORT HER WHEN SHE WENT TO THE PRIVY.
I HAD NURSED MY FATHER...
...AND I COULD ENDURE MORE THAN THE AVERAGE PERSON...
...SO IT WASN'T TERRIBLY HARD.
I NEVER THINK ABOUT HAVING FUN.
IN MY FREE TIME, I TRAIN AROUND HERE, SO PAY NO MIND.
SLOSH
SLOSH

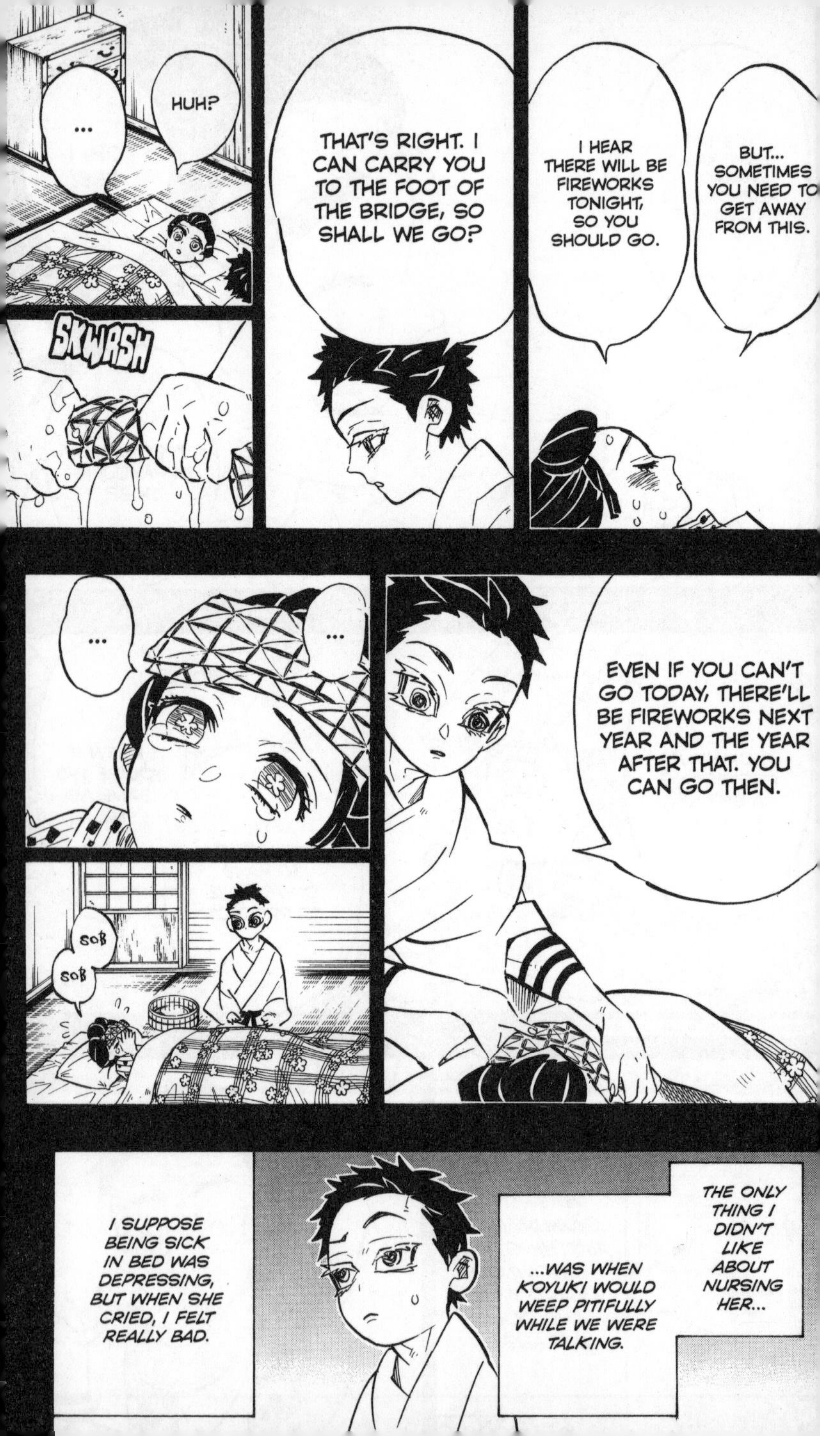
BUT... SOMETIMES YOU NEED TO GET AWAY FROM THIS.
I HEAR THERE WILL BE FIREWORKS TONIGHT, SO YOU SHOULD GO.
THAT'S RIGHT. I CAN CARRY YOU TO THE FOOT OF THE BRIDGE, SO SHALL WE GO?
HUH?
...
SKWASH
EVEN IF YOU CAN'T GO TODAY, THERE'LL BE FIREWORKS NEXT YEAR AND THE YEAR AFTER THAT. YOU CAN GO THEN.
...
...
SOB
SOB
THE ONLY THING I DIDN'T LIKE ABOUT NURSING HER...
...WAS WHEN KOYUKI WOULD WEEP PITIFULLY WHILE WE WERE TALKING.
I SUPPOSE BEING SICK IN BED WAS DEPRESSING, BUT WHEN SHE CRIED, I FELT REALLY BAD.

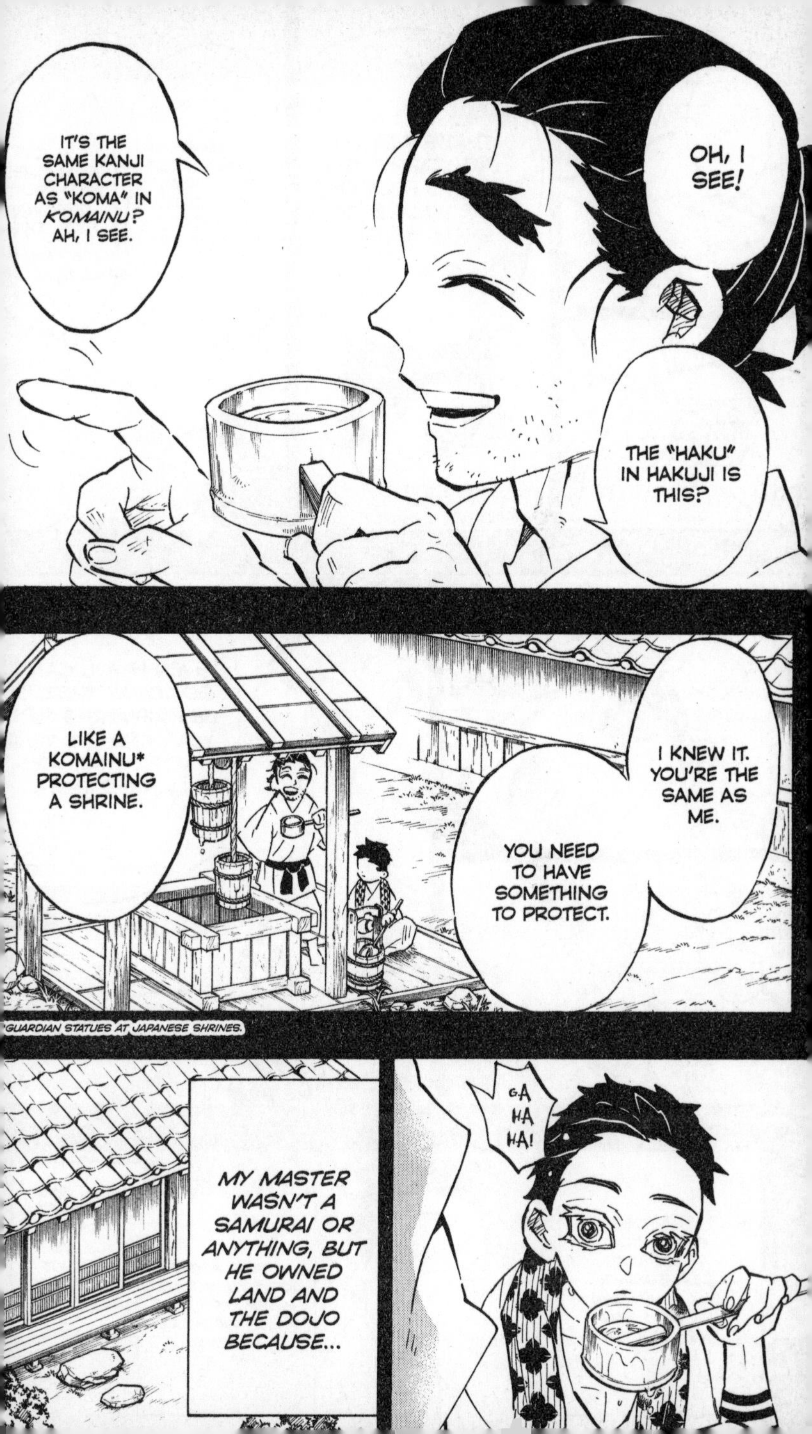
OH, I SEE!
THE "HAKU" IN HAKUJI IS THIS?
IT'S THE SAME KANJI CHARACTER AS "KOMA" IN *KOMAINU*? AH, I SEE.
I KNEW IT. YOU'RE THE SAME AS ME.
YOU NEED TO HAVE SOMETHING TO PROTECT.
LIKE A KOMAINU* PROTECTING A SHRINE.
*GUARDIAN STATUES AT JAPANESE SHRINES.
GA HA HA!
MY MASTER WASN'T A SAMURAI OR ANYTHING, BUT HE OWNED LAND AND THE DOJO BECAUSE...

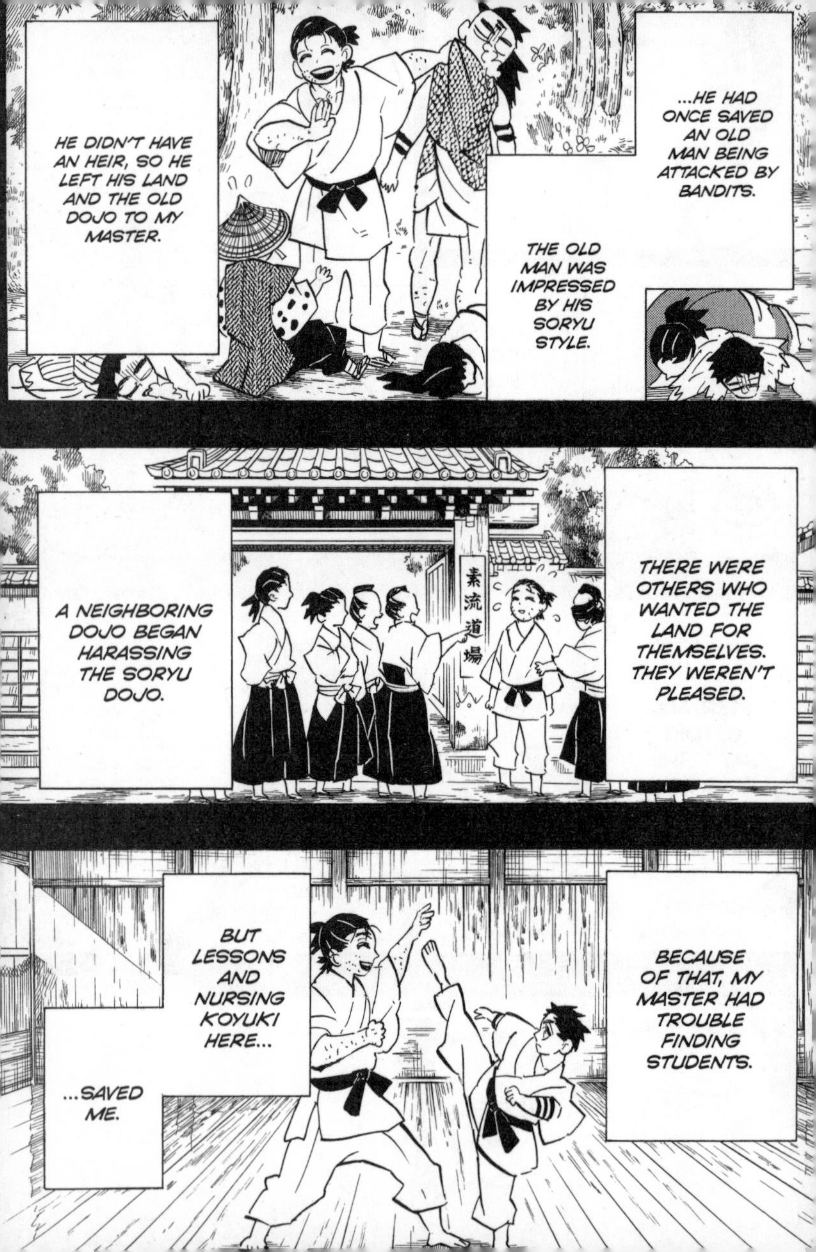
...HE HAD ONCE SAVED AN OLD MAN BEING ATTACKED BY BANDITS.
THE OLD MAN WAS IMPRESSED BY HIS SORYU STYLE.
HE DIDN'T HAVE AN HEIR, SO HE LEFT HIS LAND AND THE OLD DOJO TO MY MASTER.
THERE WERE OTHERS WHO WANTED THE LAND FOR THEMSELVES. THEY WEREN'T PLEASED.
素流道場
A NEIGHBORING DOJO BEGAN HARASSING THE SORYU DOJO.
BECAUSE OF THAT, MY MASTER HAD TROUBLE FINDING STUDENTS.
BUT LESSONS AND NURSING KOYUKI HERE...
...SAVED ME.

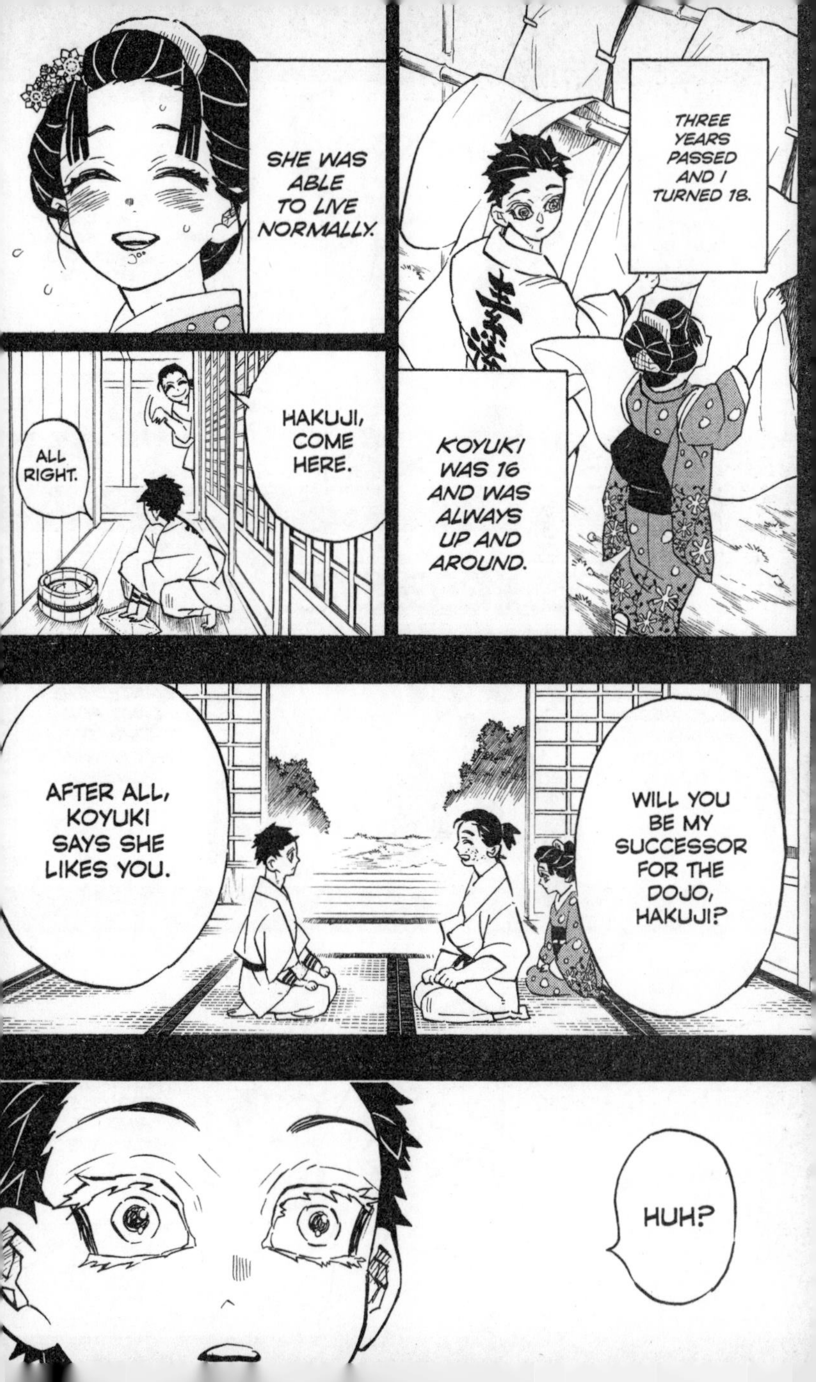
THREE YEARS PASSED AND I TURNED 18.
KOYUKI WAS 16 AND WAS ALWAYS UP AND AROUND.
SHE WAS ABLE TO LIVE NORMALLY.
HAKUJI, COME HERE.
ALL RIGHT.
WILL YOU BE MY SUCCESSOR FOR THE DOJO, HAKUJI?
AFTER ALL, KOYUKI SAYS SHE LIKES YOU.
HUH?

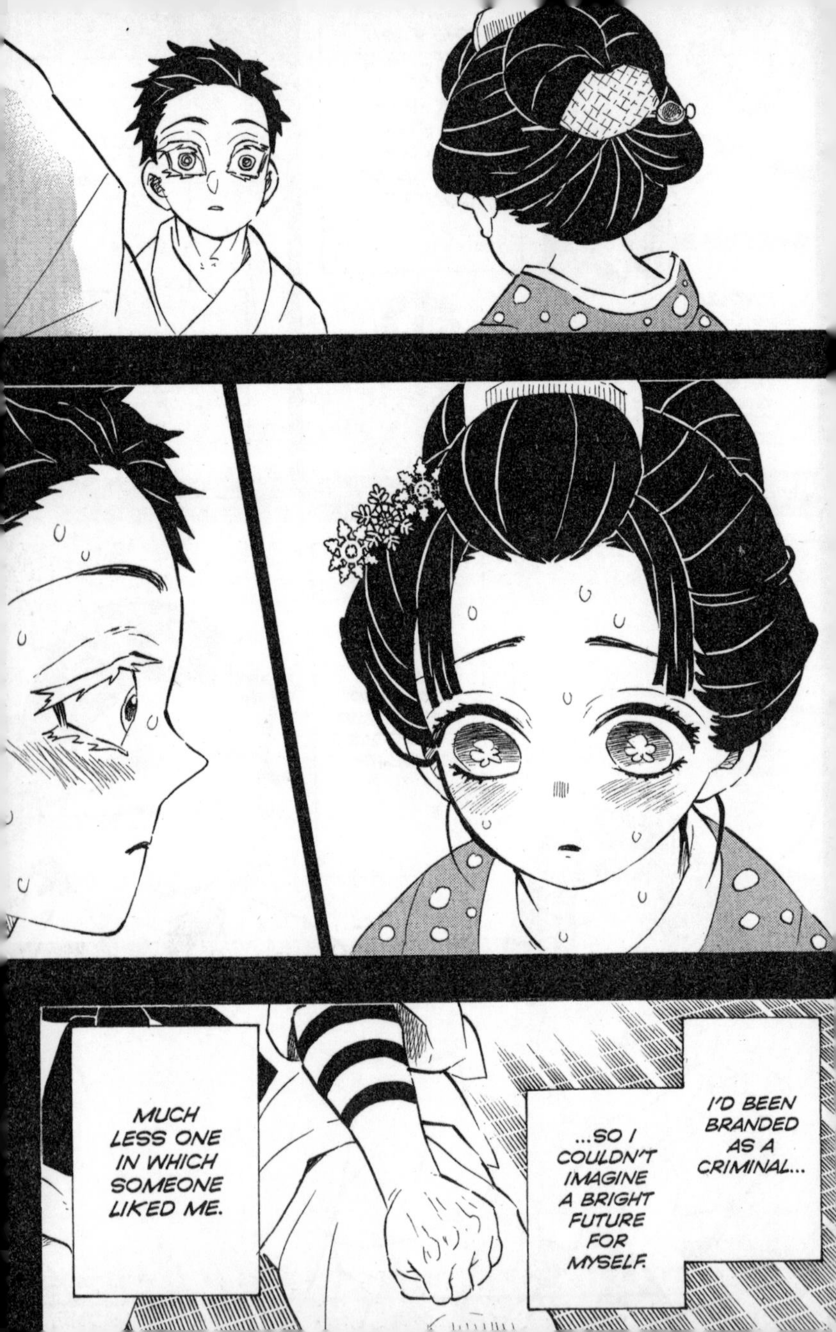
I'D BEEN BRANDED AS A CRIMINAL...
...SO I COULDN'T IMAGINE A BRIGHT FUTURE FOR MYSELF.
MUCH LESS ONE IN WHICH SOMEONE LIKED ME.

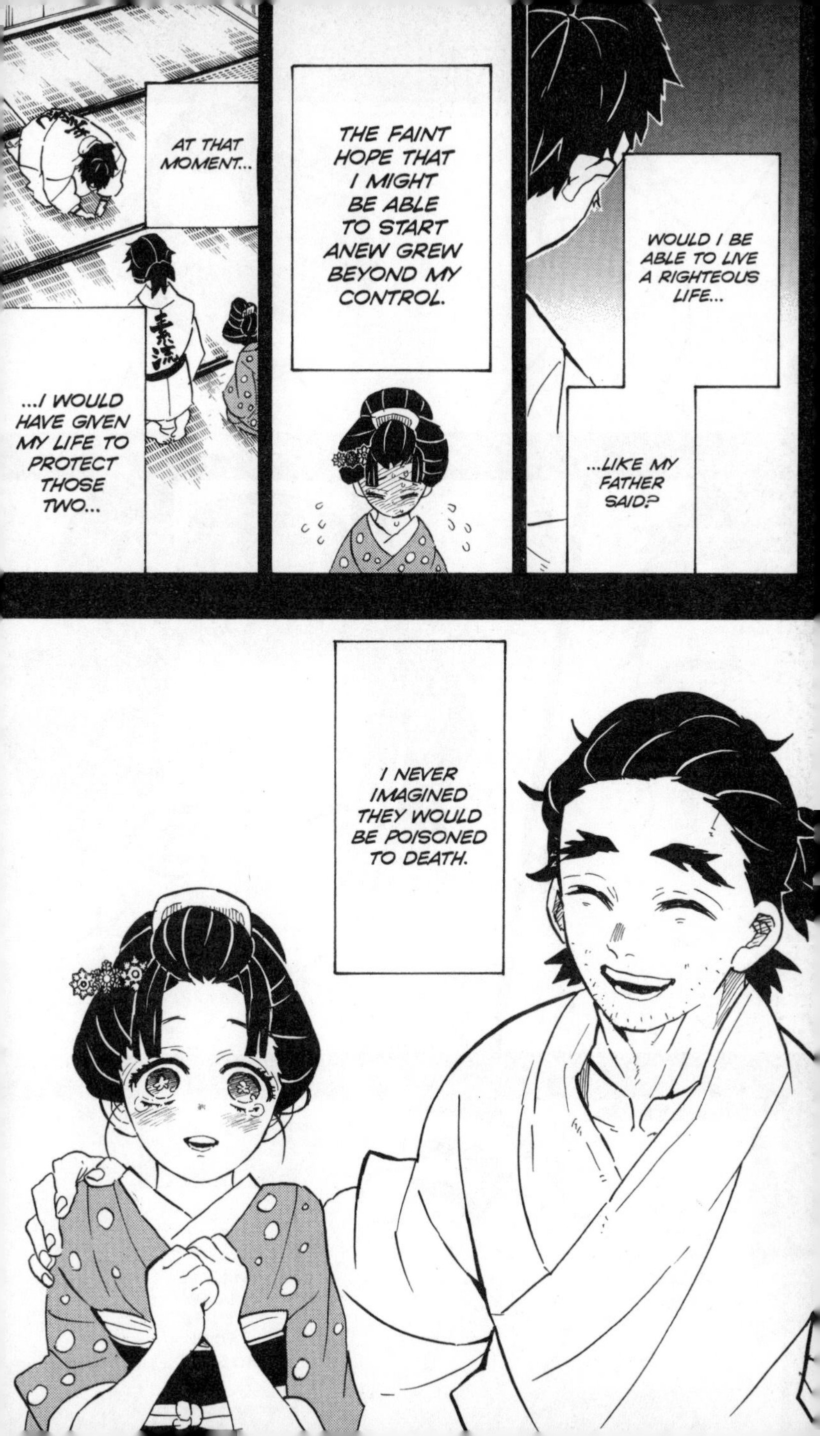
WOULD I BE ABLE TO LIVE A RIGHTEOUS LIFE...
...LIKE MY FATHER SAID?
THE FAINT HOPE THAT I MIGHT BE ABLE TO START ANEW GREW BEYOND MY CONTROL.
AT THAT MOMENT...
...I WOULD HAVE GIVEN MY LIFE TO PROTECT THOSE TWO...
I NEVER IMAGINED THEY WOULD BE POISONED TO DEATH.

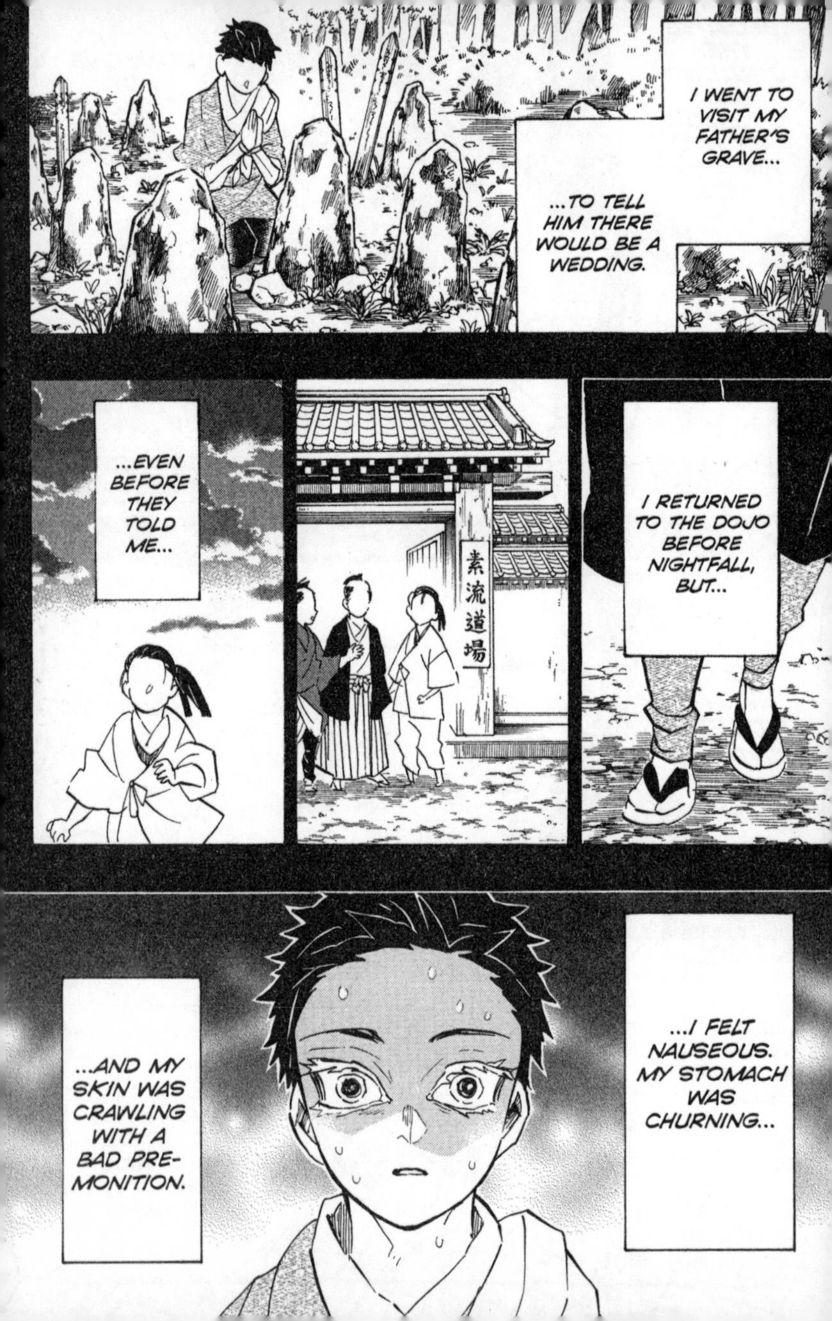

I WENT TO VISIT MY FATHER'S GRAVE...
...TO TELL HIM THERE WOULD BE A WEDDING.
I RETURNED TO THE DOJO BEFORE NIGHTFALL, BUT...
素流道場
...EVEN BEFORE THEY TOLD ME...
...I FELT NAUSEOUS. MY STOMACH WAS CHURNING...
...AND MY SKIN WAS CRAWLING WITH A BAD PRE-MONITION.

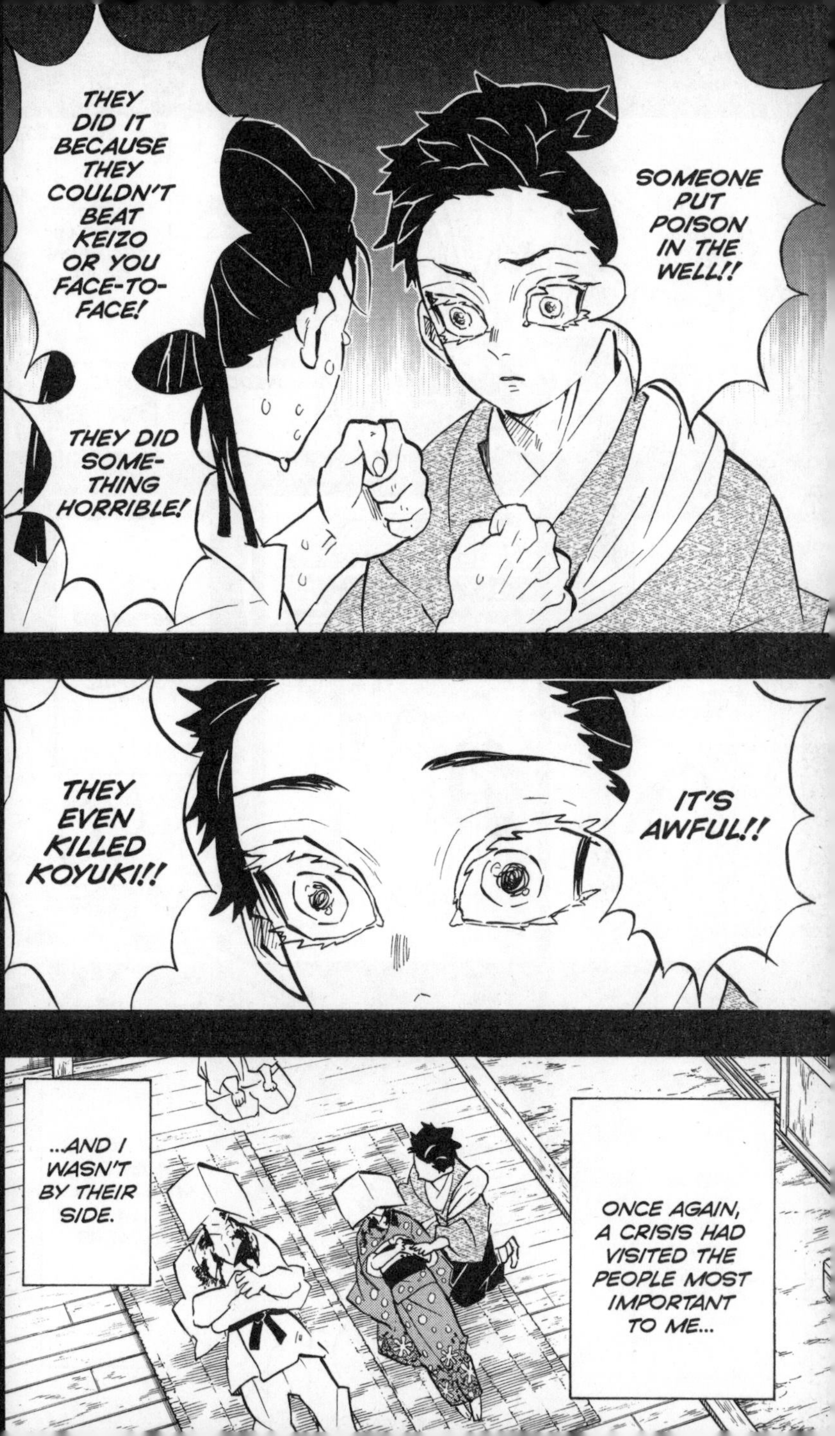
SOMEONE PUT POISON IN THE WELL!!
THEY DID IT BECAUSE THEY COULDN'T BEAT KEIZO OR YOU FACE-TO-FACE!
THEY DID SOME-THING HORRIBLE!
IT'S AWFUL!!
THEY EVEN KILLED KOYUKI!!
ONCE AGAIN, A CRISIS HAD VISITED THE PEOPLE MOST IMPORTANT TO ME...
...AND I WASN'T BY THEIR SIDE.

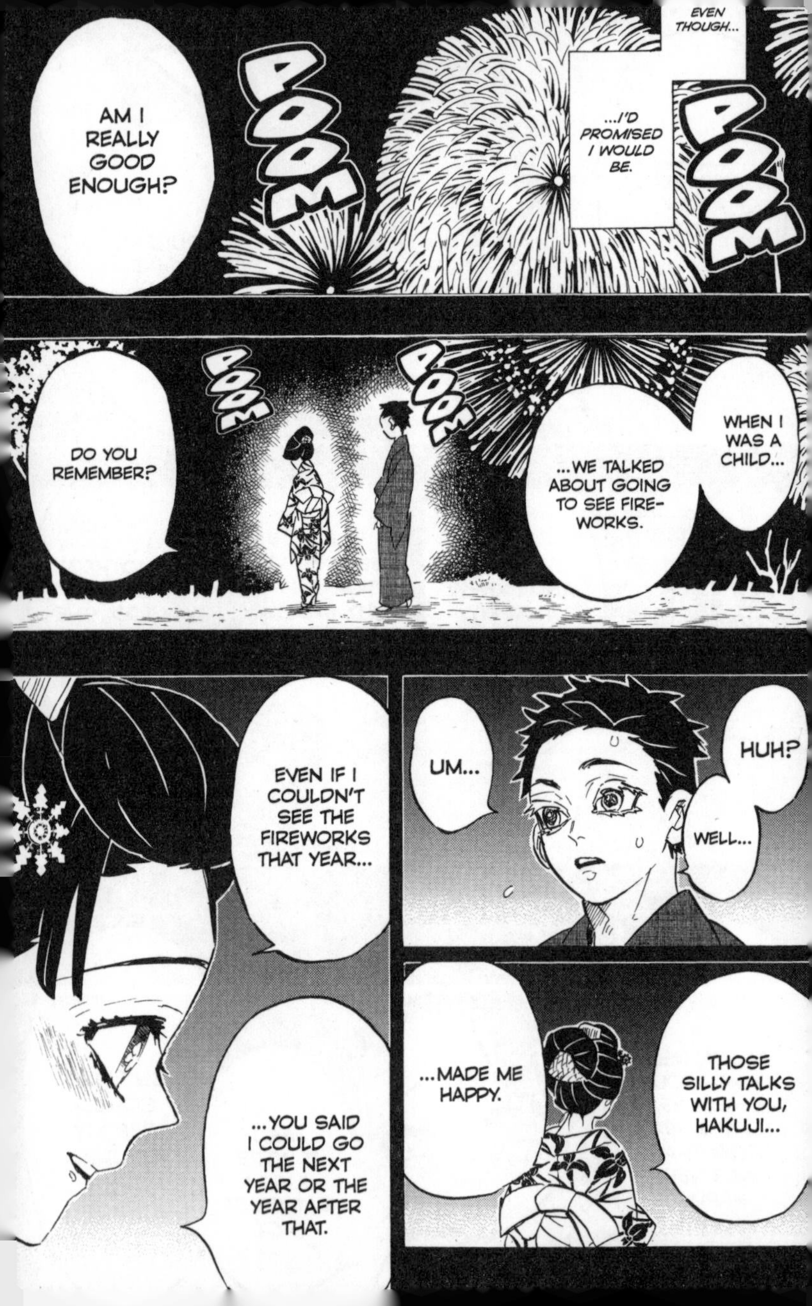
EVEN THOUGH...
...I'D PROMISED I WOULD BE.
POOM
POOM
AM I REALLY GOOD ENOUGH?
WHEN I WAS A CHILD...
...WE TALKED ABOUT GOING TO SEE FIRE-WORKS.
POOM
POOM
DO YOU REMEMBER?
HUH?
WELL...
UM...
THOSE SILLY TALKS WITH YOU, HAKUJI...
...MADE ME HAPPY.
EVEN IF I COULDN'T SEE THE FIREWORKS THAT YEAR...
...YOU SAID I COULD GO THE NEXT YEAR OR THE YEAR AFTER THAT.

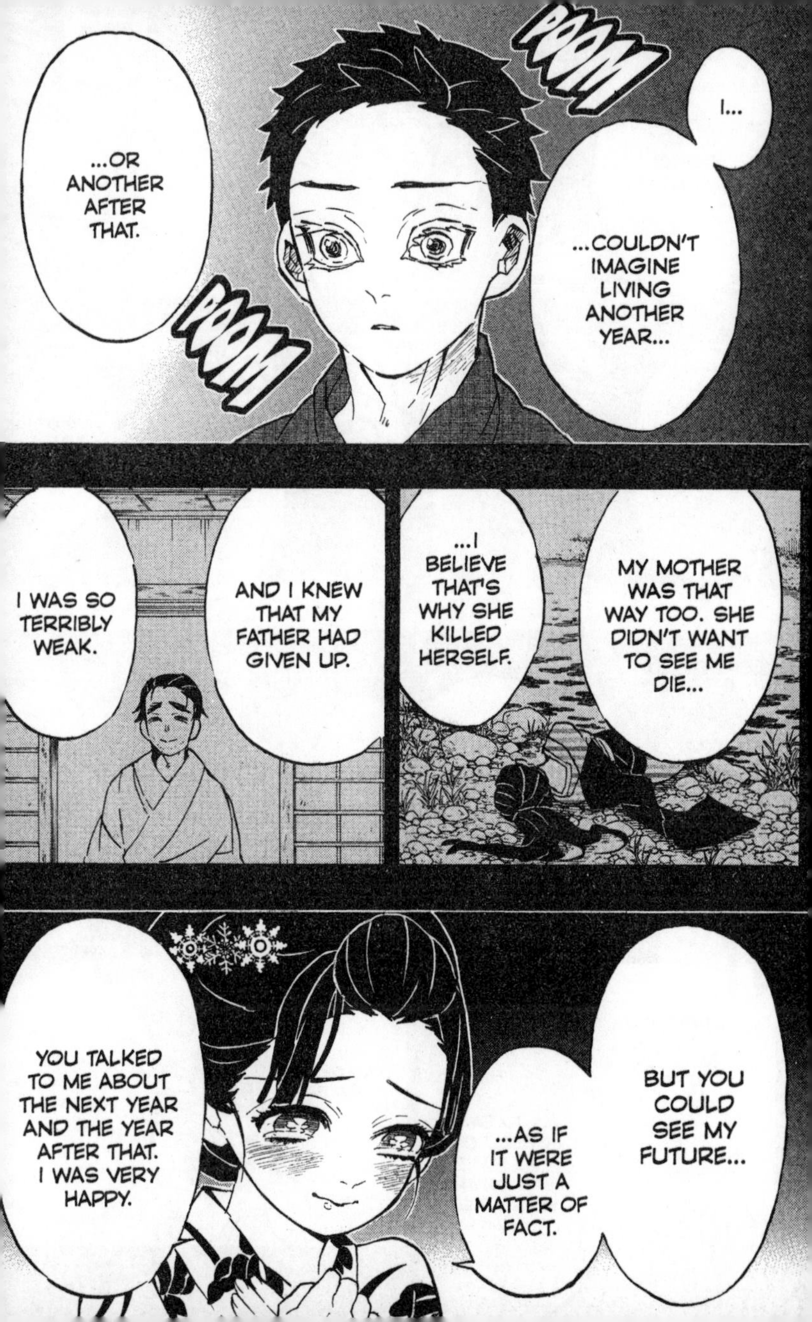
POOM
I...
...COULDN'T IMAGINE LIVING ANOTHER YEAR...
POOM
...OR ANOTHER AFTER THAT.
MY MOTHER WAS THAT WAY TOO. SHE DIDN'T WANT TO SEE ME DIE...
...I BELIEVE THAT'S WHY SHE KILLED HERSELF.
AND I KNEW THAT MY FATHER HAD GIVEN UP.
I WAS SO TERRIBLY WEAK.
BUT YOU COULD SEE MY FUTURE...
...AS IF IT WERE JUST A MATTER OF FACT.
YOU TALKED TO ME ABOUT THE NEXT YEAR AND THE YEAR AFTER THAT. I WAS VERY HAPPY.

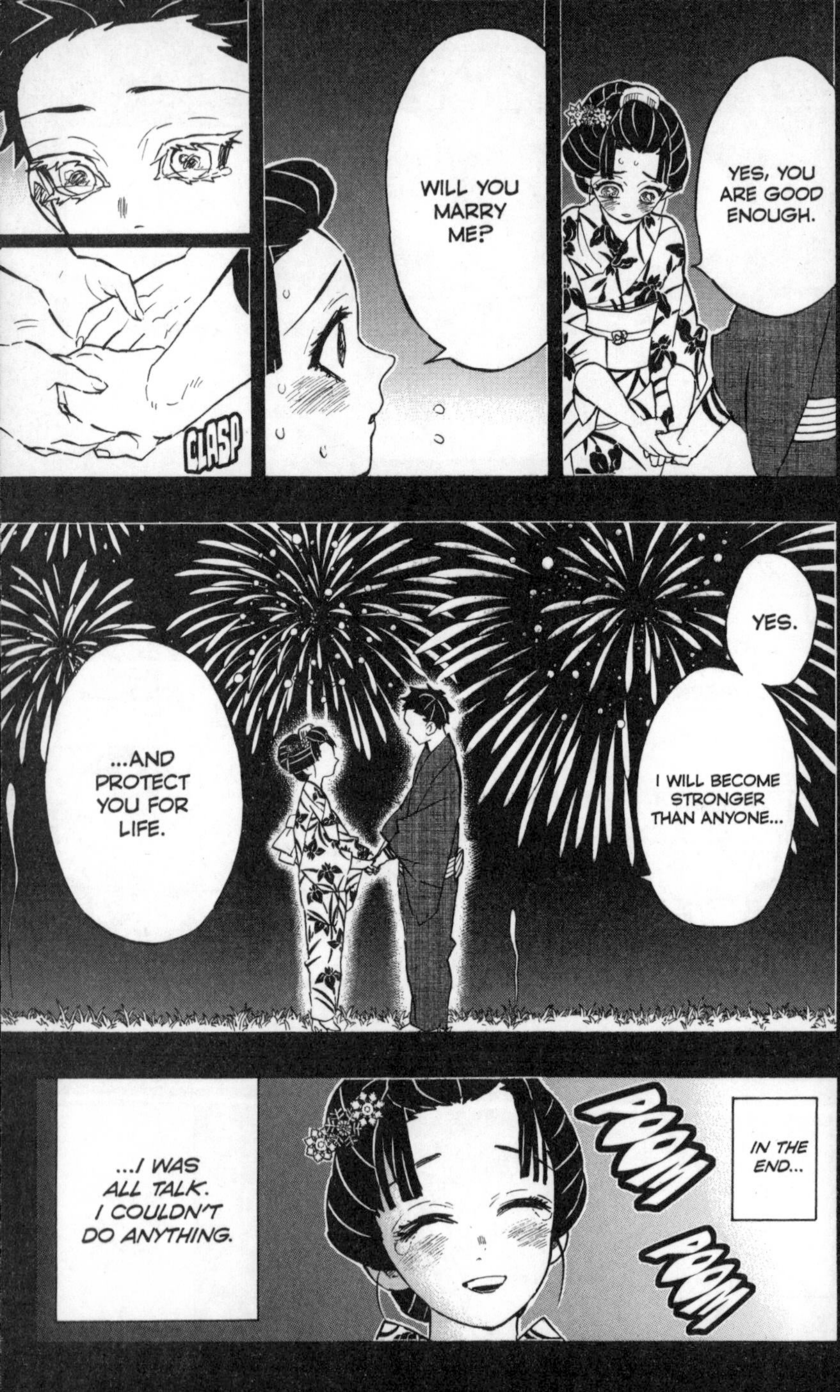
YES, YOU ARE GOOD ENOUGH.
WILL YOU MARRY ME?
CLASP
YES.
I WILL BECOME STRONGER THAN ANYONE...
...AND PROTECT YOU FOR LIFE.
IN THE END...
POOM
POOM
...I WAS ALL TALK. I COULDN'T DO ANYTHING.

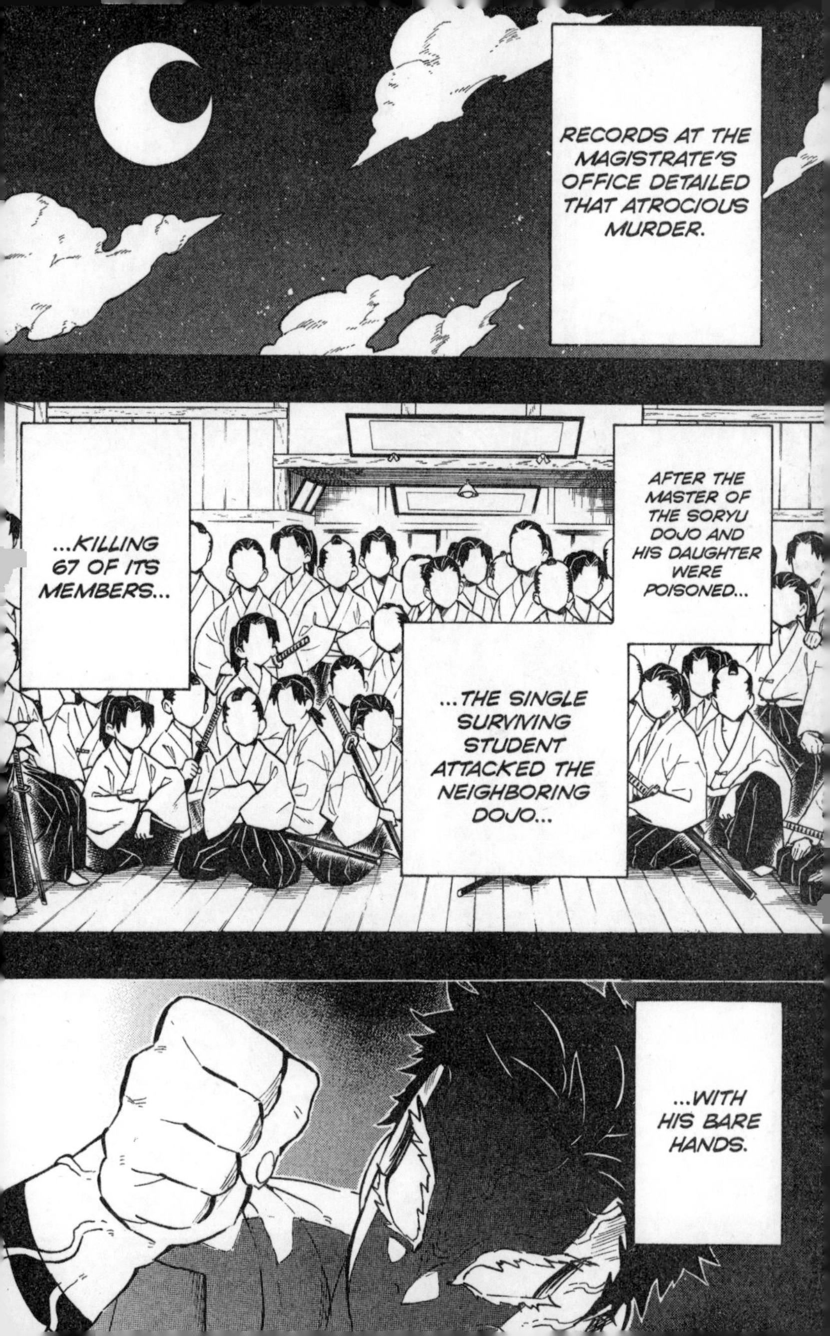
RECORDS AT THE MAGISTRATE'S OFFICE DETAILED THAT ATROCIOUS MURDER.
AFTER THE MASTER OF THE SORYU DOJO AND HIS DAUGHTER WERE POISONED...
...THE SINGLE SURVIVING STUDENT ATTACKED THE NEIGHBORING DOJO...
...KILLING 67 OF ITS MEMBERS...
...WITH HIS BARE HANDS.

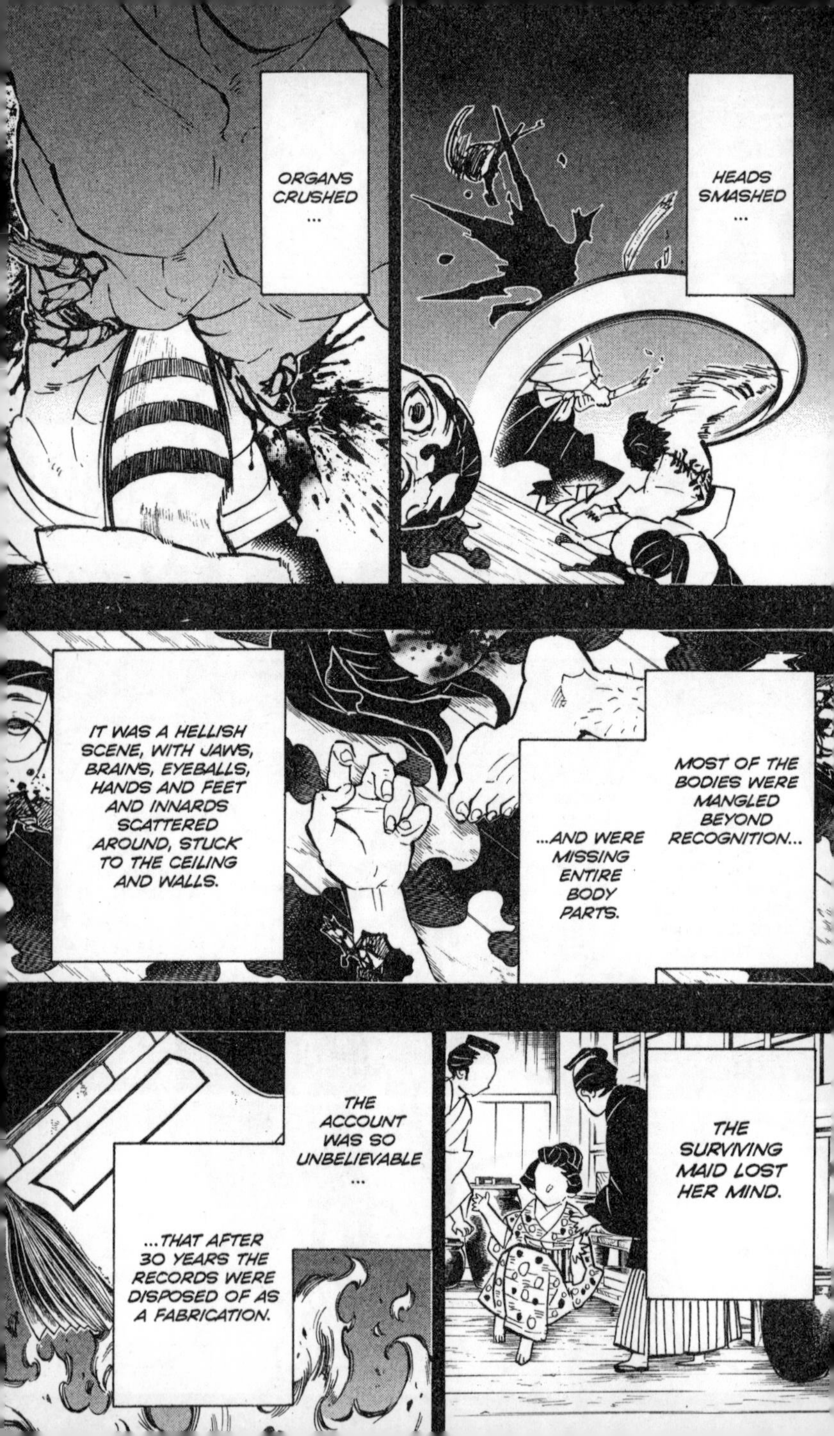
HEADS SMASHED ...
ORGANS CRUSHED ...
MOST OF THE BODIES WERE MANGLED BEYOND RECOGNITION...
...AND WERE MISSING ENTIRE BODY PARTS.
IT WAS A HELLISH SCENE, WITH JAWS, BRAINS, EYEBALLS, HANDS AND FEET AND INNARDS SCATTERED AROUND, STUCK TO THE CEILING AND WALLS.
THE SURVIVING MAID LOST HER MIND.
THE ACCOUNT WAS SO UNBELIEVABLE ...
...THAT AFTER 30 YEARS THE RECORDS WERE DISPOSED OF AS A FABRICATION.

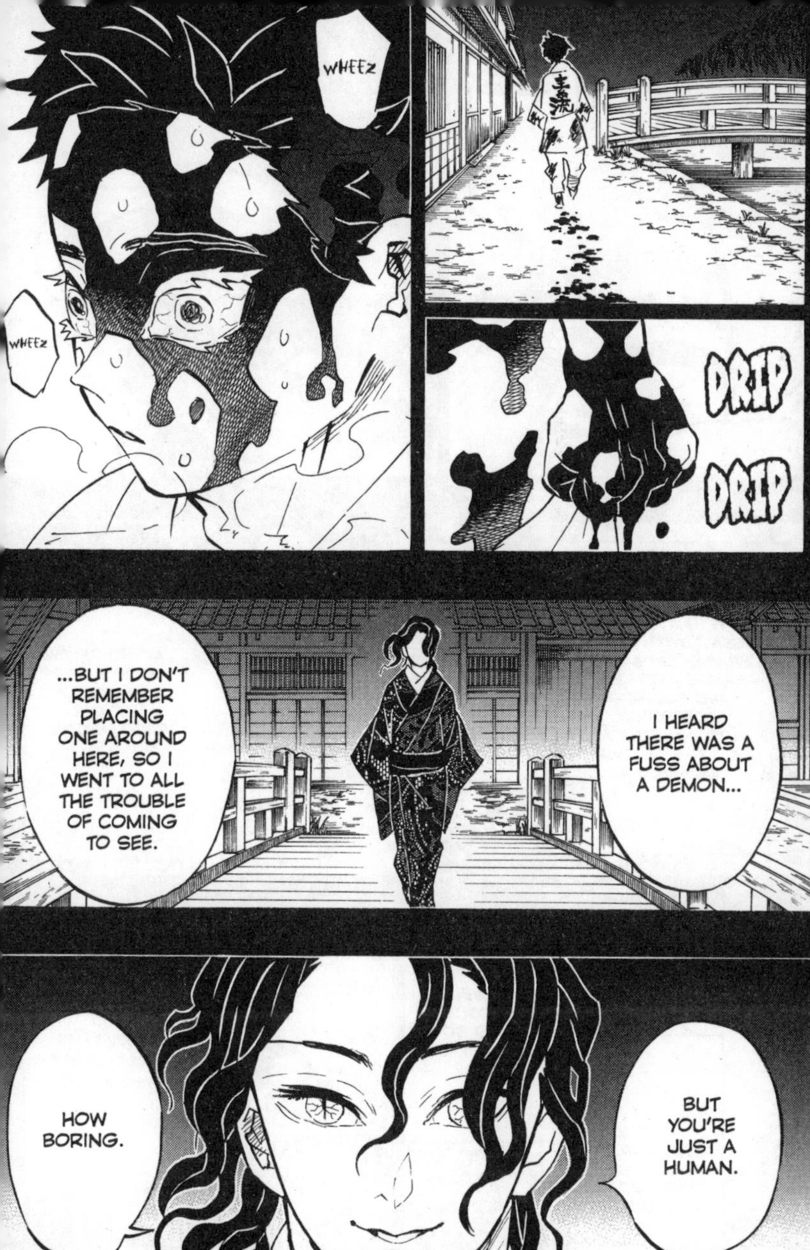
DRIP
DRIP
WHEEZ
WHEEZ
I HEARD THERE WAS A FUSS ABOUT A DEMON...
...BUT I DON'T REMEMBER PLACING ONE AROUND HERE, SO I WENT TO ALL THE TROUBLE OF COMING TO SEE.
BUT YOU'RE JUST A HUMAN.
HOW BORING.

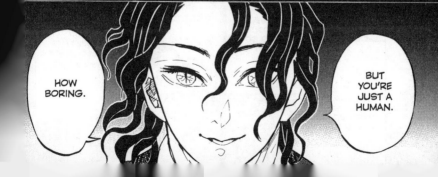

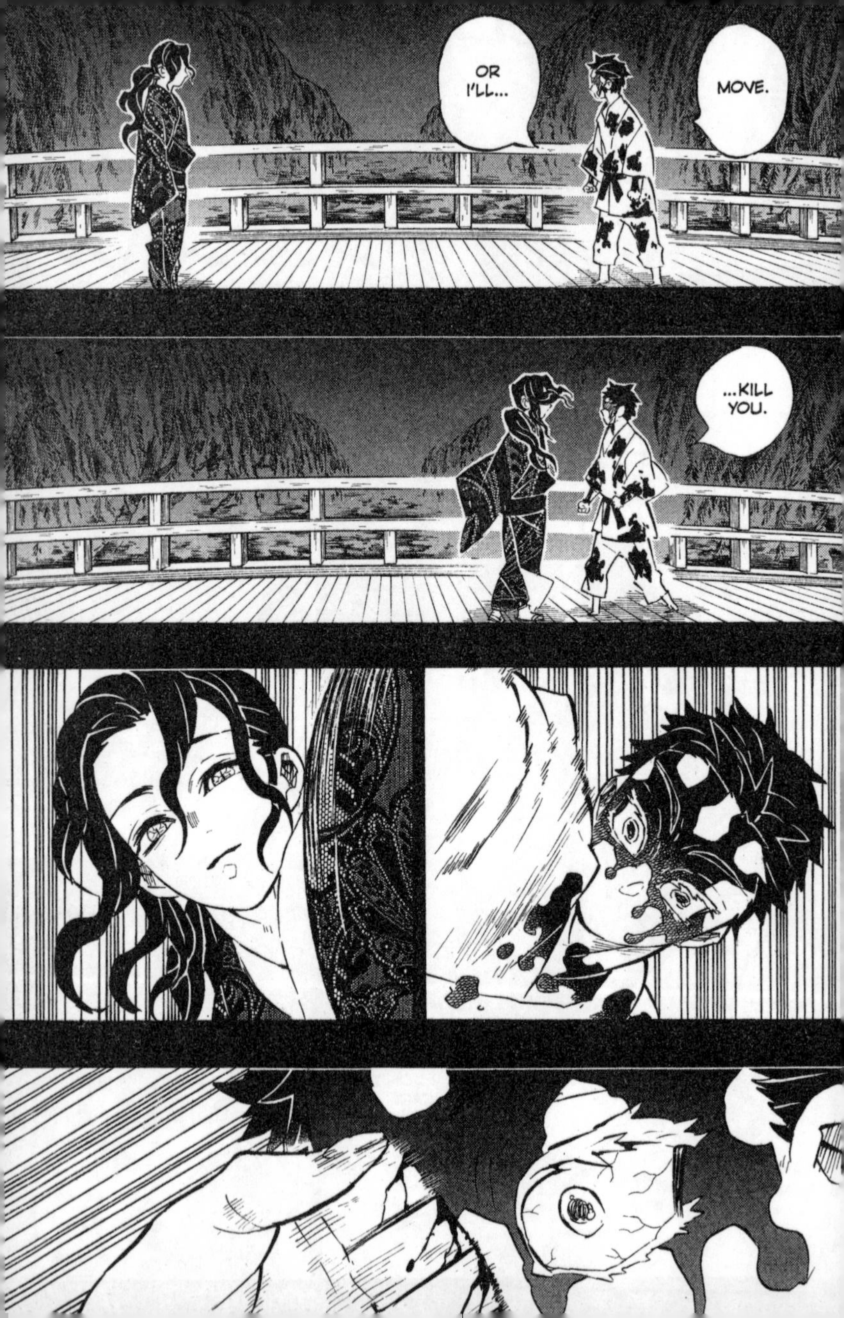
MOVE.
OR I'LL...
...KILL YOU.

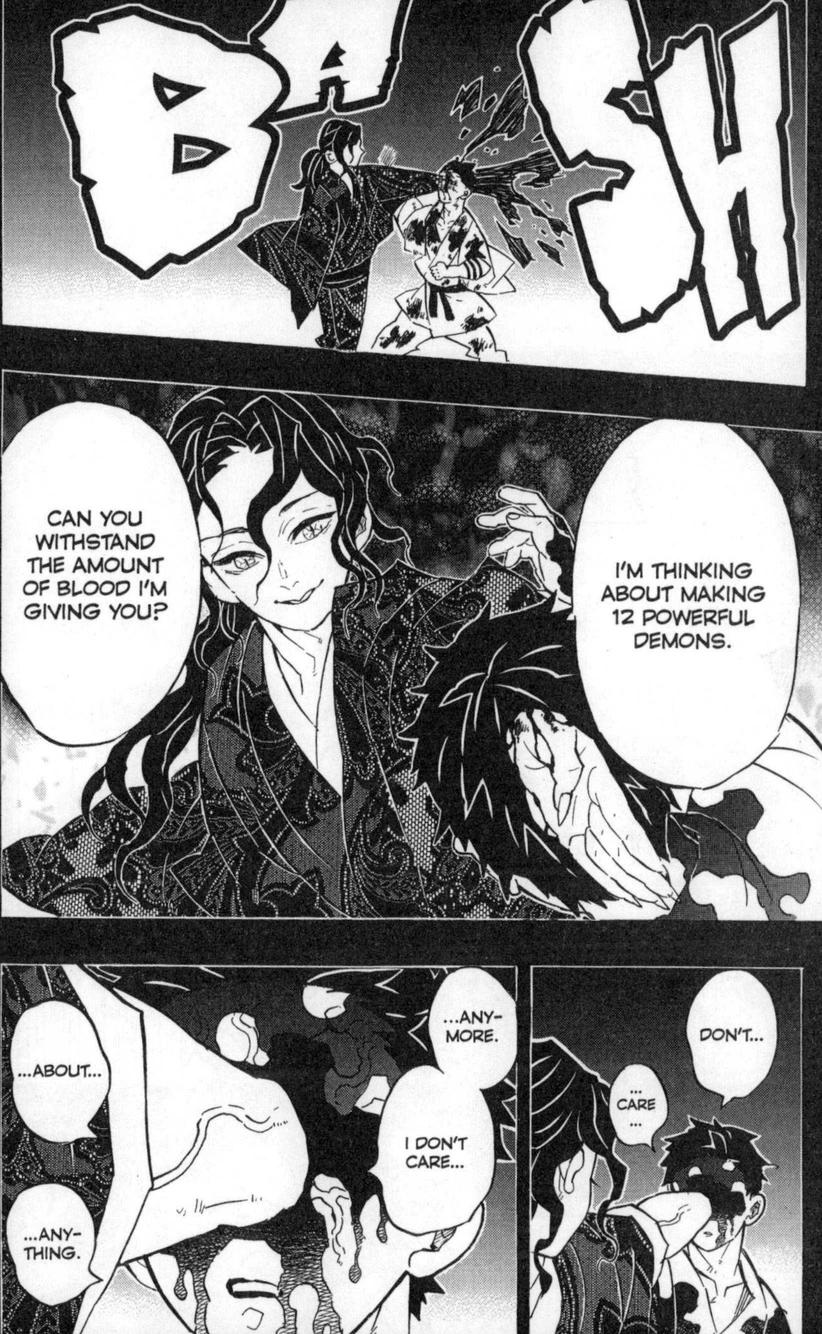
BASH
I'M THINKING ABOUT MAKING 12 POWERFUL DEMONS.
CAN YOU WITHSTAND THE AMOUNT OF BLOOD I'M GIVING YOU?
DON'T...
...CARE...
...ANY-MORE.
I DON'T CARE...
...ABOUT...
...ANY-THING.

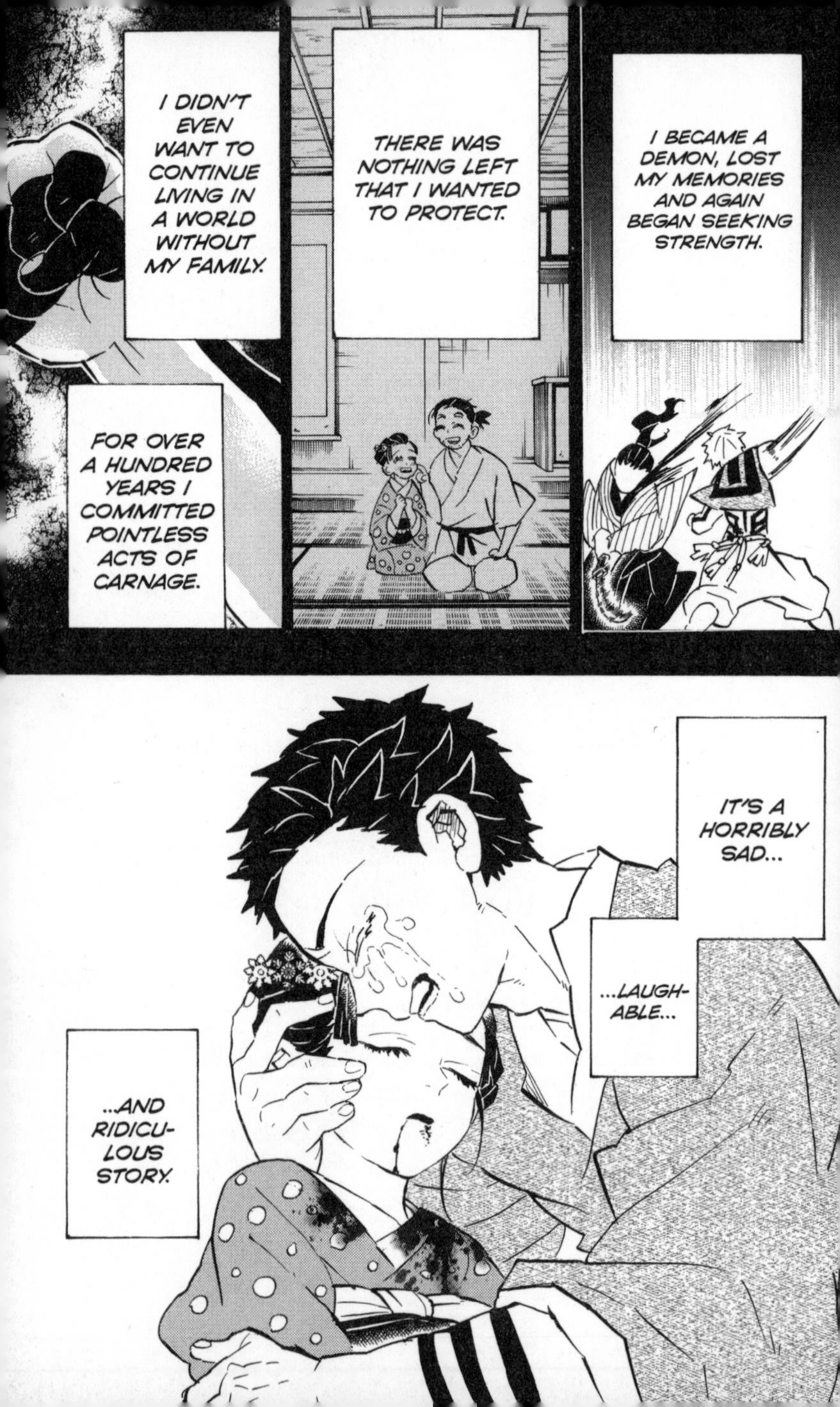
I BECAME A DEMON, LOST MY MEMORIES AND AGAIN BEGAN SEEKING STRENGTH.
THERE WAS NOTHING LEFT THAT I WANTED TO PROTECT.
I DIDN'T EVEN WANT TO CONTINUE LIVING IN A WORLD WITHOUT MY FAMILY.
FOR OVER A HUNDRED YEARS I COMMITTED POINTLESS ACTS OF CARNAGE.
IT'S A HORRIBLY SAD...
...LAUGH-ABLE...
...AND RIDICU-LOUS STORY.

Extra Tidbits

Memories are the foundation for all of Akaza's techniques.

Technique names → Come from fireworks

Technique Development pattern → Koyuki's hairpins stance

Martial arts school → Soryu

His father told him to live a righteous life, but he became a demon and committed many sins. Perhaps that's why criminal tattoos have mixed in with demon patterns and appear to be spreading all over his body.

CHAPTER 156: THANK YOU

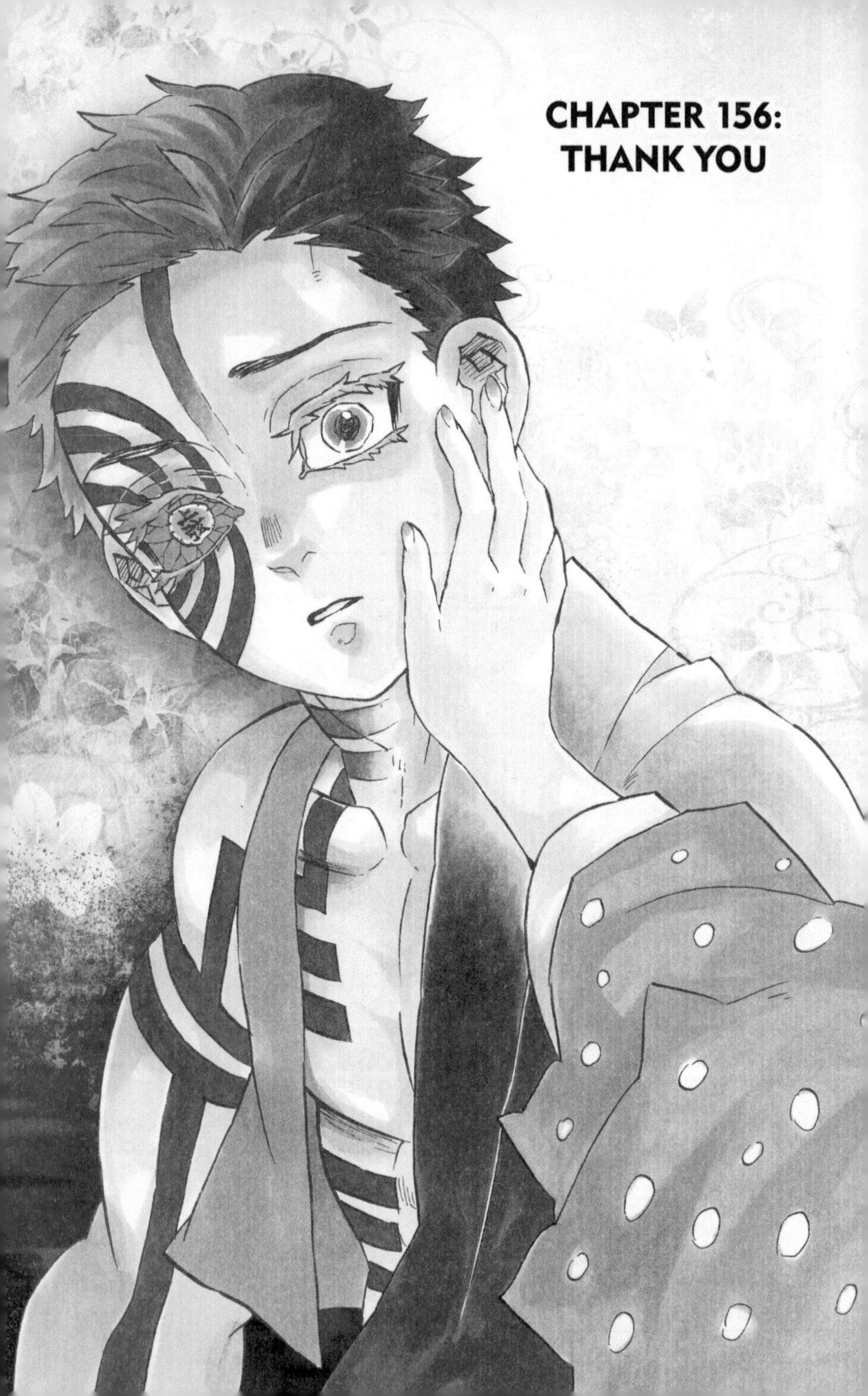

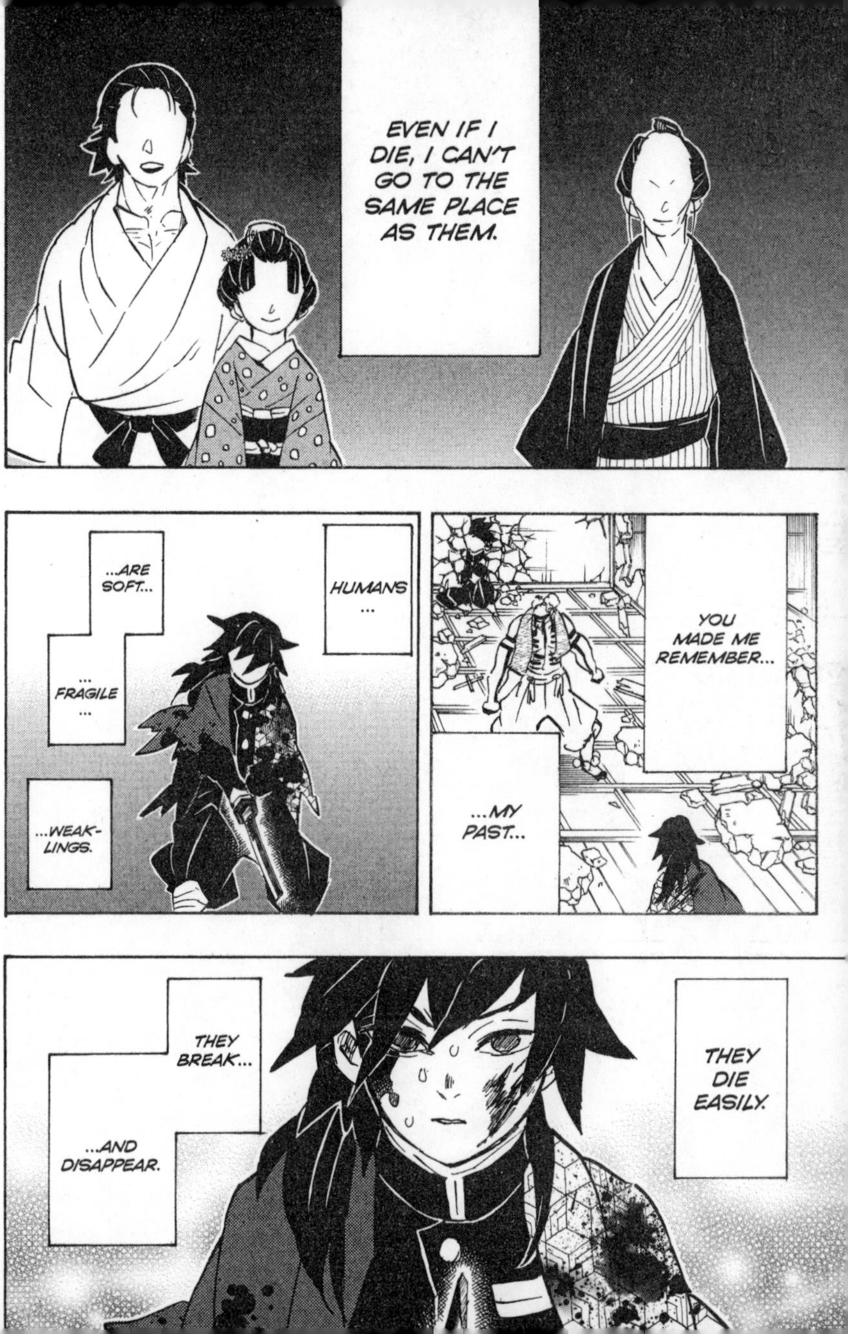

EVEN IF I DIE, I CAN'T GO TO THE SAME PLACE AS THEM.
YOU MADE ME REMEMBER...
...MY PAST...
HUMANS...
...ARE SOFT...
...FRAGILE...
...WEAKLINGS.
THEY DIE EASILY.
THEY BREAK...
...AND DISAPPEAR.

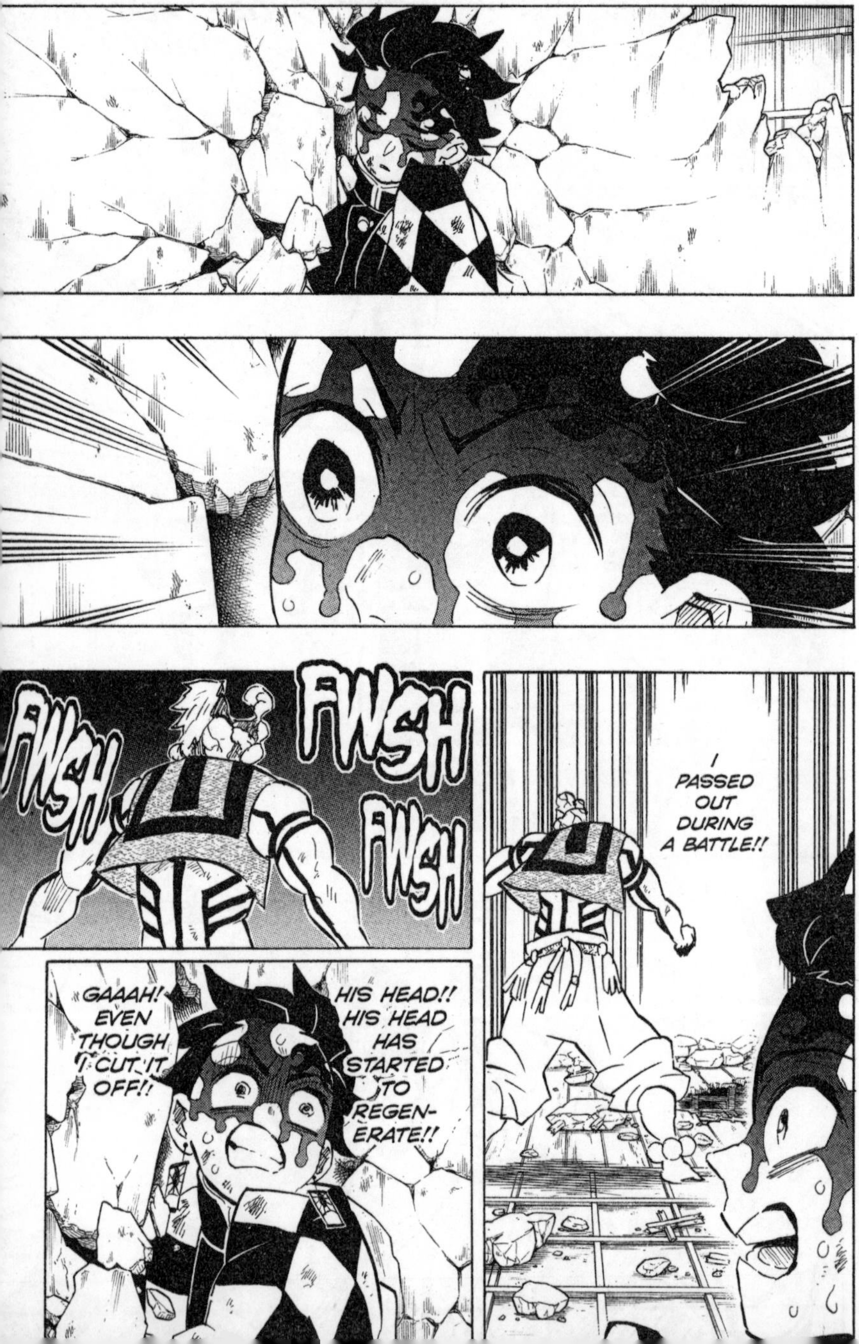
I PASSED OUT DURING A BATTLE!!
FWSH
FWSH
FWSH
HIS HEAD!! HIS HEAD HAS STARTED TO REGENERATE!!
GAAAH! EVEN THOUGH I CUT IT OFF!!

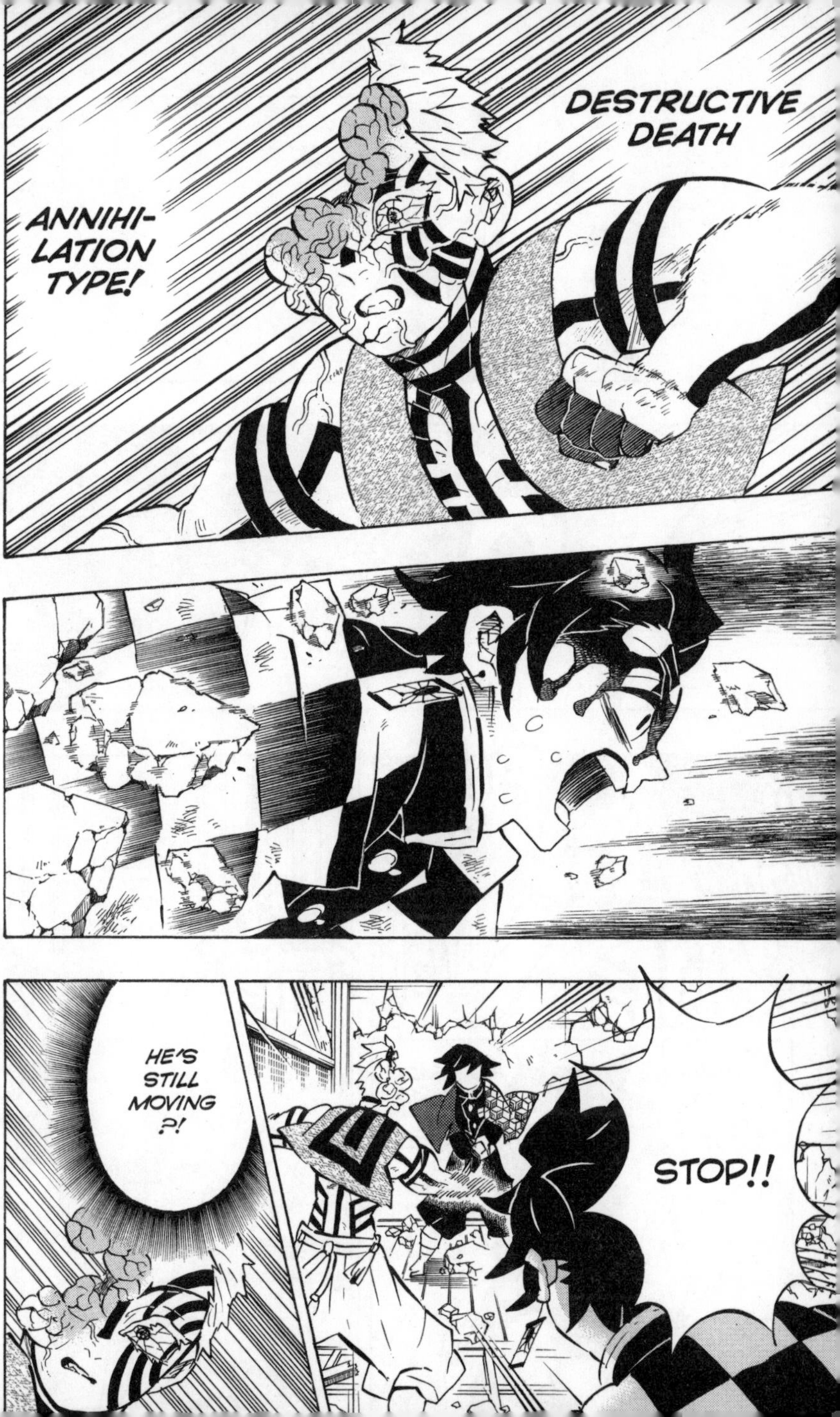
DESTRUCTIVE DEATH
ANNIHI-LATION TYPE!
STOP!!
HE'S STILL MOVING ?!

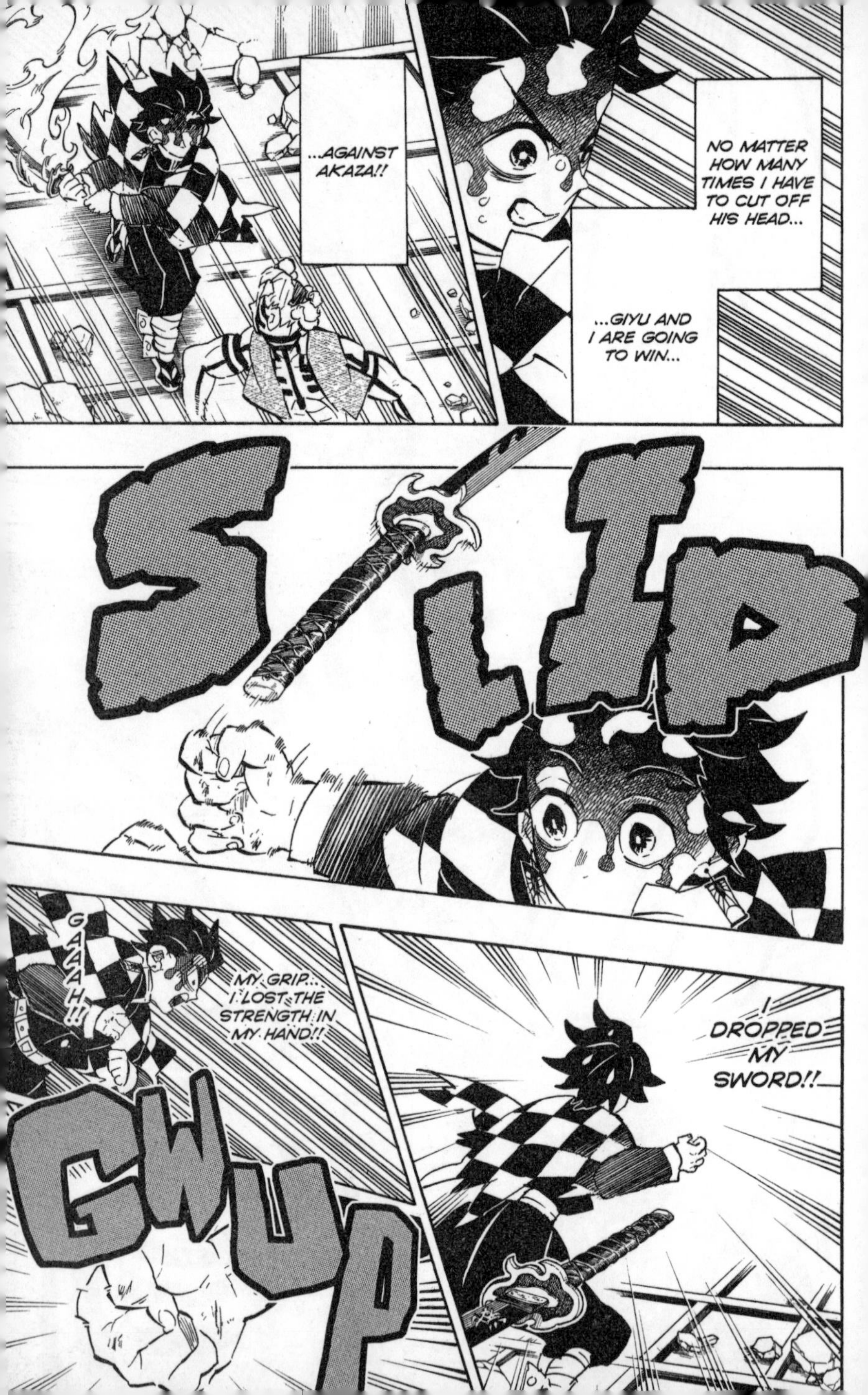
NO MATTER HOW MANY TIMES I HAVE TO CUT OFF HIS HEAD...
...GIYU AND I ARE GOING TO WIN...
...AGAINST AKAZA!!
SLIP
I DROPPED MY SWORD!!
GAAH!!
MY GRIP... I LOST THE STRENGTH IN MY HAND!!
GWUP

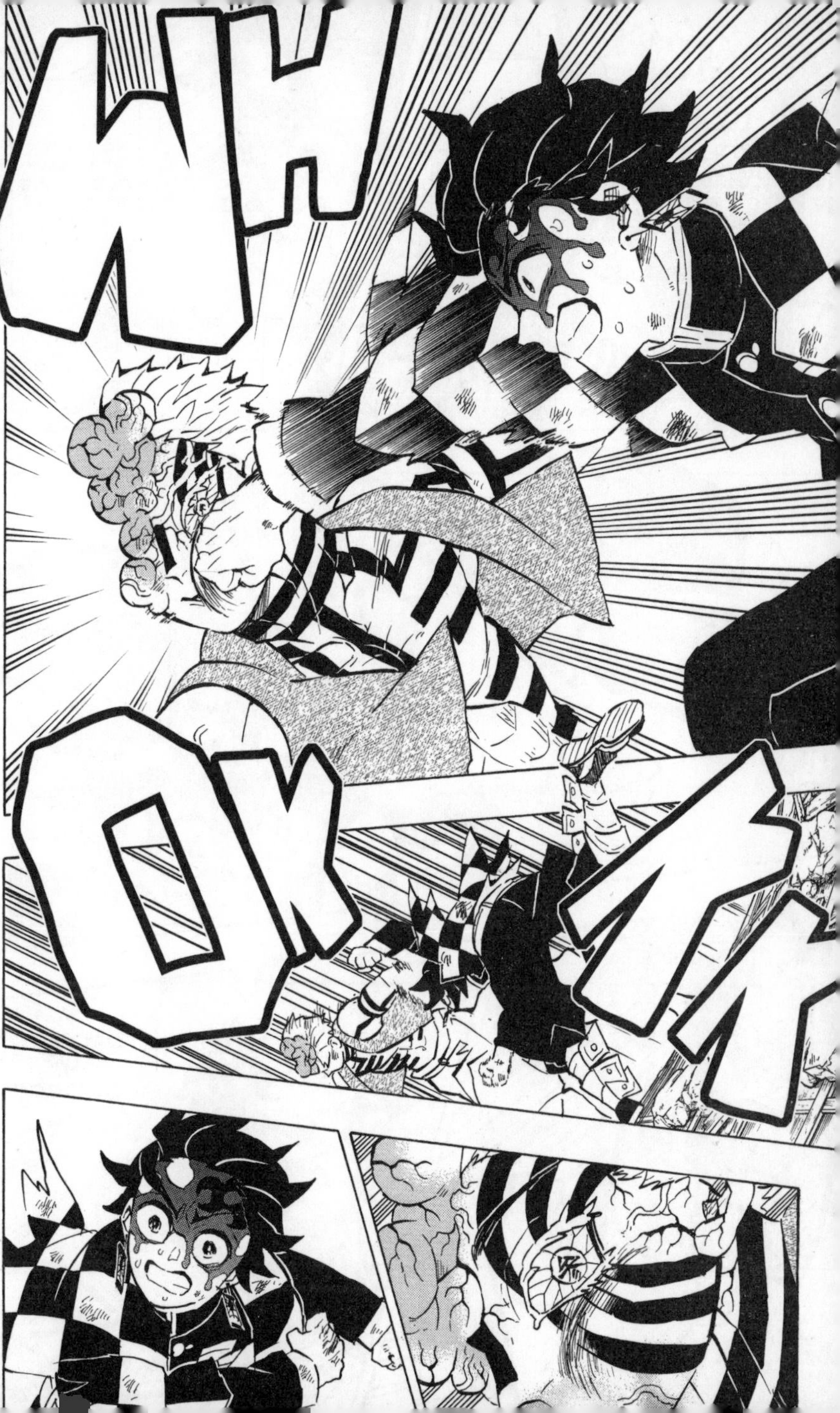

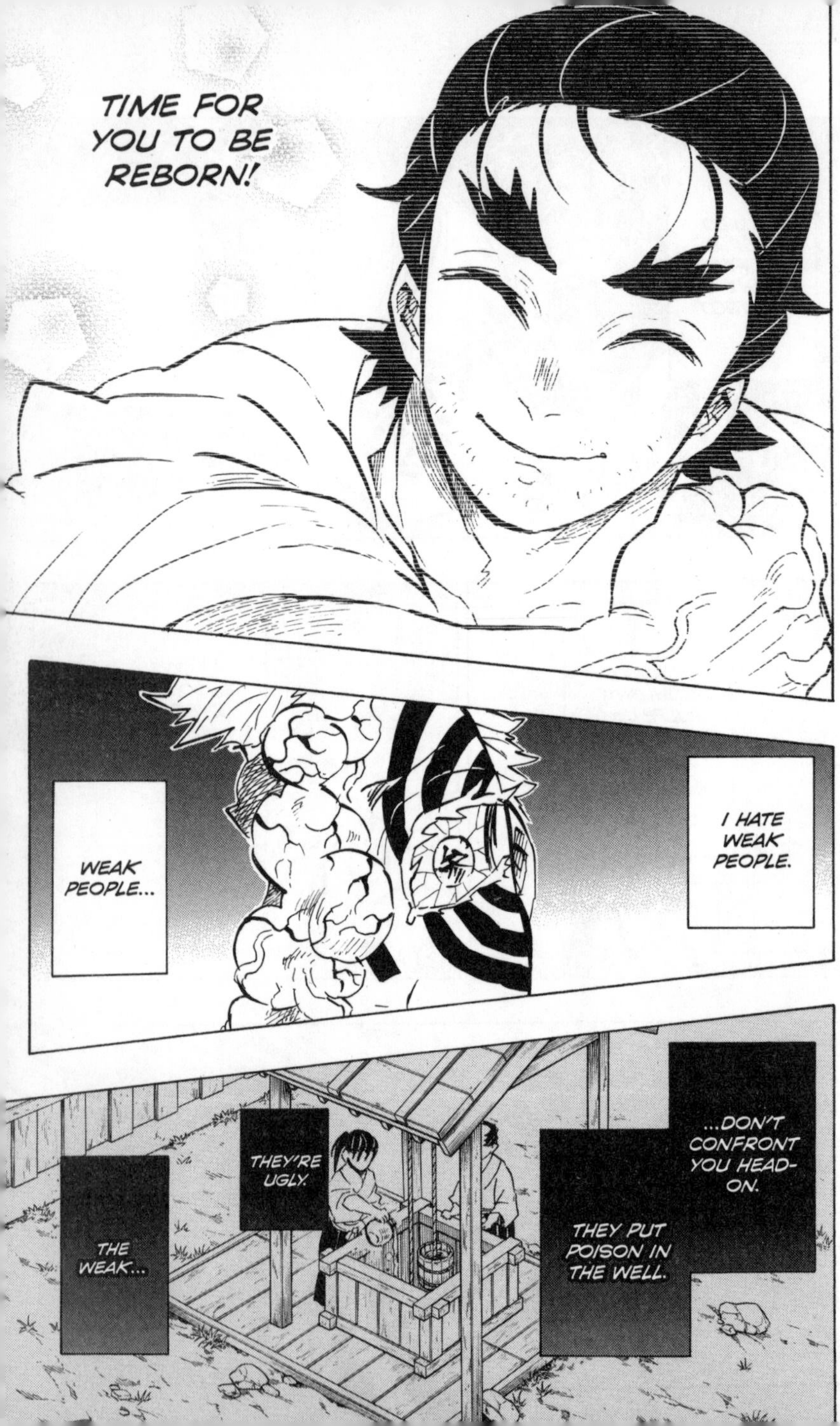
TIME FOR YOU TO BE REBORN!
I HATE WEAK PEOPLE.
WEAK PEOPLE...
...DON'T CONFRONT YOU HEAD-ON.
THEY PUT POISON IN THE WELL.
THEY'RE UGLY.
THE WEAK...

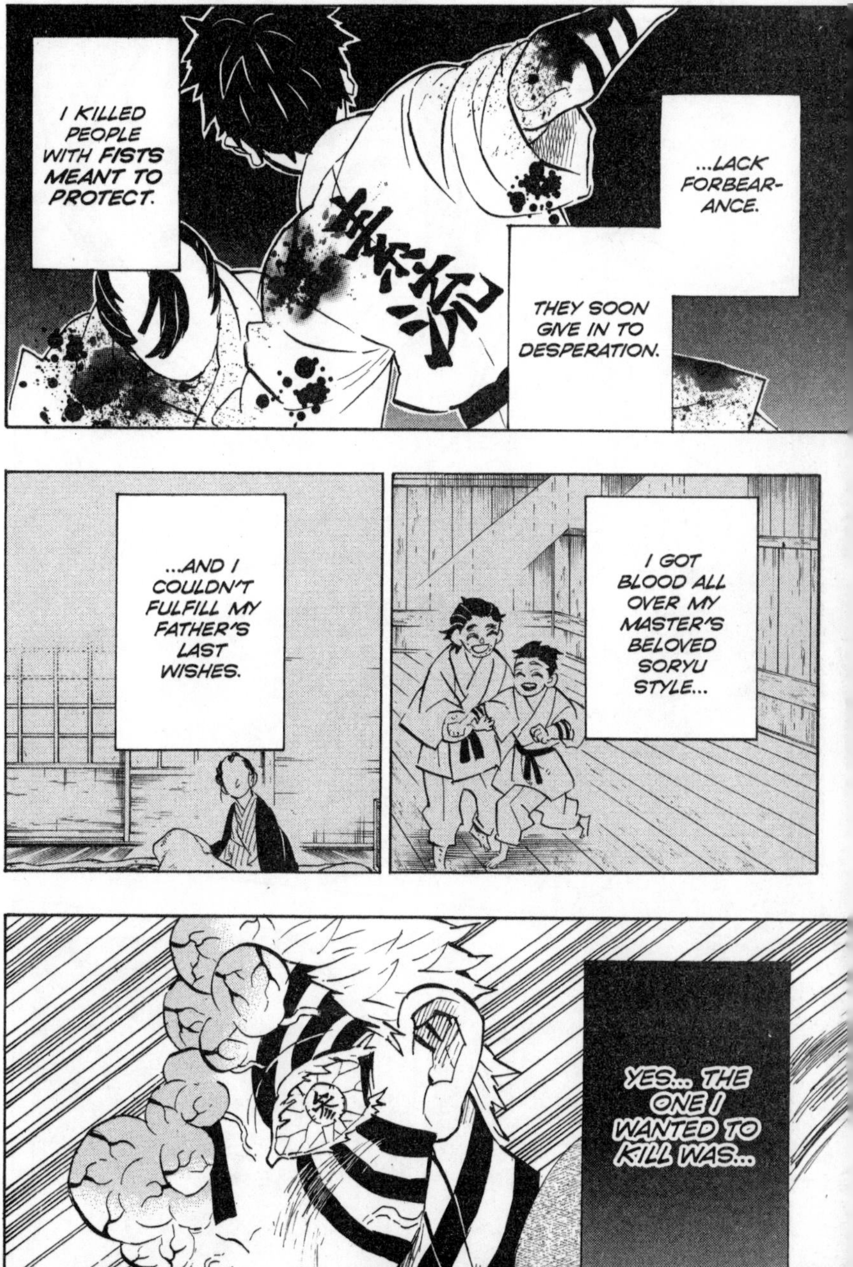
...LACK FORBEARANCE.
THEY SOON GIVE IN TO DESPERATION.
I KILLED PEOPLE WITH FISTS MEANT TO PROTECT.
I GOT BLOOD ALL OVER MY MASTER'S BELOVED SORYU STYLE...
...AND I COULDN'T FULFILL MY FATHER'S LAST WISHES.
YES... THE ONE I WANTED TO KILL WAS...

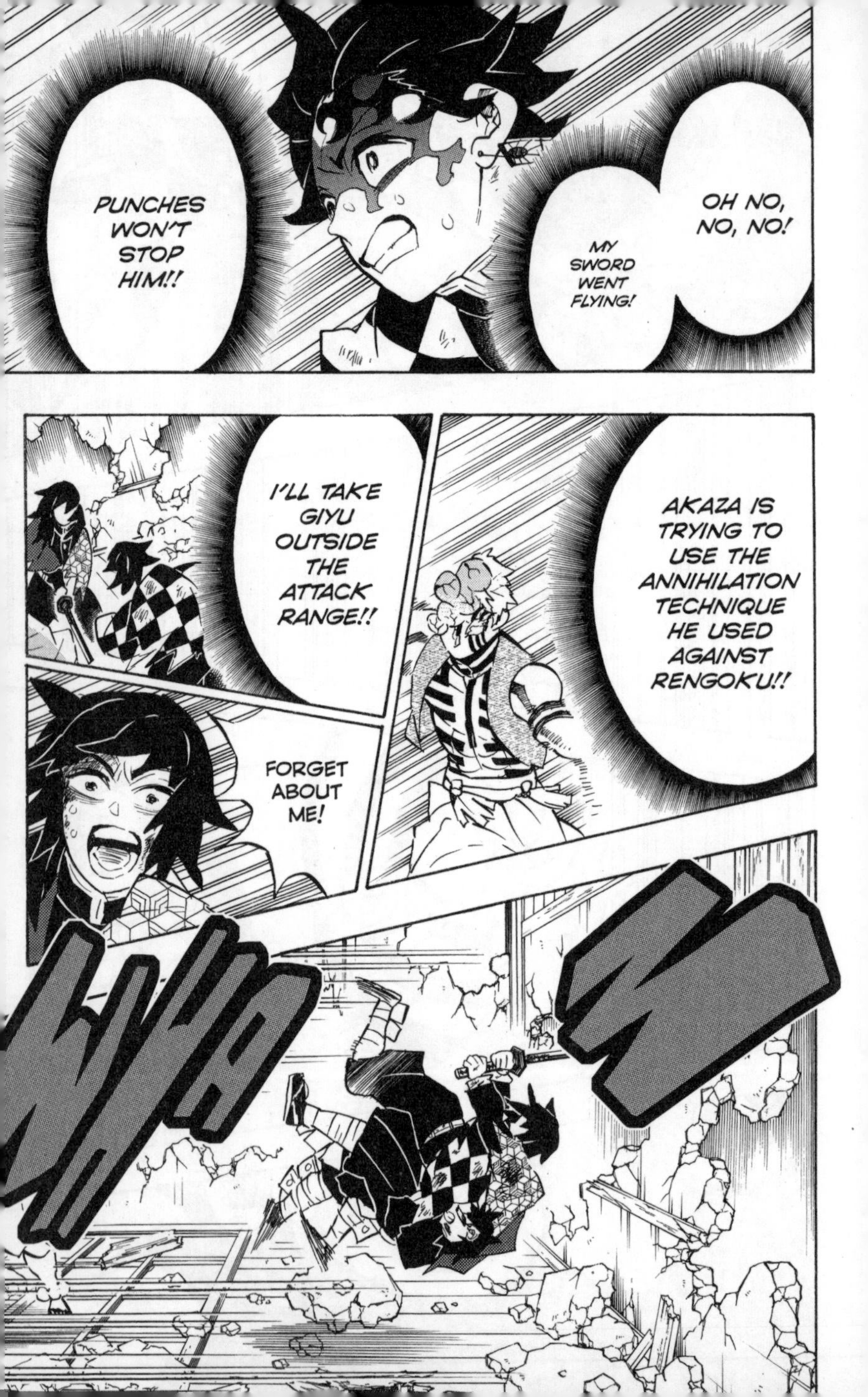
OH NO, NO, NO!
MY SWORD WENT FLYING!
PUNCHES WON'T STOP HIM!!
AKAZA IS TRYING TO USE THE ANNIHILATION TECHNIQUE HE USED AGAINST RENGOKU!!
I'LL TAKE GIYU OUTSIDE THE ATTACK RANGE!!
FORGET ABOUT ME!
WHAM

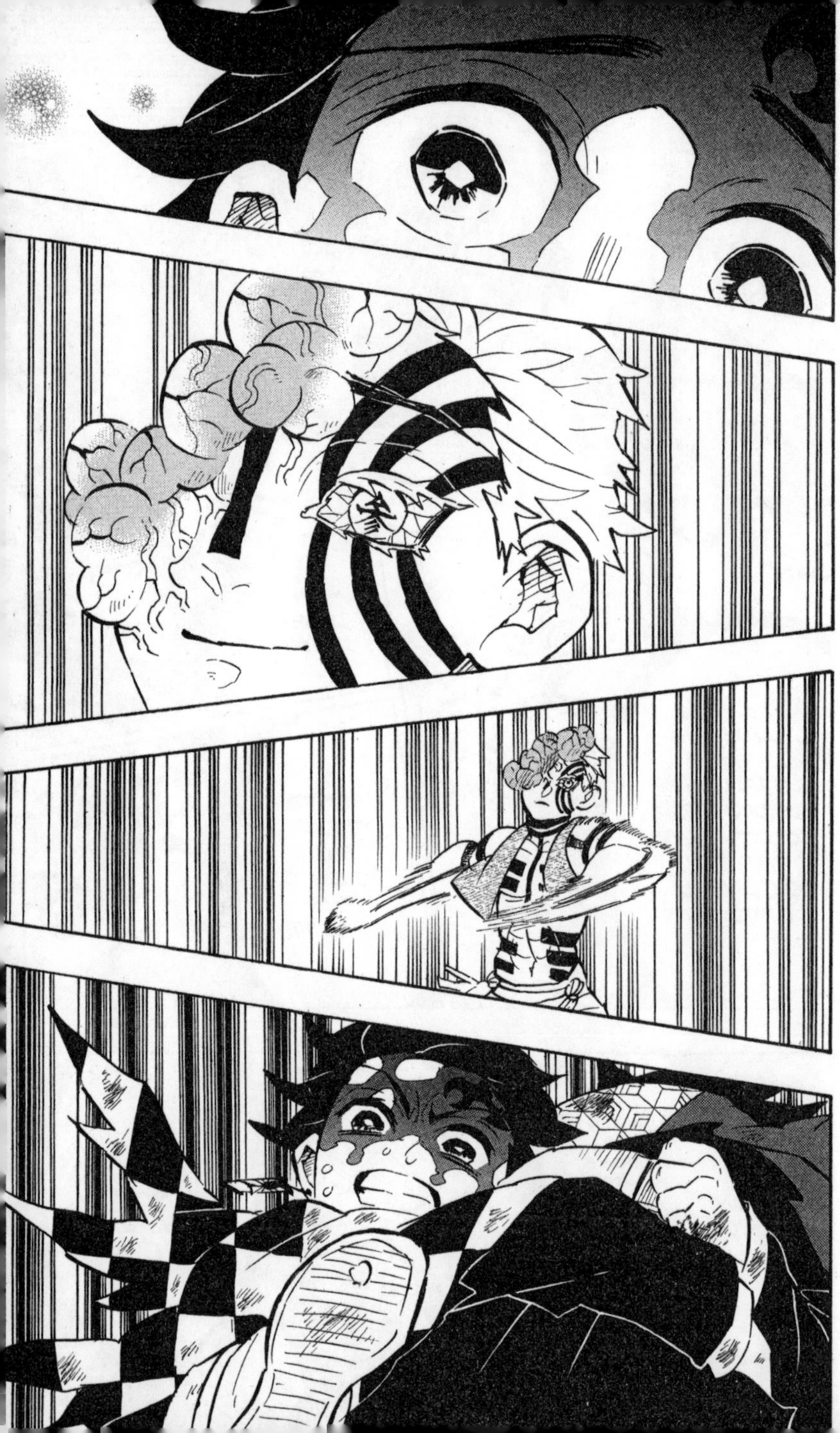

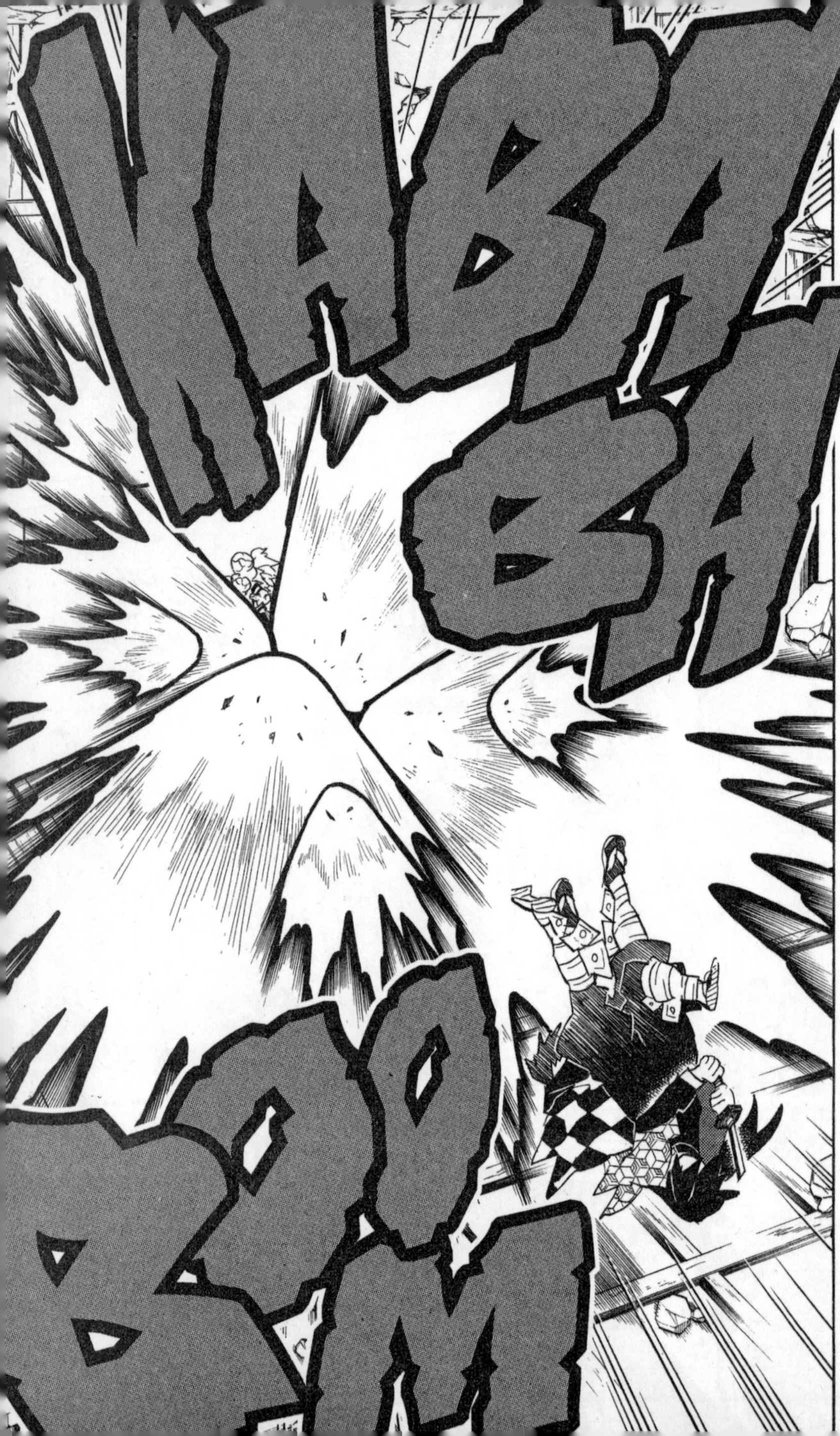
BOOM

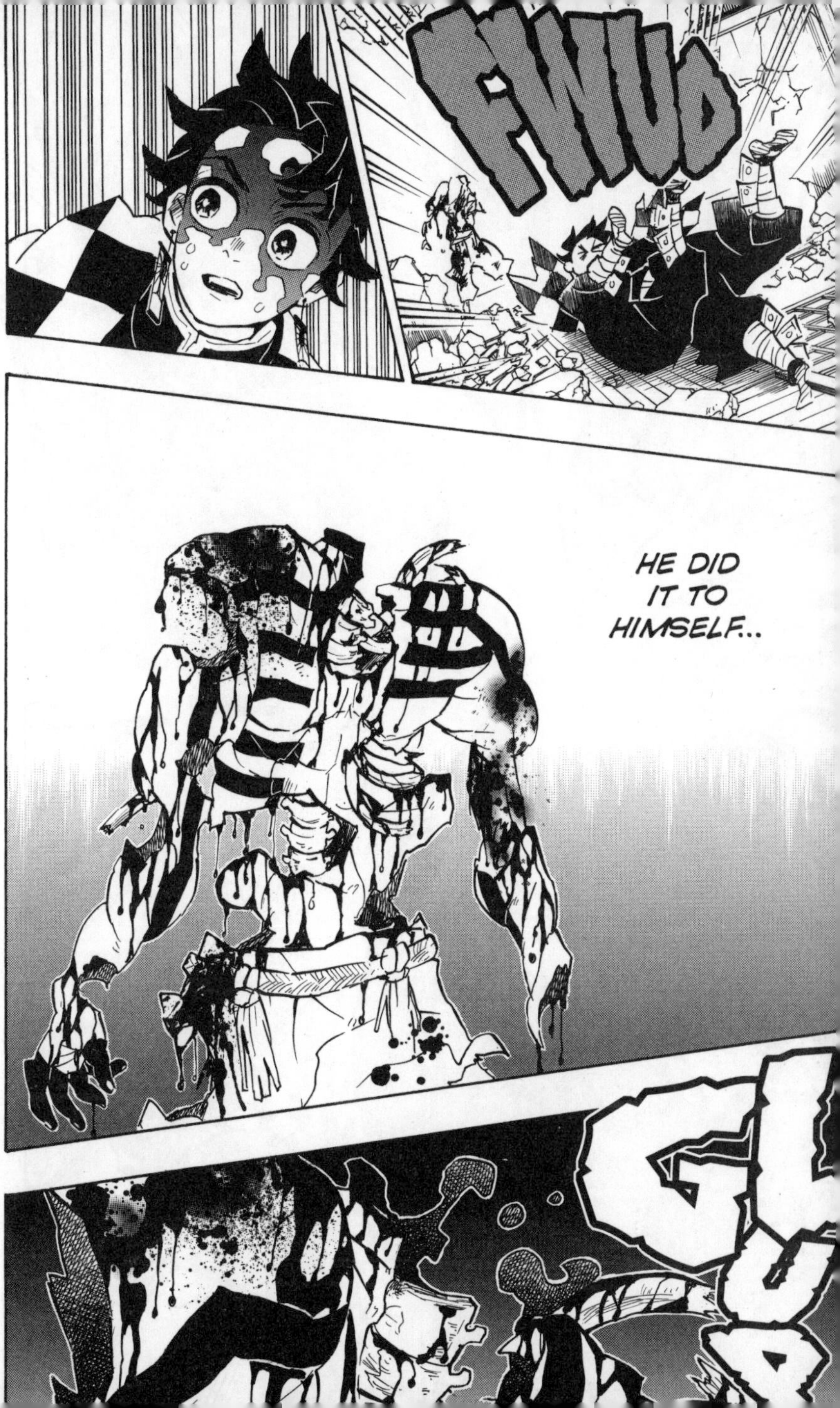
FWUD
HE DID IT TO HIMSELF...

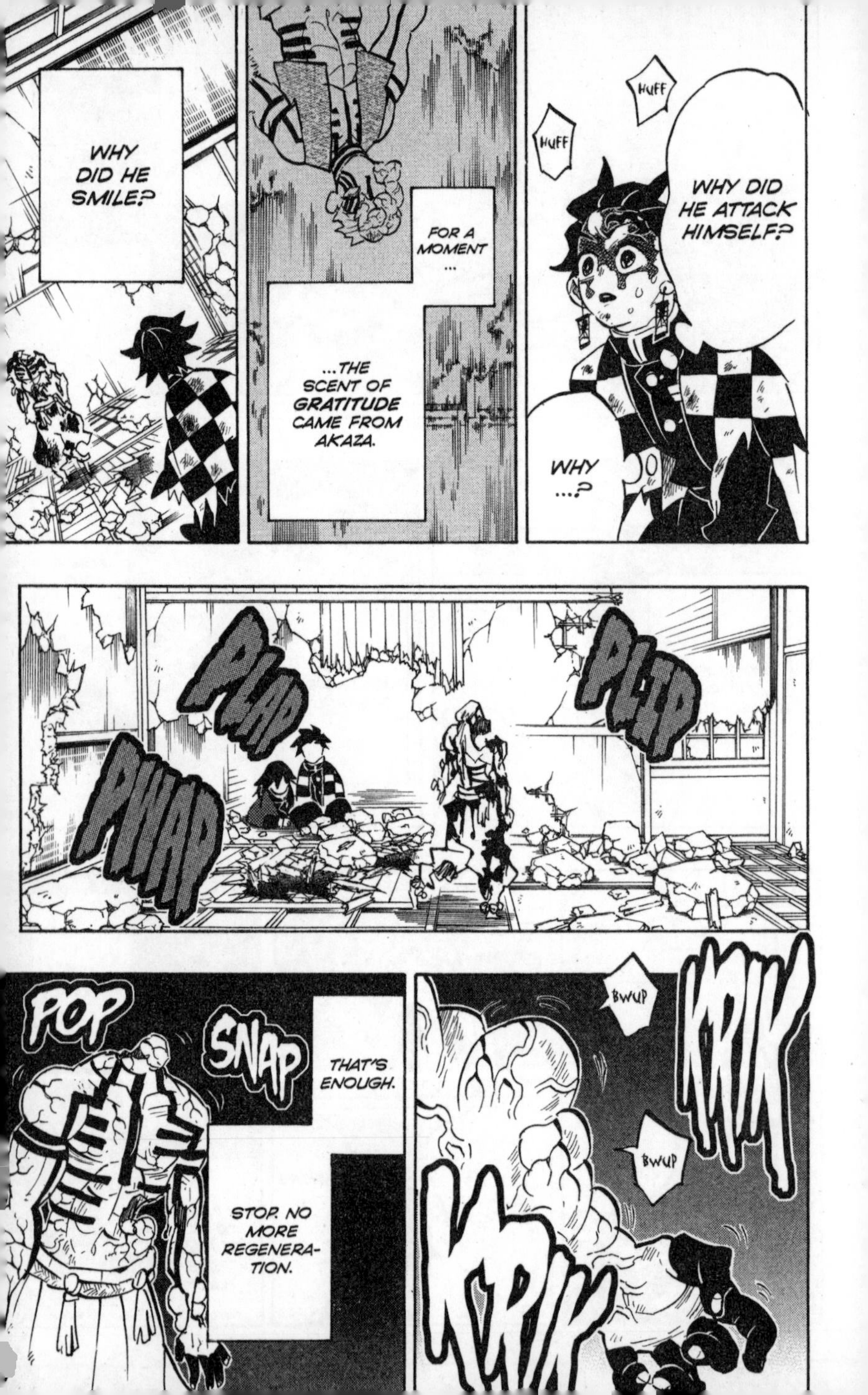
HUFF
HUFF
WHY DID HE ATTACK HIMSELF?
WHY ...?
FOR A MOMENT ...
...THE SCENT OF GRATITUDE CAME FROM AKAZA.
WHY DID HE SMILE?
PLID
PLID
PWAP
BWUP
KRIK
BWUP
KRIK
THAT'S ENOUGH.
SNAP
POP
STOP. NO MORE REGENERA-
TION.

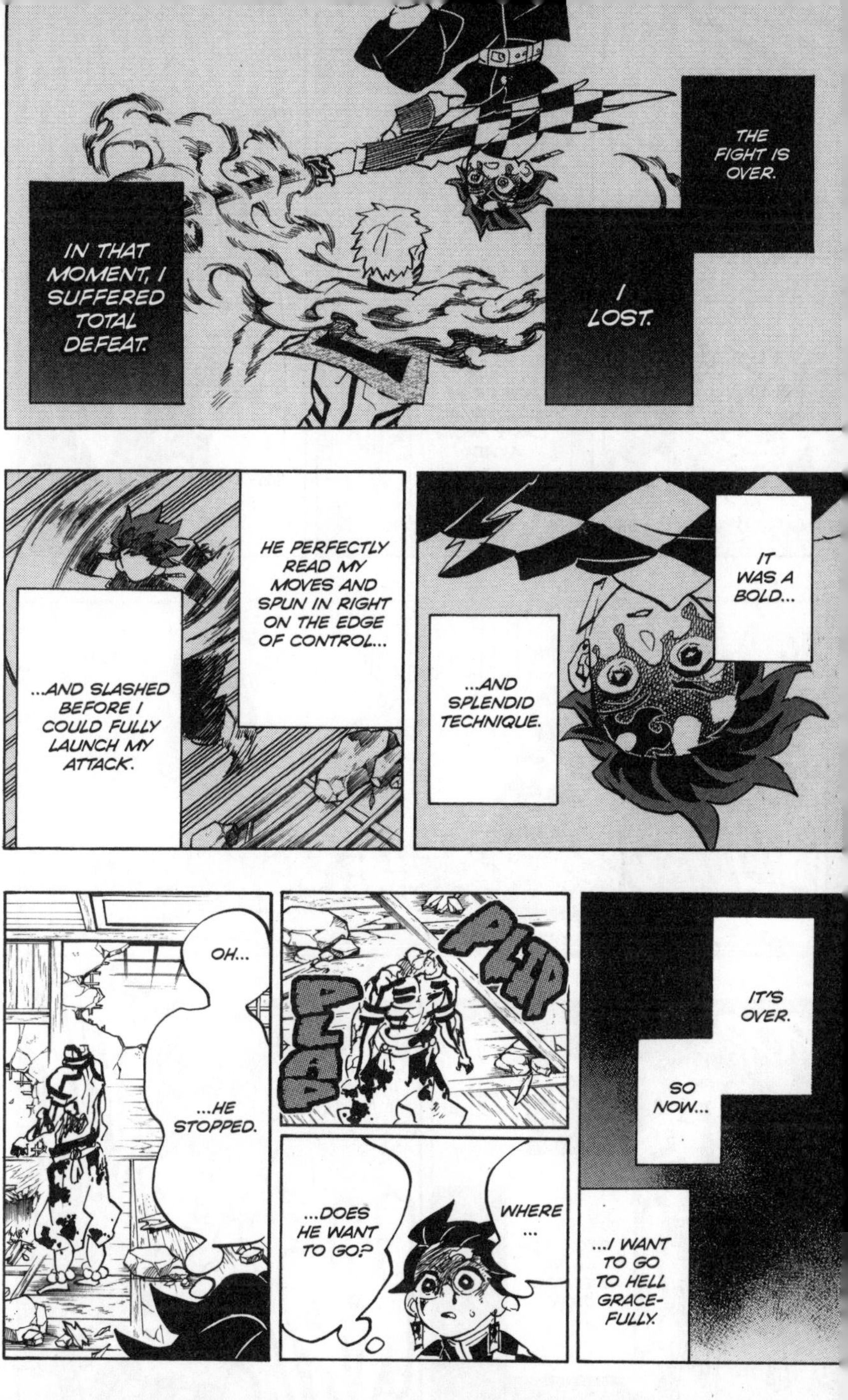
THE FIGHT IS OVER.
I LOST.
IN THAT MOMENT, I SUFFERED TOTAL DEFEAT.
IT WAS A BOLD...
...AND SPLENDID TECHNIQUE.
HE PERFECTLY READ MY MOVES AND SPUN IN RIGHT ON THE EDGE OF CONTROL...
...AND SLASHED BEFORE I COULD FULLY LAUNCH MY ATTACK.
IT'S OVER.
SO NOW...
...I WANT TO GO TO HELL GRACE-FULLY.
PLIP
PLIP
WHERE...
...DOES HE WANT TO GO?
OH...
...HE STOPPED.

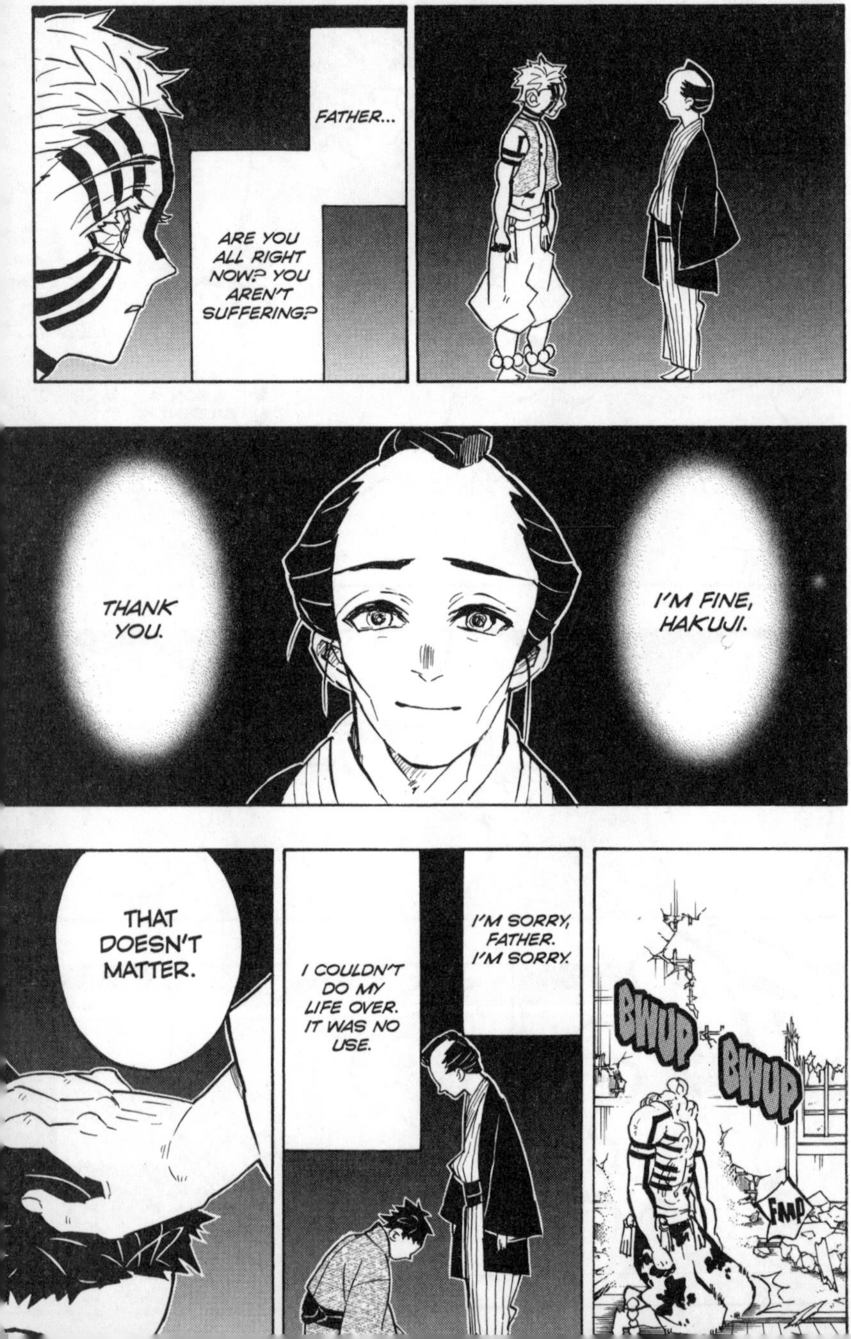
FATHER...
ARE YOU ALL RIGHT NOW? YOU AREN'T SUFFERING?
I'M FINE, HAKUJI.
THANK YOU.
BWUP
BWUP
FMP
I'M SORRY, FATHER. I'M SORRY.
I COULDN'T DO MY LIFE OVER. IT WAS NO USE.
THAT DOESN'T MATTER.

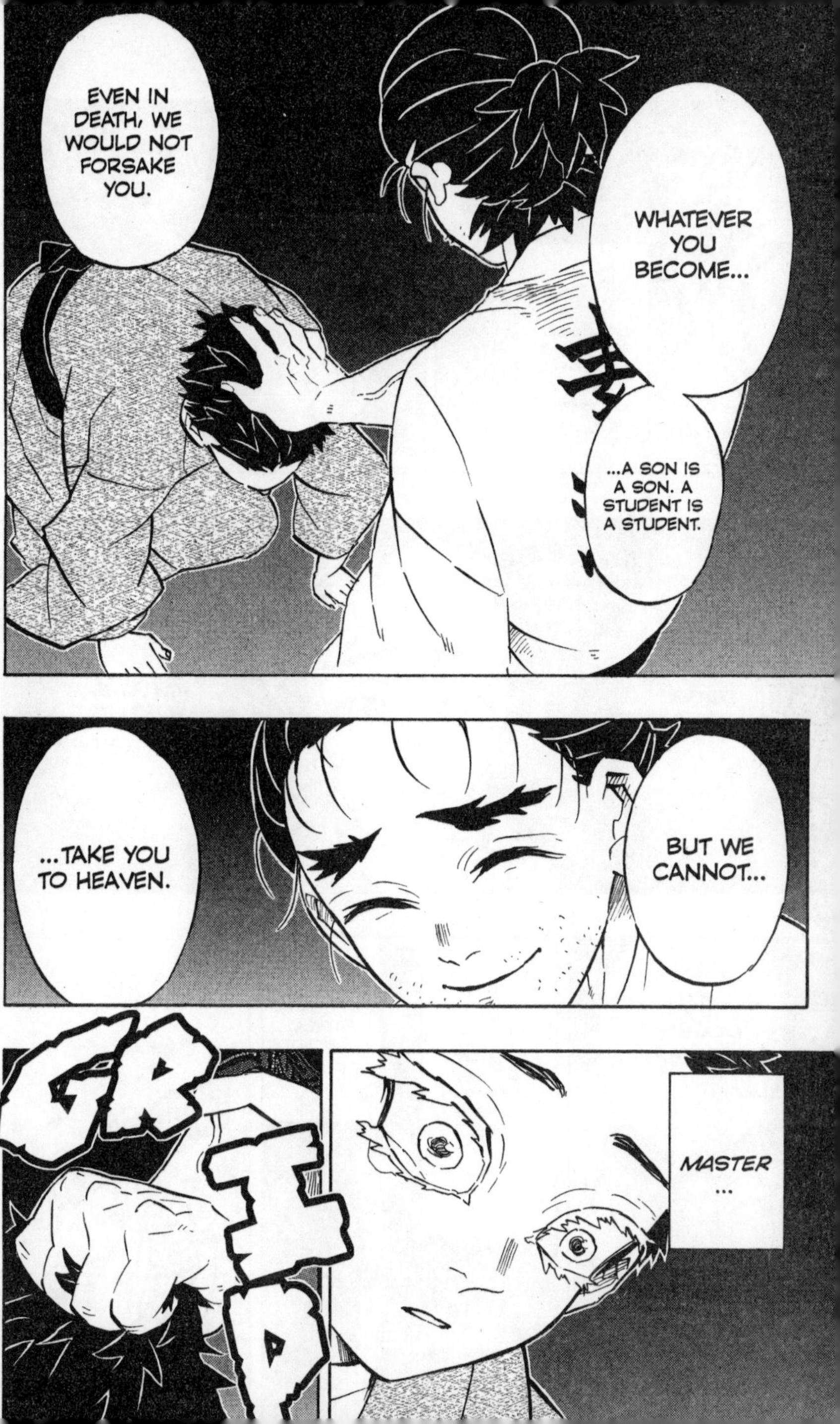
WHATEVER YOU BECOME...
...A SON IS A SON. A STUDENT IS A STUDENT.
EVEN IN DEATH, WE WOULD NOT FORSAKE YOU.
BUT WE CANNOT...
...TAKE YOU TO HEAVEN.
MASTER ...
GRIP

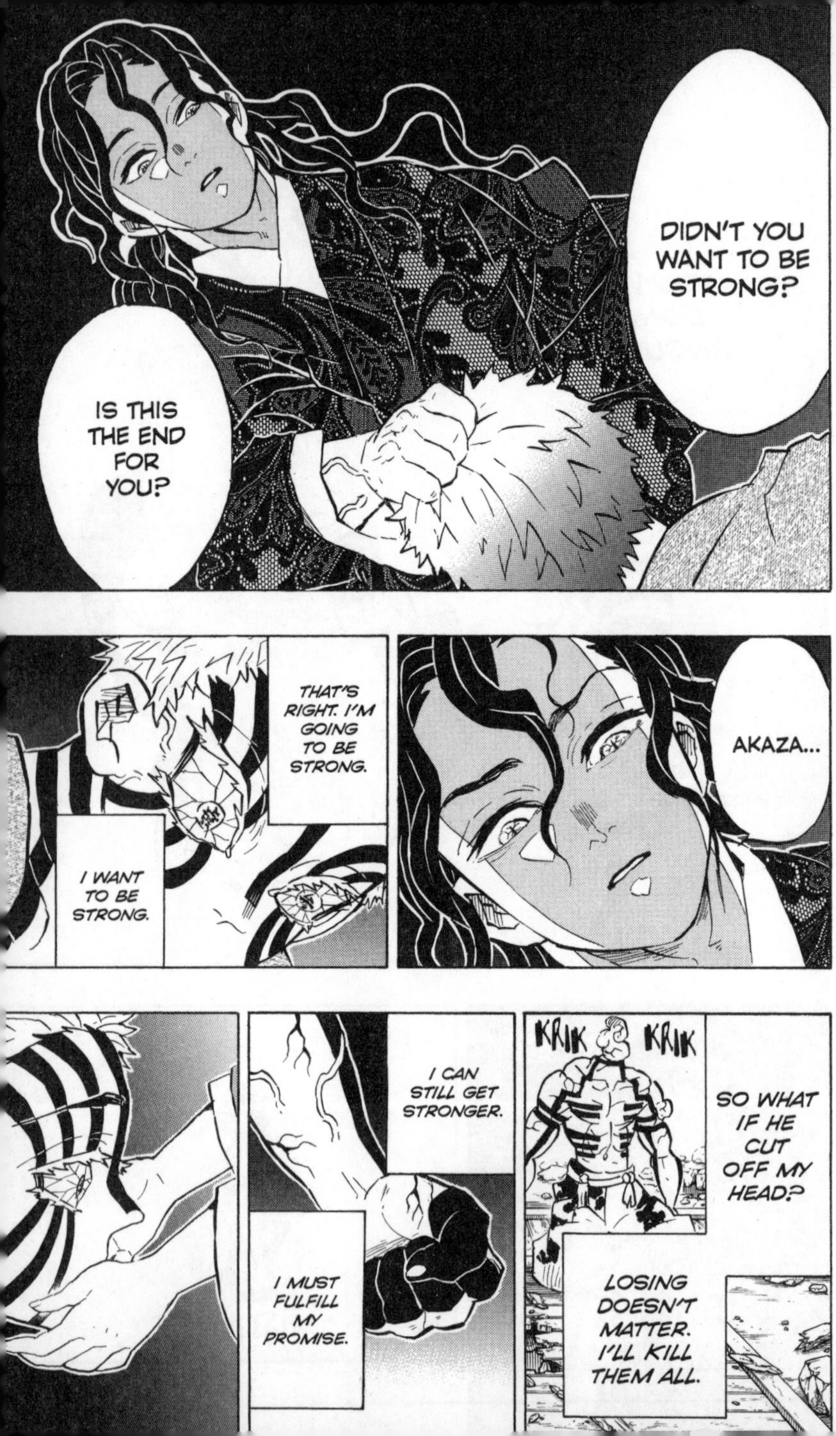
DIDN'T YOU WANT TO BE STRONG?
IS THIS THE END FOR YOU?
AKAZA...
THAT'S RIGHT. I'M GOING TO BE STRONG.
I WANT TO BE STRONG.
KRIK KRIK
SO WHAT IF HE CUT OFF MY HEAD?
LOSING DOESN'T MATTER. I'LL KILL THEM ALL.
I CAN STILL GET STRONGER.
I MUST FULFILL MY PROMISE.

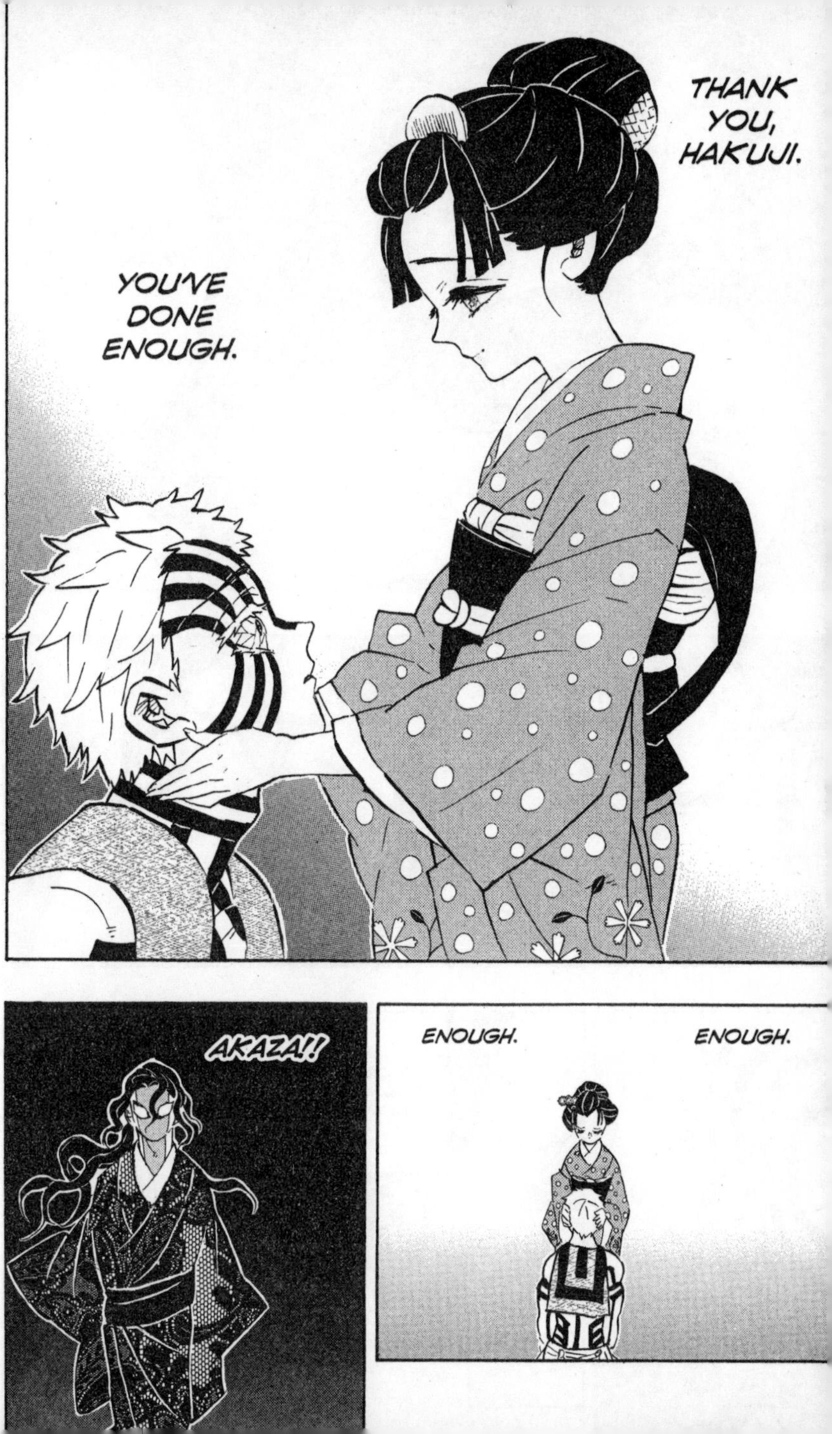
THANK YOU, HAKUJI.
YOU'VE DONE ENOUGH.
ENOUGH.
ENOUGH.
AKAZA!!

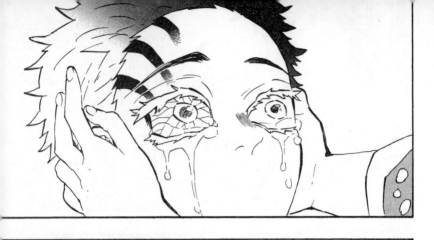

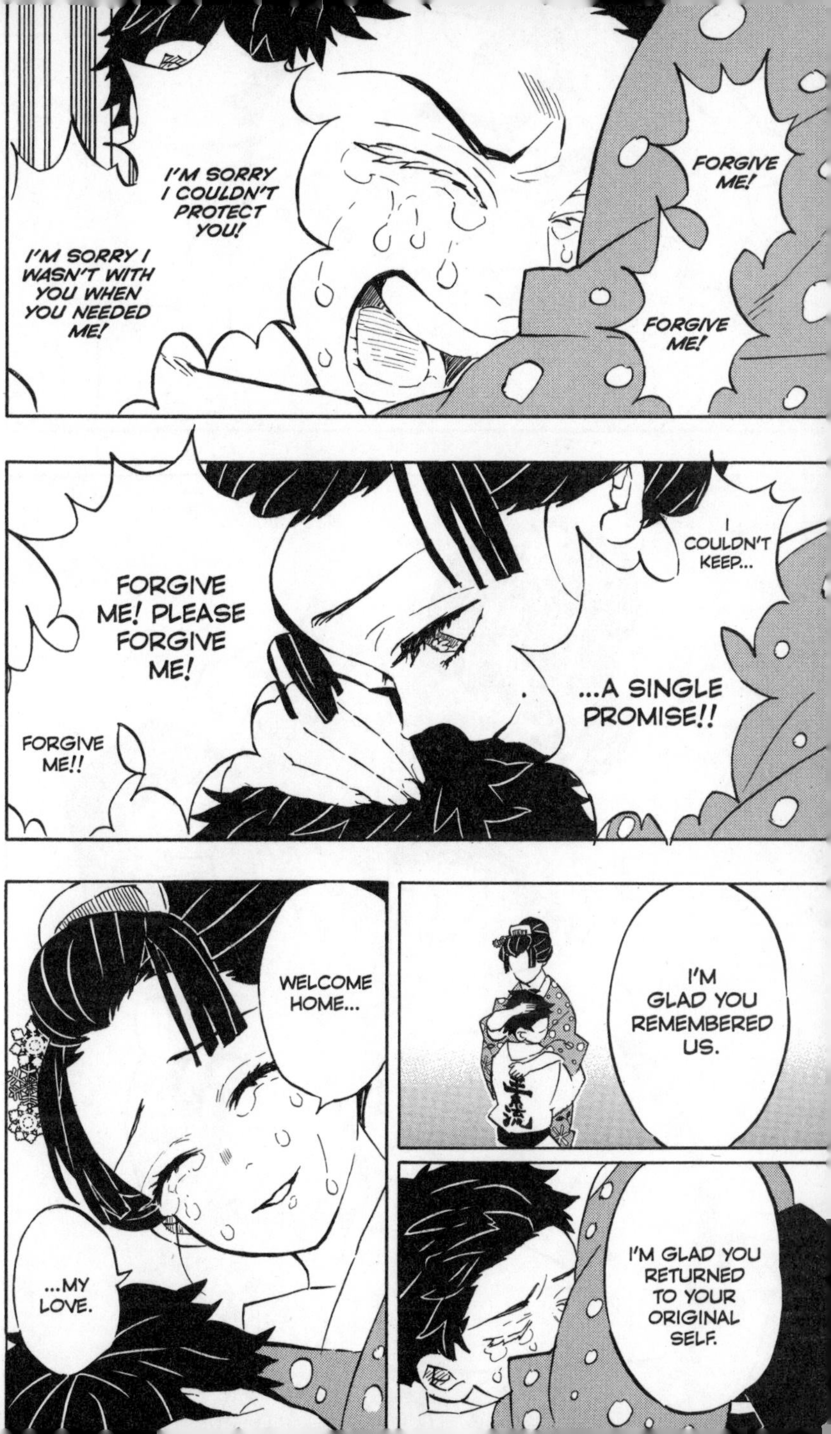
FORGIVE ME!
FORGIVE ME!
I'M SORRY I COULDN'T PROTECT YOU!
I'M SORRY I WASN'T WITH YOU WHEN YOU NEEDED ME!
I COULDN'T KEEP...
...A SINGLE PROMISE!!
FORGIVE ME! PLEASE FORGIVE ME!
FORGIVE ME!!
I'M GLAD YOU REMEMBERED US.
I'M GLAD YOU RETURNED TO YOUR ORIGINAL SELF.
WELCOME HOME...
...MY LOVE.

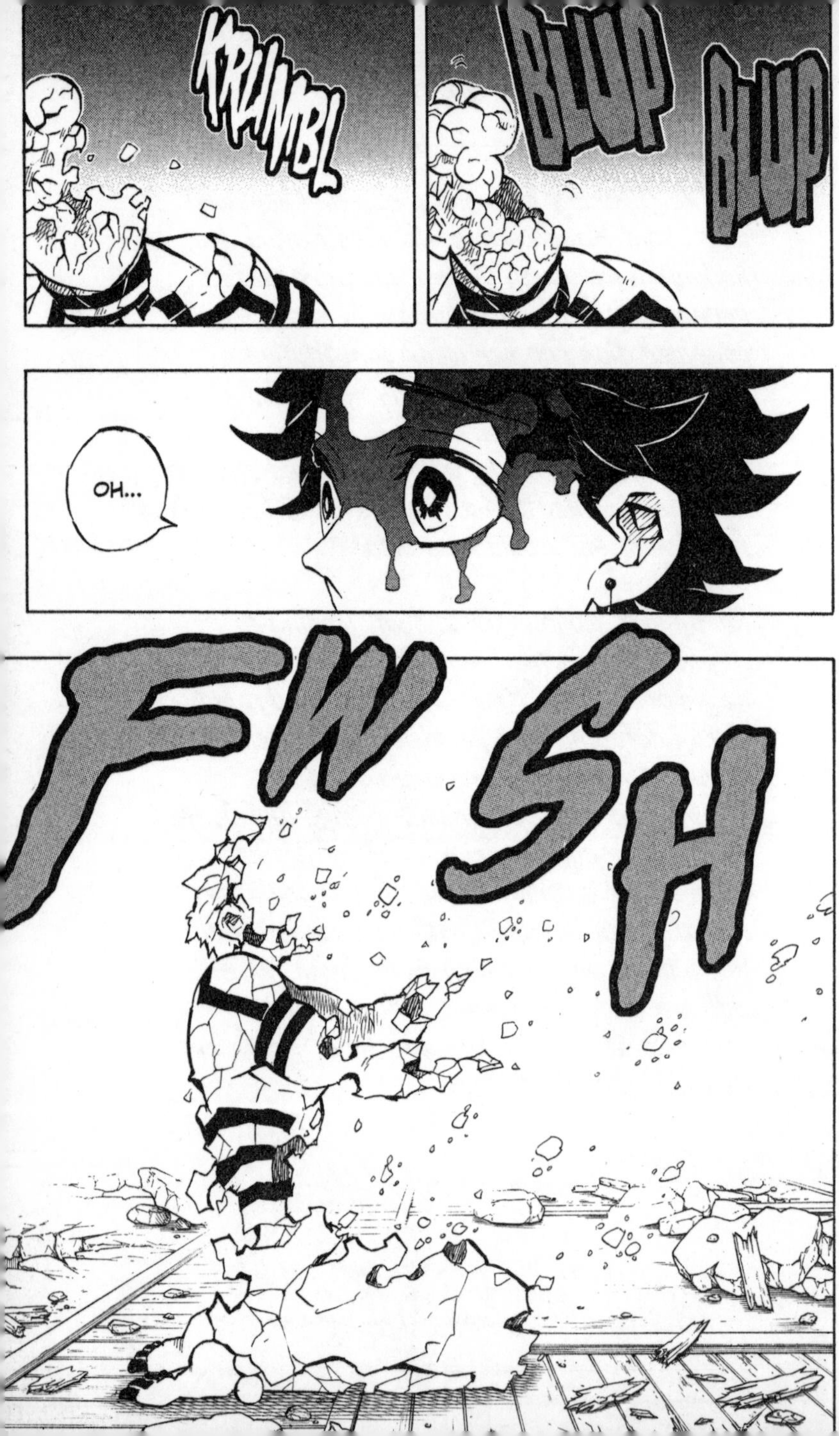
BLUP BLUP
KRUMBL
OH...
FWSH

EXTRA TIDBITS

The neighboring dojo had a son and heir who was about Koyuki's age. He liked Koyuki, but he had an extremely violent and arrogant personality, so he was unable to show proper consideration for her weak constitution. When she wasn't feeling well, he forced her to go outside with him and she had an asthma attack. Seeing that, he was frightened and ran away, leaving her to suffer. If Hakuji hadn't found her, she would have died.

Hakuji was furious about that, leading to a feud between the Soryu Dojo and the neighboring dojo. Keizo was on standby, but Hakuji defeated nine people all by himself at just 16 years of age and forbid any involvement whatsoever with Koyuki and Soryu Dojo. Incensed, the neighboring dojo's heir drew a real sword instead of a wooden one and attacked Hakuji. Hakuji defended himself by striking the oncoming blade from the side with his fist, breaking it in two. That was the technique at which Hakuji was most proficient. He called it Bell-Splitter.

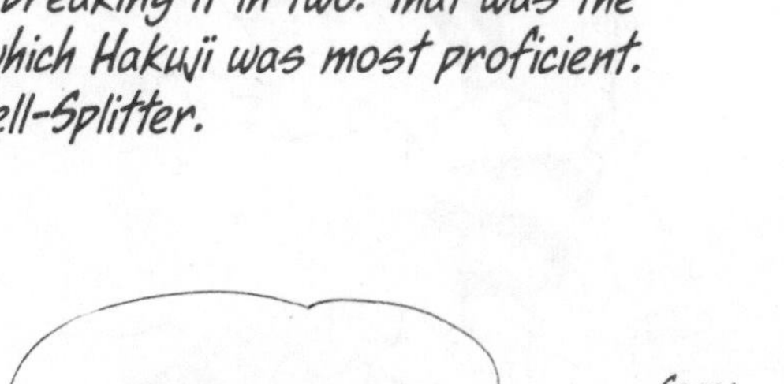
This story continues after the next chapter. Even I'm surprised at how long it is.
Sorry...

CHAPTER 157: RETURNING SPIRIT

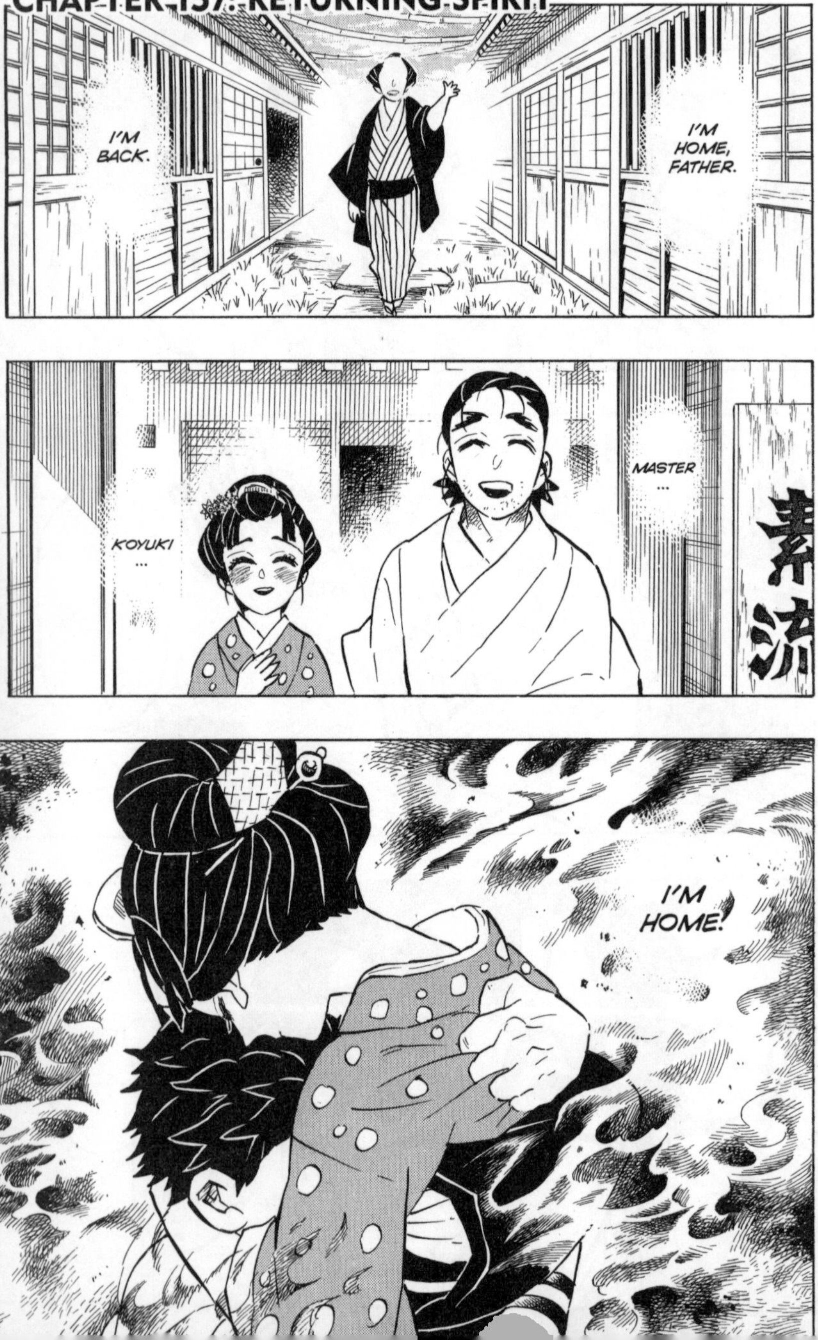
I'M HOME, FATHER.
I'M BACK.
MASTER ...
素流
KOYUKI ...
I'M HOME!

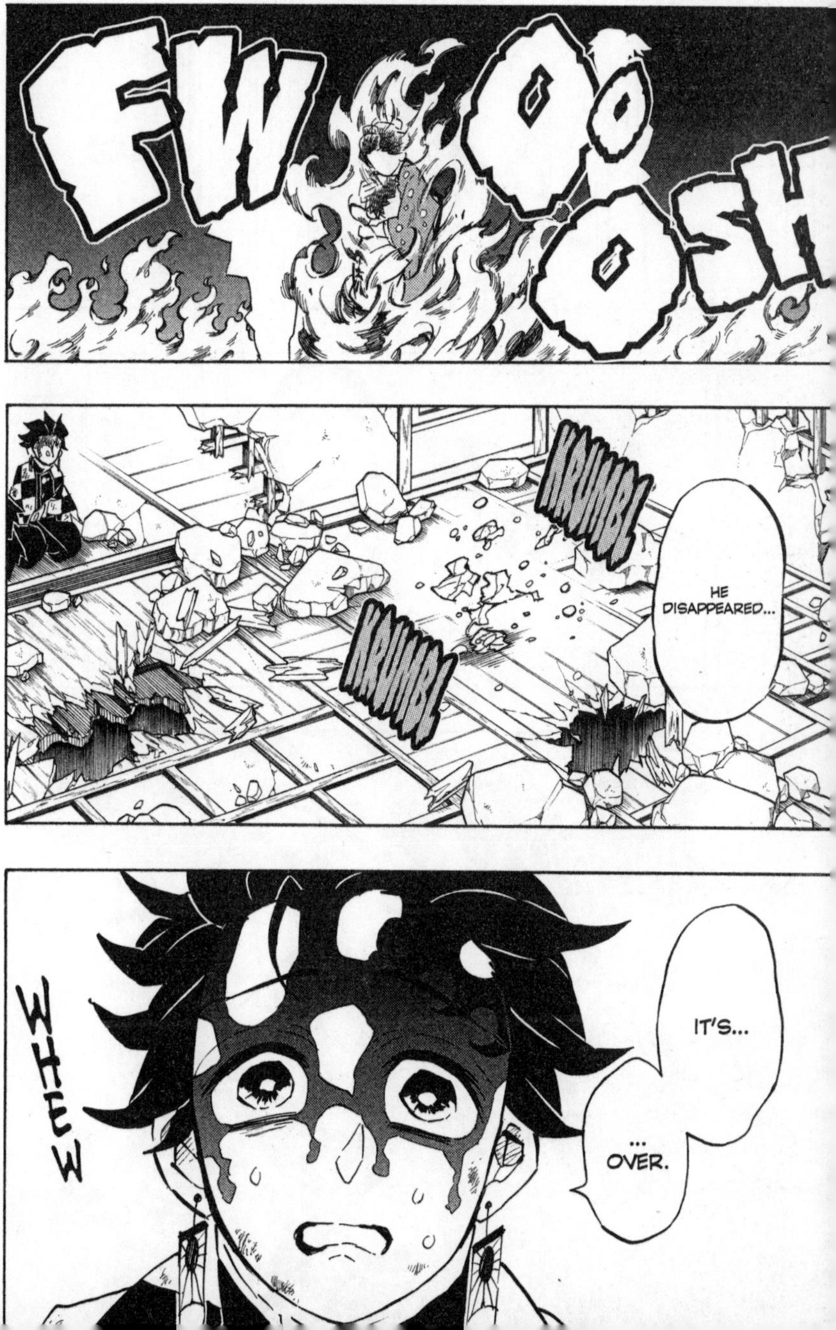
FWOOOSH
KRUMBL
KRUMBL
HE DISAPPEARED...
WHEW
IT'S...
... OVER.

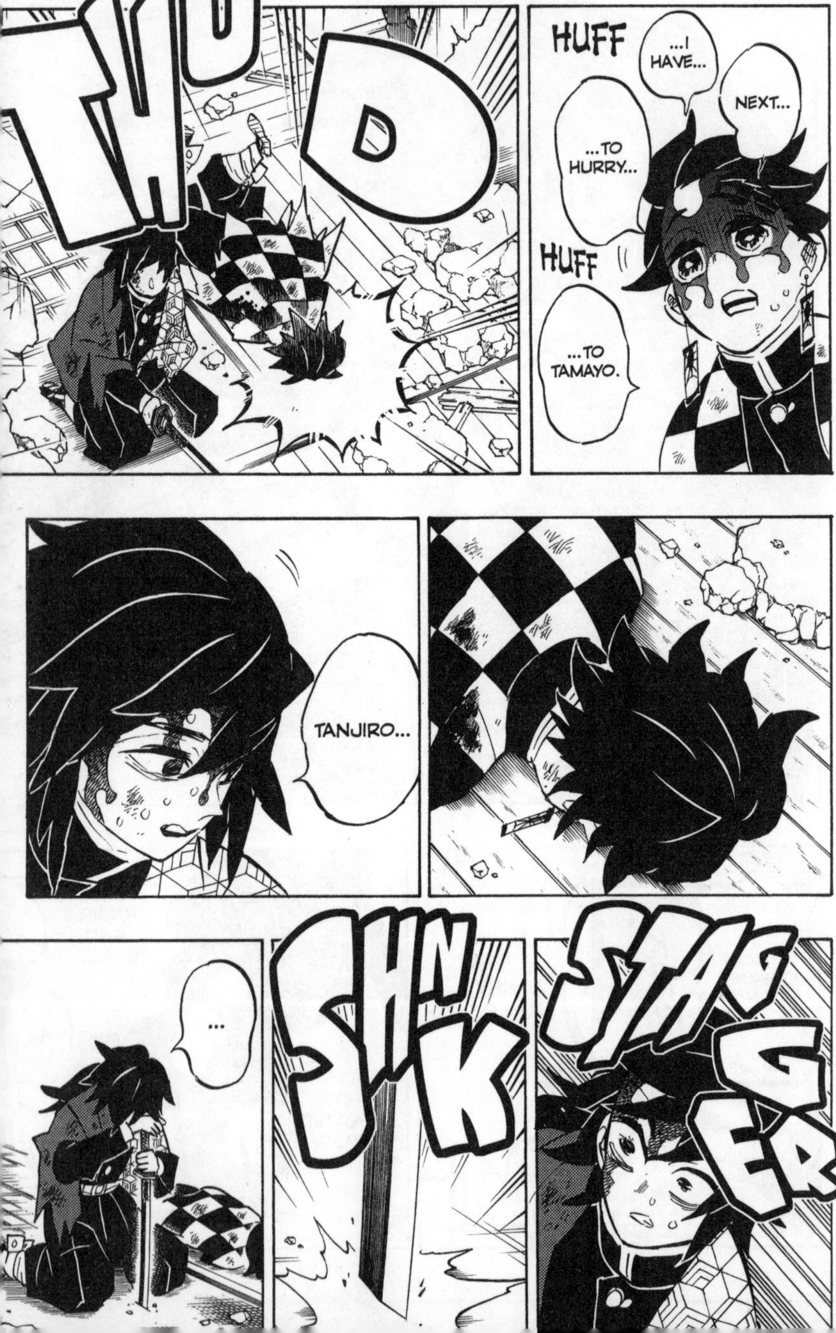
HUFF
...I HAVE...
NEXT...
...TO HURRY...
HUFF
...TO TAMAYO.
THUD
TANJIRO...
STAGGER
SHINK
...

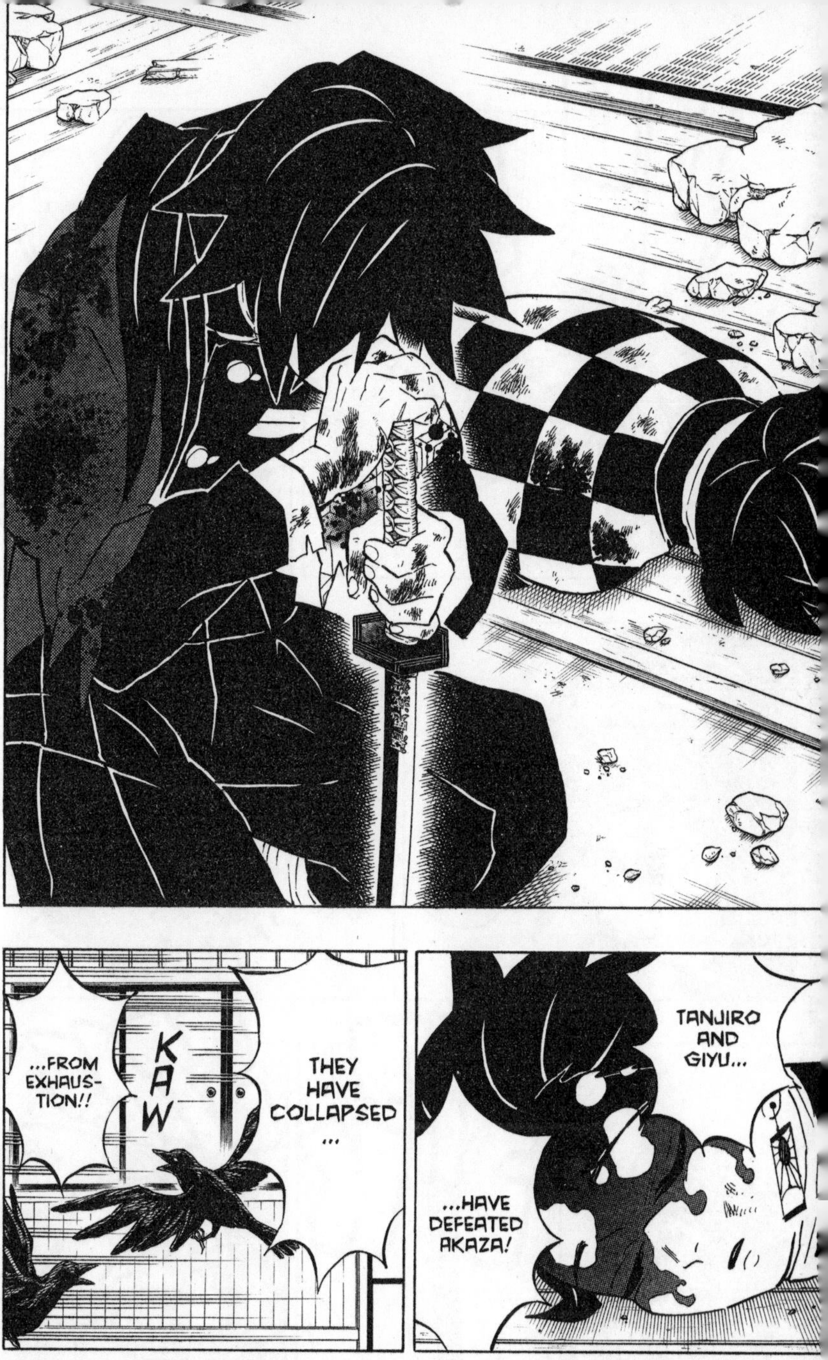
TANJIRO AND GIYU...
...HAVE DEFEATED AKAZA!
THEY HAVE COLLAPSED...
KAW
...FROM EXHAUS-TION!!

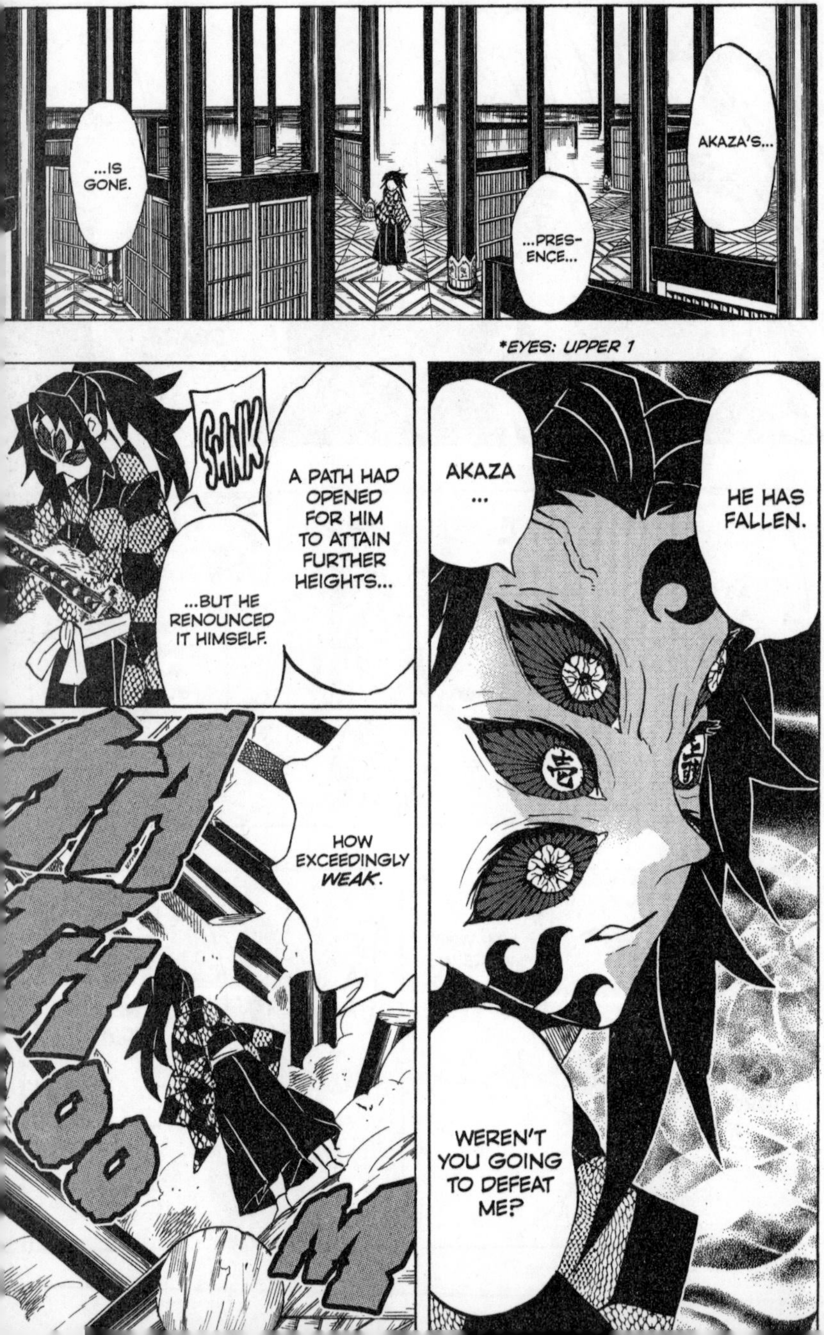
AKAZA'S...
...PRES-ENCE...
...IS GONE.
*EYES: UPPER 1
HE HAS FALLEN.
AKAZA ...
WEREN'T YOU GOING TO DEFEAT ME?
SHINK
A PATH HAD OPENED FOR HIM TO ATTAIN FURTHER HEIGHTS...
...BUT HE RENOUNCED IT HIMSELF.
HOW EXCEEDINGLY WEAK.

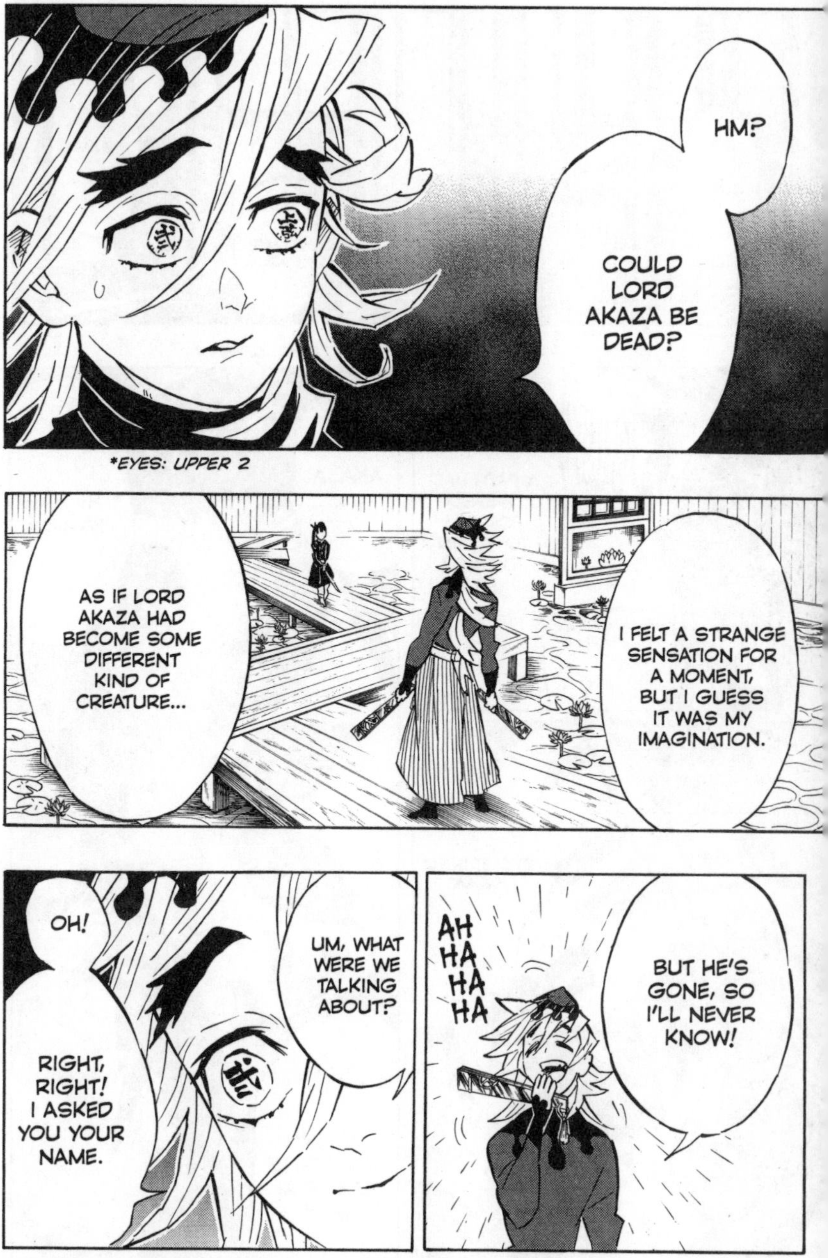
HM?
COULD LORD AKAZA BE DEAD?
*EYES: UPPER 2
I FELT A STRANGE SENSATION FOR A MOMENT, BUT I GUESS IT WAS MY IMAGINATION.
AS IF LORD AKAZA HAD BECOME SOME DIFFERENT KIND OF CREATURE...
BUT HE'S GONE, SO I'LL NEVER KNOW!
AH HA HA HA
UM, WHAT WERE WE TALKING ABOUT?
OH!
RIGHT, RIGHT! I ASKED YOU YOUR NAME.

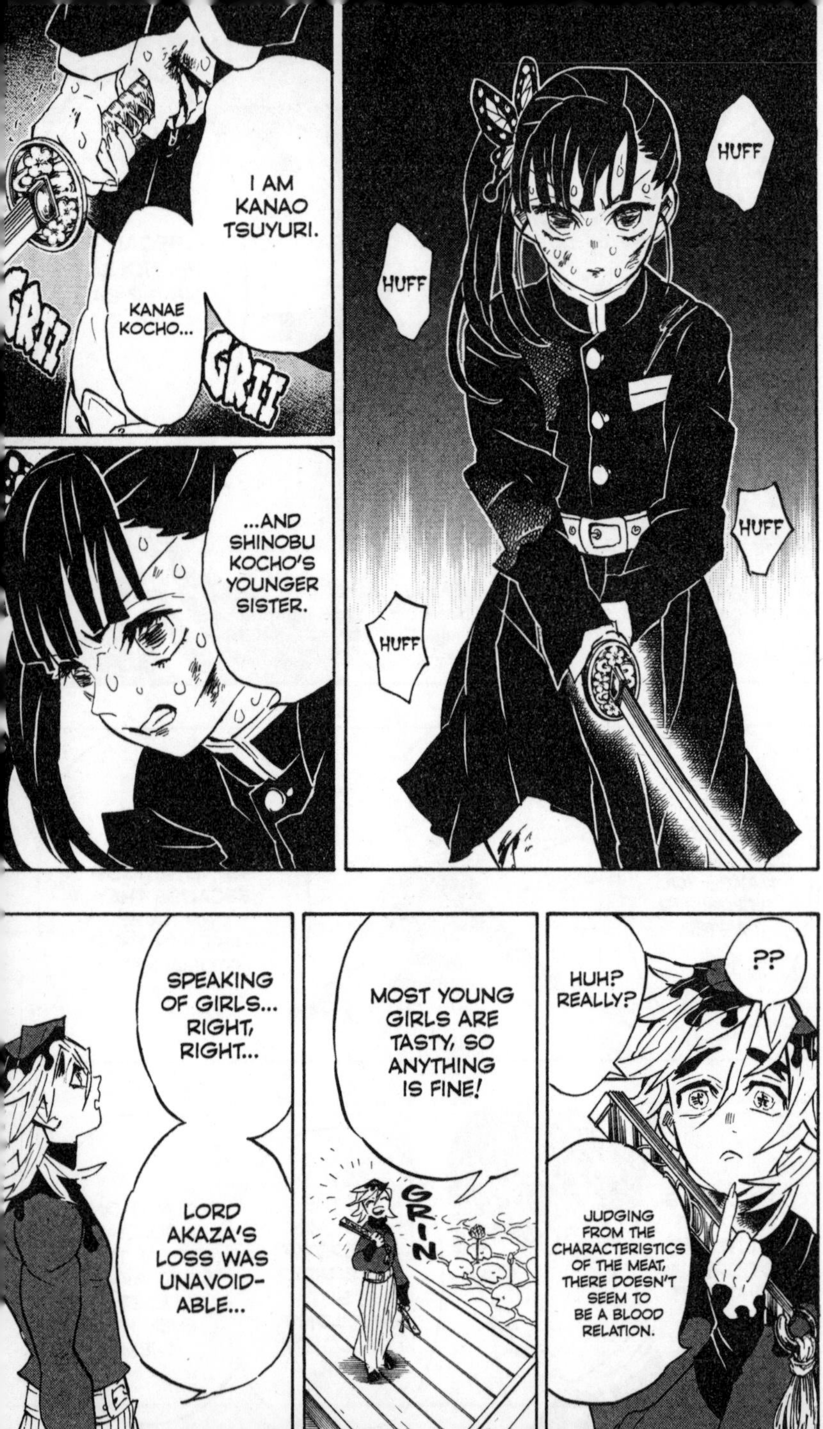
HUFF
HUFF
HUFF
HUFF
I AM KANAO TSUYURI.
KANAE KOCHO...
GRII
GRII
...AND SHINOBU KOCHO'S YOUNGER SISTER.
??
HUH? REALLY?
JUDGING FROM THE CHARACTERISTICS OF THE MEAT, THERE DOESN'T SEEM TO BE A BLOOD RELATION.
MOST YOUNG GIRLS ARE TASTY, SO ANYTHING IS FINE!
GRIN
SPEAKING OF GIRLS... RIGHT, RIGHT...
LORD AKAZA'S LOSS WAS UNAVOID-ABLE...

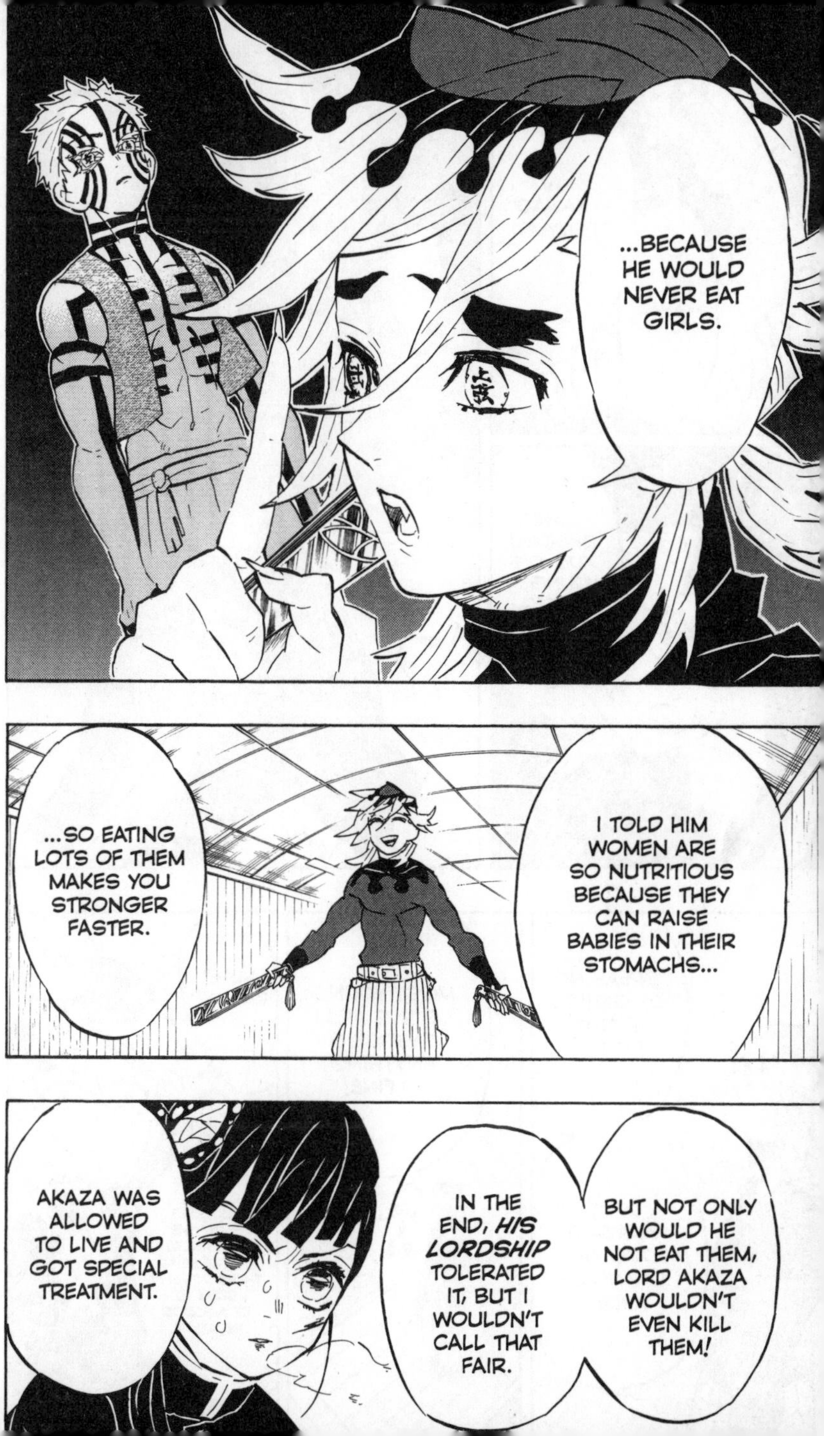
...BECAUSE HE WOULD NEVER EAT GIRLS.
I TOLD HIM WOMEN ARE SO NUTRITIOUS BECAUSE THEY CAN RAISE BABIES IN THEIR STOMACHS...
...SO EATING LOTS OF THEM MAKES YOU STRONGER FASTER.
BUT NOT ONLY WOULD HE NOT EAT THEM, LORD AKAZA WOULDN'T EVEN KILL THEM!
IN THE END, *HIS LORDSHIP* TOLERATED IT, BUT I WOULDN'T CALL THAT FAIR.
AKAZA WAS ALLOWED TO LIVE AND GOT SPECIAL TREATMENT.

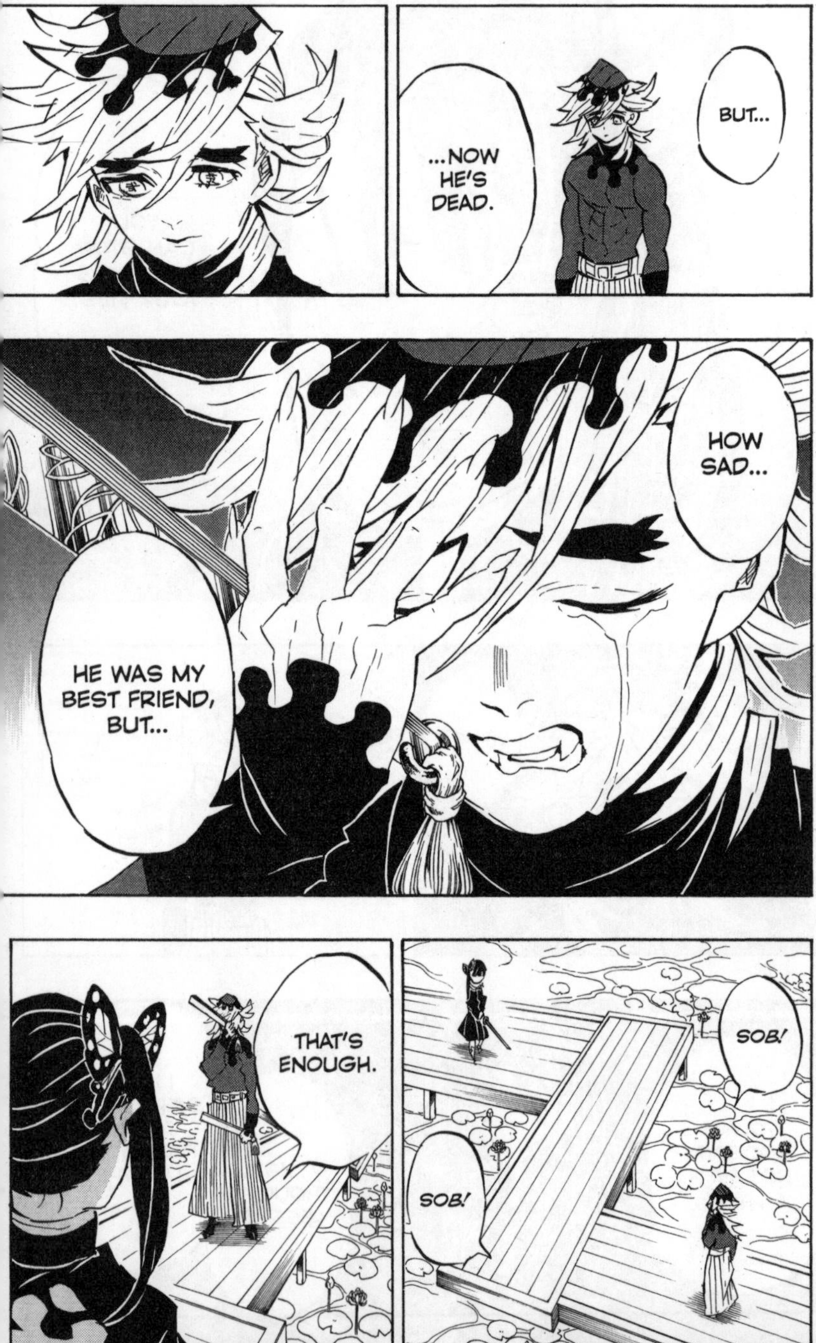
BUT...
...NOW HE'S DEAD.
HOW SAD...
HE WAS MY BEST FRIEND, BUT...
SOB!
SOB!
THAT'S ENOUGH.

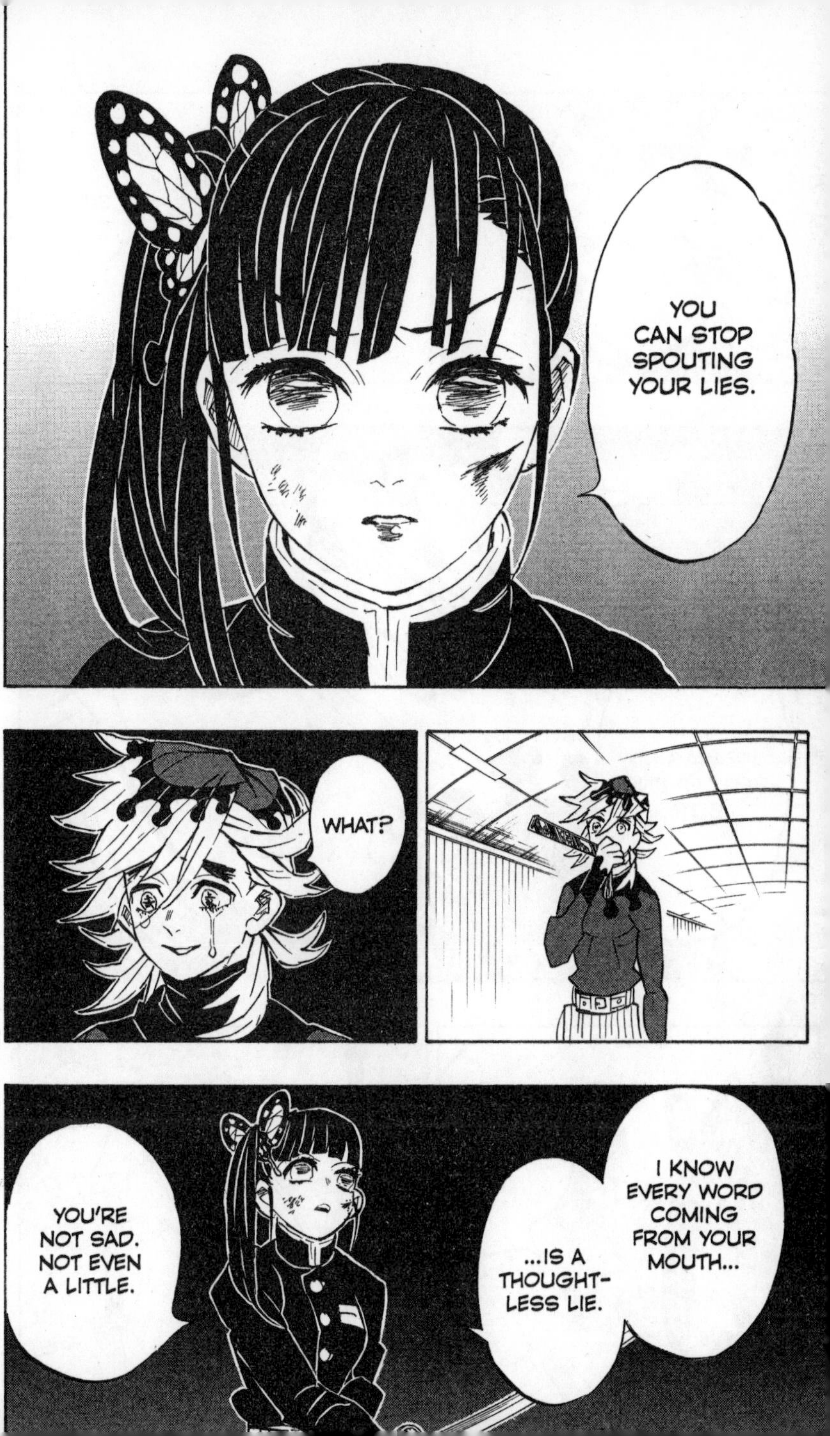
YOU CAN STOP SPOUTING YOUR LIES.
WHAT?
I KNOW EVERY WORD COMING FROM YOUR MOUTH...
...IS A THOUGHT-LESS LIE.
YOU'RE NOT SAD. NOT EVEN A LITTLE.

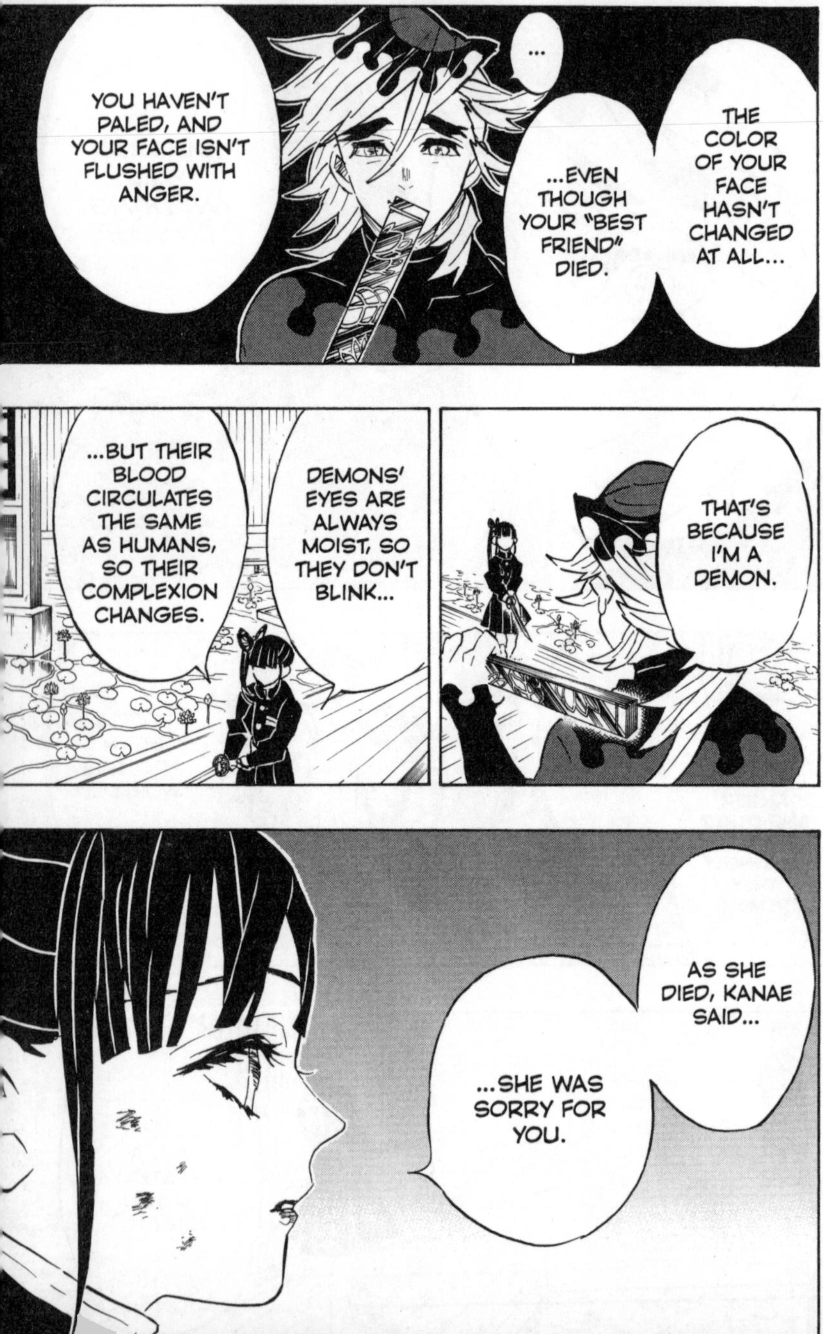
THE COLOR OF YOUR FACE HASN'T CHANGED AT ALL...
...EVEN THOUGH YOUR "BEST FRIEND" DIED.
...
YOU HAVEN'T PALED, AND YOUR FACE ISN'T FLUSHED WITH ANGER.
THAT'S BECAUSE I'M A DEMON.
DEMONS' EYES ARE ALWAYS MOIST, SO THEY DON'T BLINK...
...BUT THEIR BLOOD CIRCULATES THE SAME AS HUMANS, SO THEIR COMPLEXION CHANGES.
AS SHE DIED, KANAE SAID...
...SHE WAS SORRY FOR YOU.

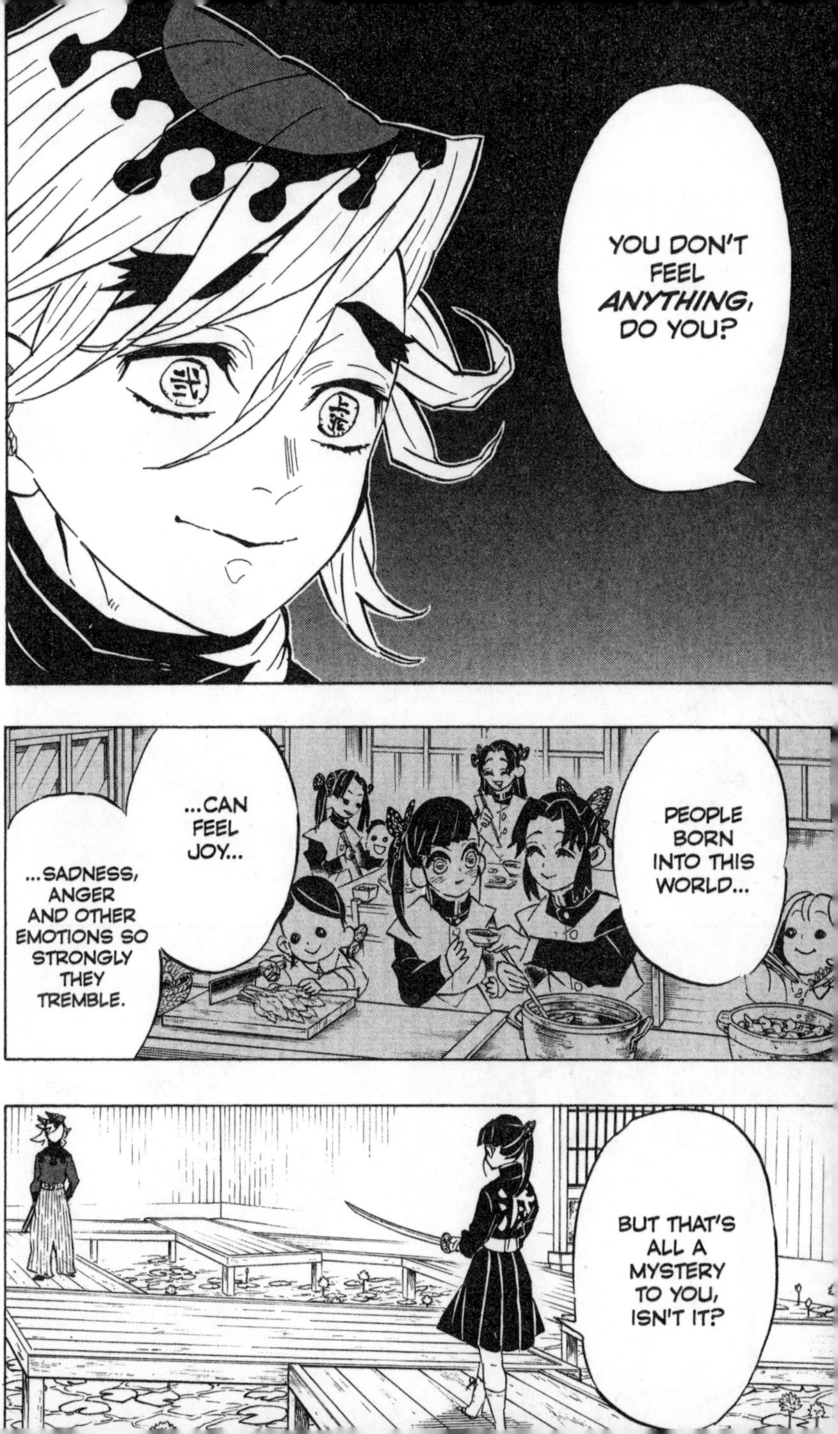
YOU DON'T FEEL *ANYTHING*, DO YOU?
PEOPLE BORN INTO THIS WORLD...
...CAN FEEL JOY...
...SADNESS, ANGER AND OTHER EMOTIONS SO STRONGLY THEY TREMBLE.
BUT THAT'S ALL A MYSTERY TO YOU, ISN'T IT?

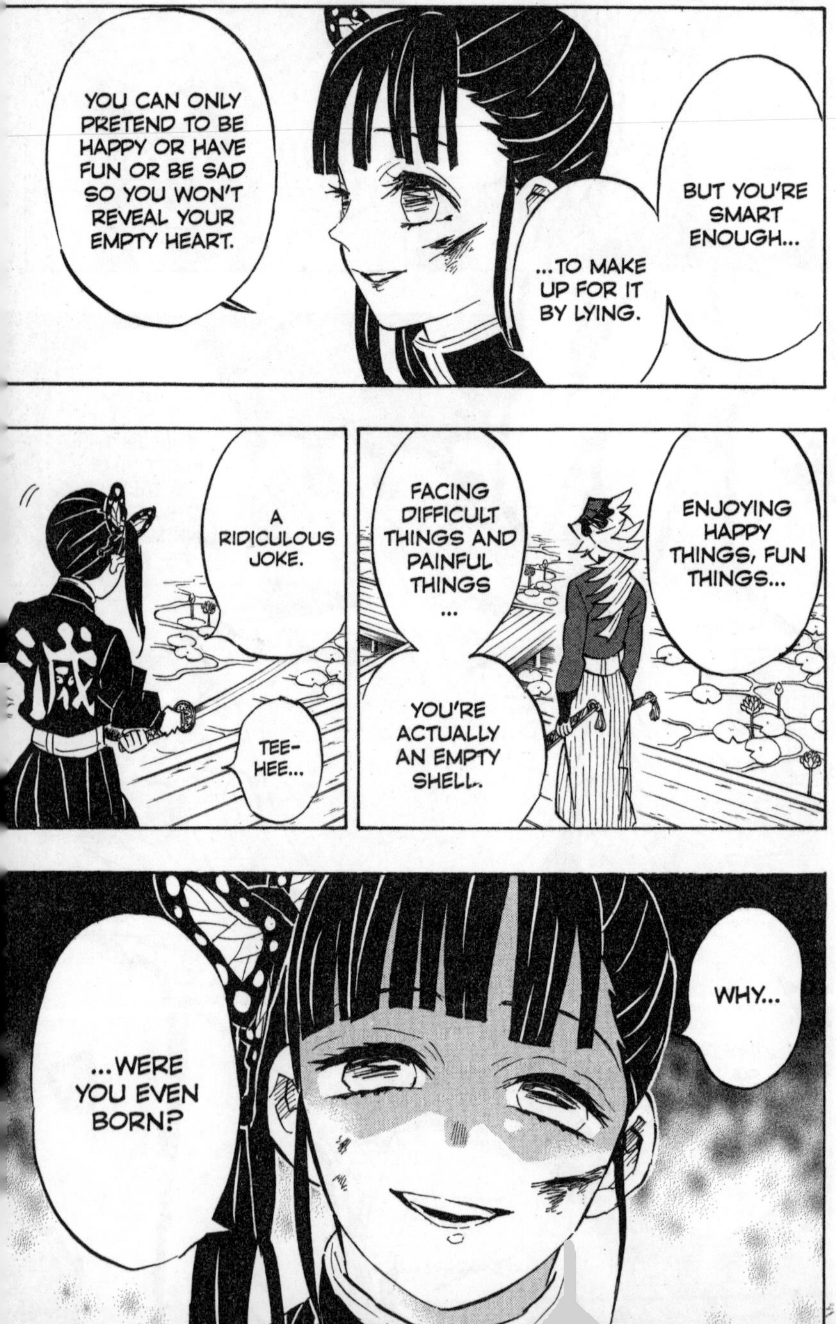
BUT YOU'RE SMART ENOUGH...
...TO MAKE UP FOR IT BY LYING.
YOU CAN ONLY PRETEND TO BE HAPPY OR HAVE FUN OR BE SAD SO YOU WON'T REVEAL YOUR EMPTY HEART.
ENJOYING HAPPY THINGS, FUN THINGS...
FACING DIFFICULT THINGS AND PAINFUL THINGS ...
YOU'RE ACTUALLY AN EMPTY SHELL.
A RIDICULOUS JOKE.
TEE-HEE...
WHY...
...WERE YOU EVEN BORN?

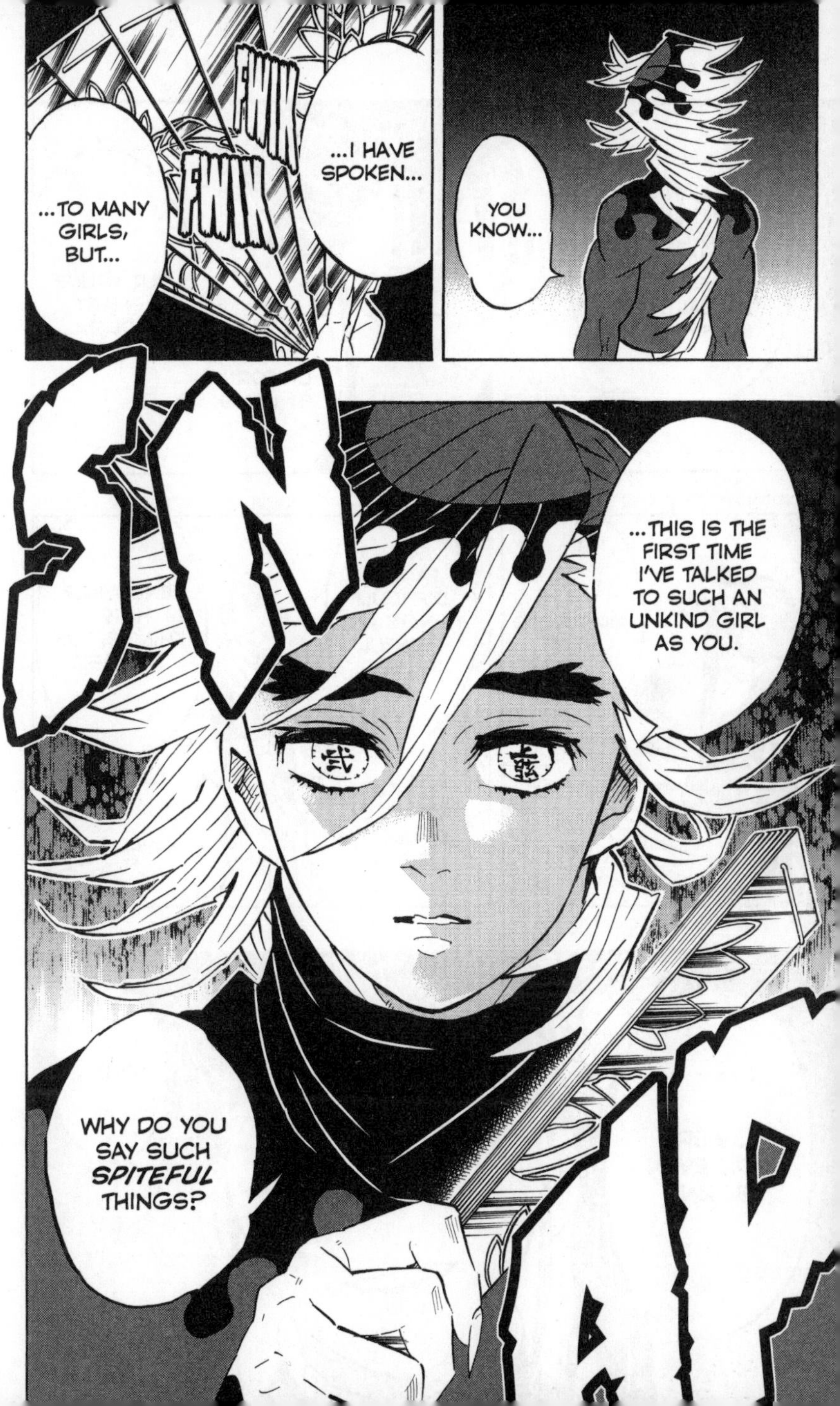
YOU KNOW...
...I HAVE SPOKEN...
FWIK
FWIK
...TO MANY GIRLS, BUT...
...THIS IS THE FIRST TIME I'VE TALKED TO SUCH AN UNKIND GIRL AS YOU.
SN
WHY DO YOU SAY SUCH *SPITEFUL* THINGS?
AP

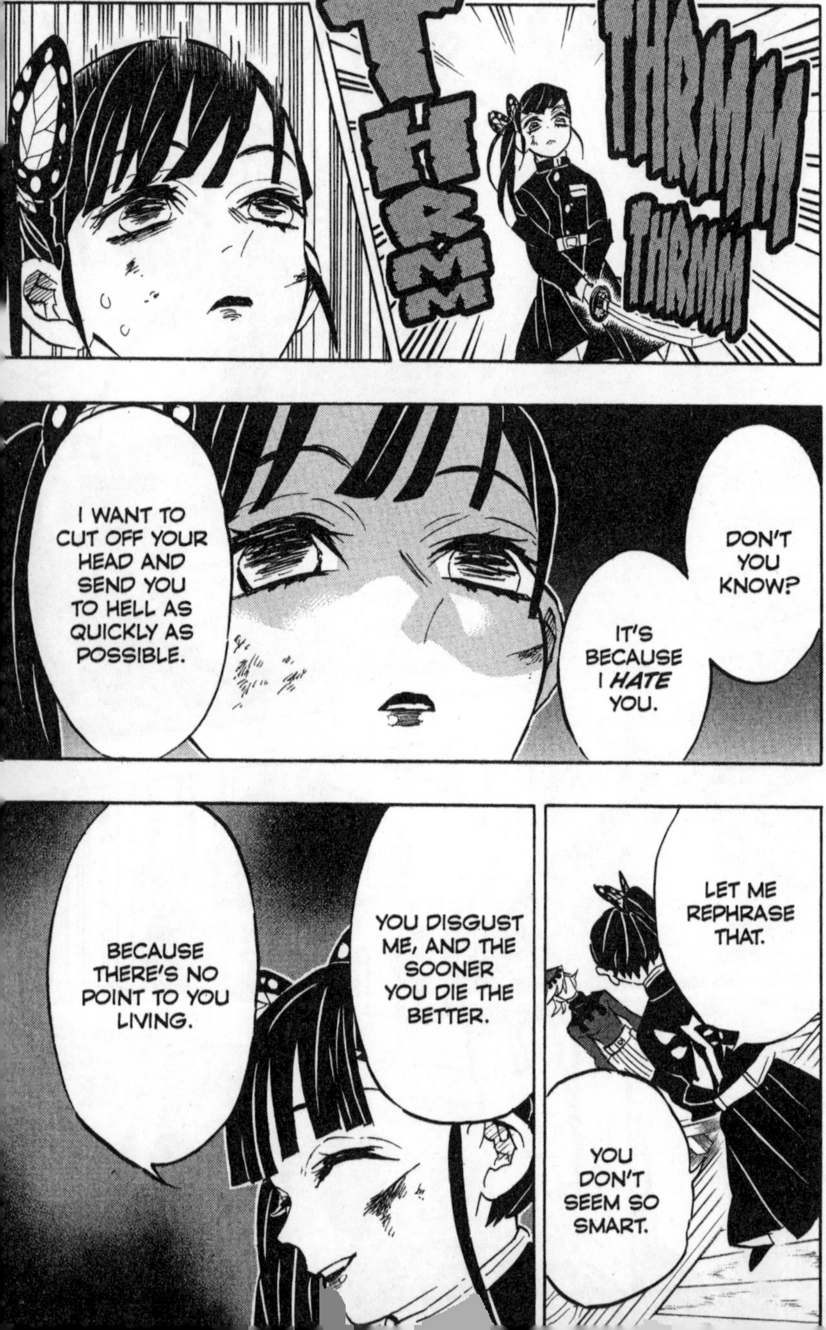
THRMMM
THRMM
THRMM
DON'T YOU KNOW?
IT'S BECAUSE I *HATE* YOU.
I WANT TO CUT OFF YOUR HEAD AND SEND YOU TO HELL AS QUICKLY AS POSSIBLE.
LET ME REPHRASE THAT.
YOU DON'T SEEM SO SMART.
YOU DISGUST ME, AND THE SOONER YOU DIE THE BETTER.
BECAUSE THERE'S NO POINT TO YOU LIVING.

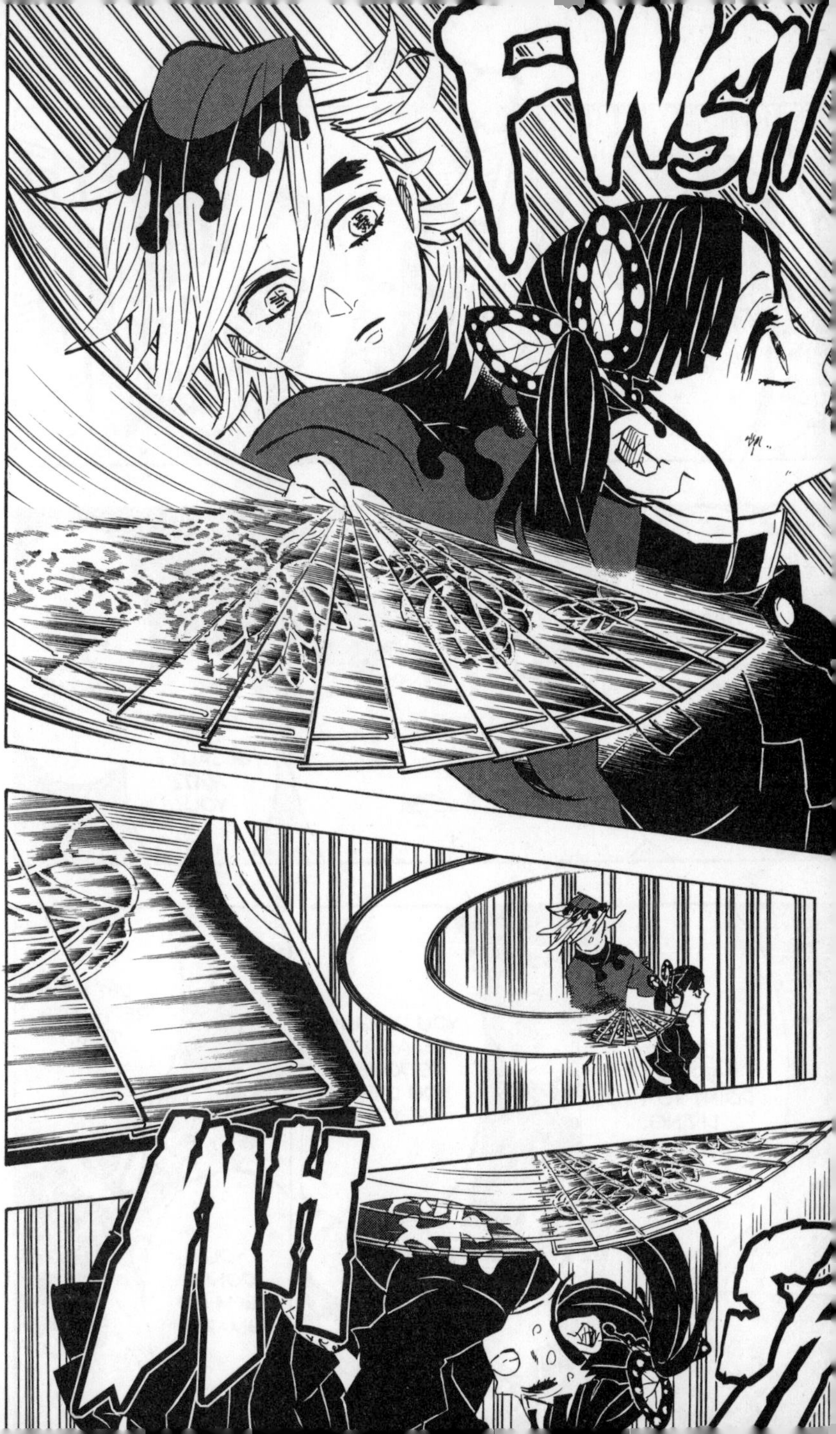
FWSH
WH

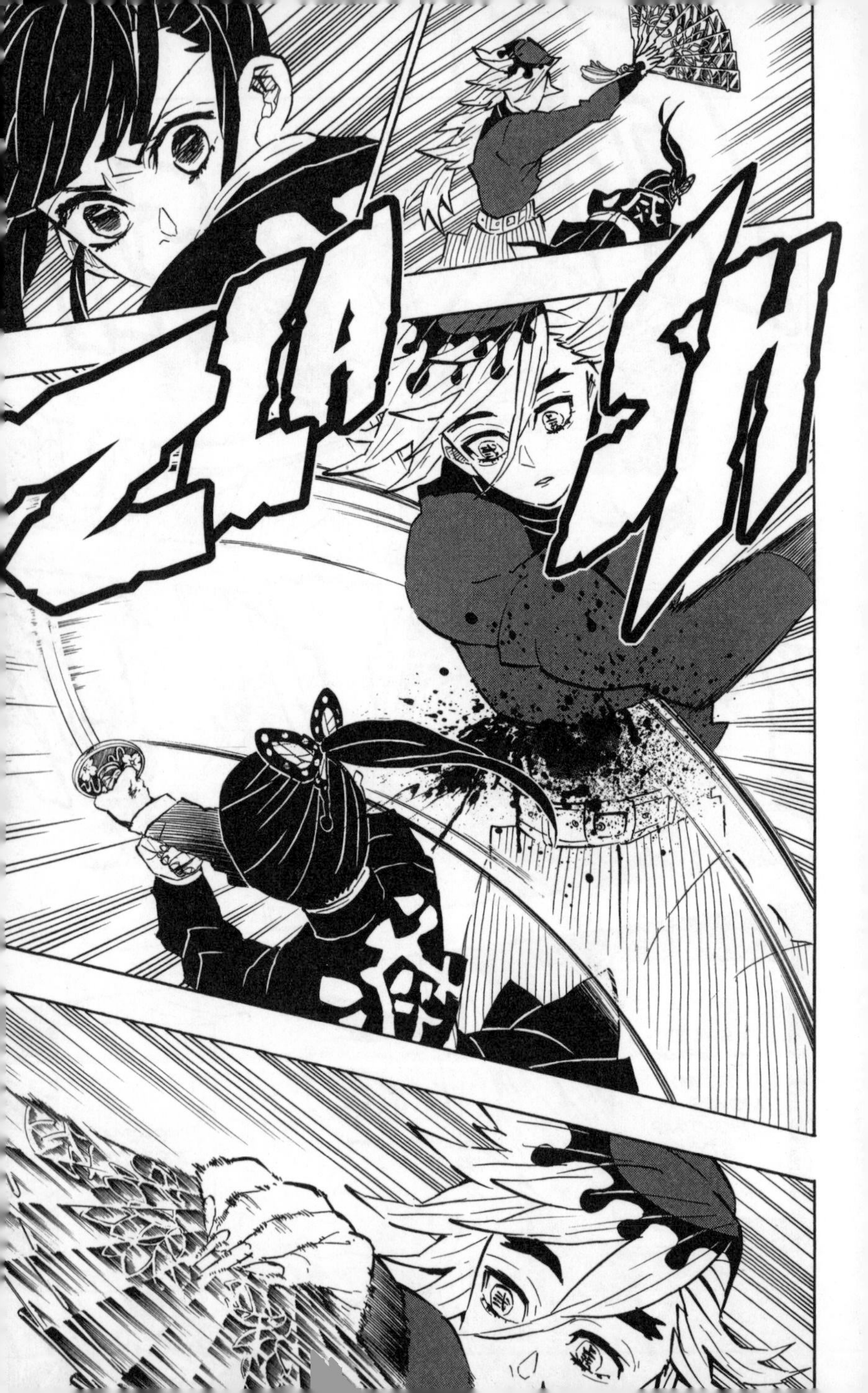
ZWOOSH

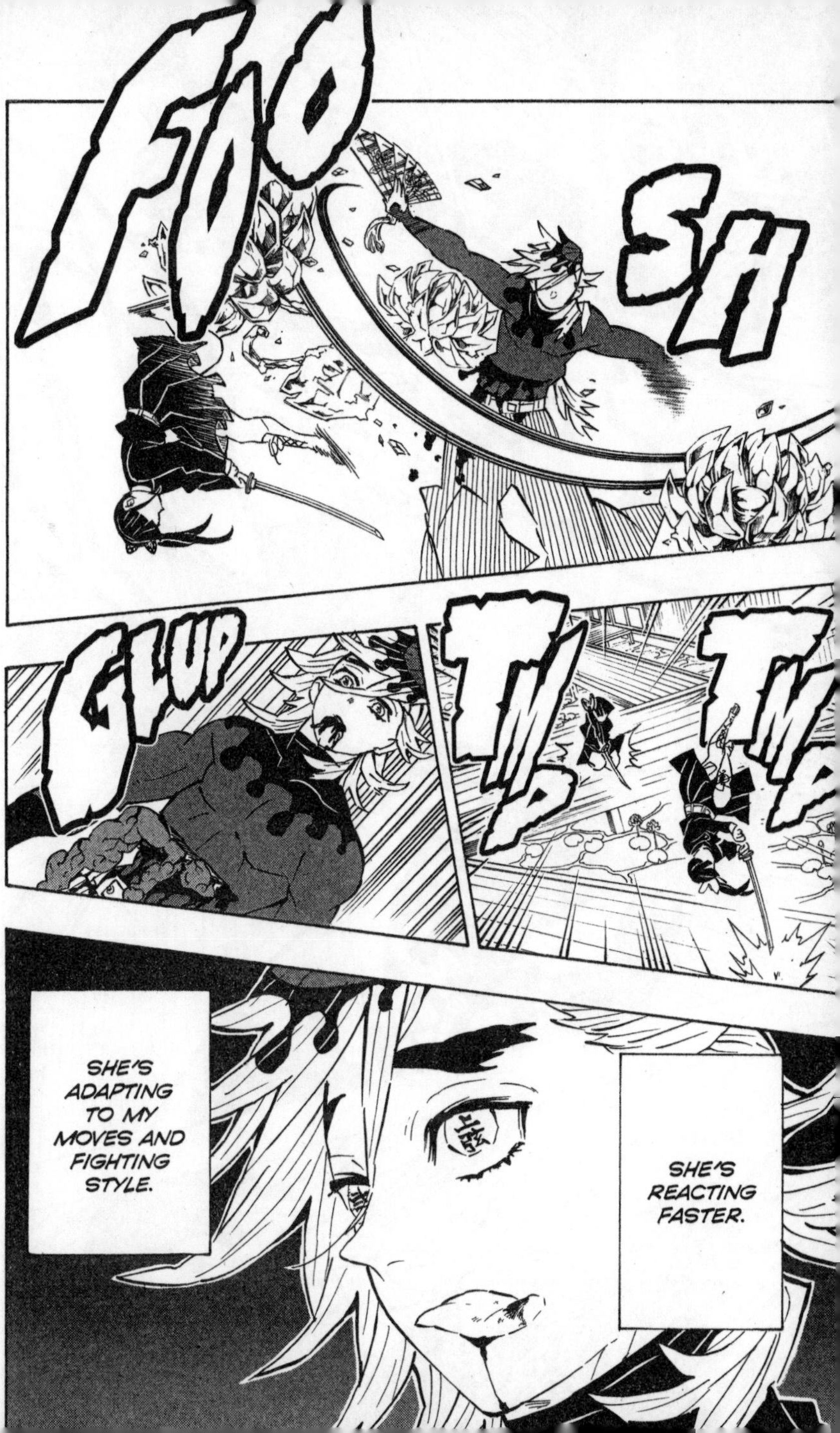

SH
GLUP
SHE'S REACTING FASTER.
SHE'S ADAPTING TO MY MOVES AND FIGHTING STYLE.

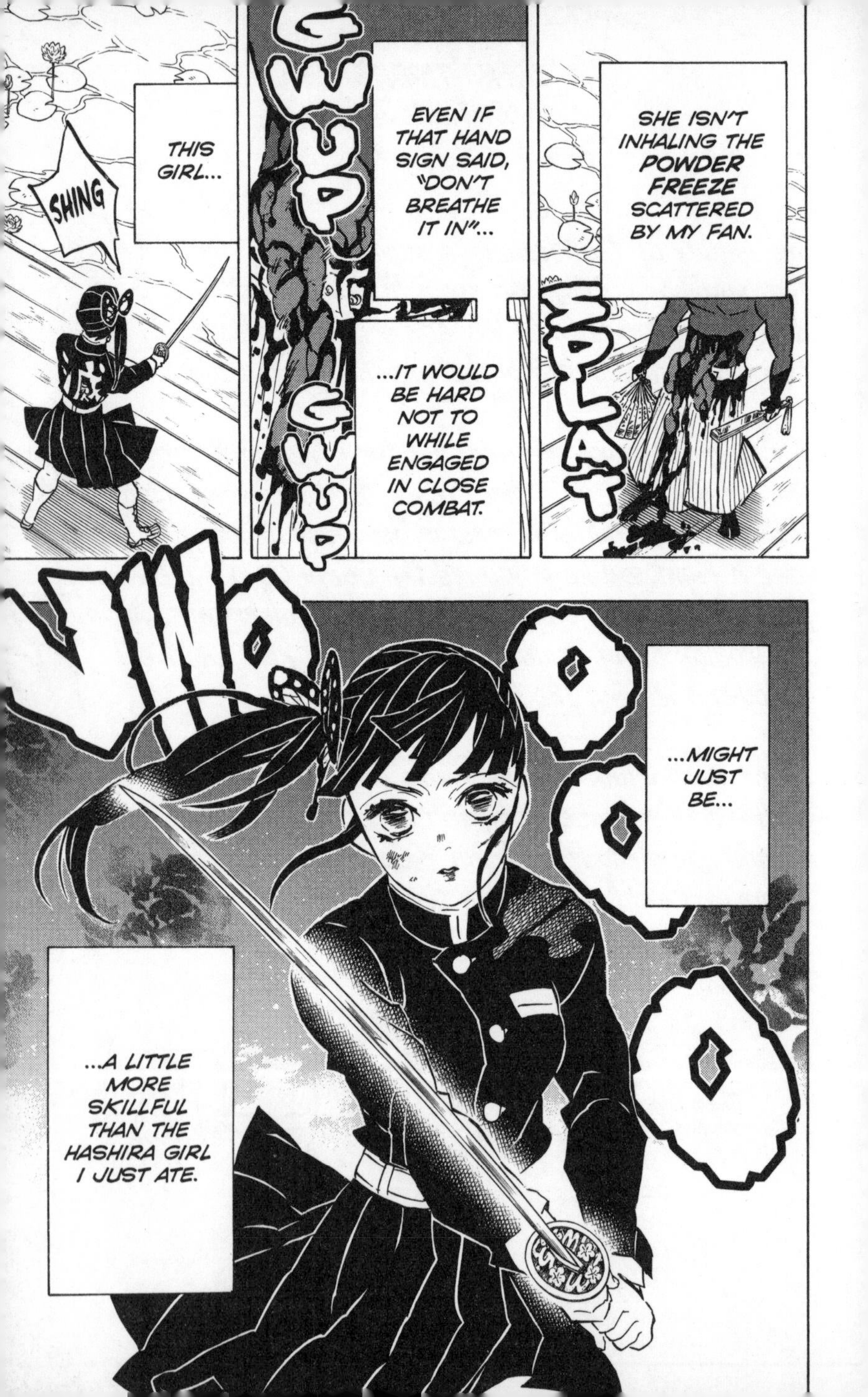
SHE ISN'T INHALING THE POWDER FREEZE SCATTERED BY MY FAN.
SPLAT
EVEN IF THAT HAND SIGN SAID, "DON'T BREATHE IT IN"...
...IT WOULD BE HARD NOT TO WHILE ENGAGED IN CLOSE COMBAT.
GWUP
GWUP
THIS GIRL...
SHING
...MIGHT JUST BE...
...A LITTLE MORE SKILLFUL THAN THE HASHIRA GIRL I JUST ATE.

EXTRA TIDBITS CONTINUED

The beauty of that technique moved the master of the neighboring dojo so much that he admitted defeat, apologized for his son's inappropriate behavior and stopped bothering the Soryu Dojo.

A few quiet years passed, but then the master of the neighboring dojo died. When the heir heard about Hakuji and Koyuki's marriage, he knew he would lose a fight, so he poisoned the Soryu Dojo's well, partially at the prompting of the dojo adherents. An old woman living nearby witnessed the heir and his followers leaving the Soryu Dojo.

After they drank poison, Keizo carried Koyuki to a physician's house, coughing up blood as he ran. Koyuki had already died, but Keizo took a few hours to die and suffered a long time.

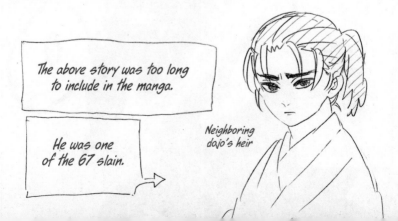

The above story was too long to include in the manga.

He was one of the 67 slain.

Neighboring dojo's heir

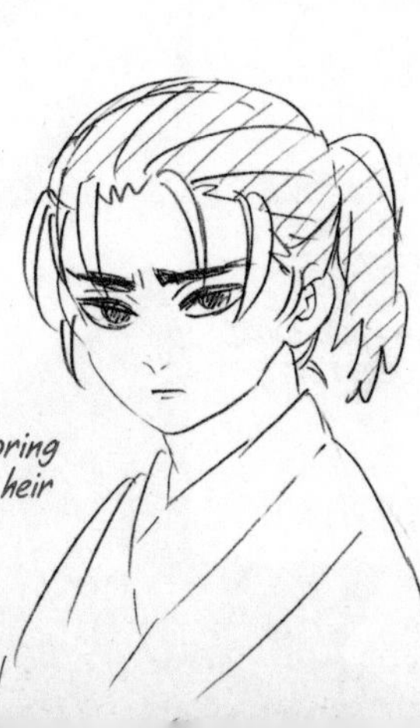

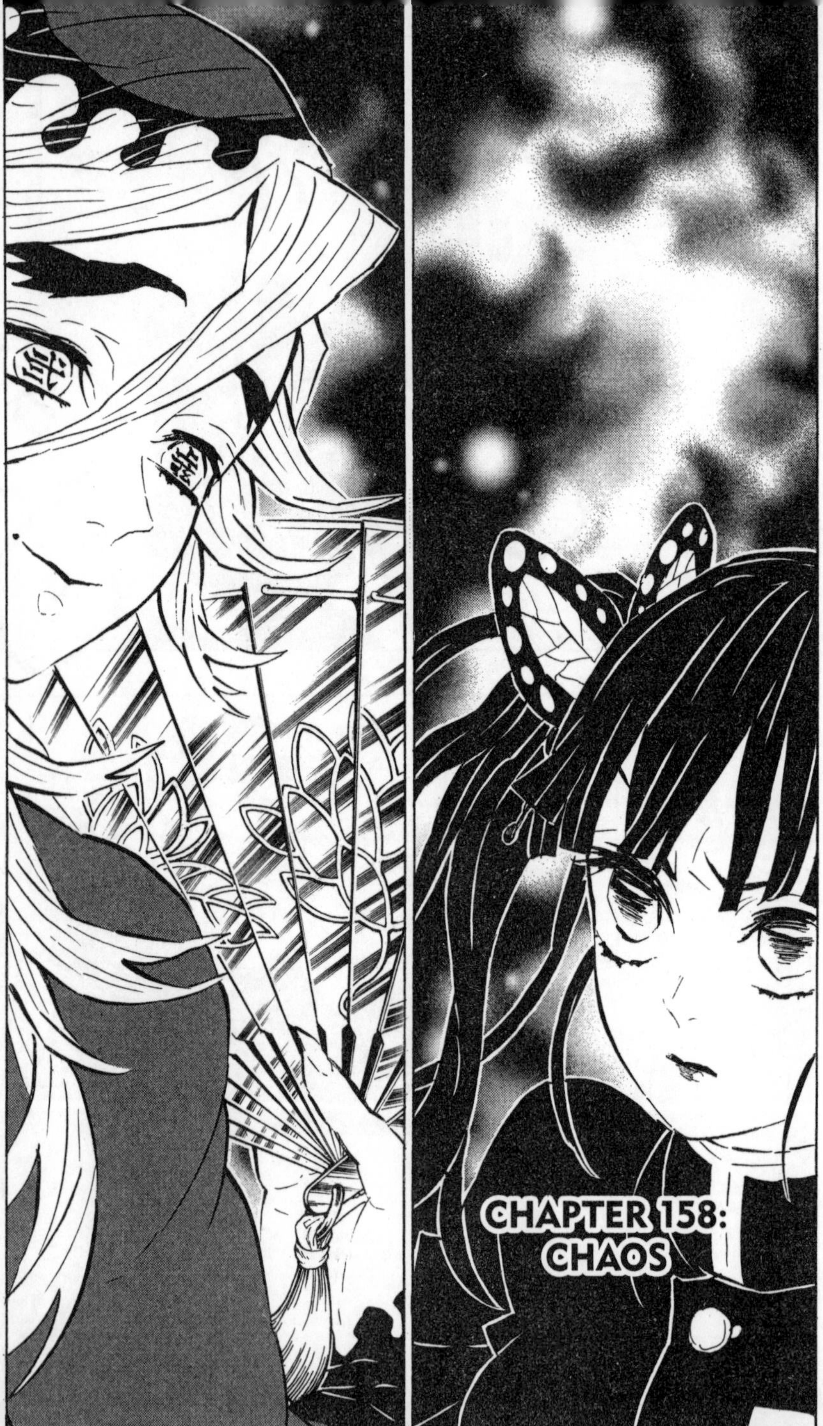
CHAPTER 158:
CHAOS

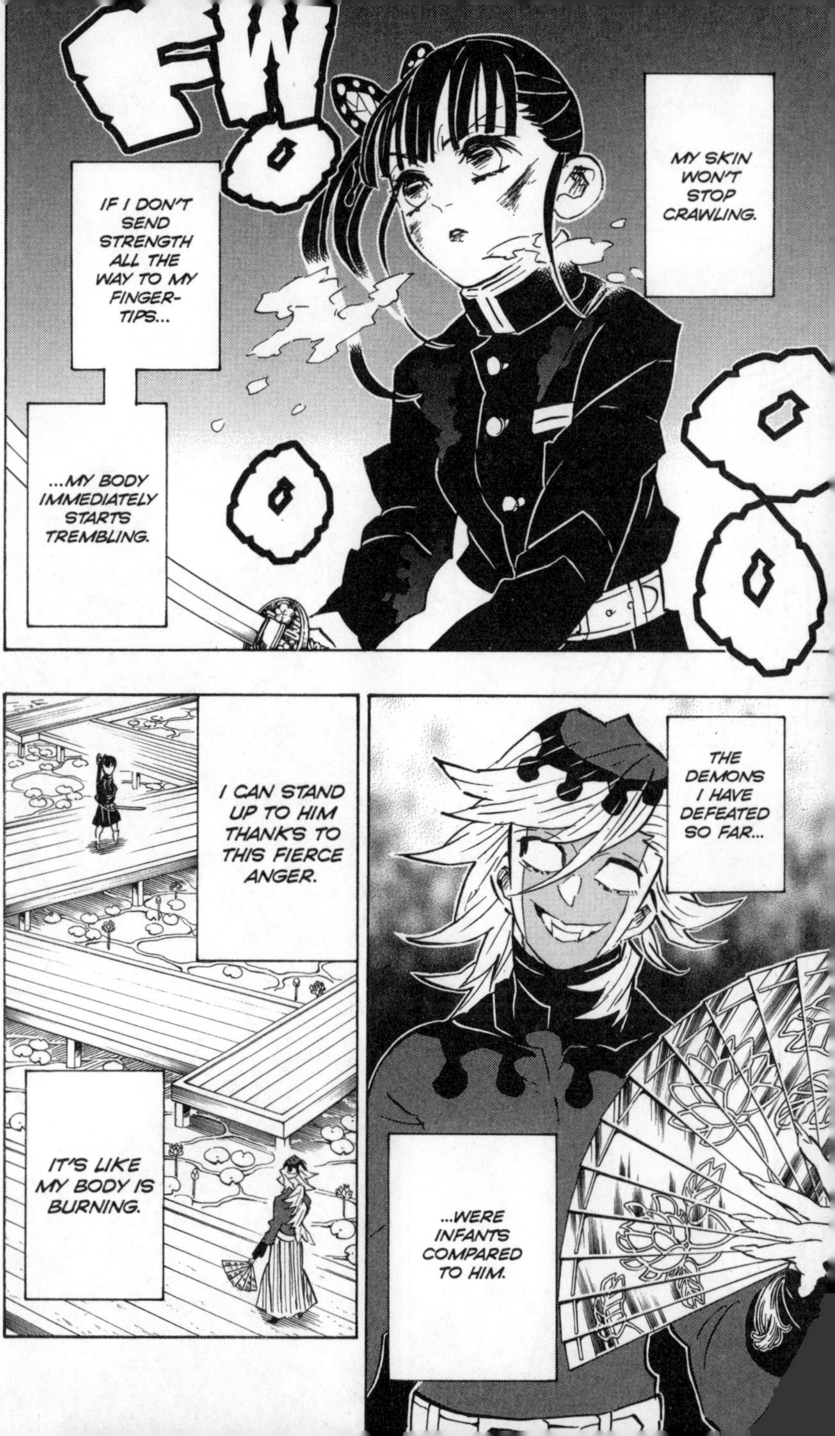
MY SKIN WON'T STOP CRAWLING.
FW
IF I DON'T SEND STRENGTH ALL THE WAY TO MY FINGER-TIPS...
...MY BODY IMMEDIATELY STARTS TREMBLING.
THE DEMONS I HAVE DEFEATED SO FAR...
...WERE INFANTS COMPARED TO HIM.
I CAN STAND UP TO HIM THANKS TO THIS FIERCE ANGER.
IT'S LIKE MY BODY IS BURNING.

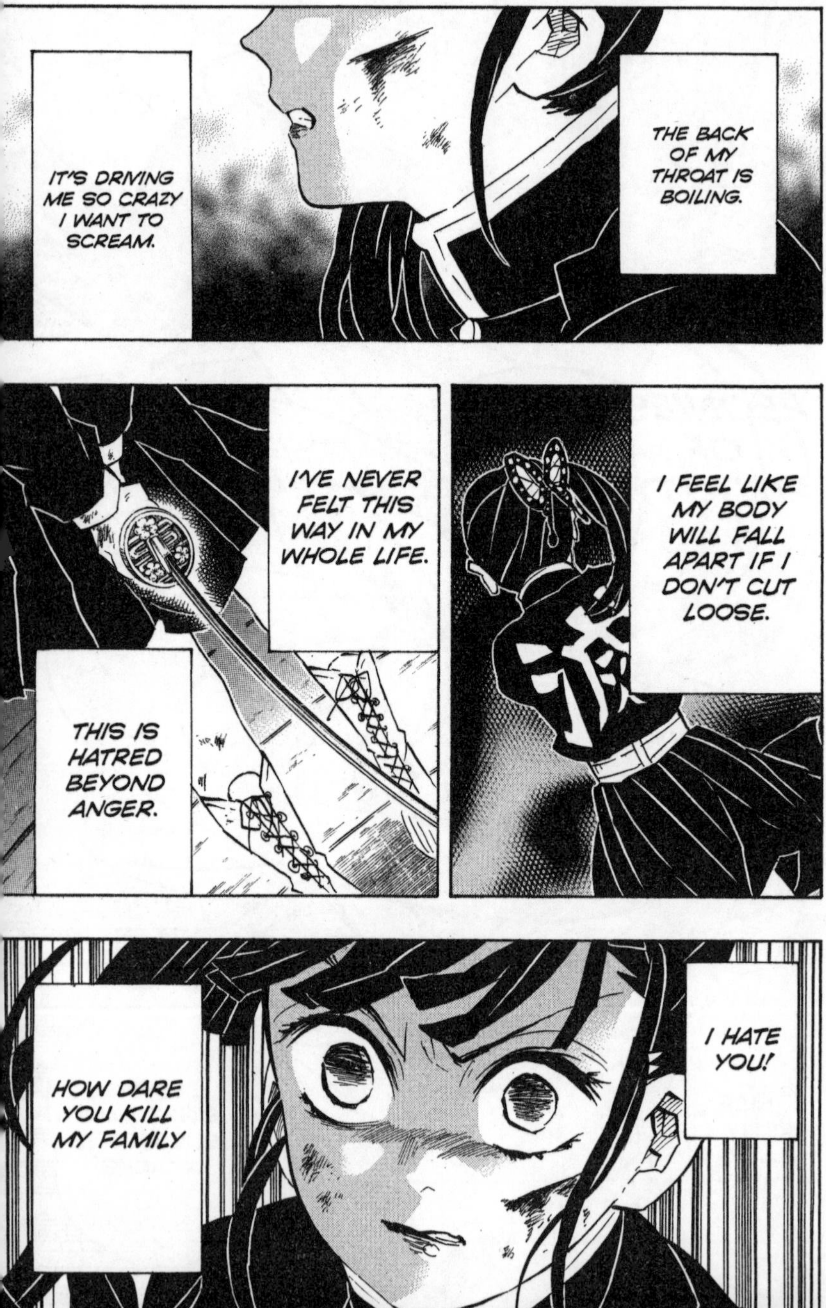
THE BACK OF MY THROAT IS BOILING.
IT'S DRIVING ME SO CRAZY I WANT TO SCREAM.
I FEEL LIKE MY BODY WILL FALL APART IF I DON'T CUT LOOSE.
I'VE NEVER FELT THIS WAY IN MY WHOLE LIFE.
THIS IS HATRED BEYOND ANGER.
I HATE YOU!
HOW DARE YOU KILL MY FAMILY

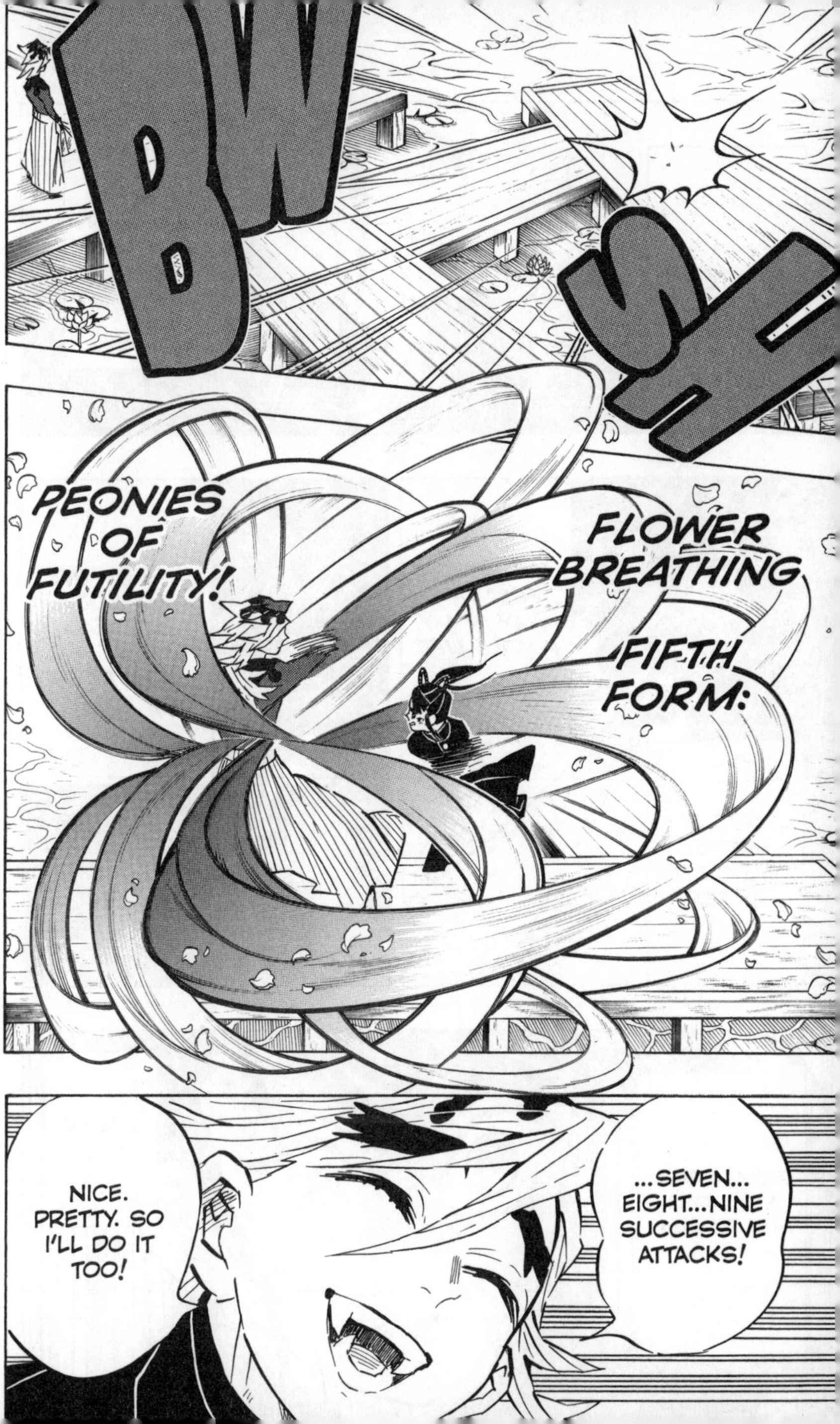
BWSH
FLOWER BREATHING
FIFTH FORM:
PEONIES OF FUTILITY!
...SEVEN... EIGHT...NINE SUCCESSIVE ATTACKS!
NICE. PRETTY. SO I'LL DO IT TOO!

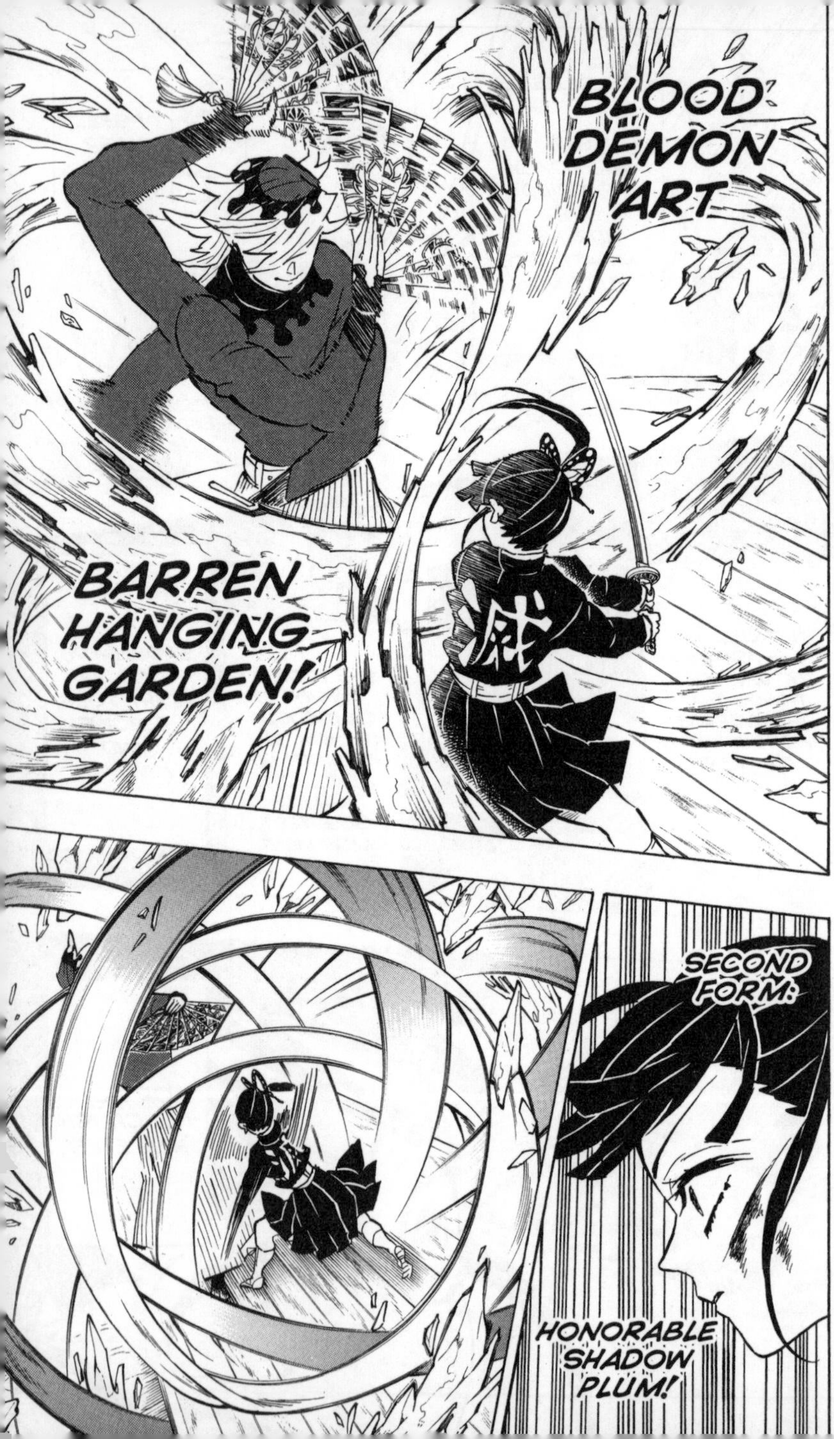
BLOOD DEMON ART
BARREN HANGING GARDEN!
SECOND FORM:
HONORABLE SHADOW PLUM!

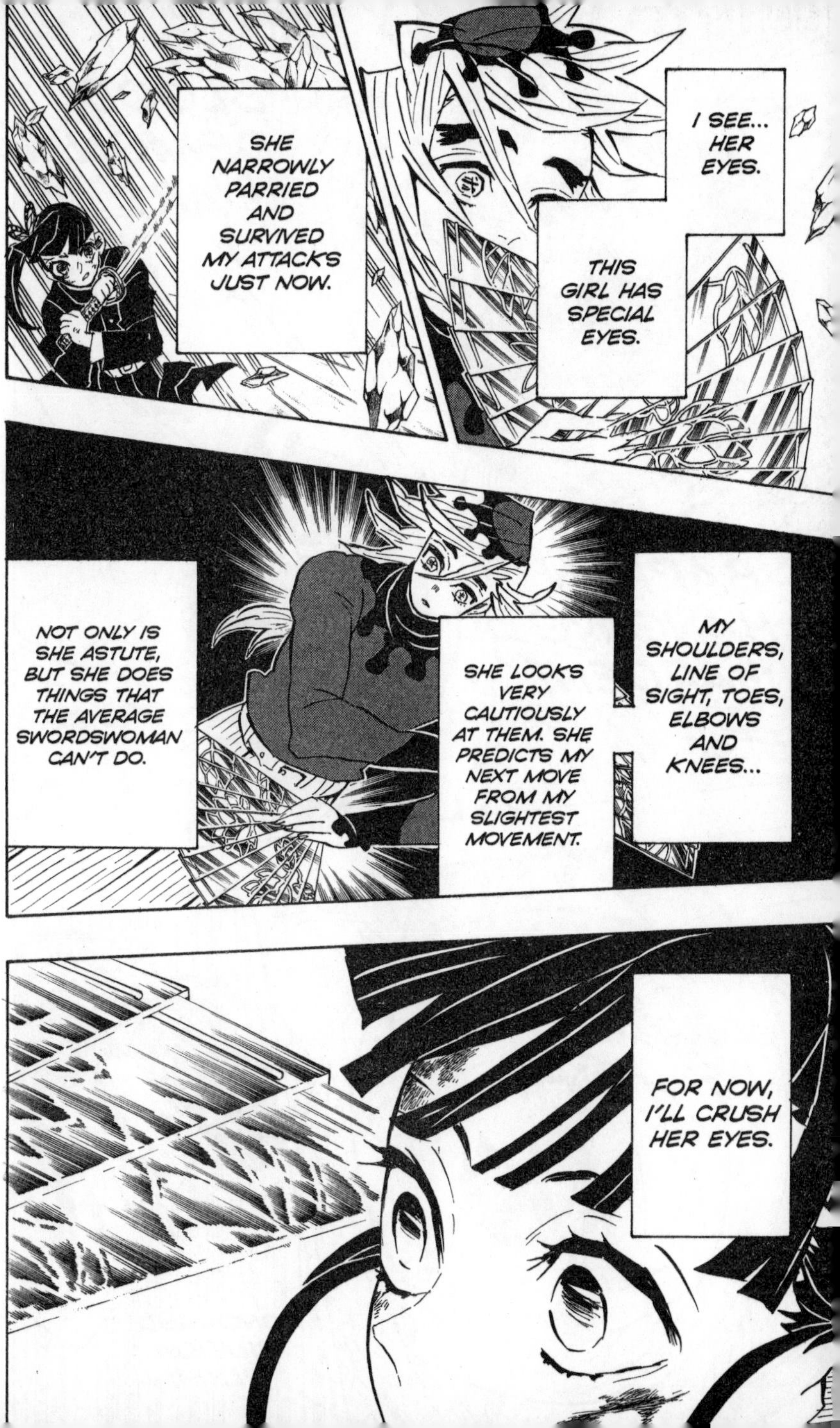
I SEE... HER EYES.
THIS GIRL HAS SPECIAL EYES.
SHE NARROWLY PARRIED AND SURVIVED MY ATTACKS JUST NOW.
MY SHOULDERS, LINE OF SIGHT, TOES, ELBOWS AND KNEES...
SHE LOOKS VERY CAUTIOUSLY AT THEM. SHE PREDICTS MY NEXT MOVE FROM MY SLIGHTEST MOVEMENT.
NOT ONLY IS SHE ASTUTE, BUT SHE DOES THINGS THAT THE AVERAGE SWORDSWOMAN CAN'T DO.
FOR NOW, I'LL CRUSH HER EYES.

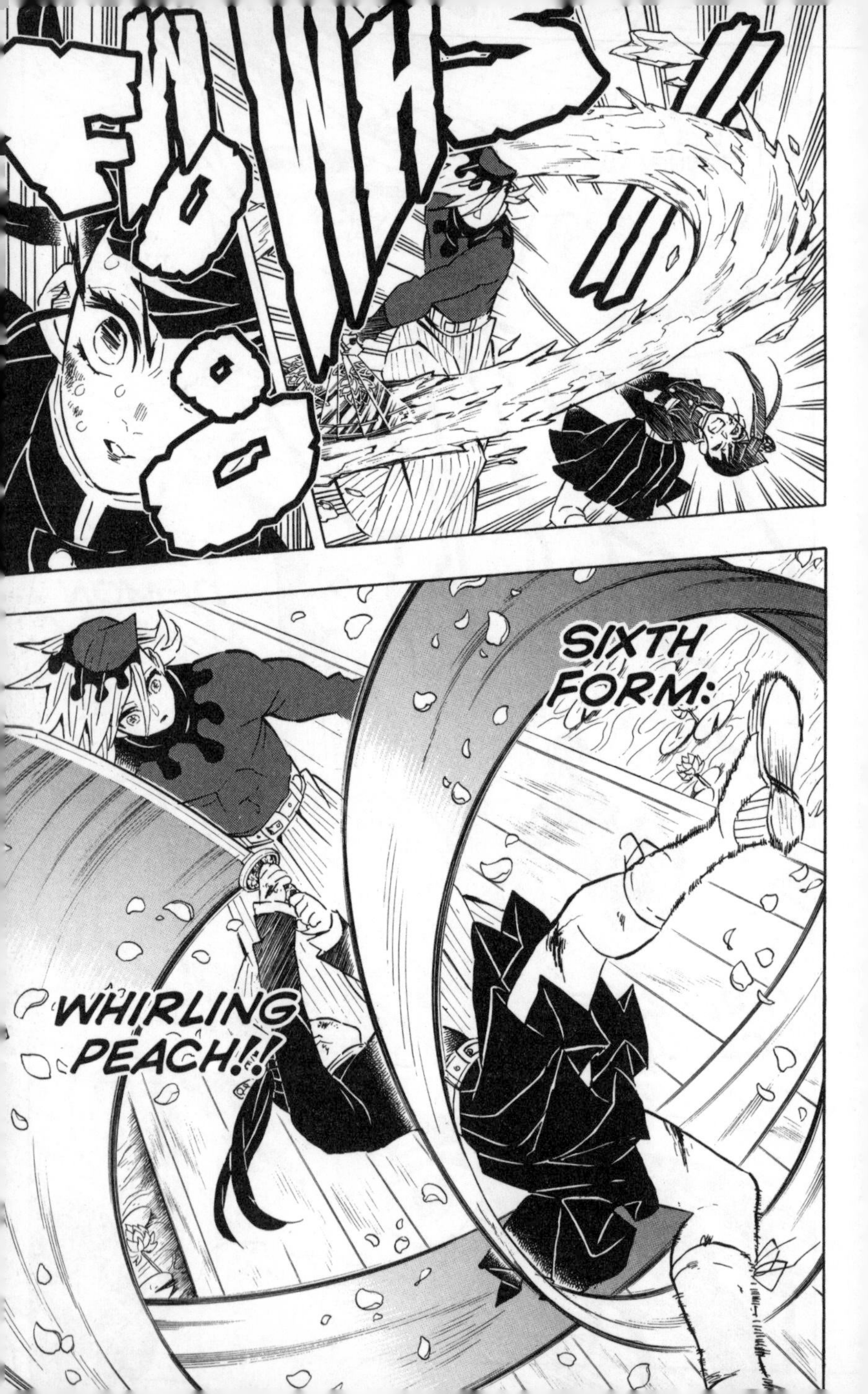
SIXTH FORM:
WHIRLING PEACH!!

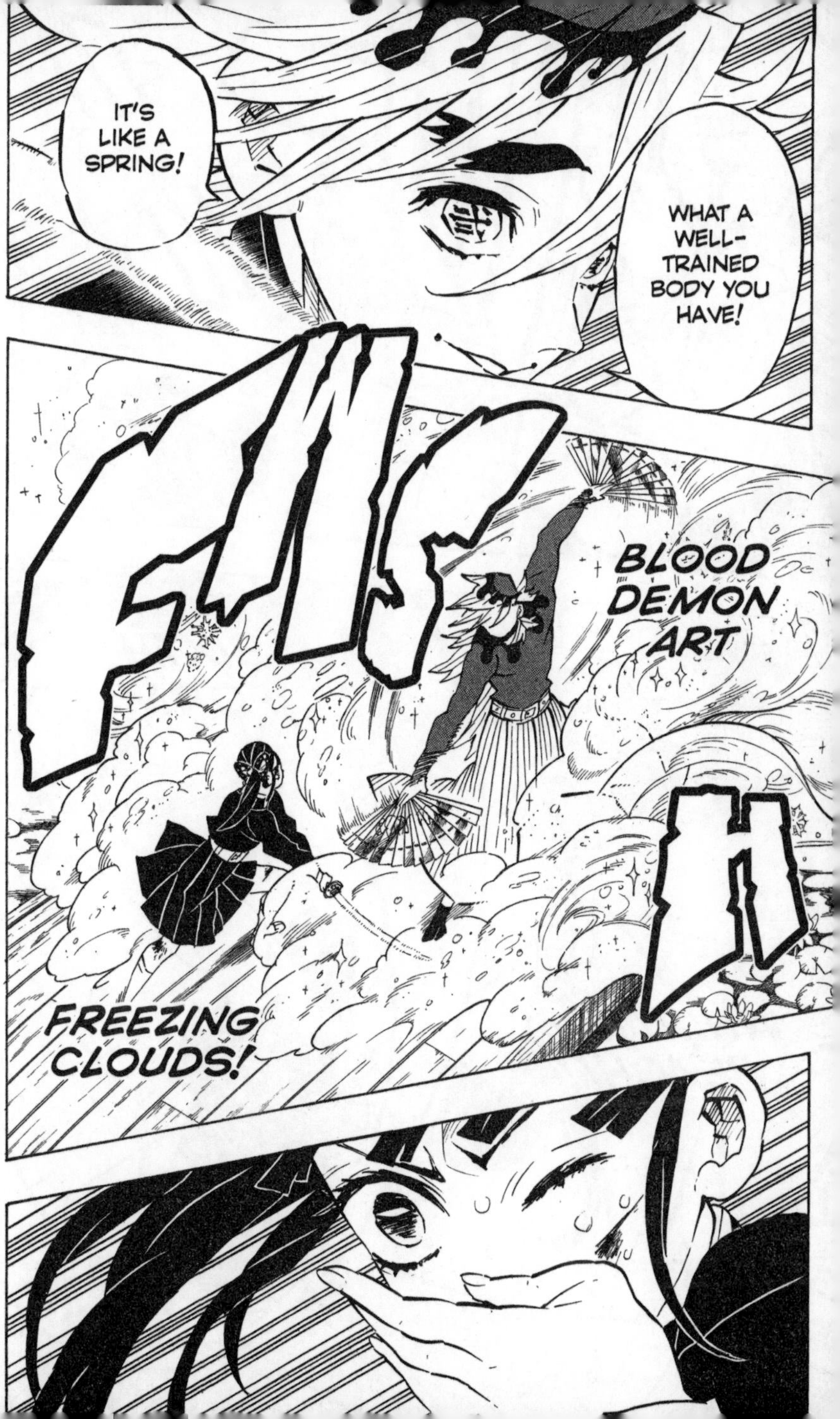
WHAT A WELL-TRAINED BODY YOU HAVE!
IT'S LIKE A SPRING!
BLOOD DEMON ART
FREEZING CLOUDS!

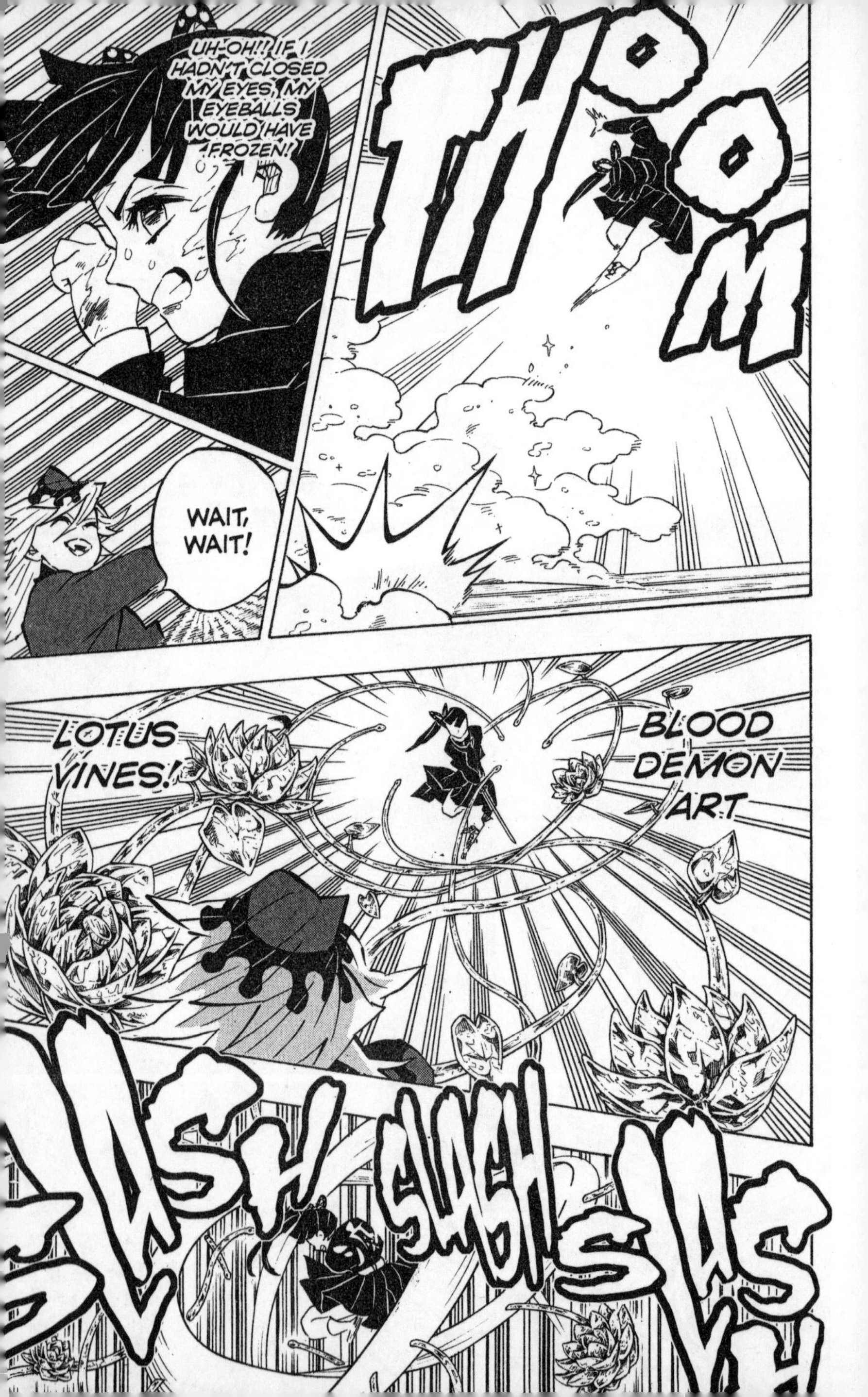
THOOM
UH-OH!! IF I HADN'T CLOSED MY EYES, MY EYEBALLS WOULD HAVE FROZEN!
WAIT, WAIT!
BLOOD DEMON ART
LOTUS VINES!
SLASH
SLASH
SLASH

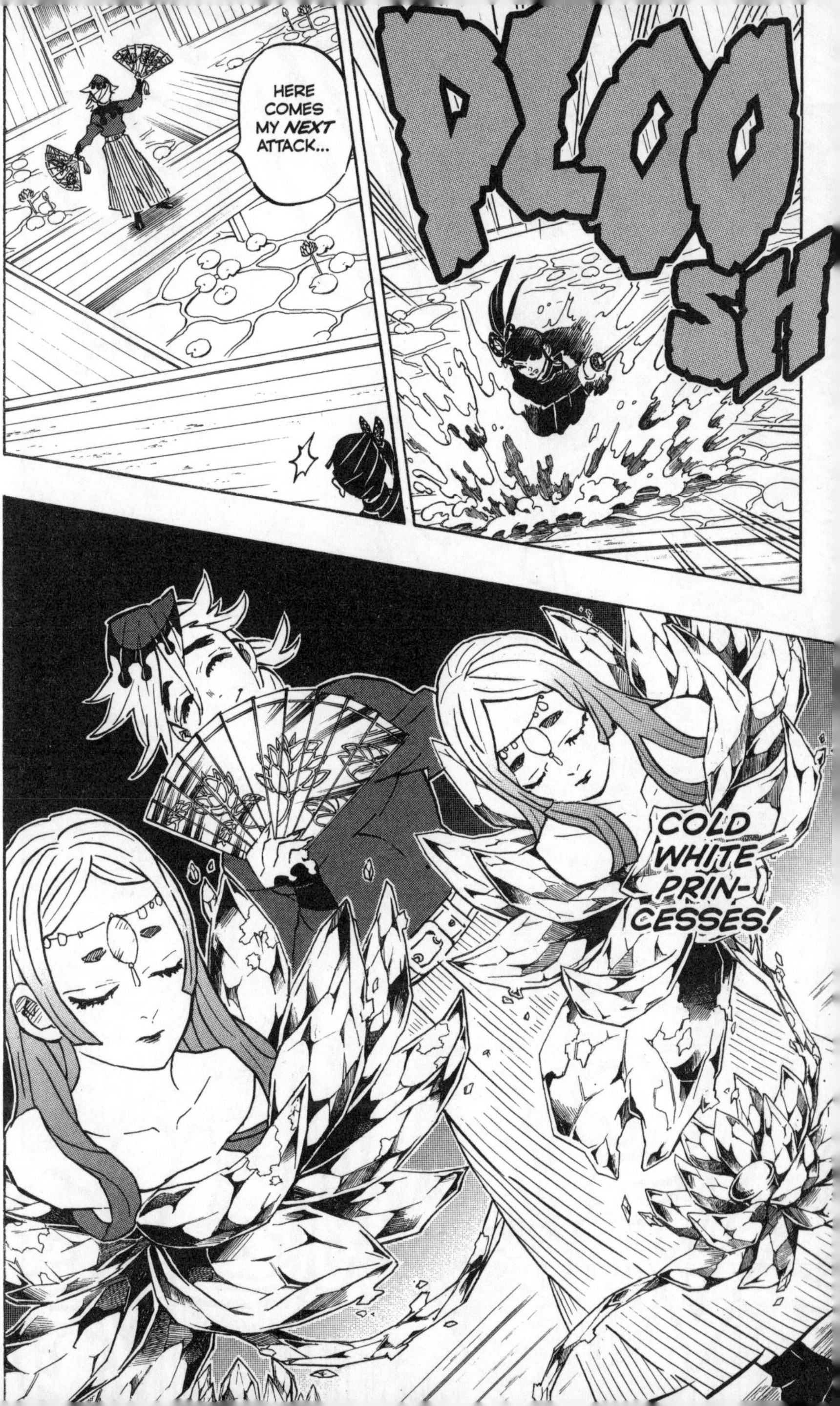
PLOOSH
HERE COMES MY *NEXT* ATTACK...
COLD WHITE PRINCESSES!

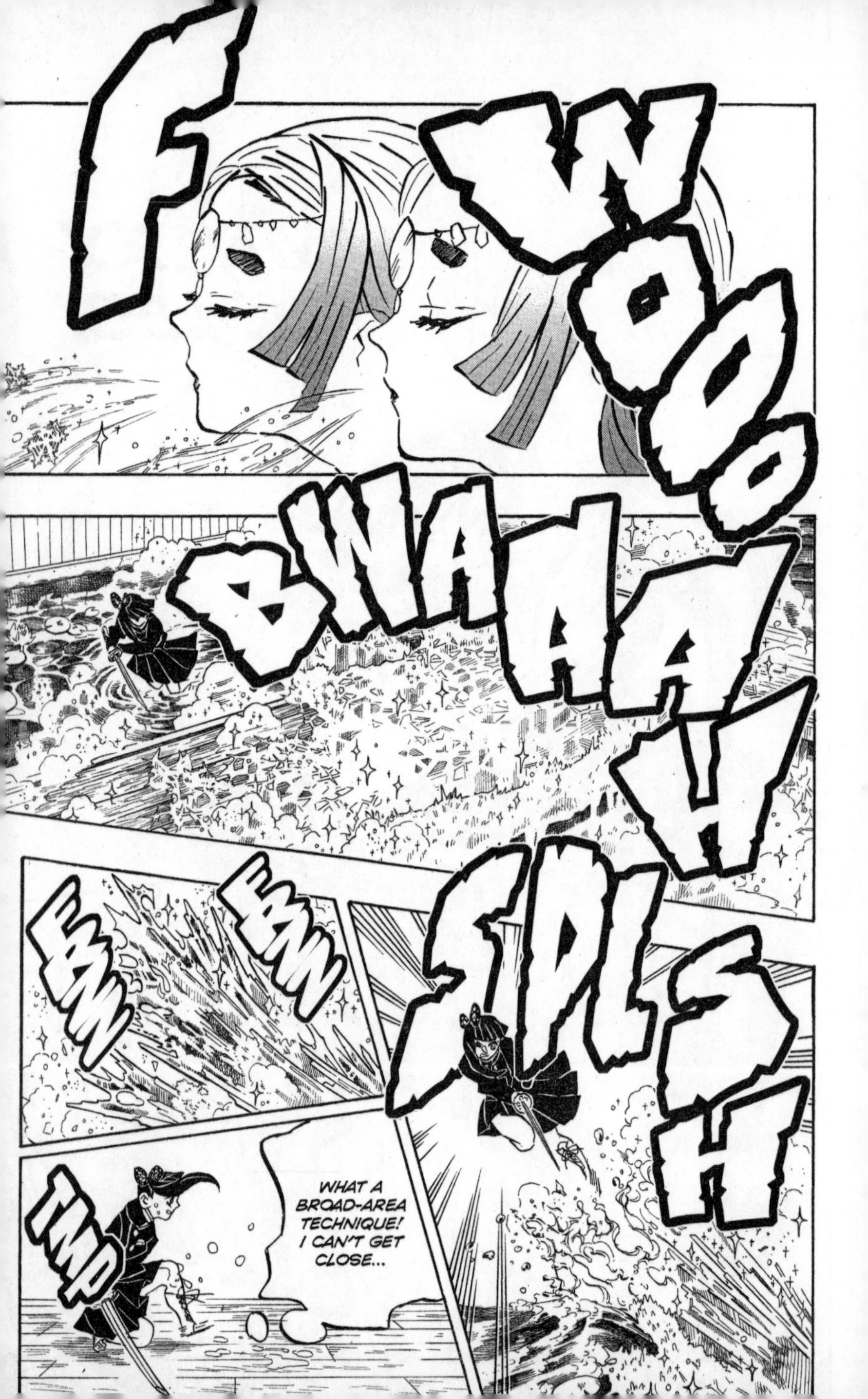
FWOOO
BWAAH
TMP
WHAT A BROAD-AREA TECHNIQUE! I CAN'T GET CLOSE...

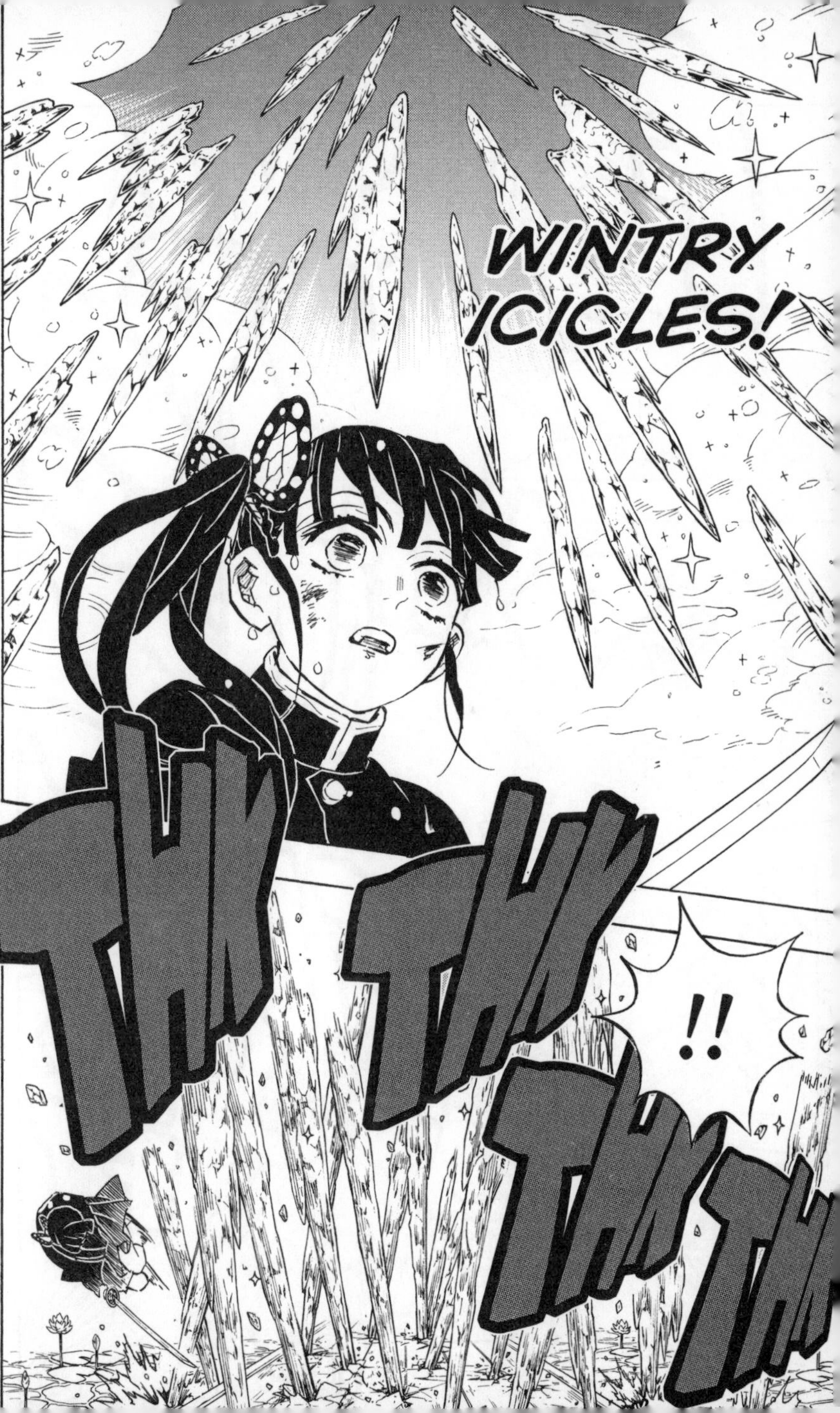
WINTRY ICICLES!
!!
THK
THK
THK
THK

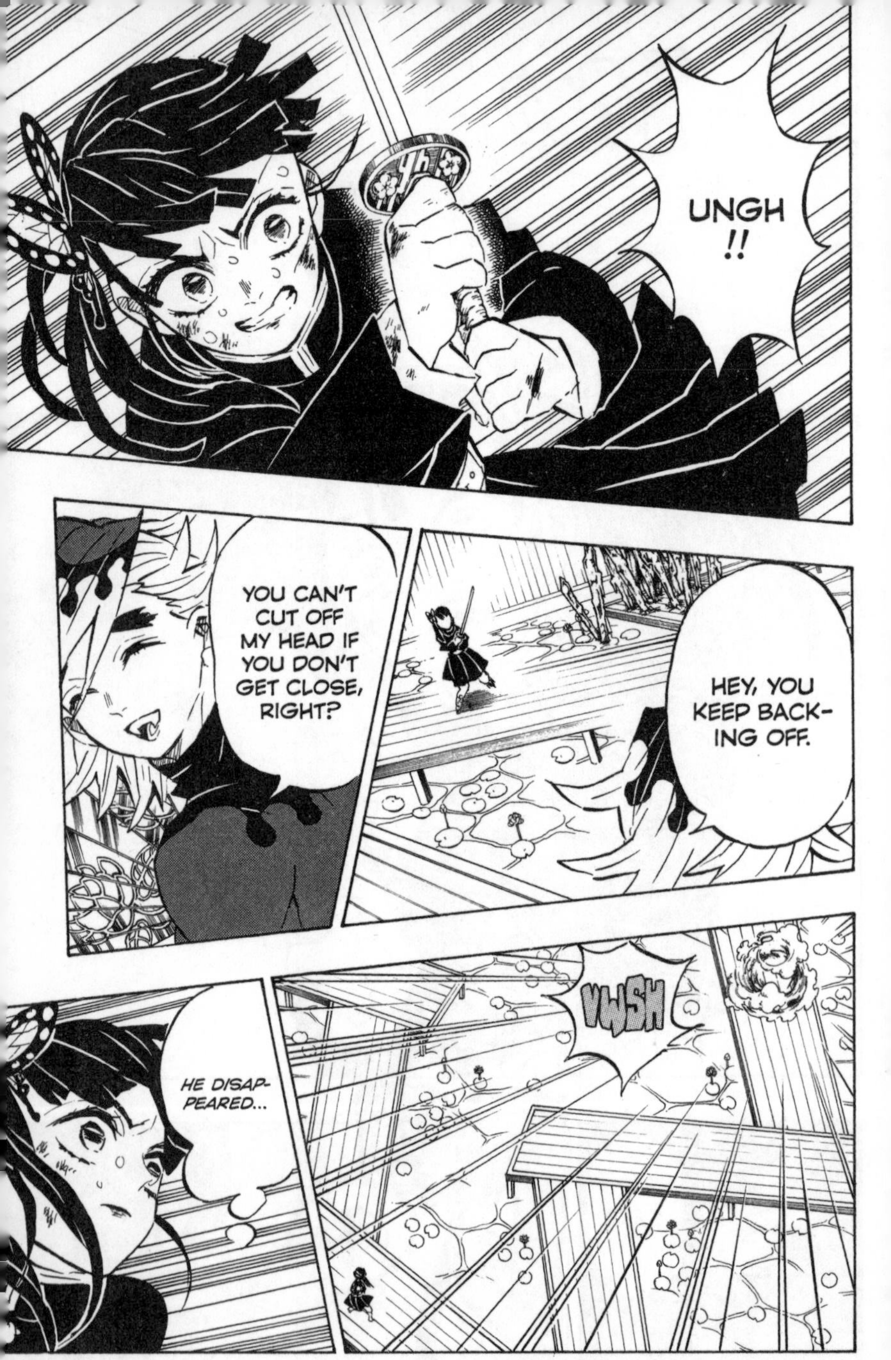
UNGH!!
HEY, YOU KEEP BACK-ING OFF.
YOU CAN'T CUT OFF MY HEAD IF YOU DON'T GET CLOSE, RIGHT?
VWSH
HE DISAP-PEARED...

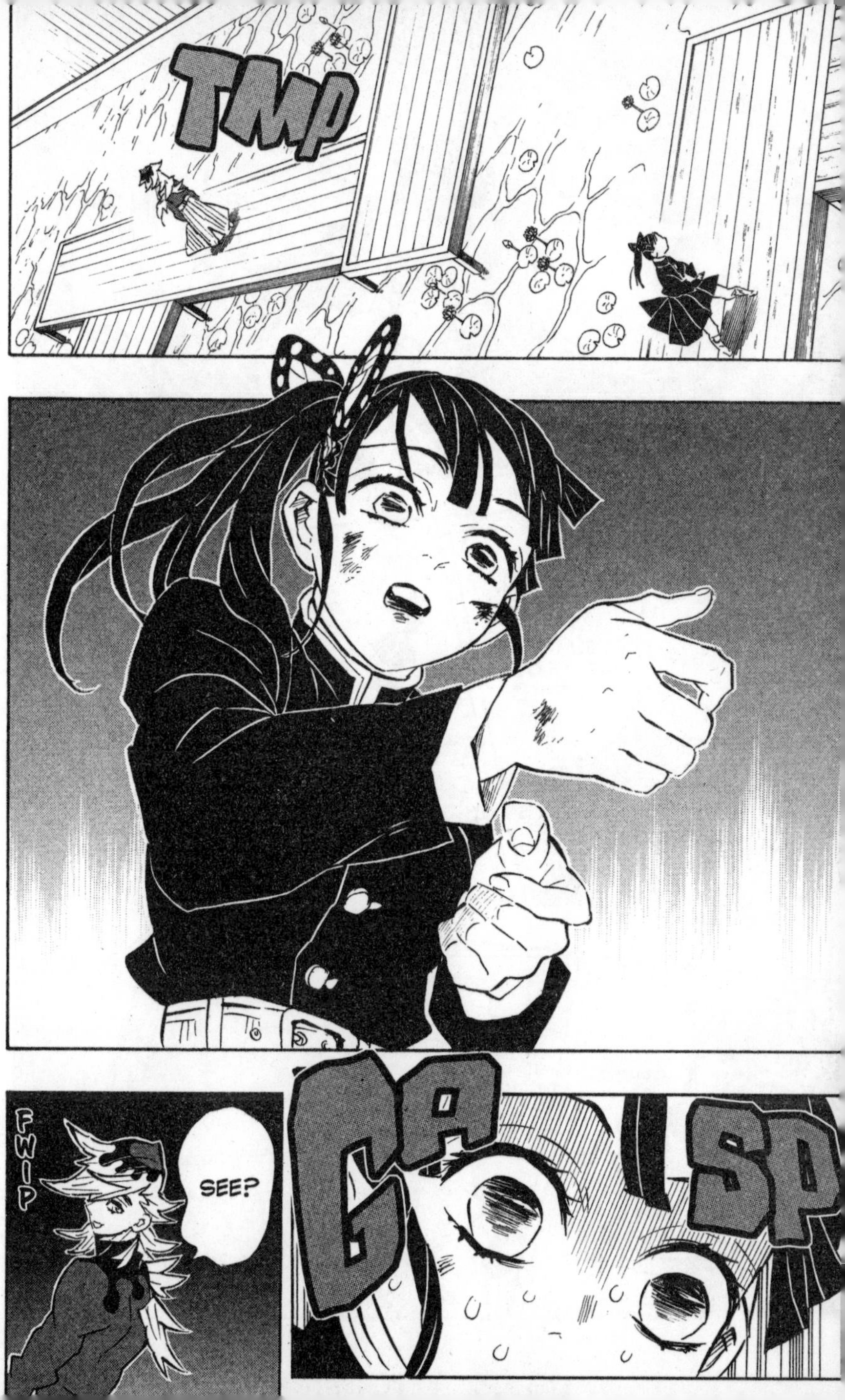
TMP
GA
SP
FWIP
SEE?

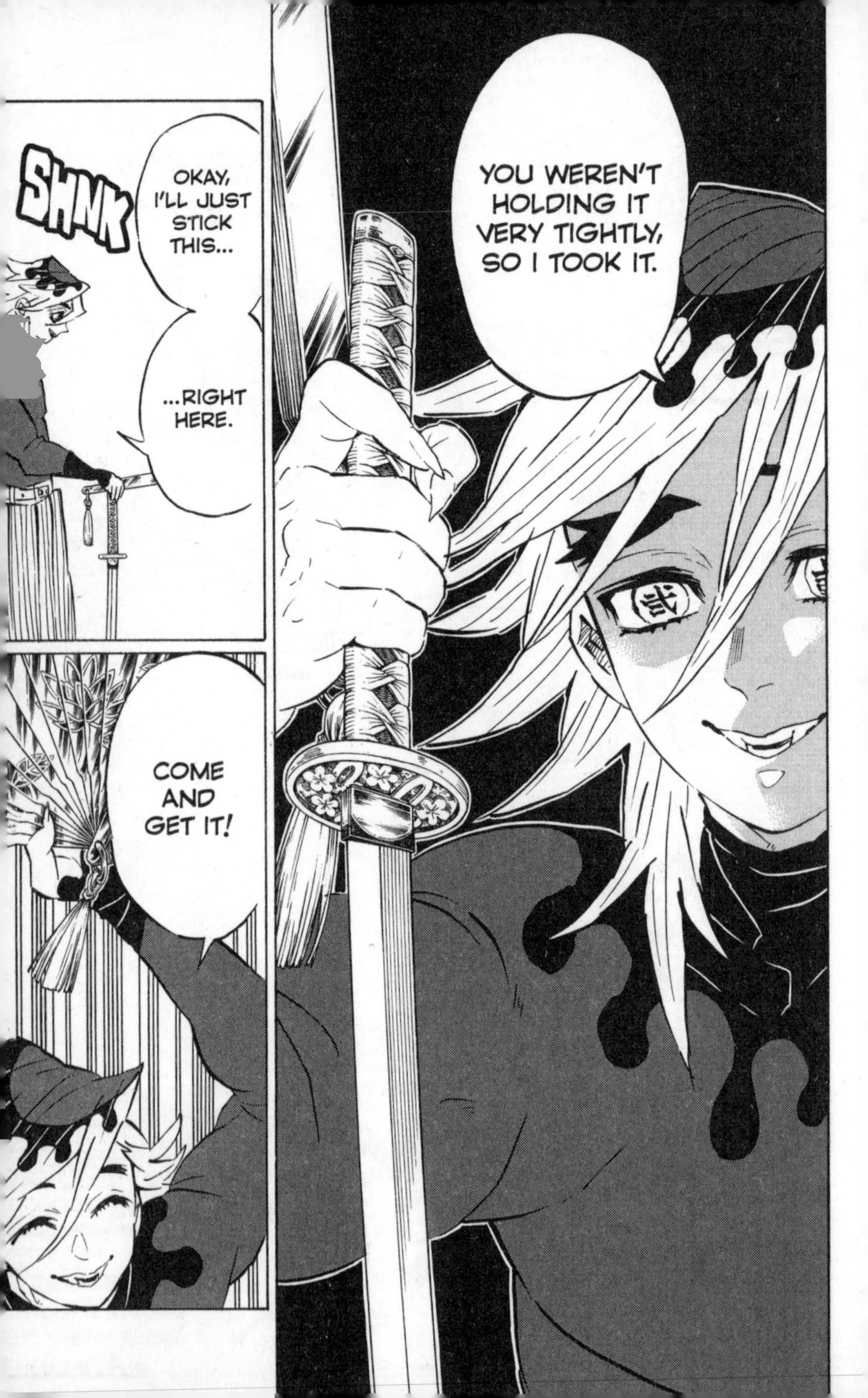
YOU WEREN'T HOLDING IT VERY TIGHTLY, SO I TOOK IT.
SHNK
OKAY, I'LL JUST STICK THIS...
...RIGHT HERE.
COME AND GET IT!

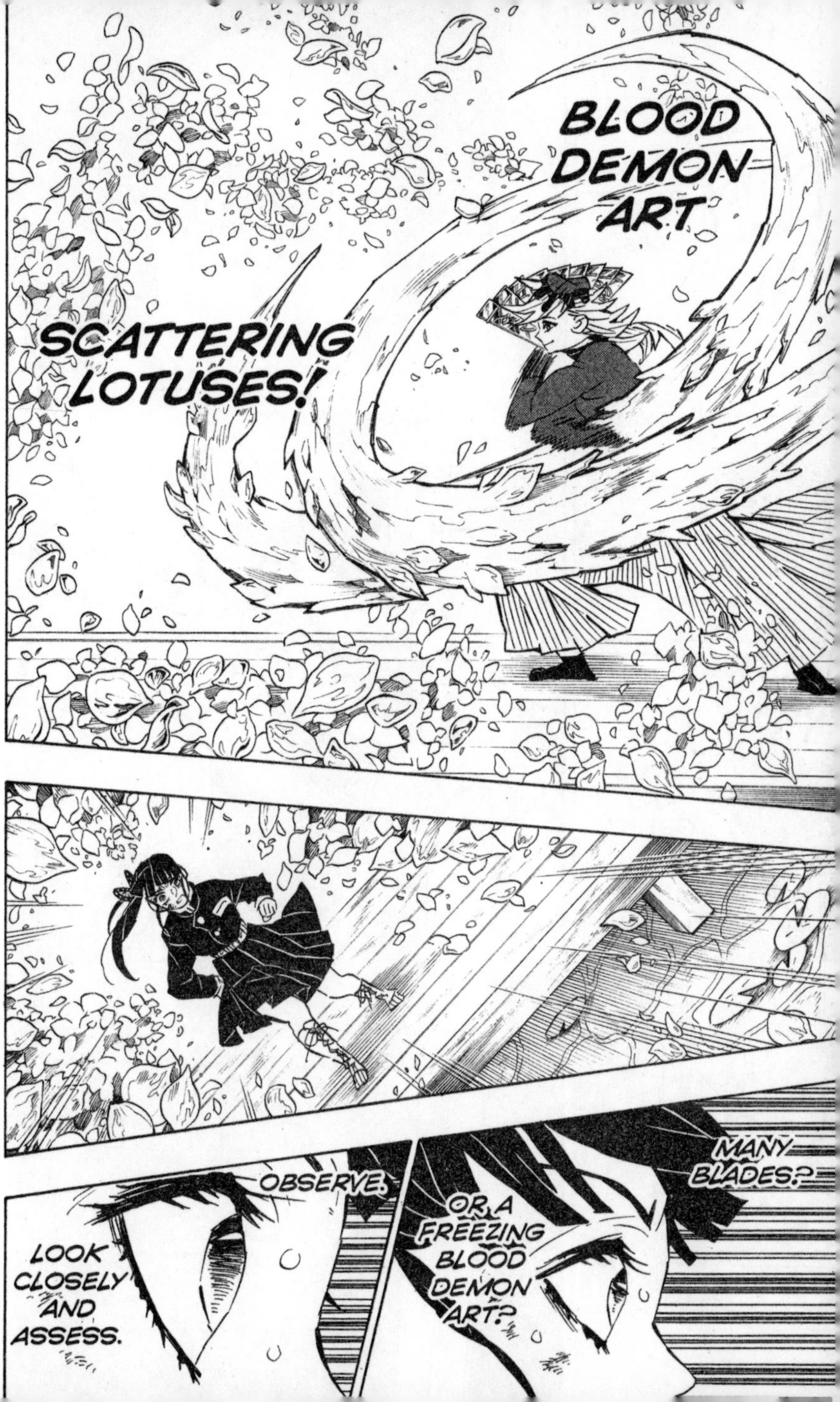
BLOOD DEMON ART
SCATTERING LOTUSES!
MANY BLADES?
OR A FREEZING BLOOD DEMON ART?
OBSERVE.
LOOK CLOSELY AND ASSESS.

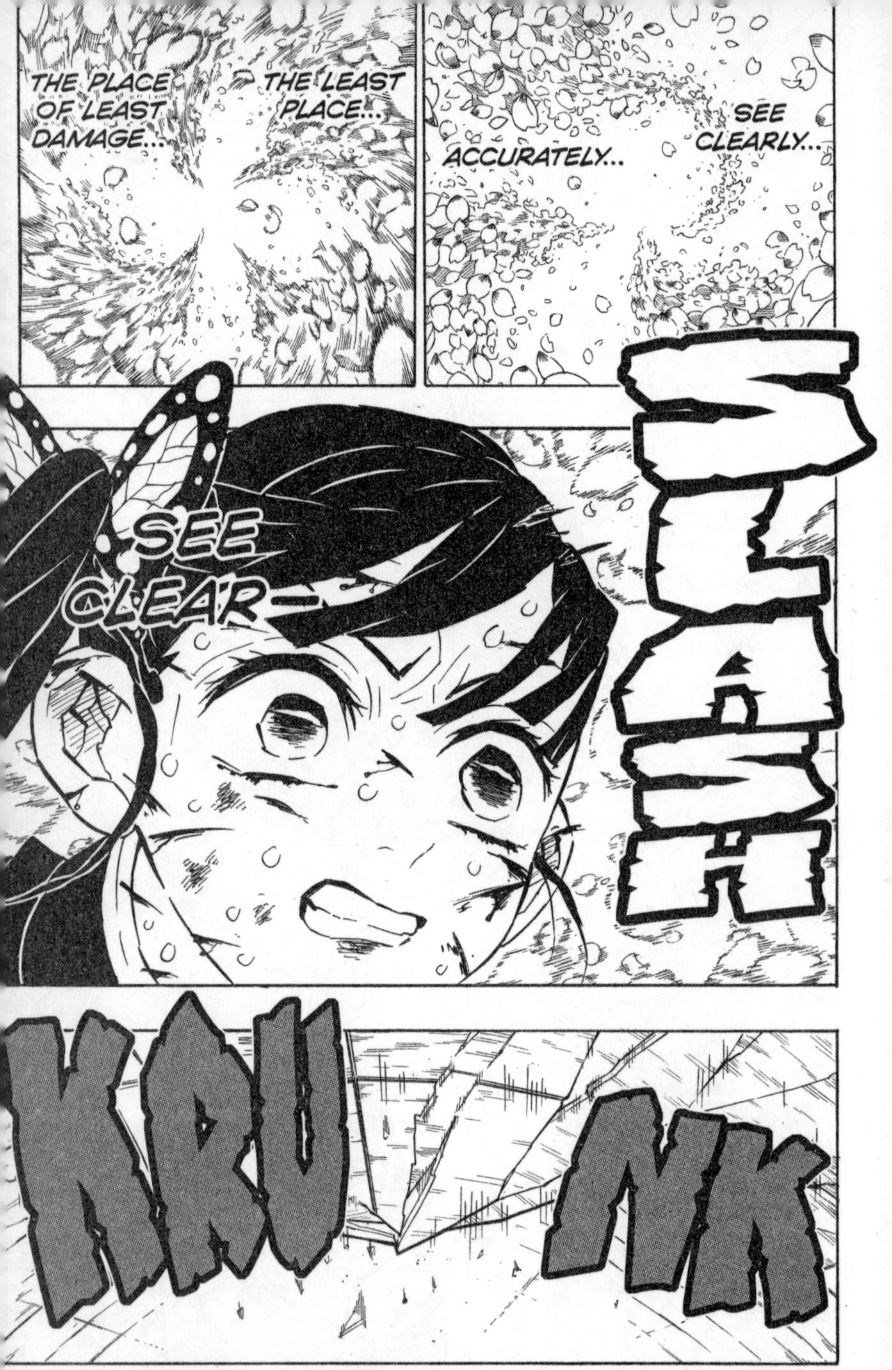
SEE CLEARLY...
ACCURATELY...
THE LEAST PLACE...
THE PLACE OF LEAST DAMAGE...
FLASH
SEE CLEAR—
KRUNK

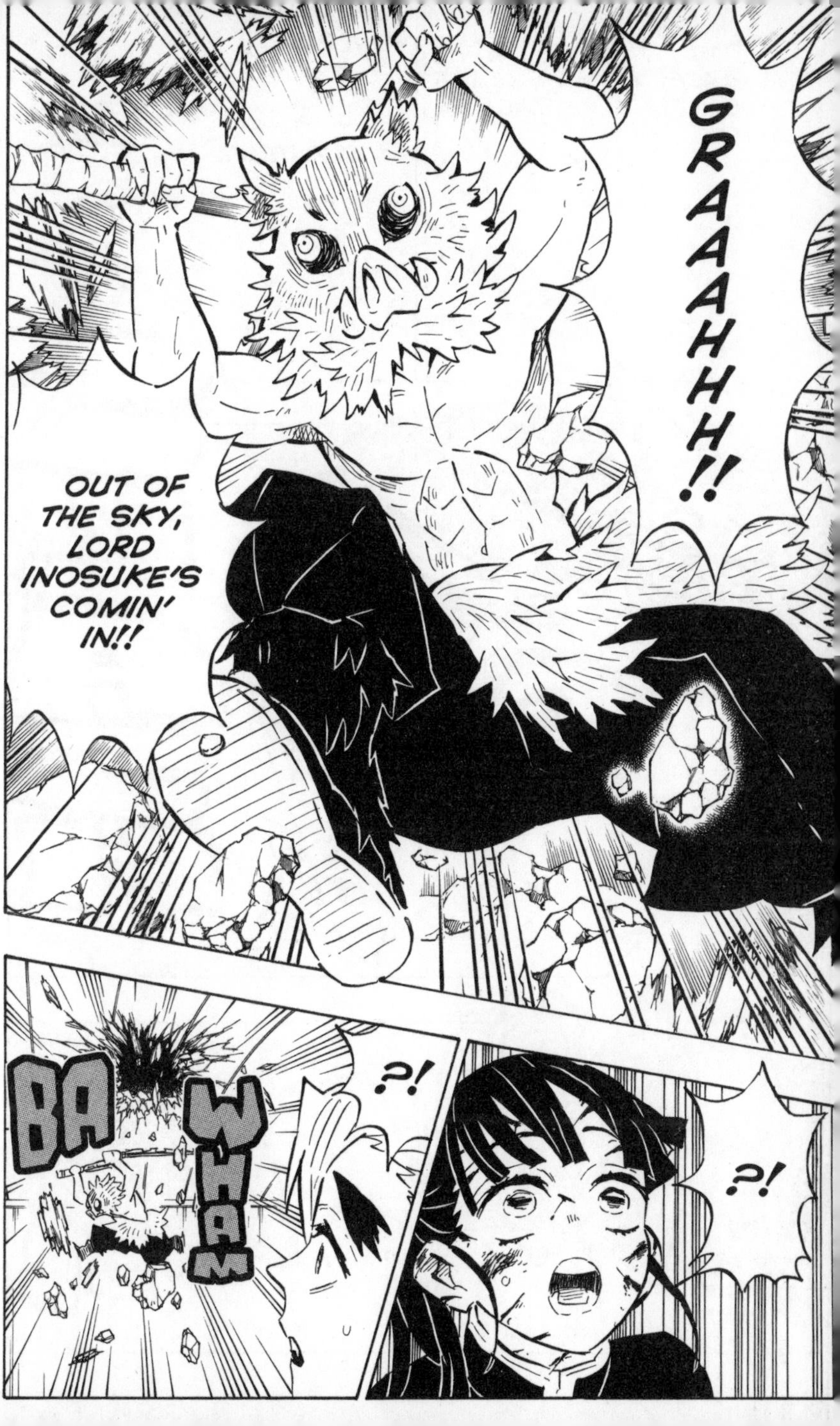
GRAAAHHH!!
OUT OF THE SKY, LORD INOSUKE'S COMIN' IN!!
?!
?!
BA
WHAM

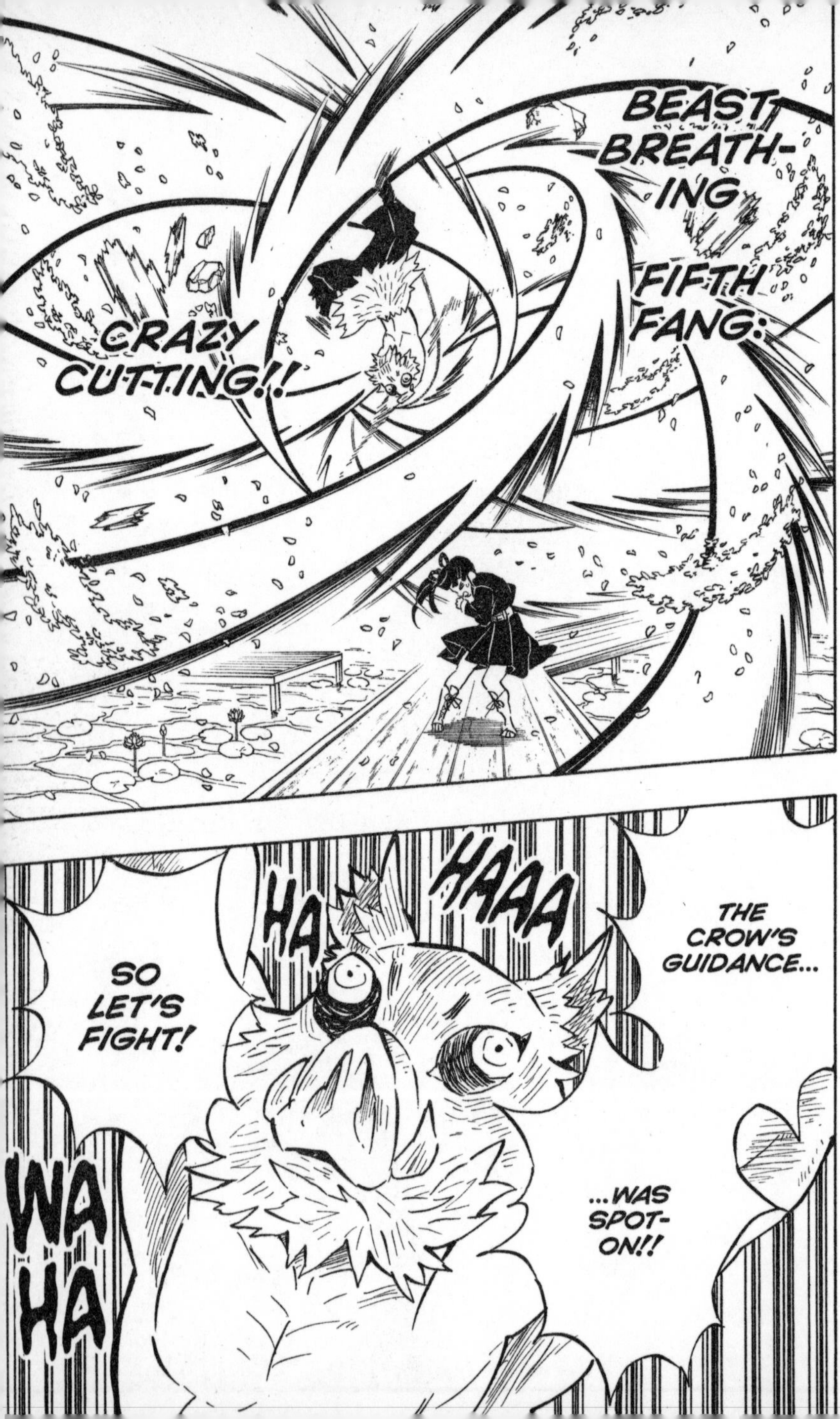
BEAST BREATHING FIFTH FANG:
CRAZY CUTTING!!
THE CROW'S GUIDANCE...
HAAA
HA
...WAS SPOT-ON!!
SO LET'S FIGHT!
WA HA HA

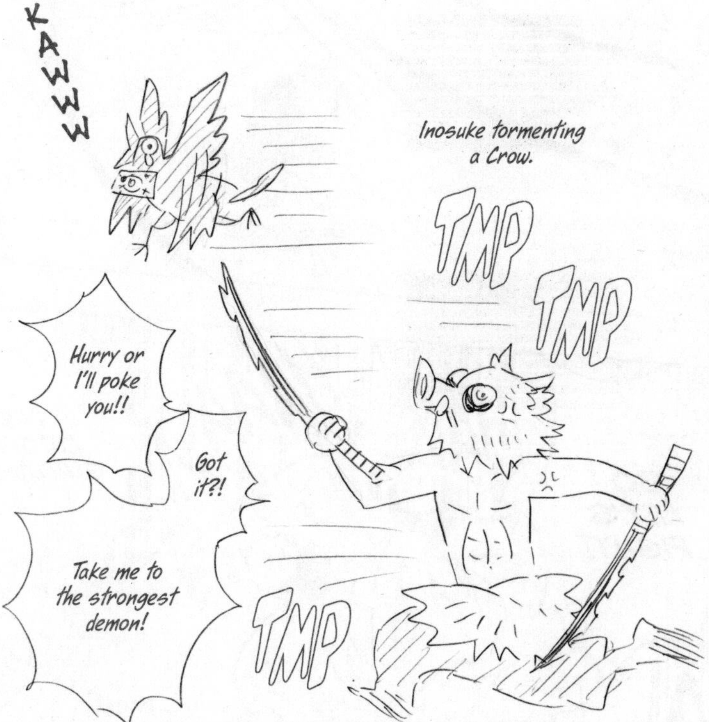
Inosuke tormenting a Crow.
TMP
TMP
KAWWW
Take me to the strongest demon!
Hurry or I'll poke you!!
Got it?!
TMP

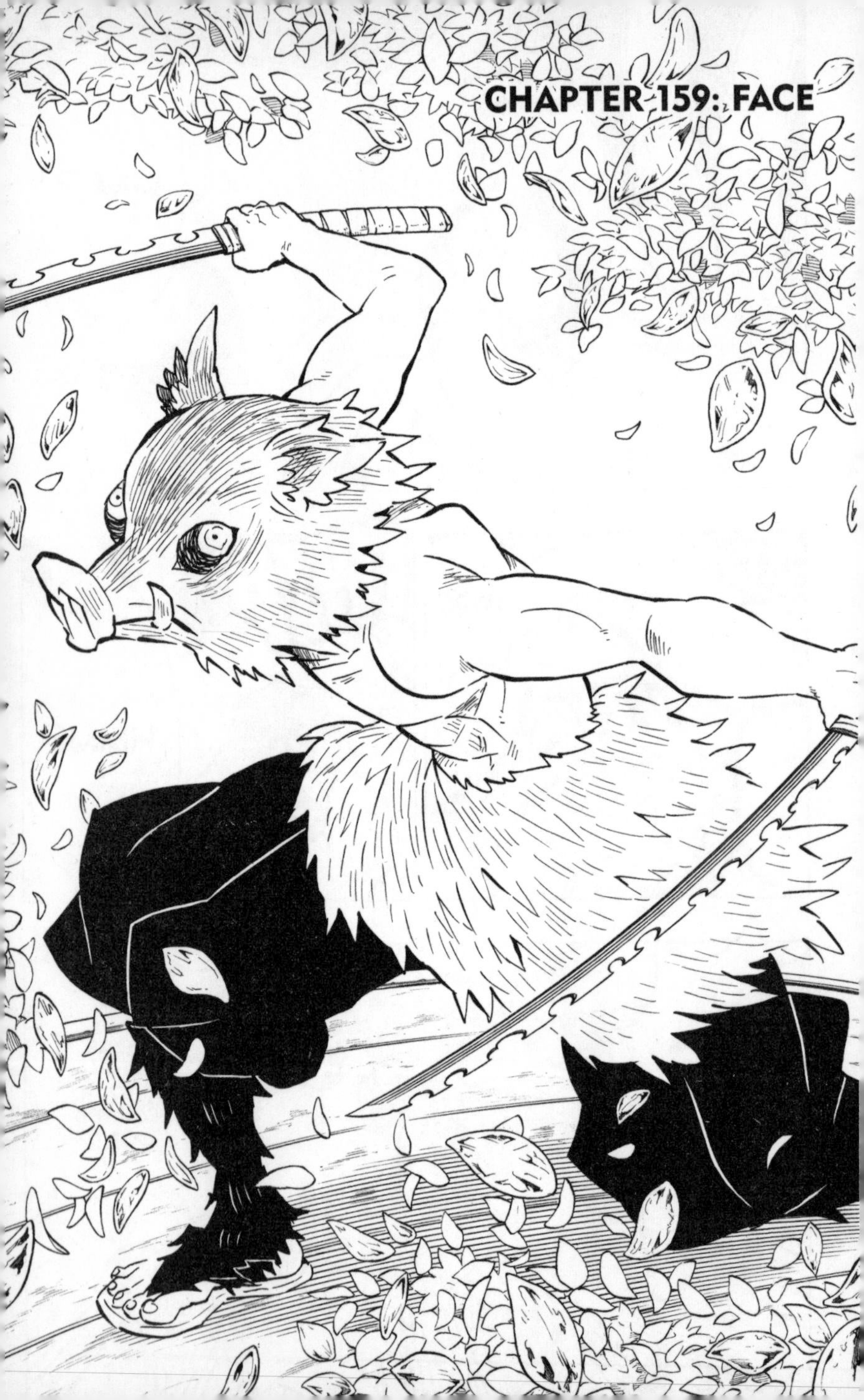
CHAPTER 159: FACE

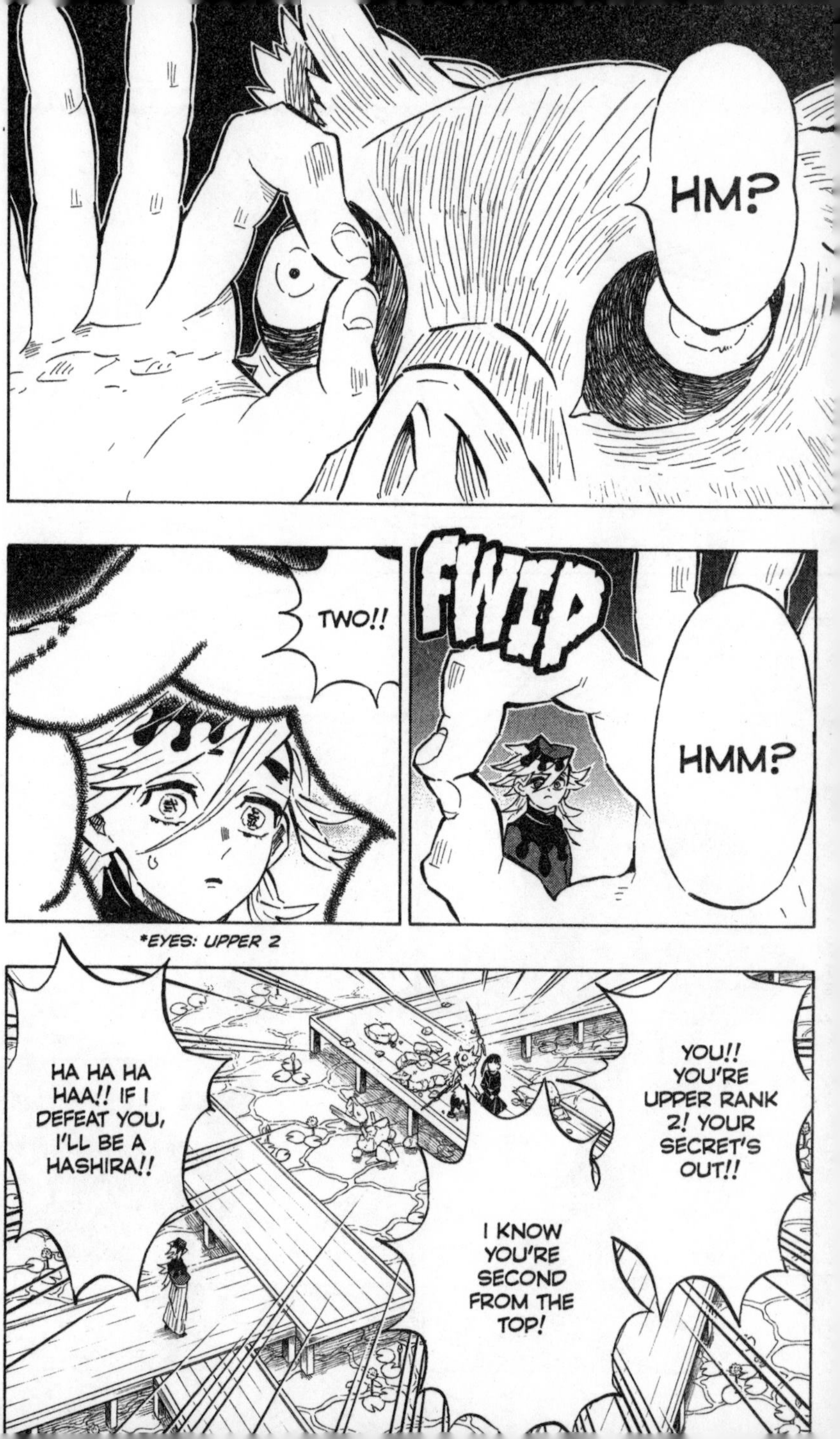
HM?
FWIP
HMM?
TWO!!
*EYES: UPPER 2
YOU!! YOU'RE UPPER RANK 2! YOUR SECRET'S OUT!!
I KNOW YOU'RE SECOND FROM THE TOP!
HA HA HA HAA!! IF I DEFEAT YOU, I'LL BE A HASHIRA!!

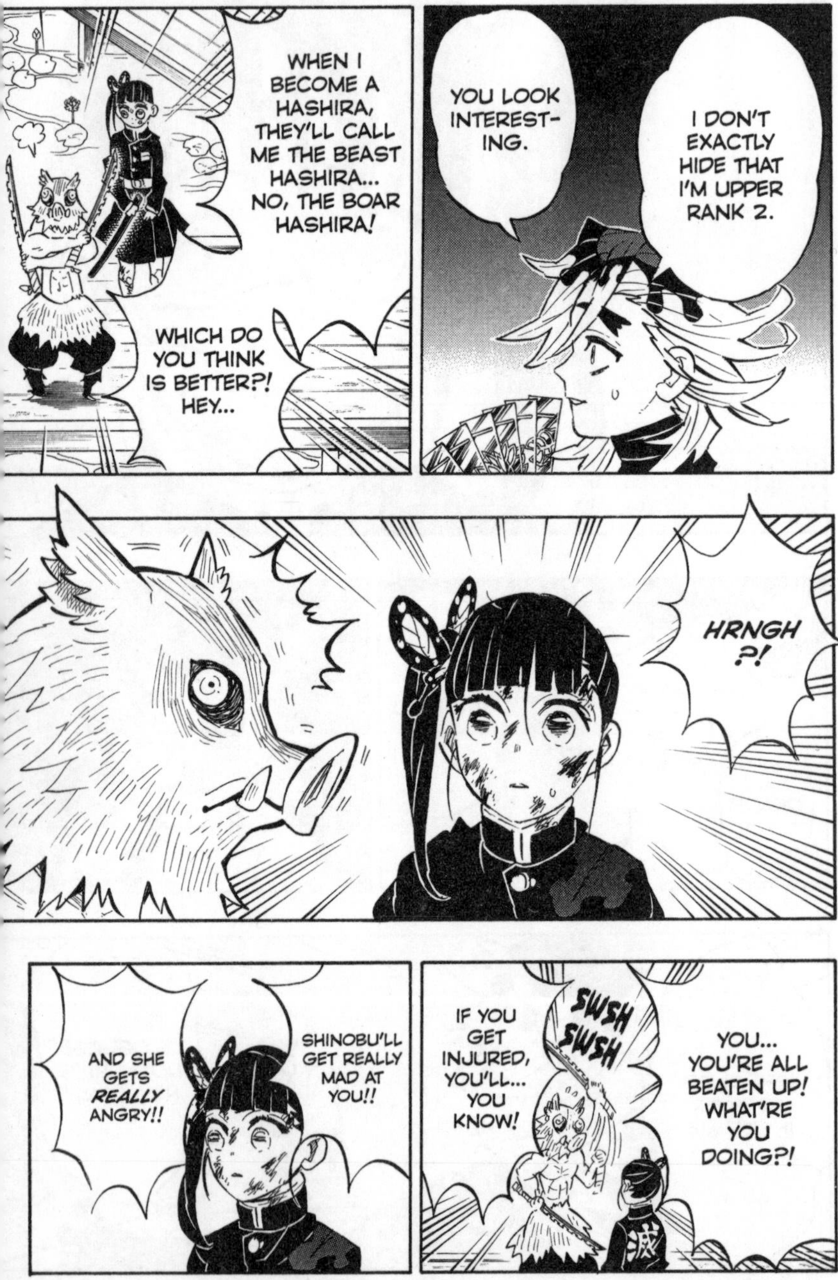
I DON'T EXACTLY HIDE THAT I'M UPPER RANK 2.
YOU LOOK INTEREST-ING.
WHEN I BECOME A HASHIRA, THEY'LL CALL ME THE BEAST HASHIRA... NO, THE BOAR HASHIRA!
WHICH DO YOU THINK IS BETTER?! HEY...
HRNGH ?!
YOU... YOU'RE ALL BEATEN UP! WHAT'RE YOU DOING?!
SWSH SWSH
IF YOU GET INJURED, YOU'LL... YOU KNOW!
SHINOBU'LL GET REALLY MAD AT YOU!!
AND SHE GETS *REALLY* ANGRY!!

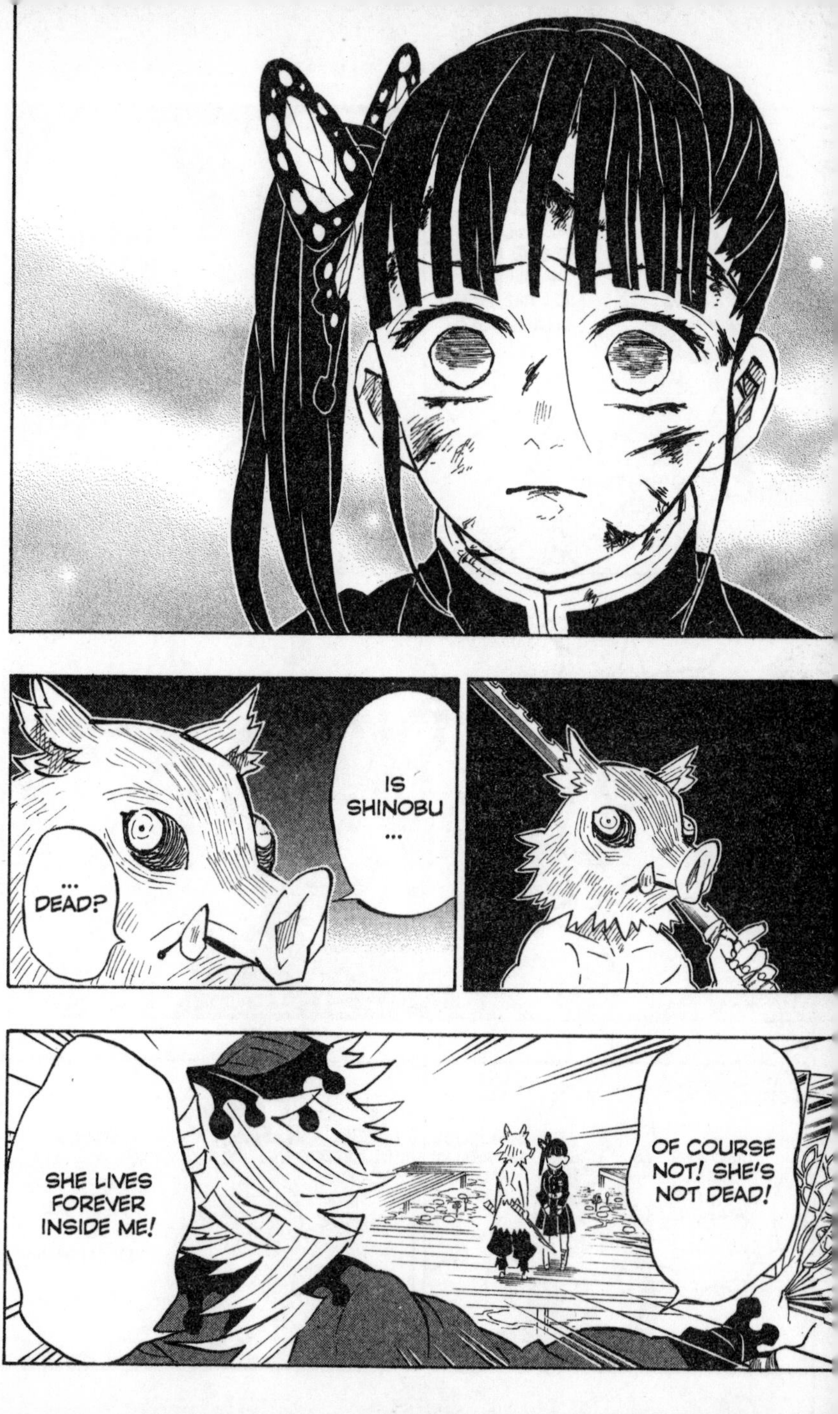
IS SHINOBU ...
... DEAD?
OF COURSE NOT! SHE'S NOT DEAD!
SHE LIVES FOREVER INSIDE ME!

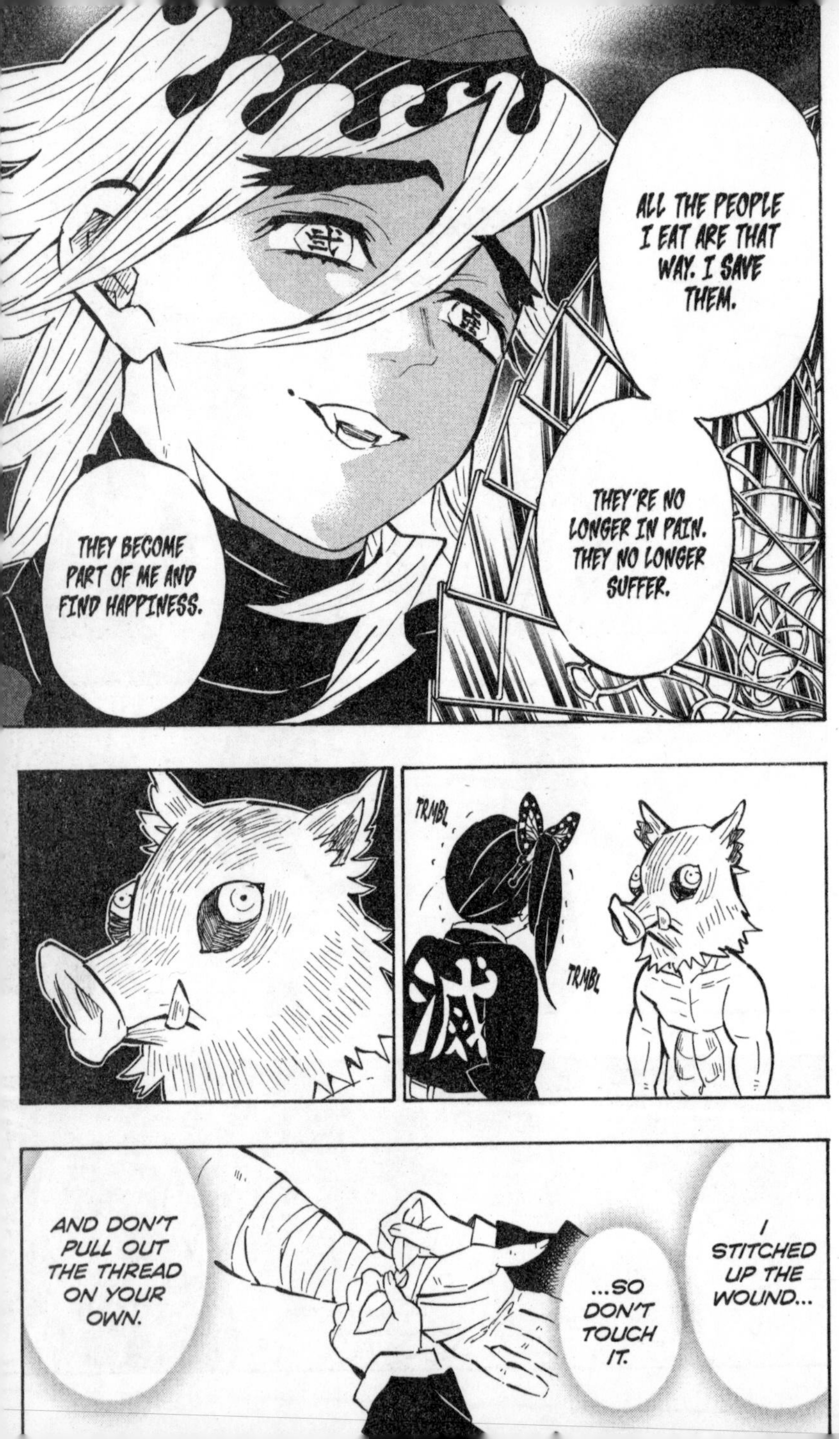
ALL THE PEOPLE I EAT ARE THAT WAY. I SAVE THEM.
THEY'RE NO LONGER IN PAIN. THEY NO LONGER SUFFER.
THEY BECOME PART OF ME AND FIND HAPPINESS.
TRMBL
TRMBL
I STITCHED UP THE WOUND...
...SO DON'T TOUCH IT.
AND DON'T PULL OUT THE THREAD ON YOUR OWN.

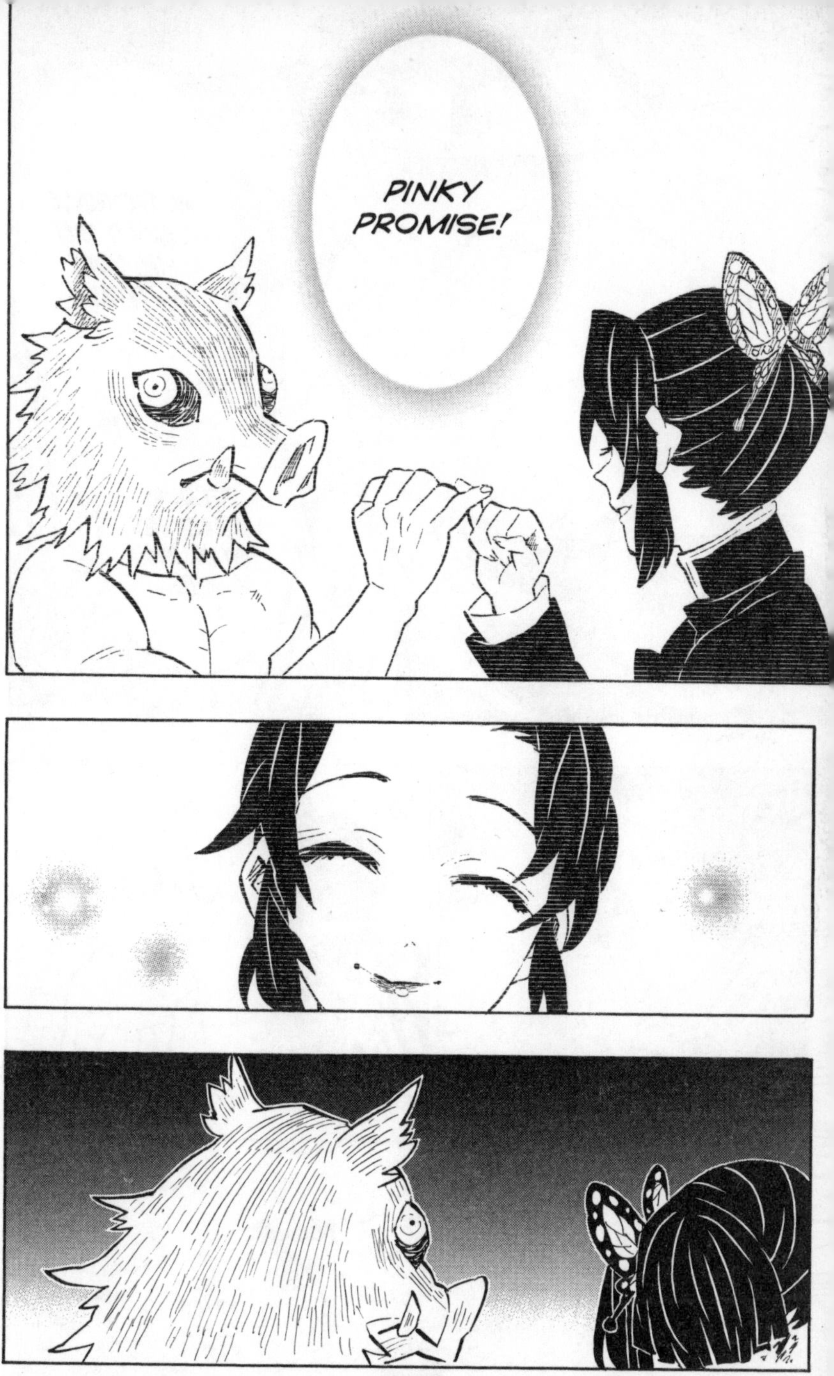
PINKY PROMISE!

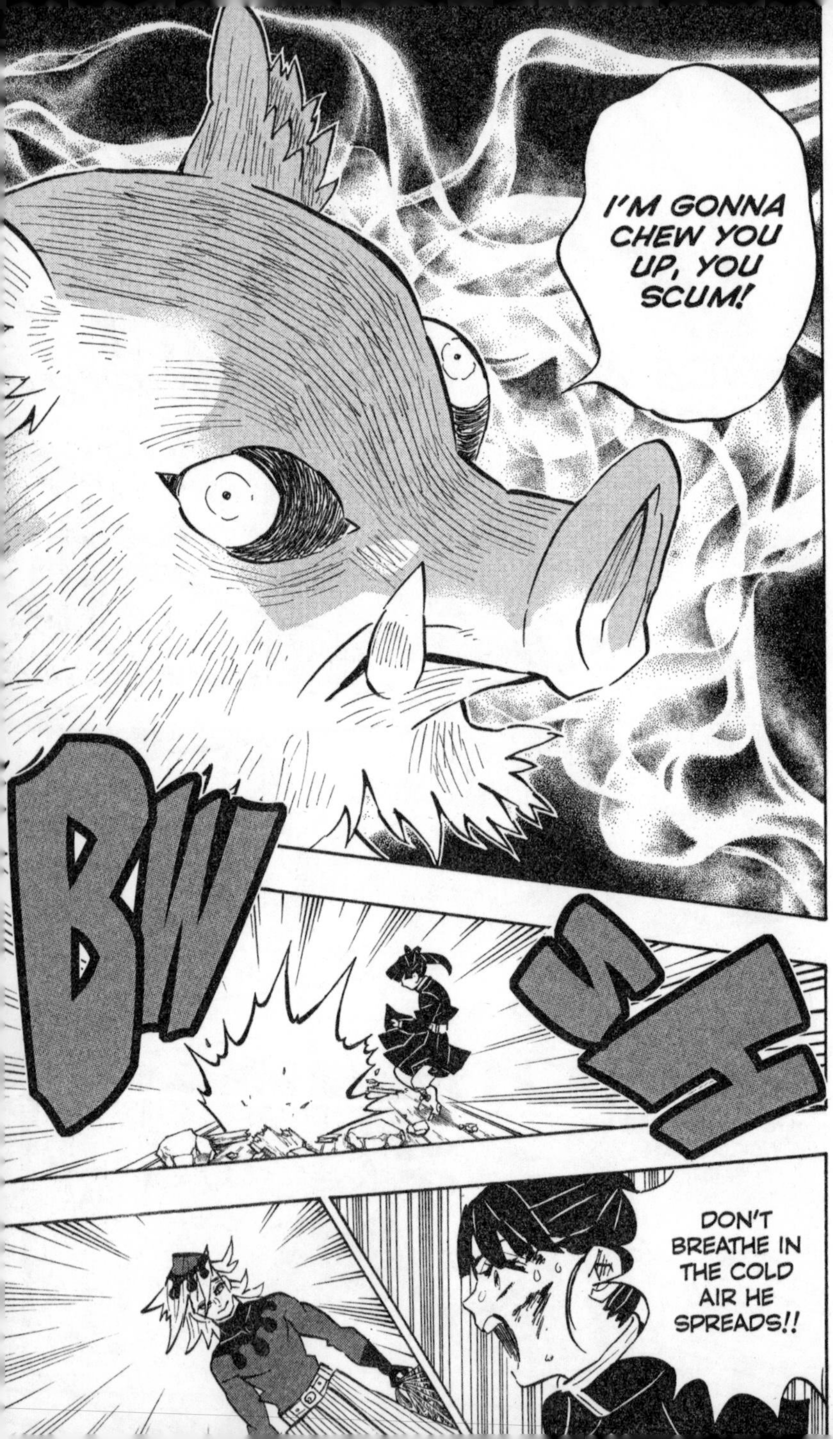
I'M GONNA CHEW YOU UP, YOU SCUM!
SH
BW
DON'T BREATHE IN THE COLD AIR HE SPREADS!!

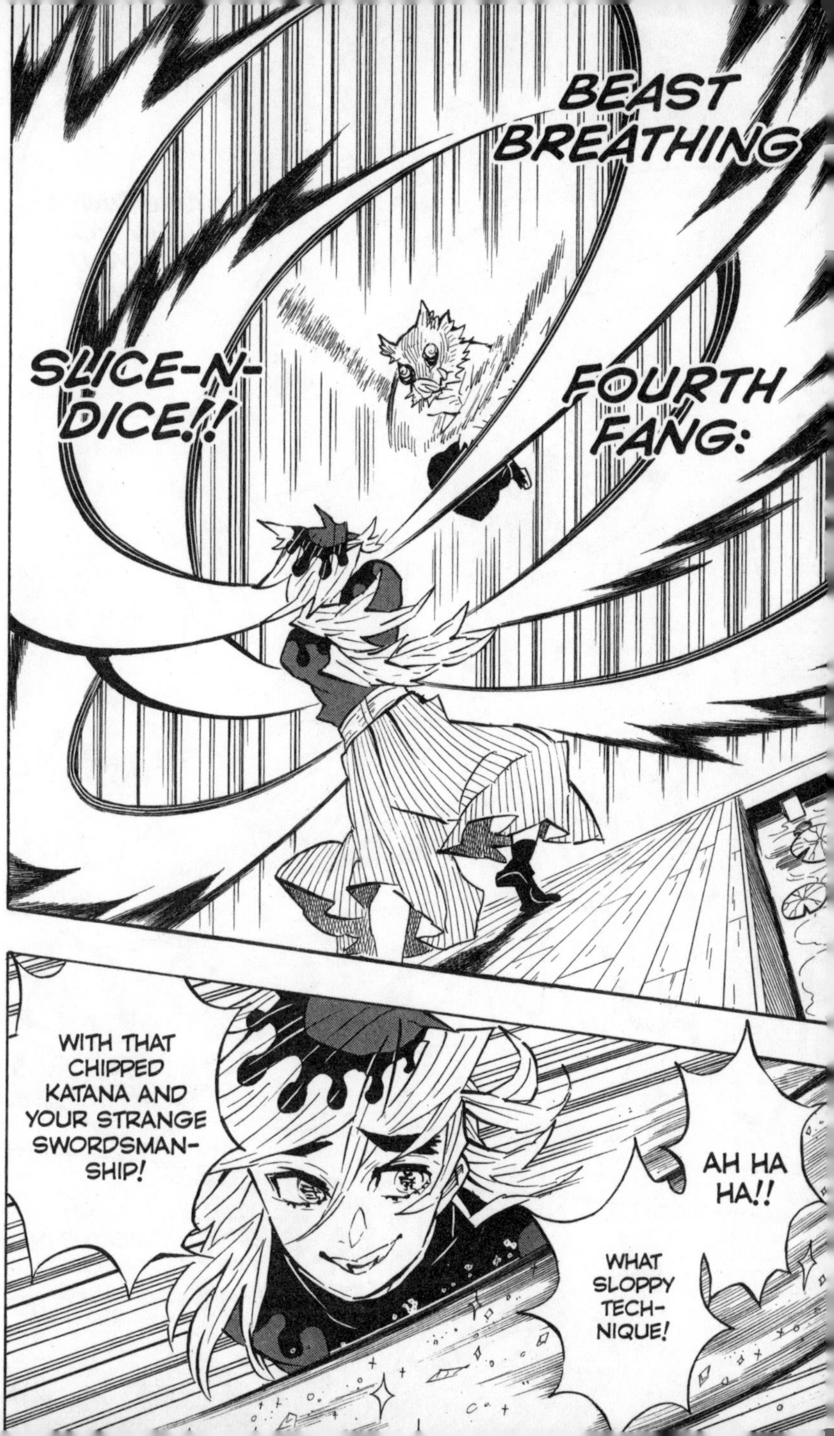
BEAST BREATHING
FOURTH FANG:
SLICE-N-DICE!!
AH HA HA!!
WHAT SLOPPY TECHNIQUE!
WITH THAT CHIPPED KATANA AND YOUR STRANGE SWORDSMANSHIP!

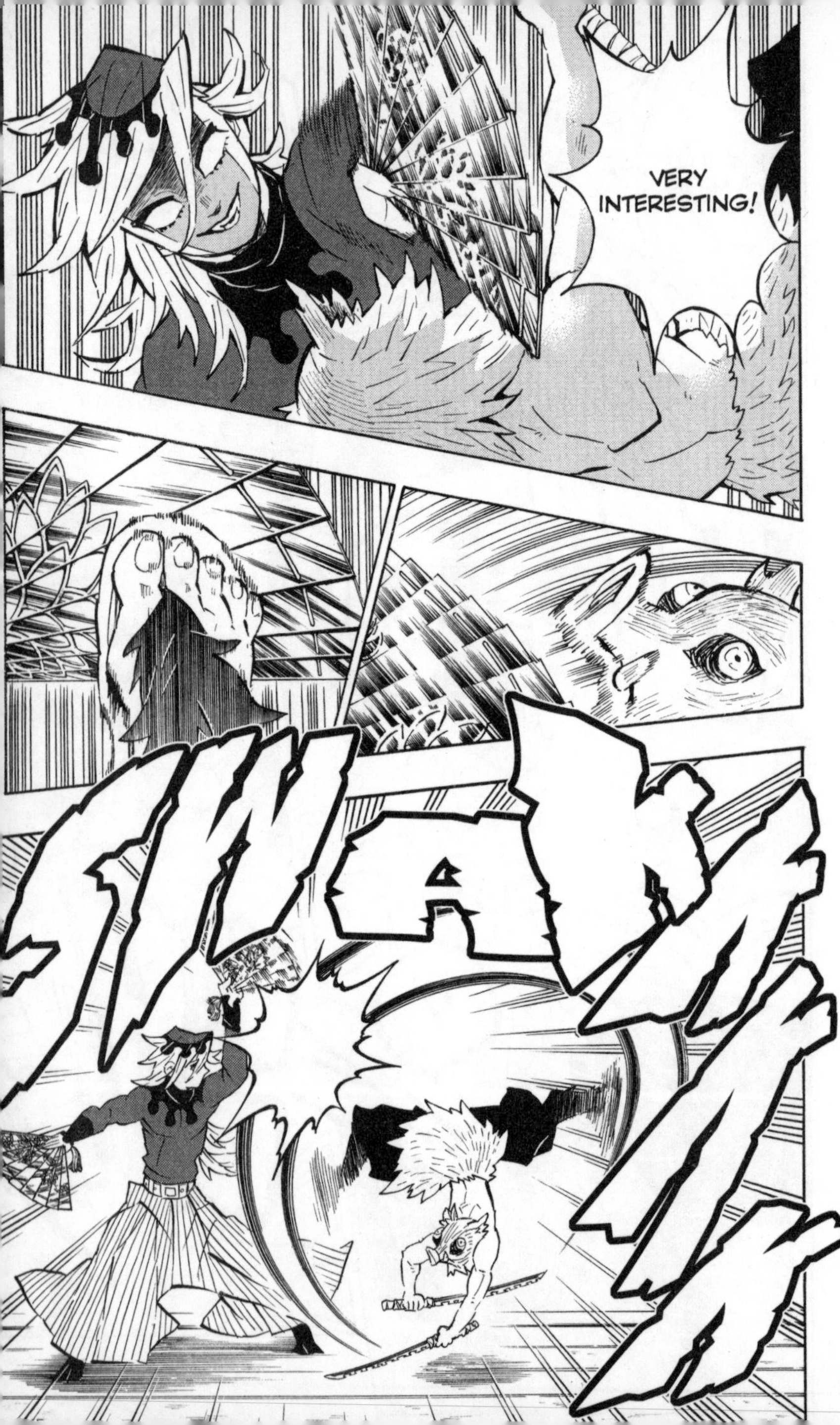
VERY INTERESTING!

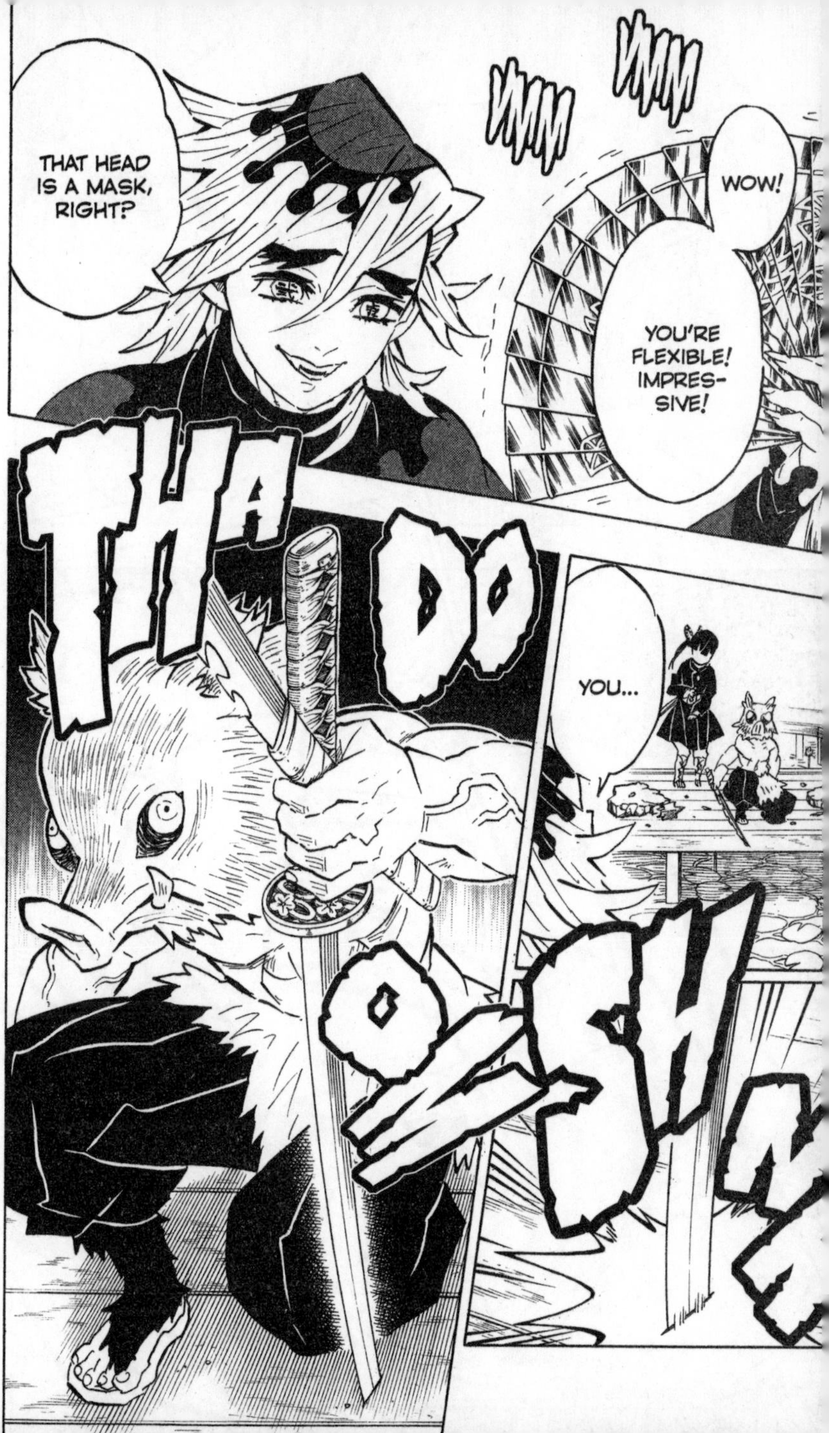
VNM
VNM
WOW!
YOU'RE FLEXIBLE! IMPRES-SIVE!
THAT HEAD IS A MASK, RIGHT?
YOU...
THA
DO
SH

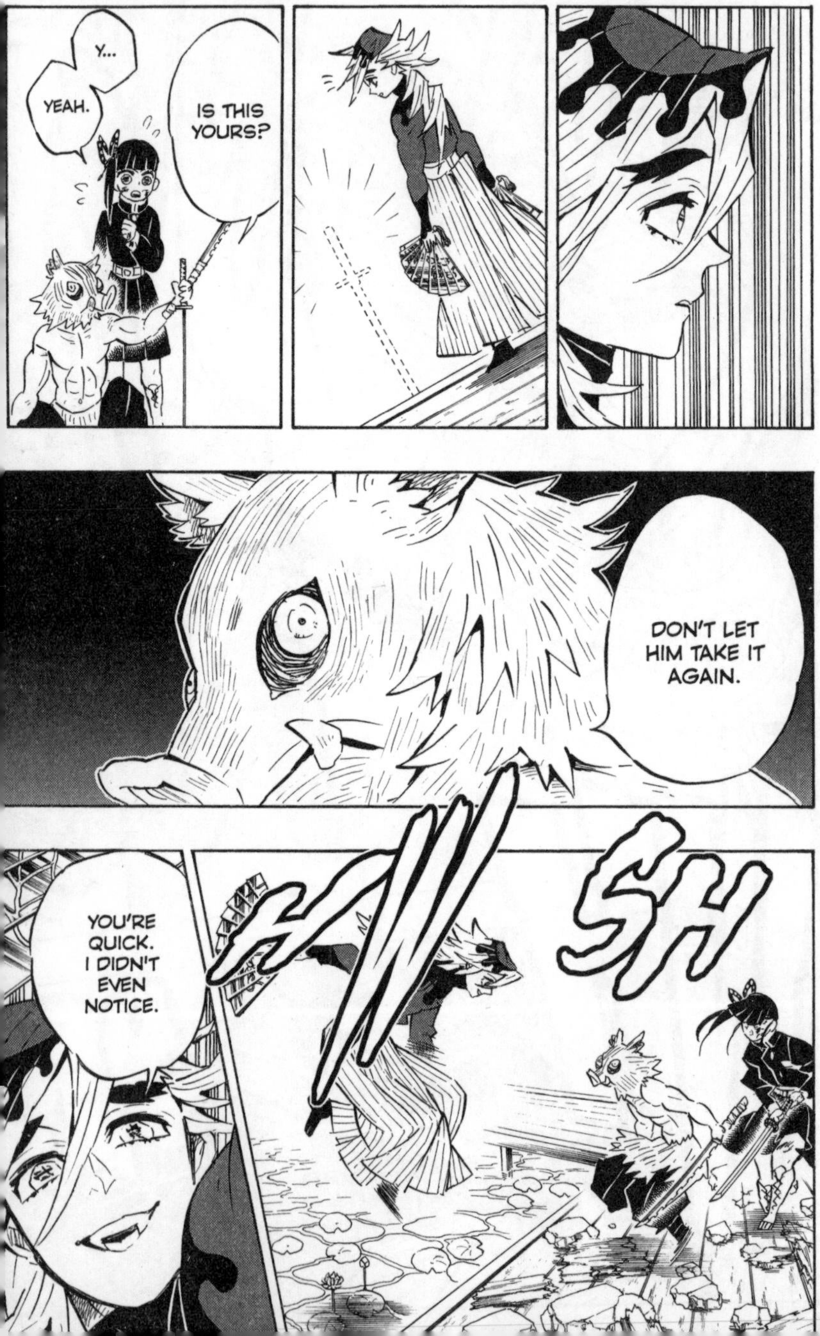
IS THIS YOURS?
Y... YEAH.
DON'T LET HIM TAKE IT AGAIN.
SHH
YOU'RE QUICK. I DIDN'T EVEN NOTICE.

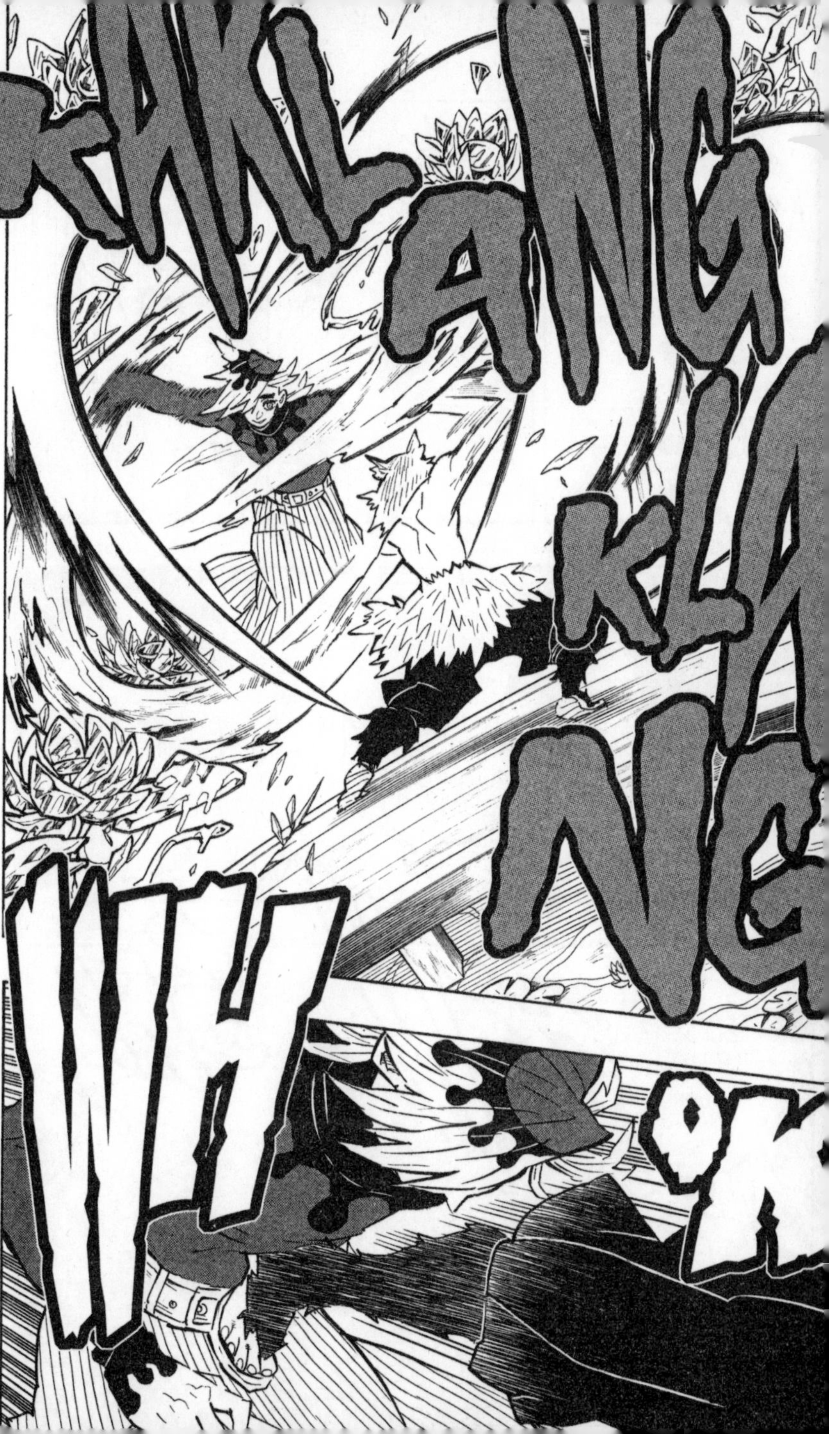
KAKLANG
KLANG
WH
OK

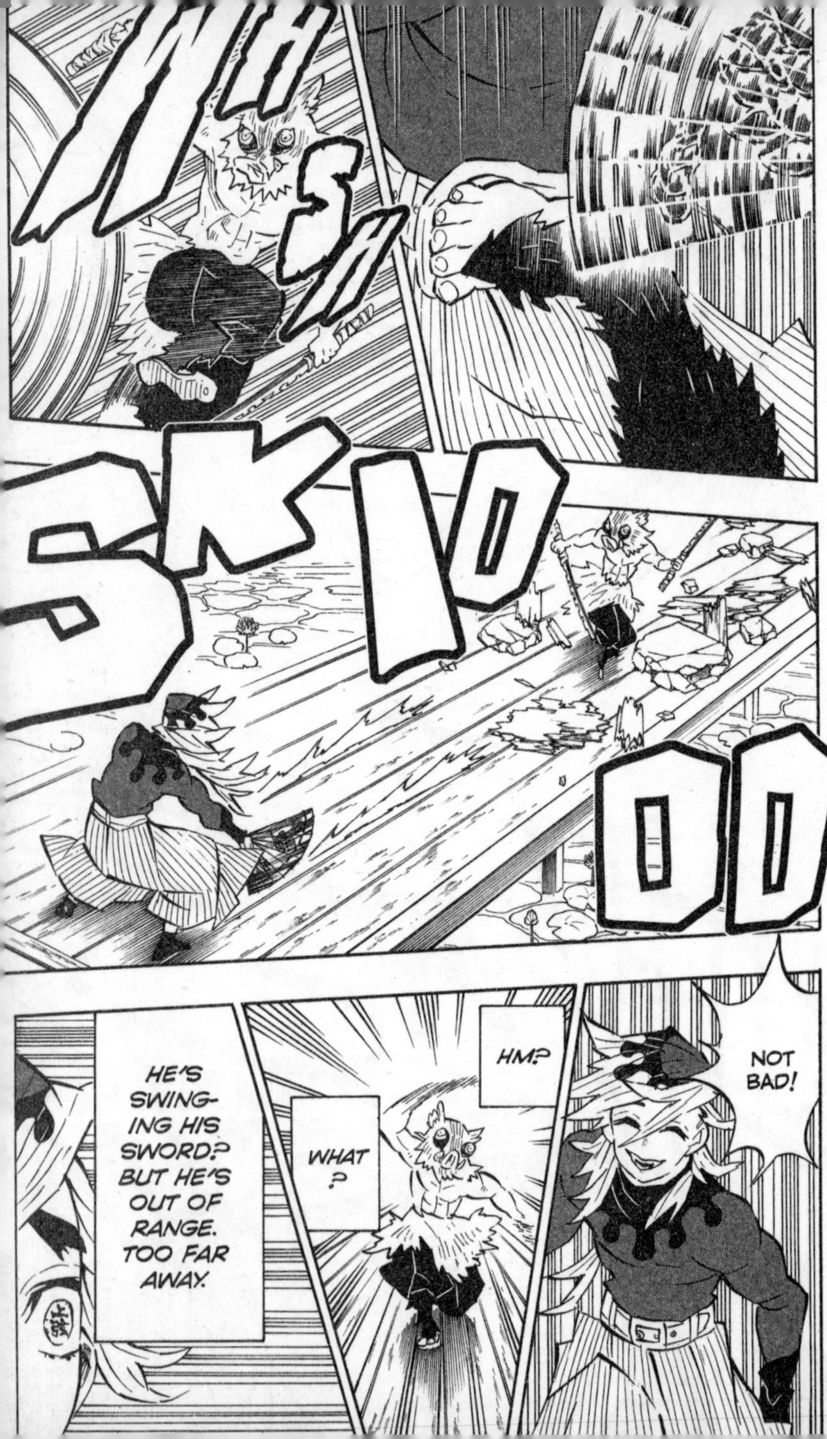
NOT BAD!
HM?
WHAT ?
HE'S SWING-ING HIS SWORD? BUT HE'S OUT OF RANGE. TOO FAR AWAY.

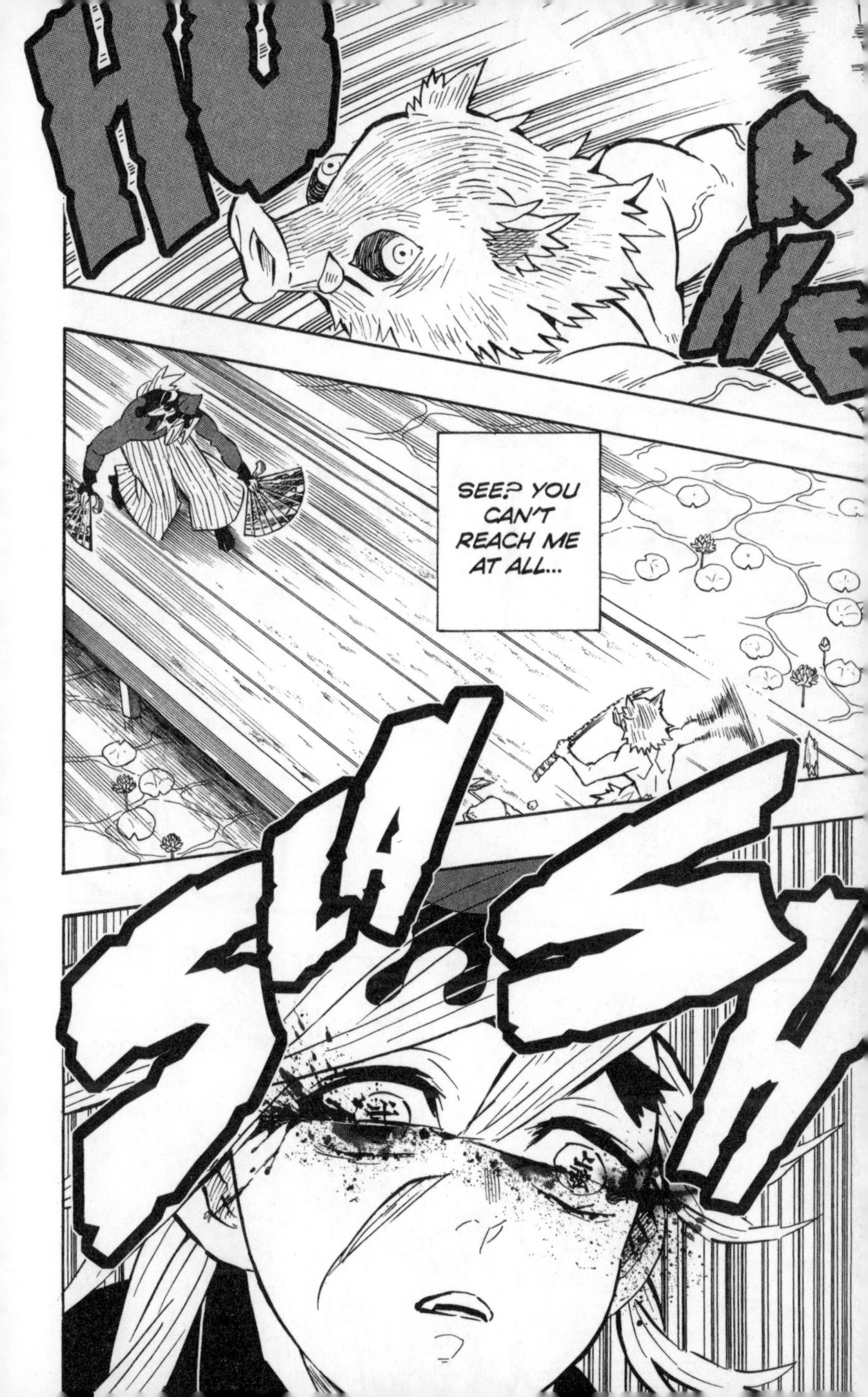
SEE? YOU CAN'T REACH ME AT ALL...
SLASH

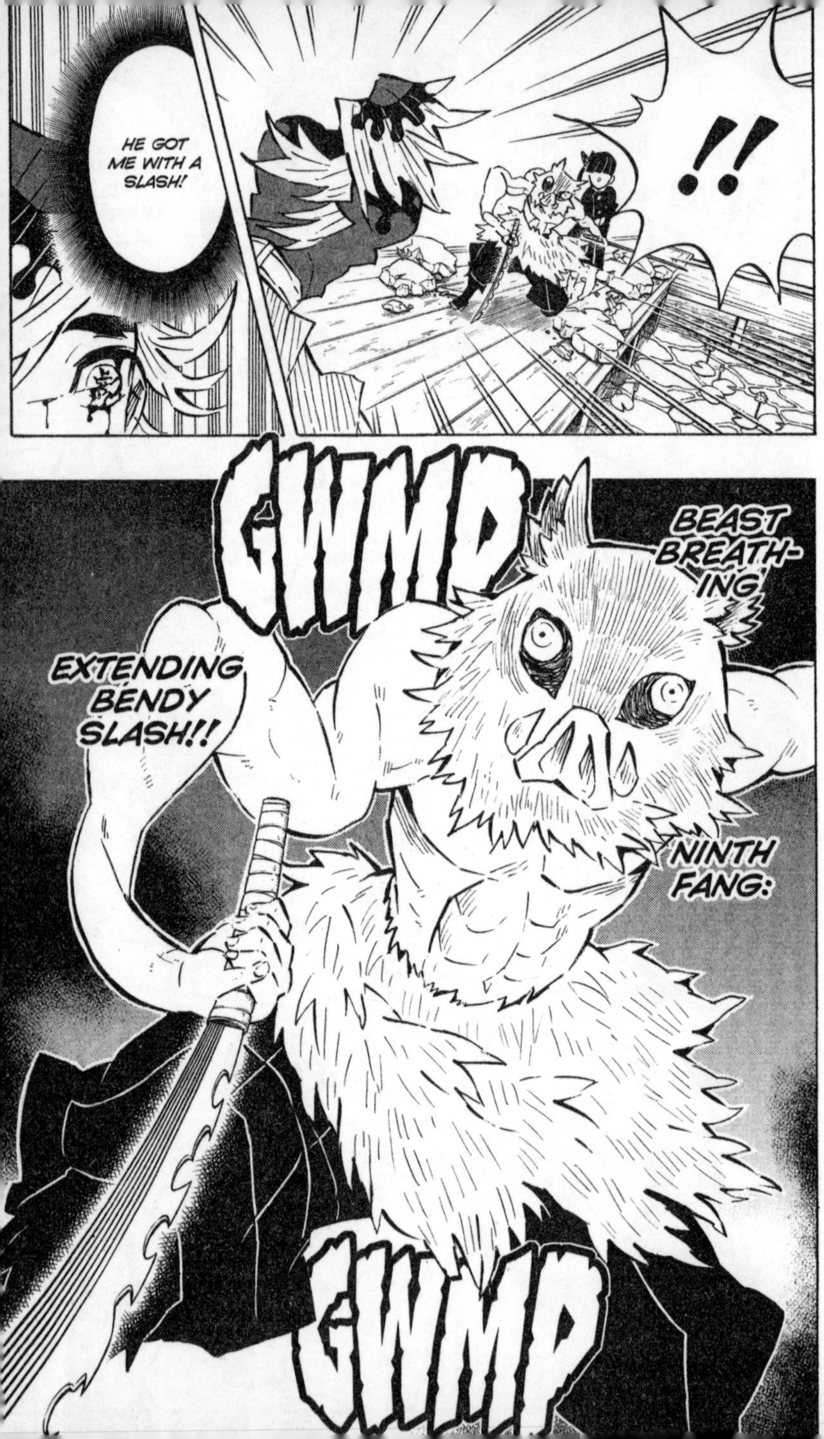
!!
HE GOT ME WITH A SLASH!
GWMD
BEAST BREATH-ING
NINTH FANG:
EXTENDING BENDY SLASH!!
GWMP

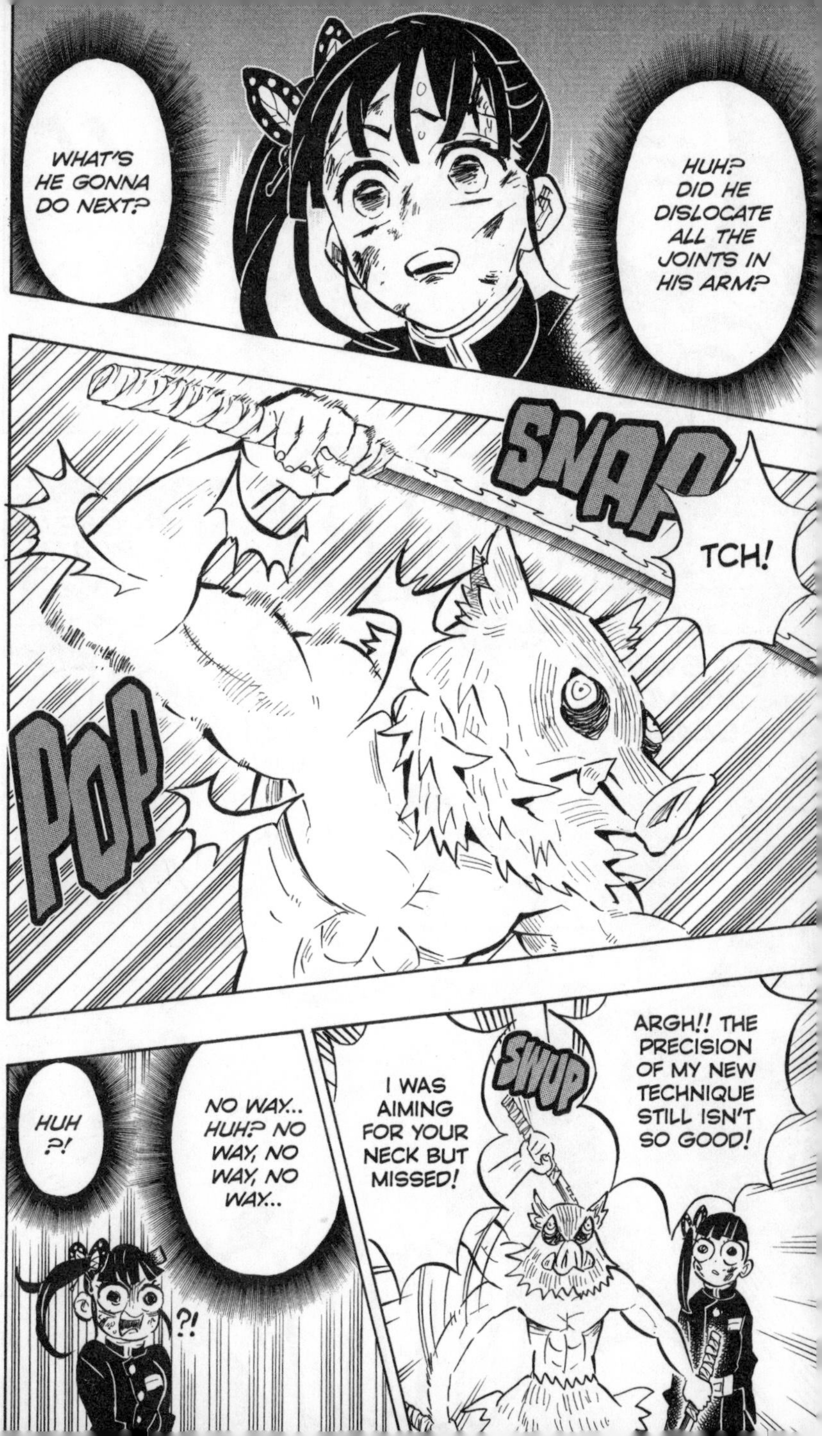
HUH? DID HE DISLOCATE ALL THE JOINTS IN HIS ARM?
WHAT'S HE GONNA DO NEXT?
SNAP
TCH!
POP
ARGH!! THE PRECISION OF MY NEW TECHNIQUE STILL ISN'T SO GOOD!
SWUP
I WAS AIMING FOR YOUR NECK BUT MISSED!
NO WAY... HUH? NO WAY, NO WAY, NO WAY...
HUH ?!
?!

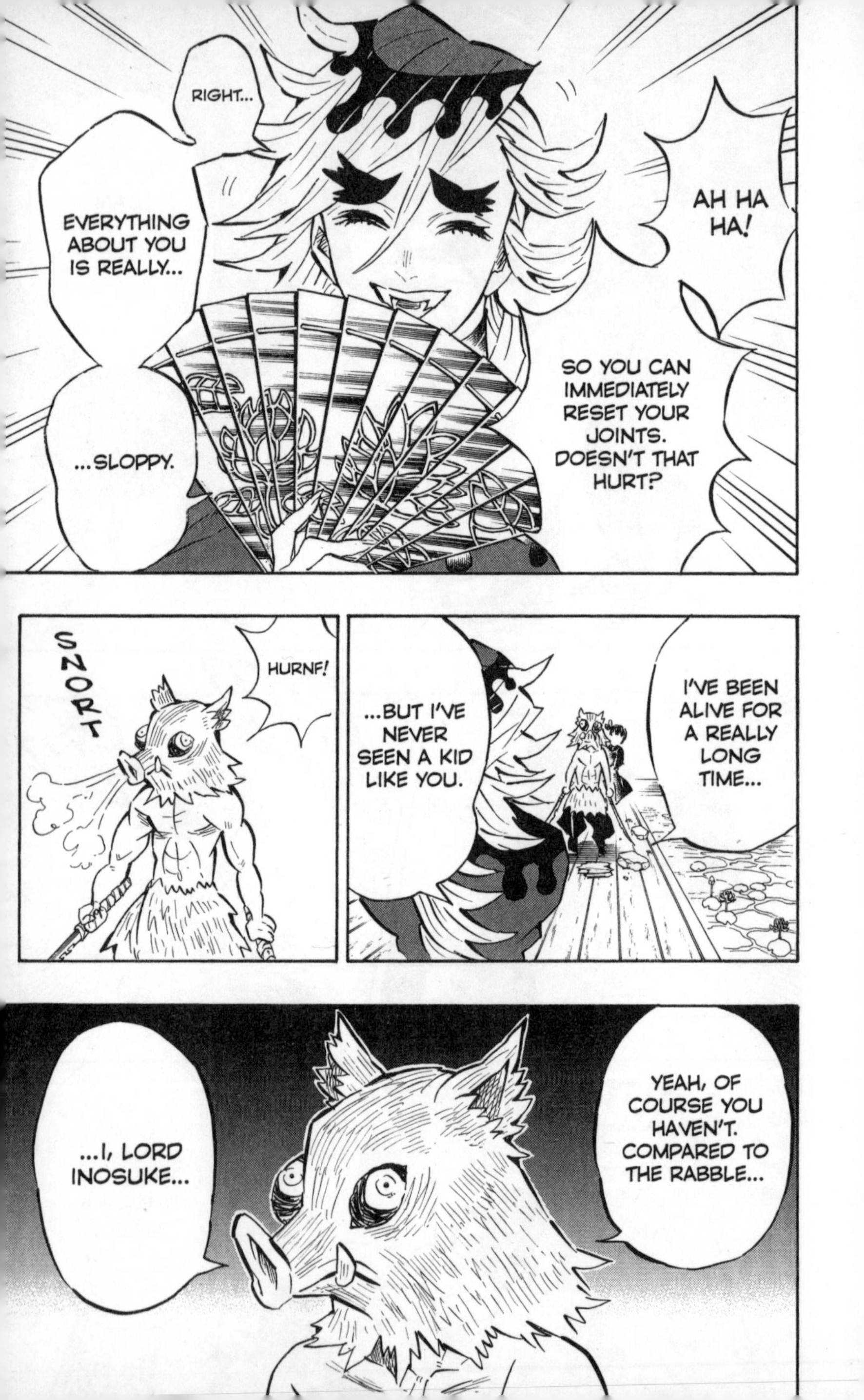
AH HA HA!
SO YOU CAN IMMEDIATELY RESET YOUR JOINTS. DOESN'T THAT HURT?
RIGHT...
EVERYTHING ABOUT YOU IS REALLY...
...SLOPPY.
I'VE BEEN ALIVE FOR A REALLY LONG TIME...
...BUT I'VE NEVER SEEN A KID LIKE YOU.
HURNF!
SNORT
YEAH, OF COURSE YOU HAVEN'T. COMPARED TO THE RABBLE...
...I, LORD INOSUKE...

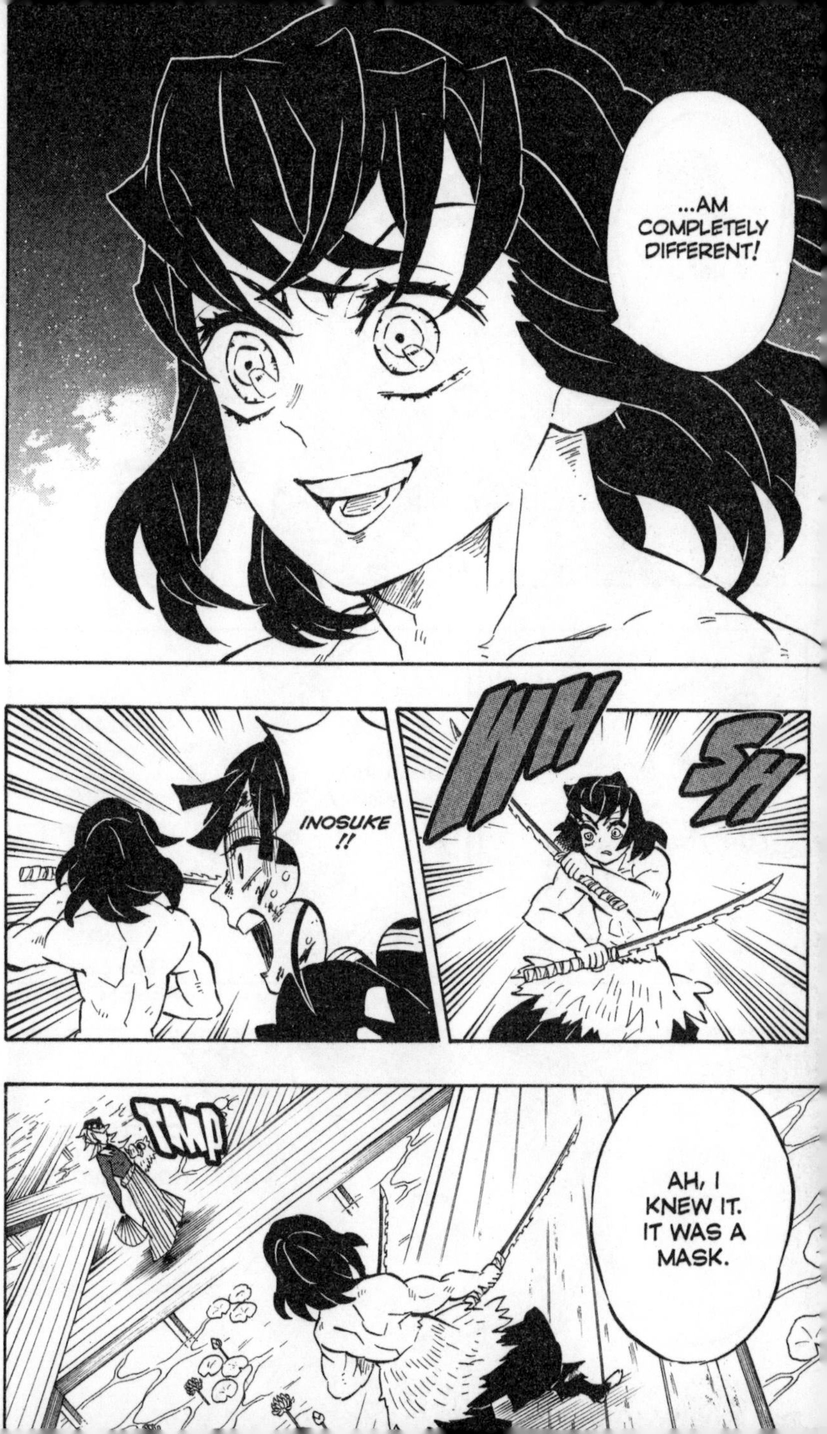
...AM COMPLETELY DIFFERENT!
SH
WHH
INOSUKE !!
AH, I KNEW IT. IT WAS A MASK.
TMP

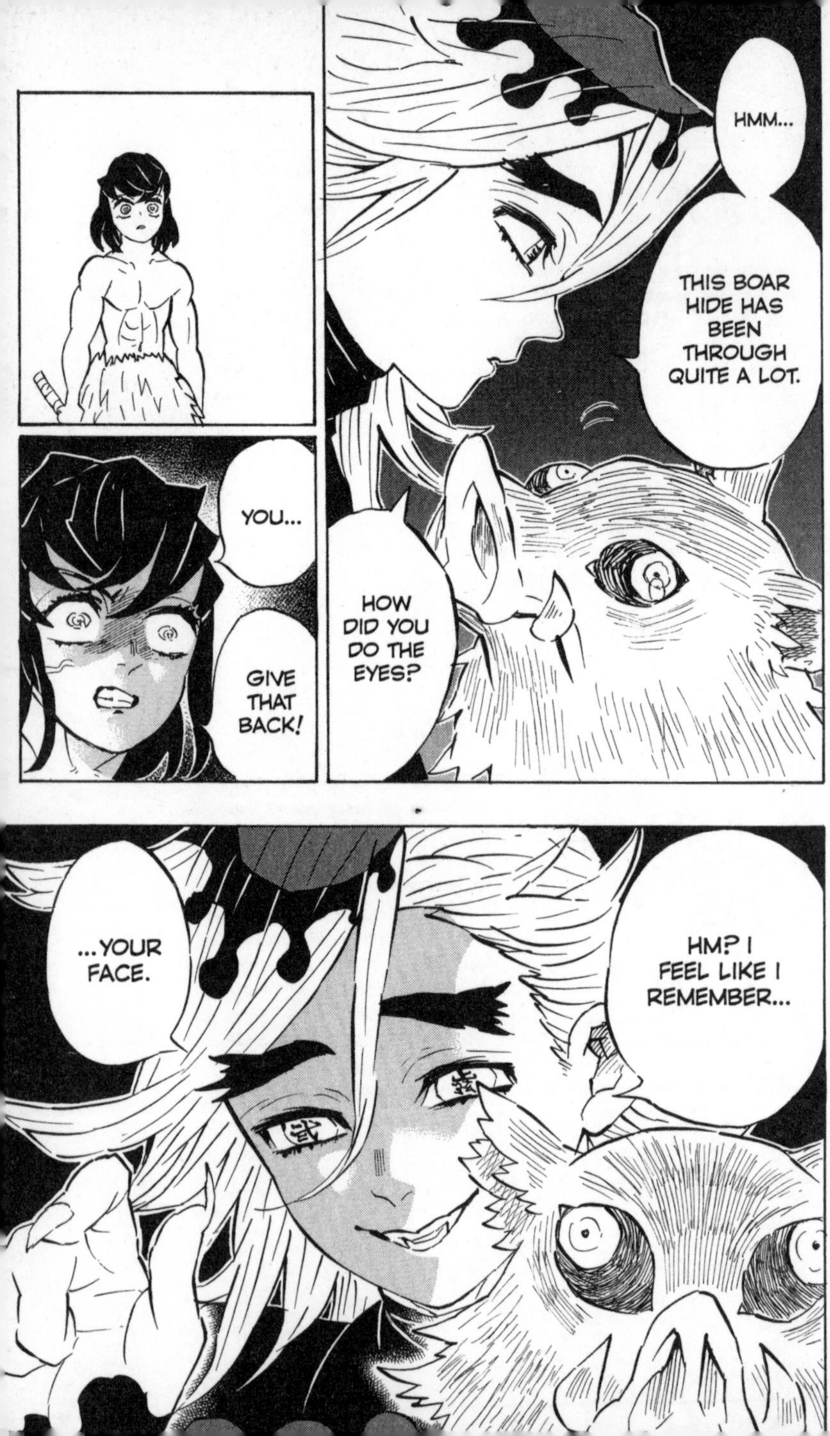
HMM...
THIS BOAR HIDE HAS BEEN THROUGH QUITE A LOT.
HOW DID YOU DO THE EYES?
YOU...
GIVE THAT BACK!
HM? I FEEL LIKE I REMEMBER...
...YOUR FACE.

JUNIOR HIGH AND HIGH SCHOOL !! KIMETSU ACADEMY

Genya Shinazugawa (16 yrs) First-year, Class Kabosu. The ace of the marksmanship club. He's no good at math, so his older brother always gets angry at him.

He won the marksmanship competition, but when he received his award at school, his brother stepped in and broke it, saying it was useless and Genya should study math more. Genya trembled as he stood on stage. Everyone had been afraid of him because of his large size and face, but this incident made his classmates sympathize with him, so he got more friends.

His hairstyle is against school rules, but when he shaved his head, his shots stopped hitting the target, so he received special permission.

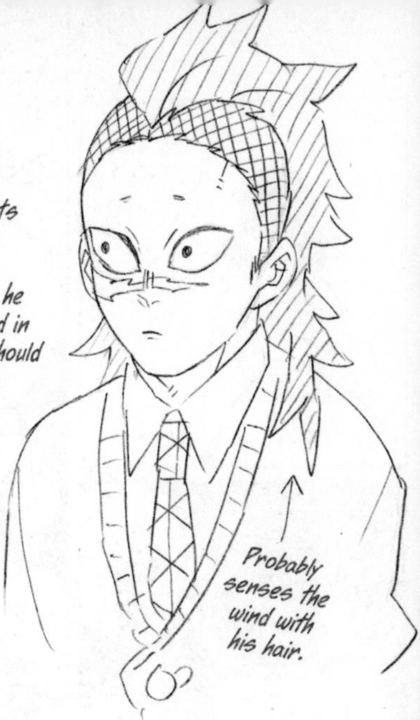
Probably senses the wind with his hair.

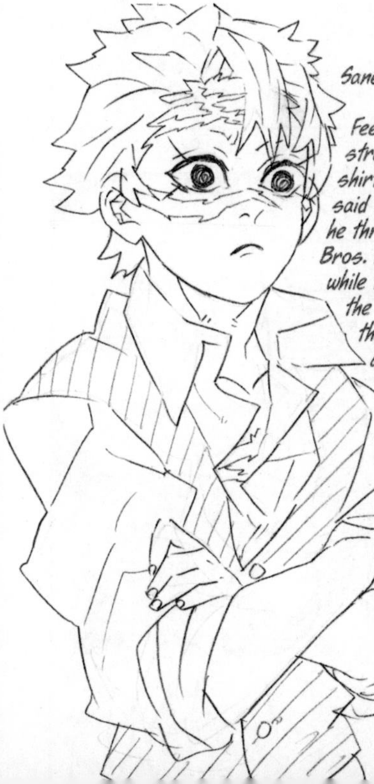

Sanemi Shinazugawa. Math teacher.

Feeling constricted around his neck stresses him out, so he always leaves his shirt unbuttoned. Once when his students said they wouldn't need math in the future, he threw them out the window like in Smash Bros. He talks to Ms. Kanae a lot, so for a while there was a plan to bump him off, but the Smash Bros. incident put an end to that. He's incredibly kind to the women, children and the elderly, but whenever he approaches children, they burst into tears. He doesn't even button his shirt for ceremonial occasions.

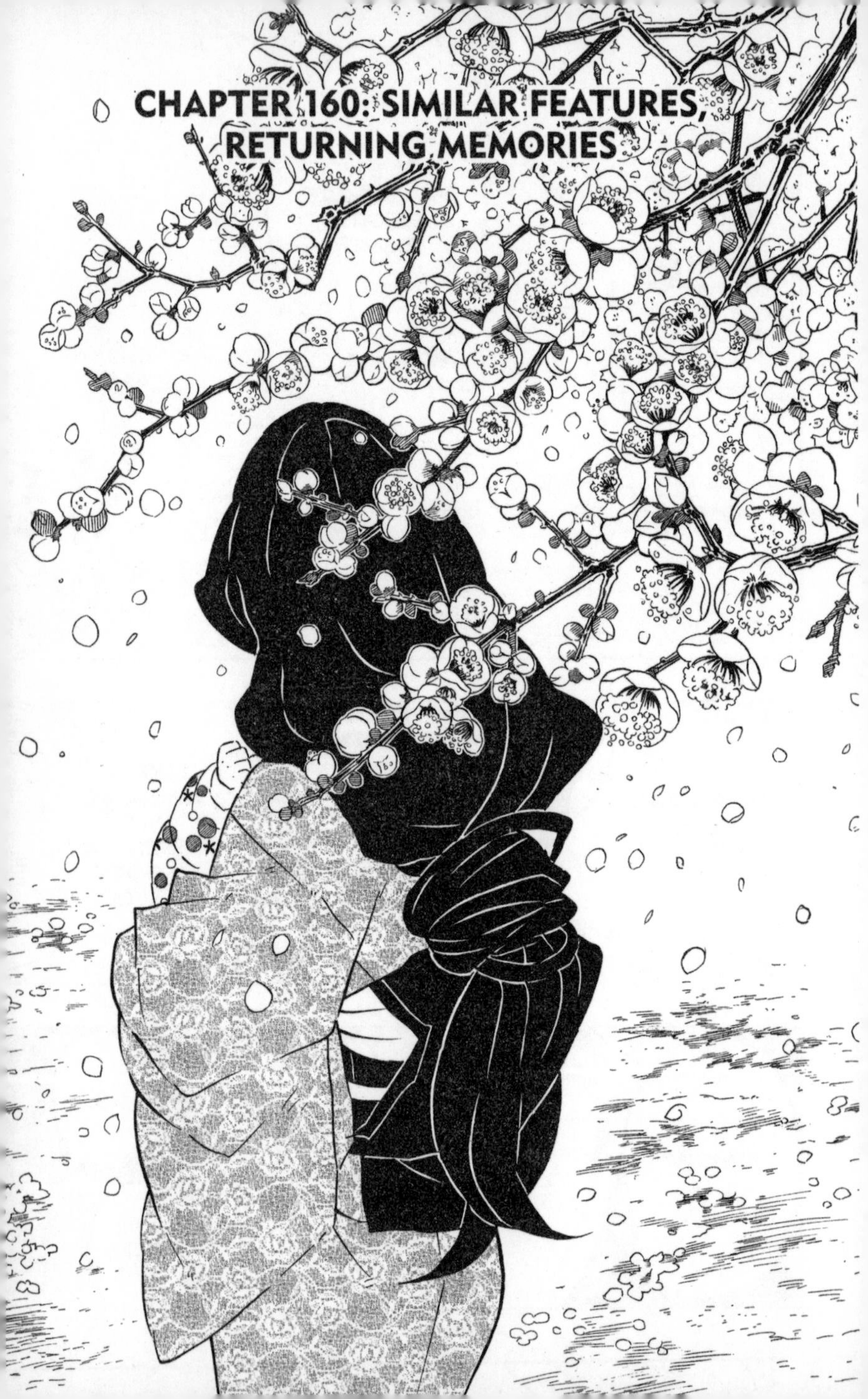
CHAPTER 160: SIMILAR FEATURES, RETURNING MEMORIES

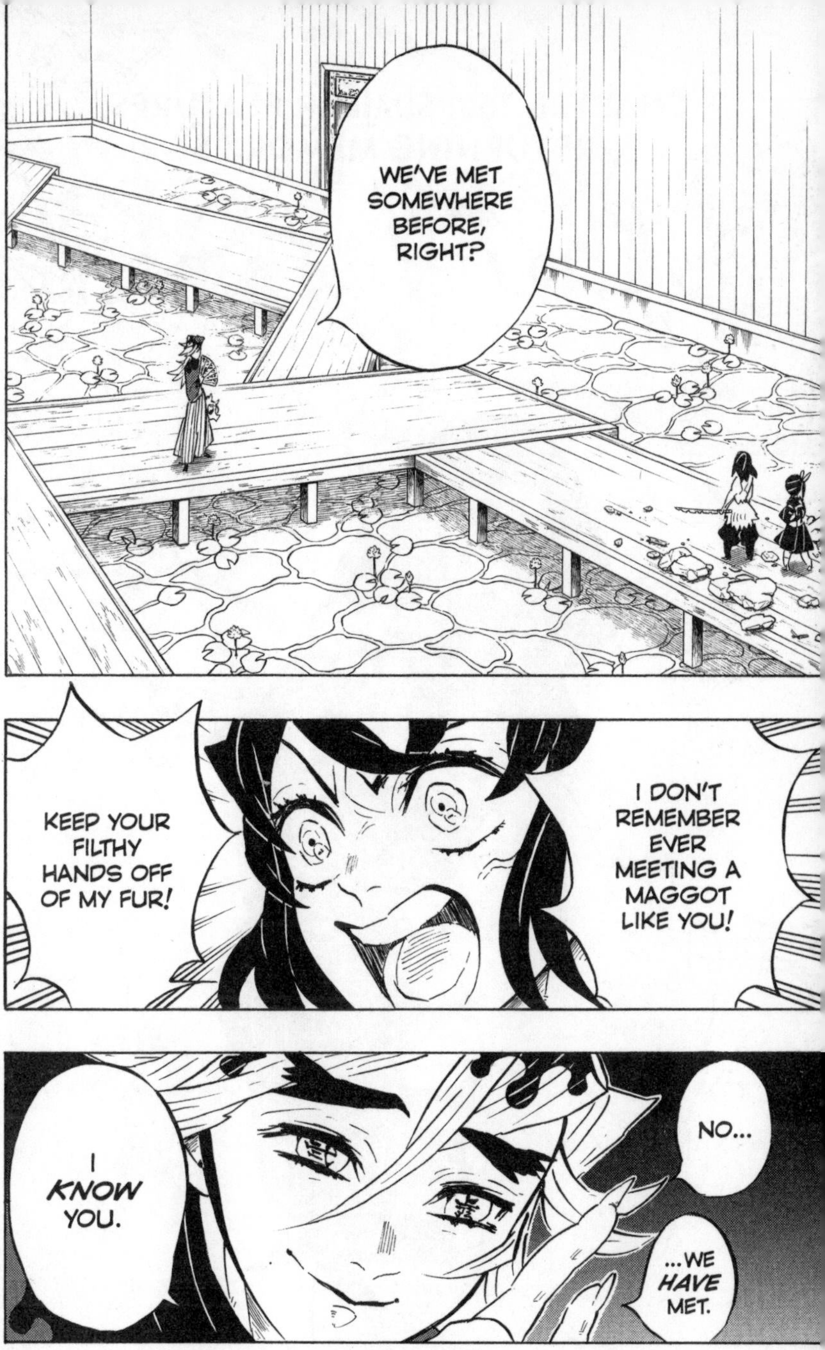
WE'VE MET SOMEWHERE BEFORE, RIGHT?
I DON'T REMEMBER EVER MEETING A MAGGOT LIKE YOU!
KEEP YOUR FILTHY HANDS OFF OF MY FUR!
NO...
...WE *HAVE* MET.
I *KNOW* YOU.

**EYES: UPPER 2*

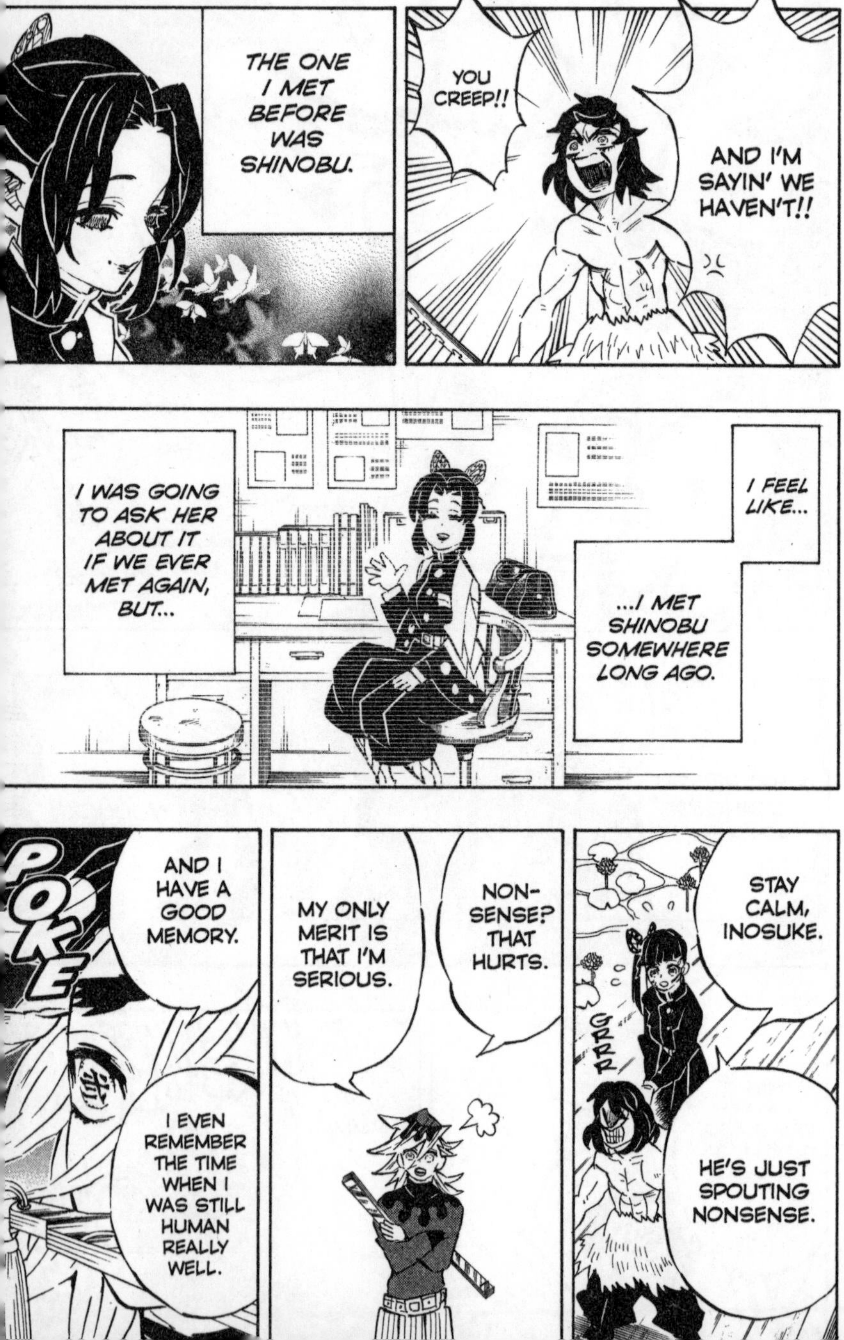
YOU CREEP!!
AND I'M SAYIN' WE HAVEN'T!!
THE ONE I MET BEFORE WAS SHINOBU.
I FEEL LIKE...
...I MET SHINOBU SOMEWHERE LONG AGO.
I WAS GOING TO ASK HER ABOUT IT IF WE EVER MET AGAIN, BUT...
STAY CALM, INOSUKE.
GRRR
HE'S JUST SPOUTING NONSENSE.
NON-SENSE? THAT HURTS.
MY ONLY MERIT IS THAT I'M SERIOUS.
POKE
AND I HAVE A GOOD MEMORY.
I EVEN REMEMBER THE TIME WHEN I WAS STILL HUMAN REALLY WELL.

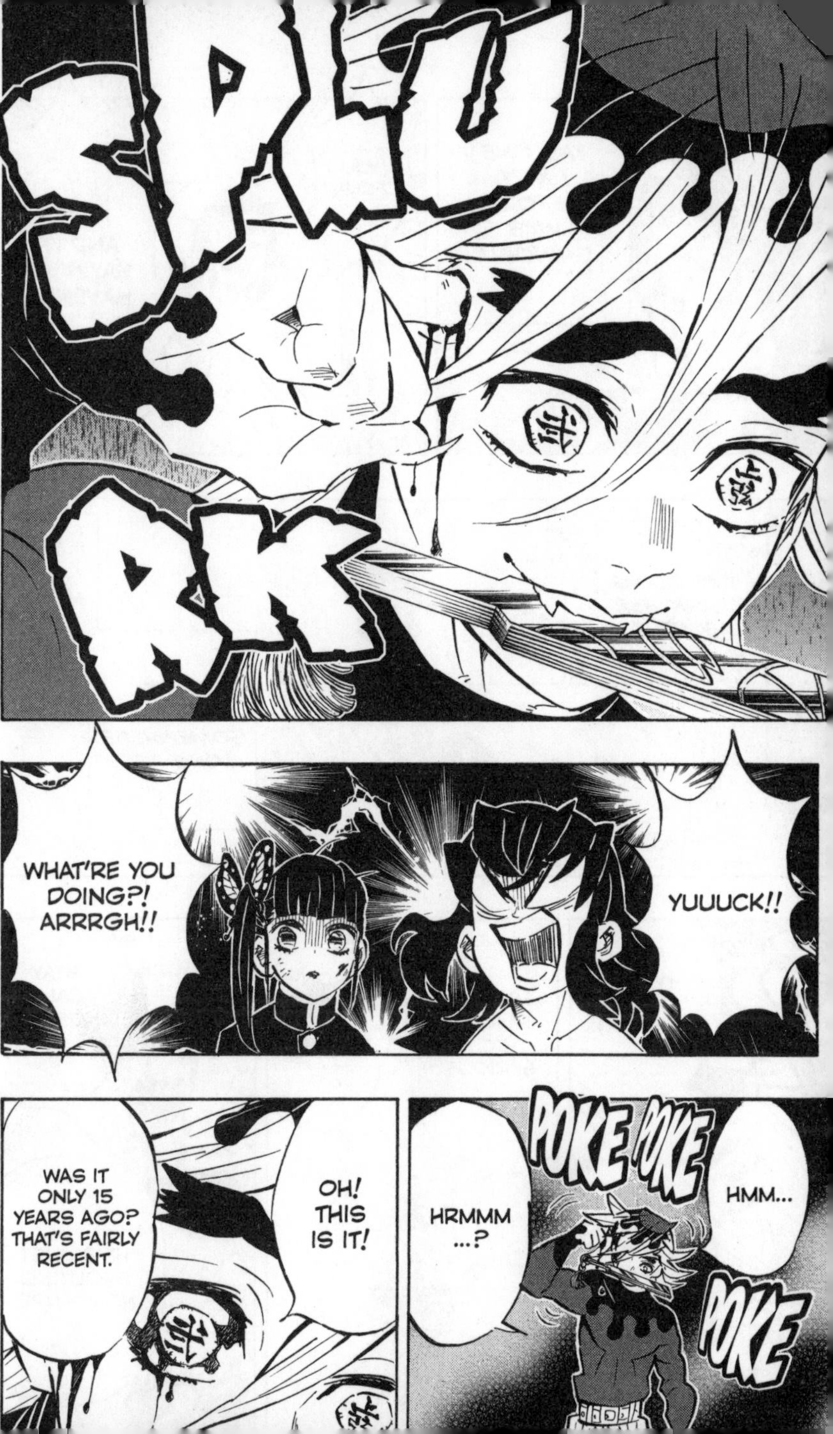
SPLU
RK
YUUUCK!!
WHAT'RE YOU DOING?! ARRRGH!!
POKE POKE
HMM...
POKE
HRMMM ...?
OH! THIS IS IT!
WAS IT ONLY 15 YEARS AGO? THAT'S FAIRLY RECENT.

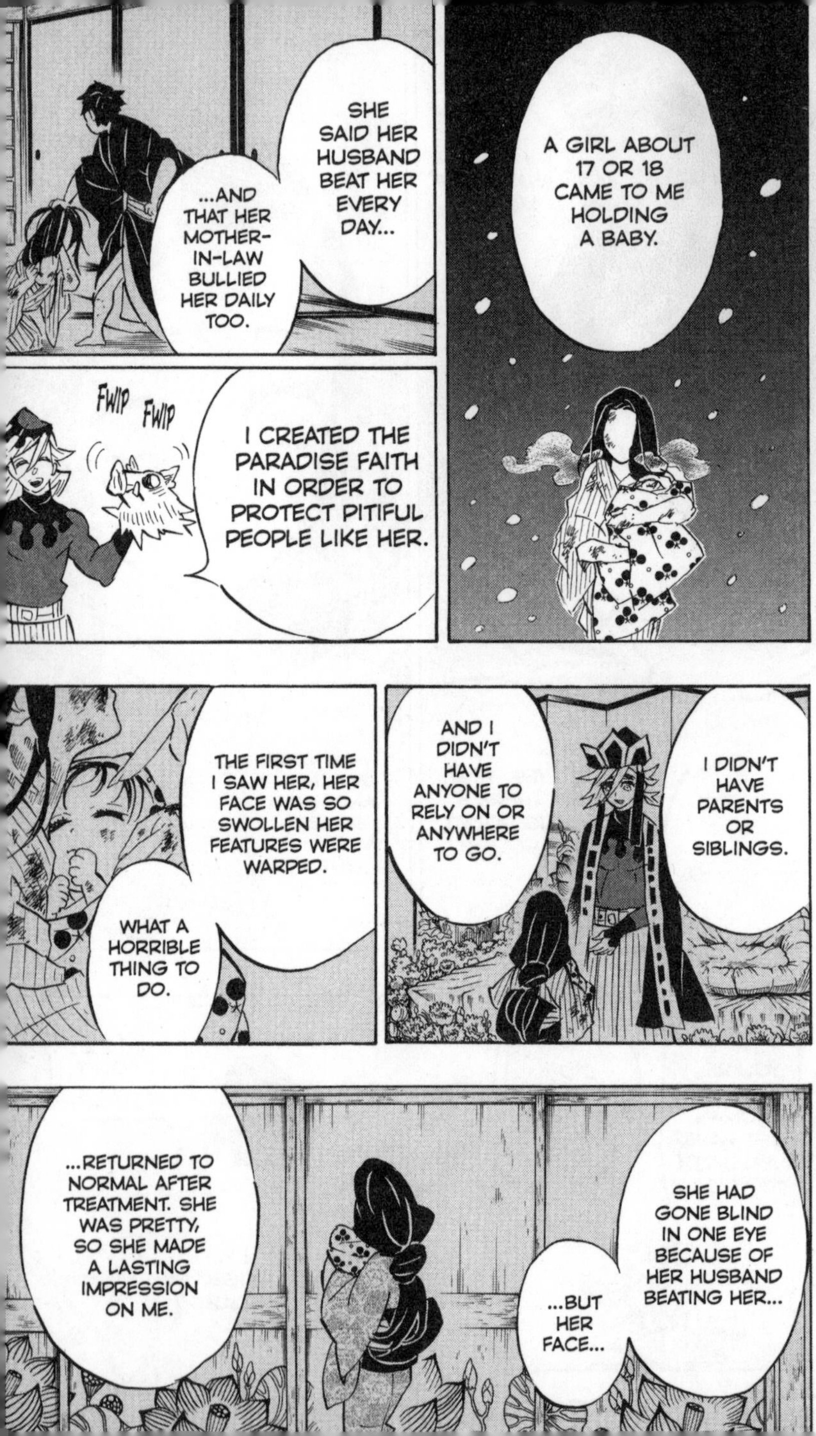
A GIRL ABOUT 17 OR 18 CAME TO ME HOLDING A BABY.
SHE SAID HER HUSBAND BEAT HER EVERY DAY...
...AND THAT HER MOTHER-IN-LAW BULLIED HER DAILY TOO.
I CREATED THE PARADISE FAITH IN ORDER TO PROTECT PITIFUL PEOPLE LIKE HER.
FWIP
FWIP
I DIDN'T HAVE PARENTS OR SIBLINGS.
AND I DIDN'T HAVE ANYONE TO RELY ON OR ANYWHERE TO GO.
THE FIRST TIME I SAW HER, HER FACE WAS SO SWOLLEN HER FEATURES WERE WARPED.
WHAT A HORRIBLE THING TO DO.
SHE HAD GONE BLIND IN ONE EYE BECAUSE OF HER HUSBAND BEATING HER...
...BUT HER FACE...
...RETURNED TO NORMAL AFTER TREATMENT. SHE WAS PRETTY, SO SHE MADE A LASTING IMPRESSION ON ME.

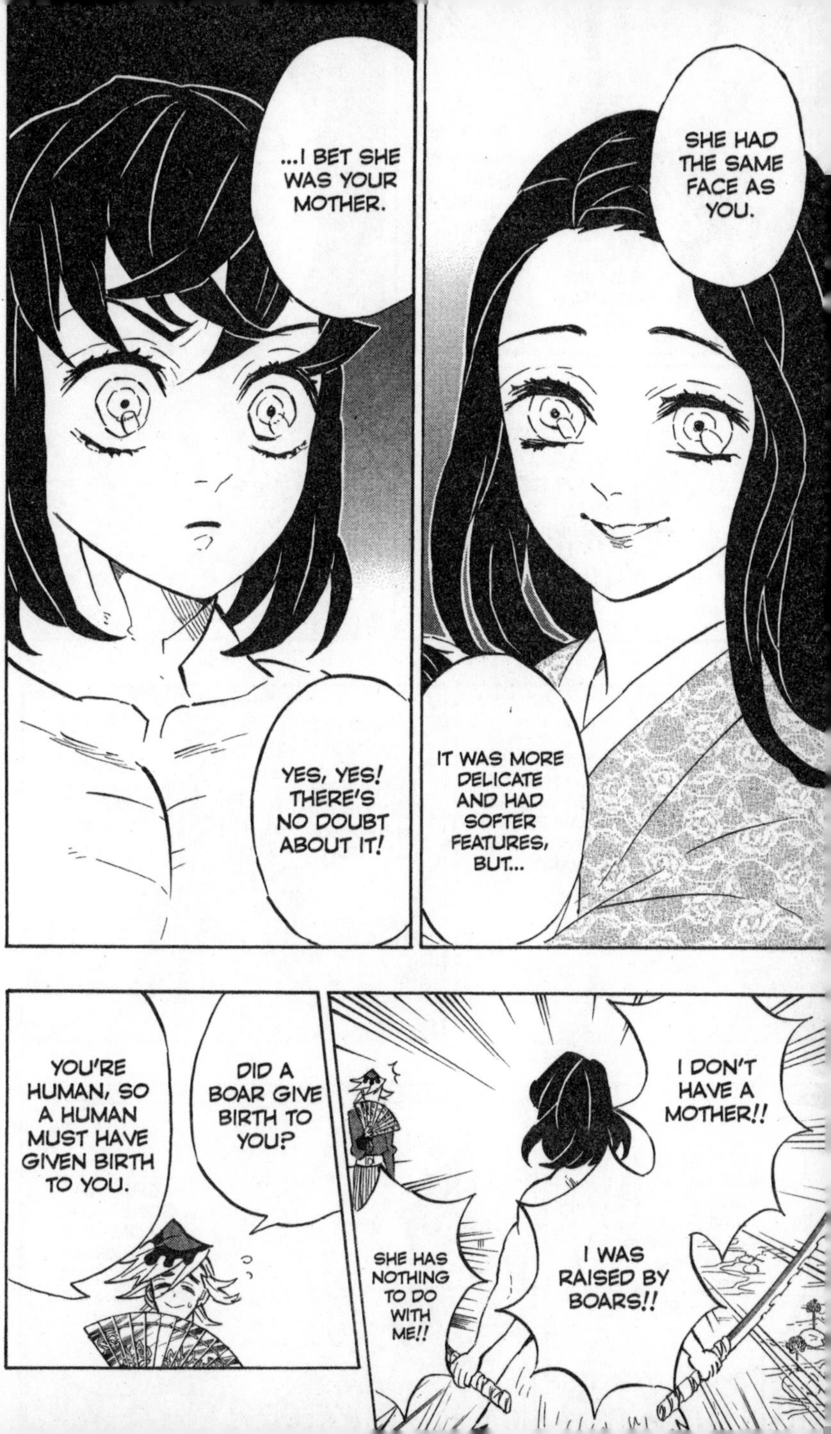
SHE HAD THE SAME FACE AS YOU.
IT WAS MORE DELICATE AND HAD SOFTER FEATURES, BUT...
...I BET SHE WAS YOUR MOTHER.
YES, YES! THERE'S NO DOUBT ABOUT IT!
I DON'T HAVE A MOTHER!!
I WAS RAISED BY BOARS!!
SHE HAS NOTHING TO DO WITH ME!!
DID A BOAR GIVE BIRTH TO YOU?
YOU'RE HUMAN, SO A HUMAN MUST HAVE GIVEN BIRTH TO YOU.

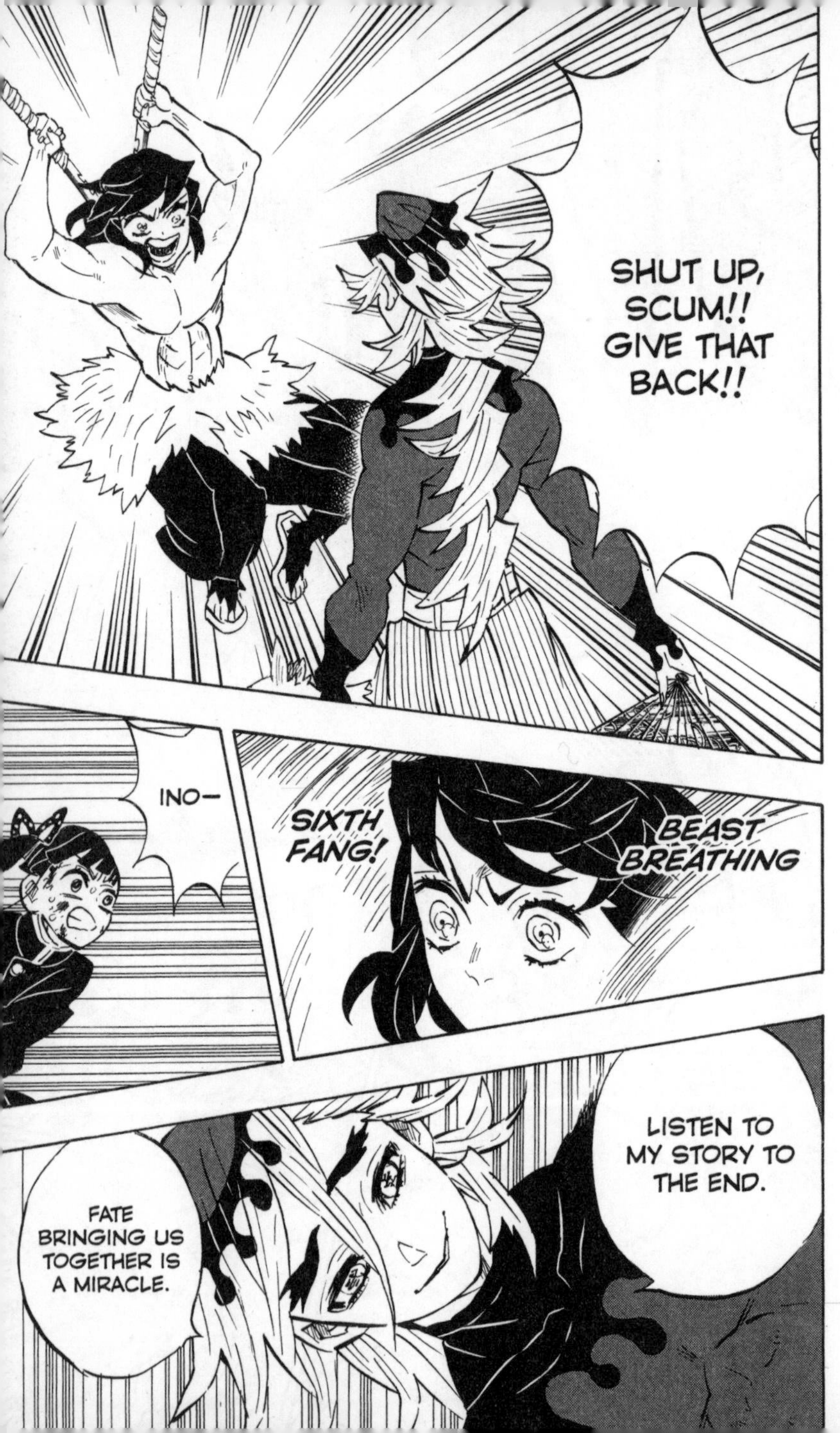
SHUT UP, SCUM!! GIVE THAT BACK!!
BEAST BREATHING
SIXTH FANG!
INO—
LISTEN TO MY STORY TO THE END.
FATE BRINGING US TOGETHER IS A MIRACLE.

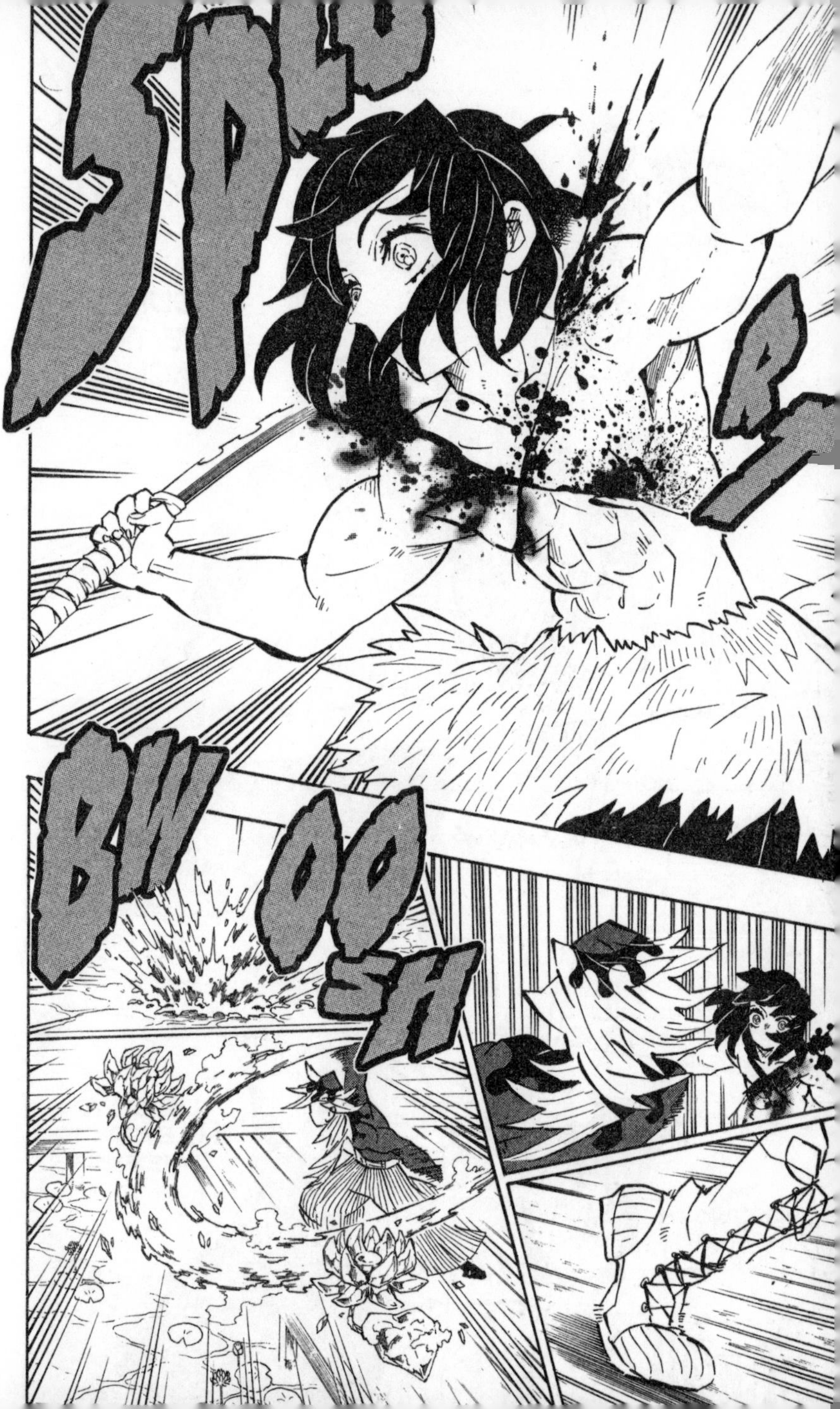
BWOOSH

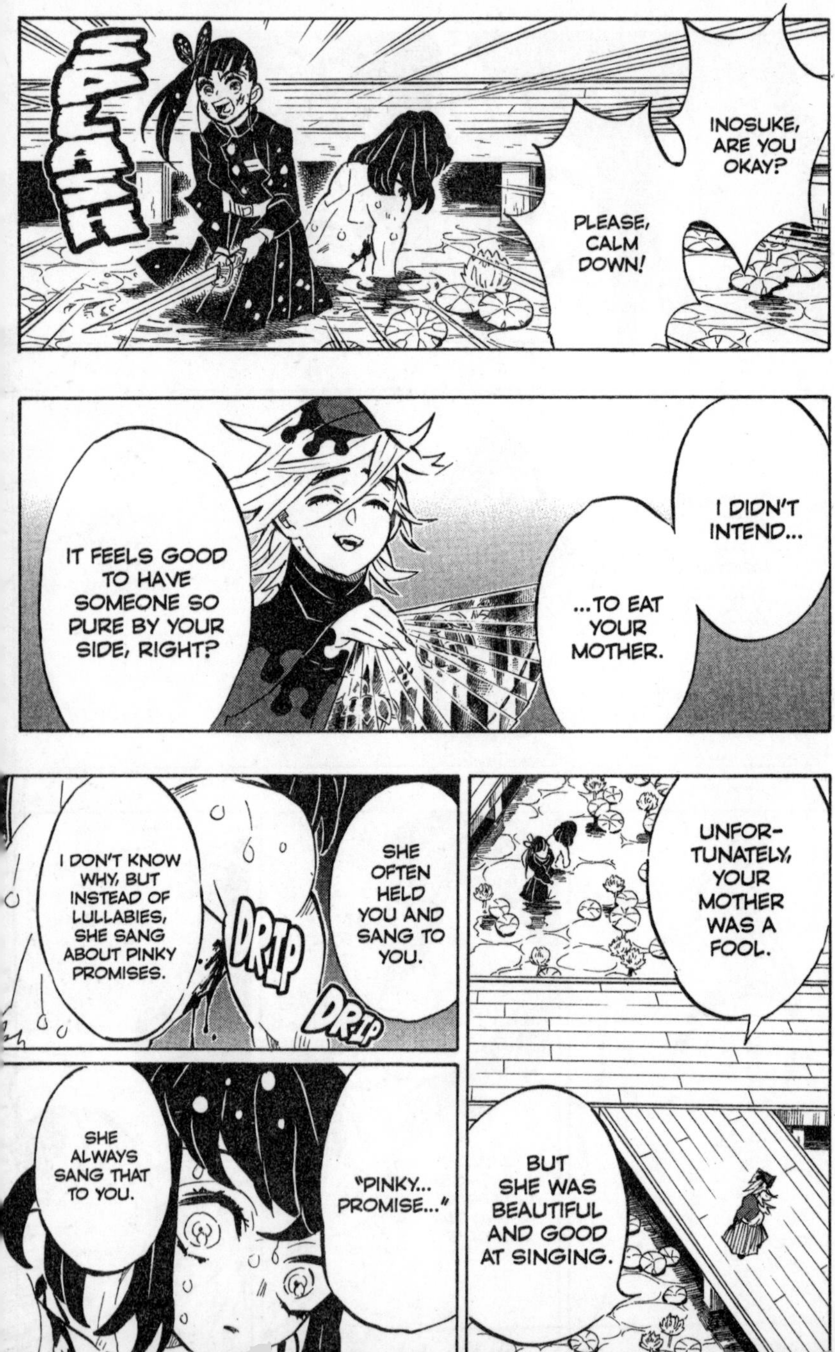
INOSUKE, ARE YOU OKAY?
PLEASE, CALM DOWN!
SPLASH
I DIDN'T INTEND...
...TO EAT YOUR MOTHER.
IT FEELS GOOD TO HAVE SOMEONE SO PURE BY YOUR SIDE, RIGHT?
UNFORTUNATELY, YOUR MOTHER WAS A FOOL.
SHE OFTEN HELD YOU AND SANG TO YOU.
I DON'T KNOW WHY, BUT INSTEAD OF LULLABIES, SHE SANG ABOUT PINKY PROMISES.
DRIP
DRIP
BUT SHE WAS BEAUTIFUL AND GOOD AT SINGING.
"PINKY... PROMISE..."
SHE ALWAYS SANG THAT TO YOU.

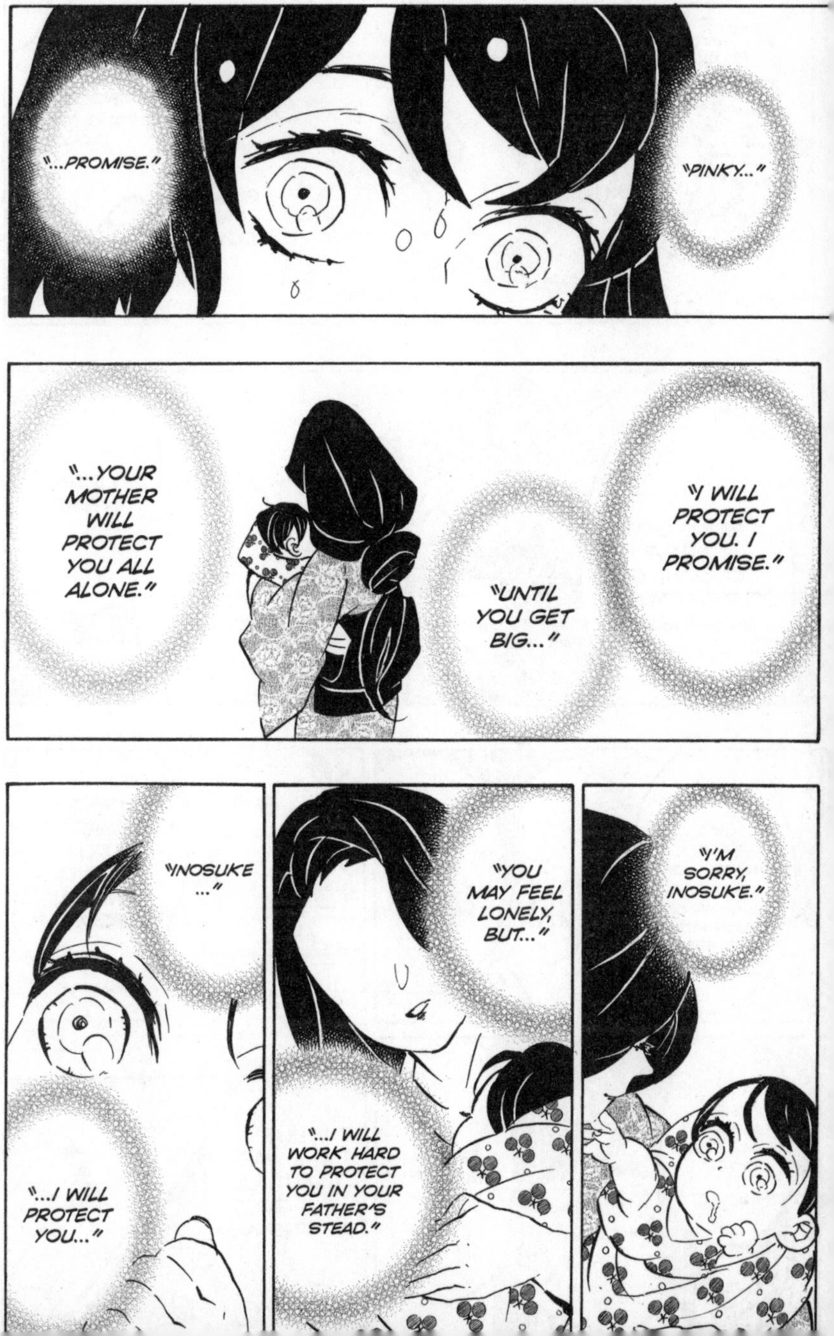
"PINKY..."
"...PROMISE."
"I WILL PROTECT YOU. I PROMISE."
"UNTIL YOU GET BIG..."
"...YOUR MOTHER WILL PROTECT YOU ALL ALONE."
"I'M SORRY, INOSUKE."
"YOU MAY FEEL LONELY, BUT..."
"...I WILL WORK HARD TO PROTECT YOU IN YOUR FATHER'S STEAD."
"INOSUKE..."
"...I WILL PROTECT YOU..."

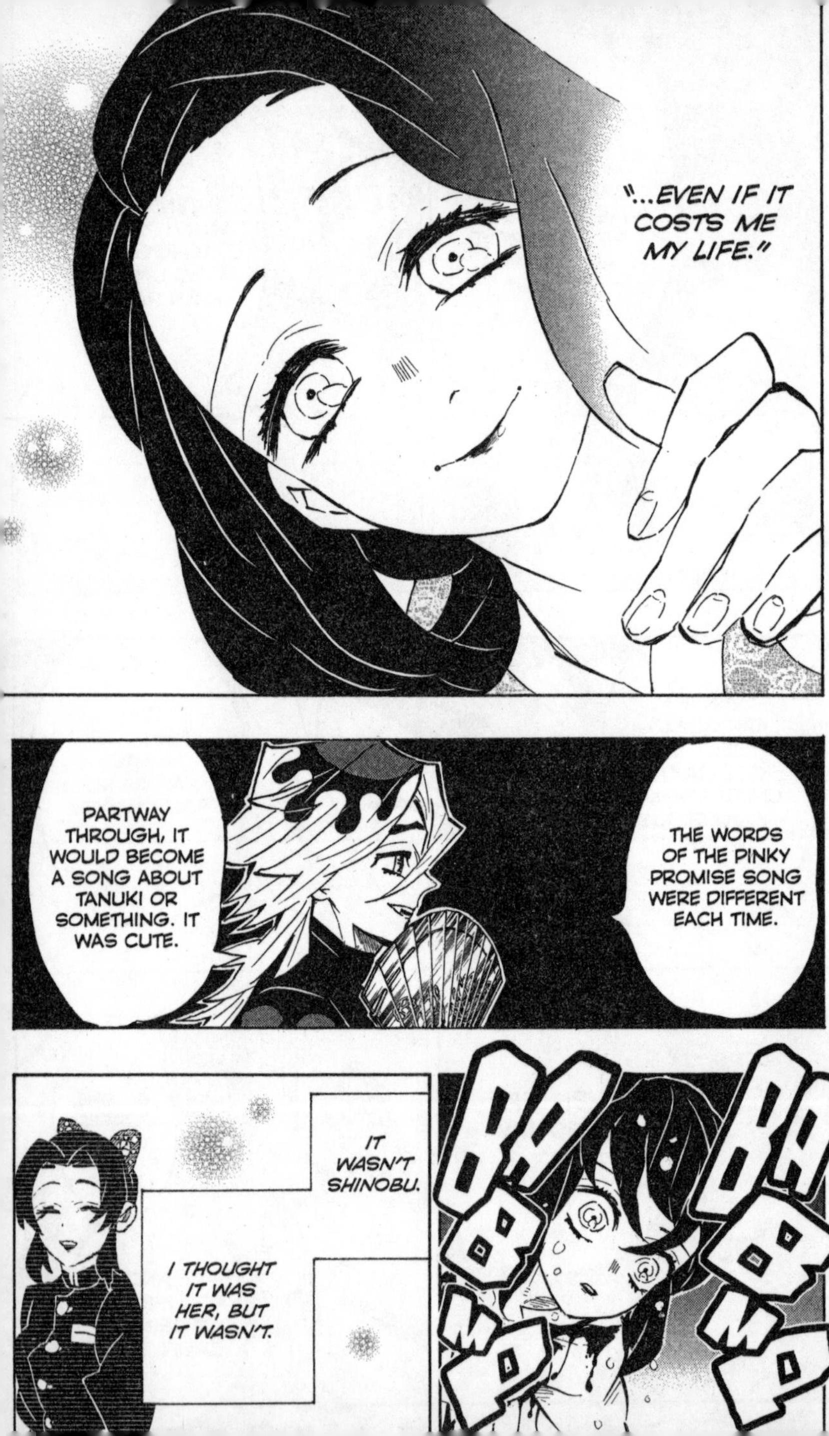
"...EVEN IF IT COSTS ME MY LIFE."
THE WORDS OF THE PINKY PROMISE SONG WERE DIFFERENT EACH TIME.
PARTWAY THROUGH, IT WOULD BECOME A SONG ABOUT TANUKI OR SOMETHING. IT WAS CUTE.
BA BMP
BA BMP
IT WASN'T SHINOBU.
I THOUGHT IT WAS HER, BUT IT WASN'T.

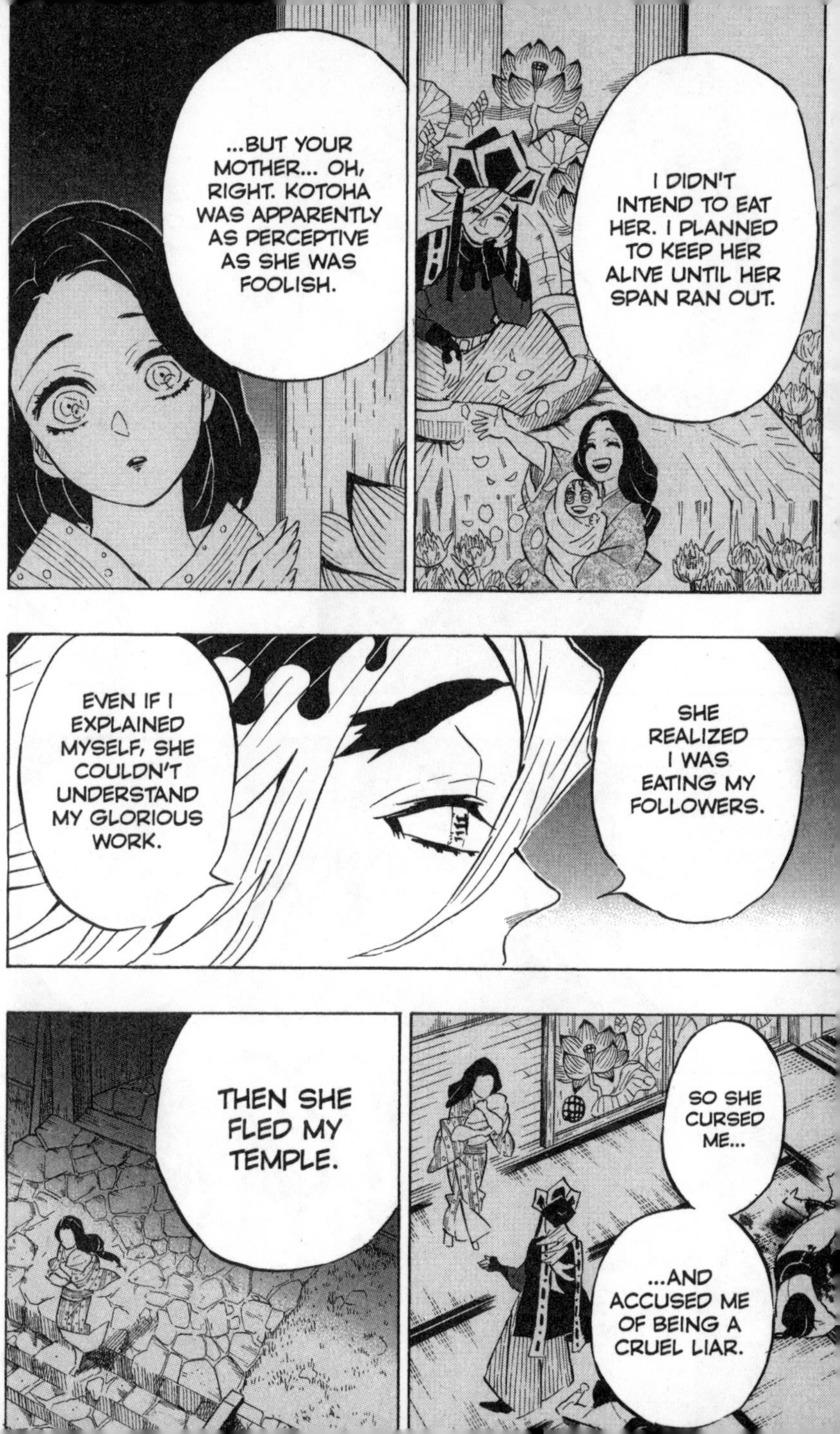
I DIDN'T INTEND TO EAT HER. I PLANNED TO KEEP HER ALIVE UNTIL HER SPAN RAN OUT.
...BUT YOUR MOTHER... OH, RIGHT. KOTOHA WAS APPARENTLY AS PERCEPTIVE AS SHE WAS FOOLISH.
SHE REALIZED I WAS EATING MY FOLLOWERS.
EVEN IF I EXPLAINED MYSELF, SHE COULDN'T UNDERSTAND MY GLORIOUS WORK.
SO SHE CURSED ME...
...AND ACCUSED ME OF BEING A CRUEL LIAR.
THEN SHE FLED MY TEMPLE.

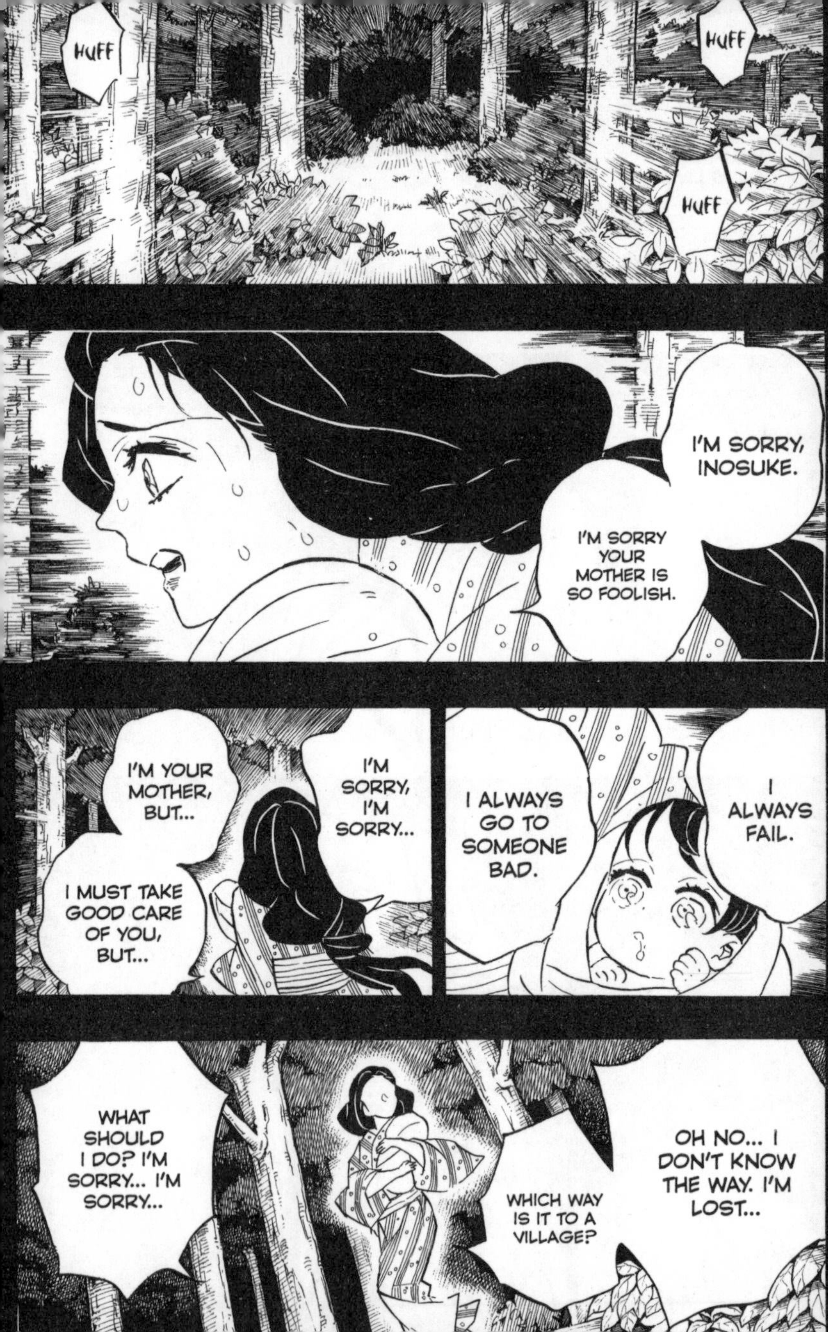
HUFF
HUFF
HUFF
I'M SORRY, INOSUKE.
I'M SORRY YOUR MOTHER IS SO FOOLISH.
I ALWAYS FAIL.
I ALWAYS GO TO SOMEONE BAD.
I'M SORRY, I'M SORRY...
I'M YOUR MOTHER, BUT...
I MUST TAKE GOOD CARE OF YOU, BUT...
OH NO... I DON'T KNOW THE WAY. I'M LOST...
WHICH WAY IS IT TO A VILLAGE?
WHAT SHOULD I DO? I'M SORRY... I'M SORRY...

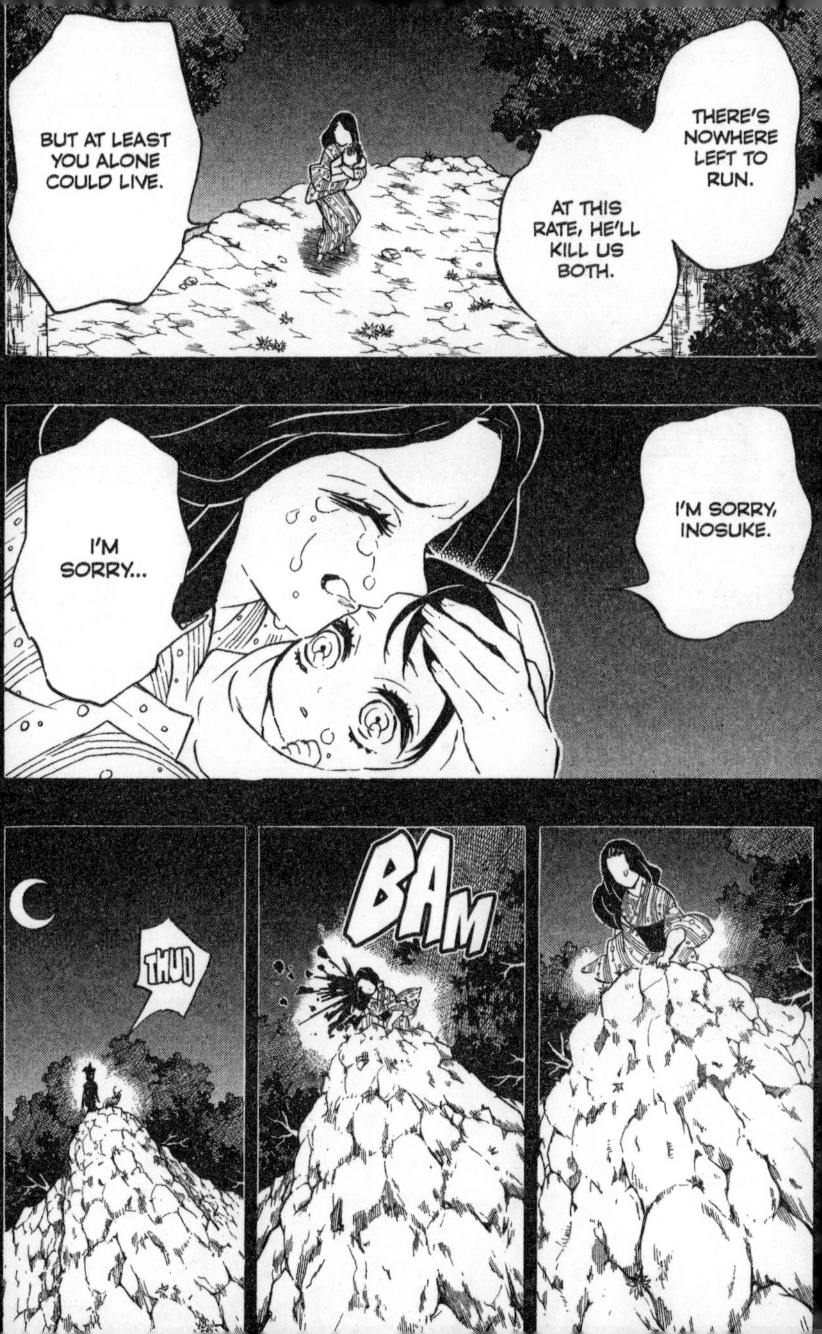
THERE'S NOWHERE LEFT TO RUN.
AT THIS RATE, HE'LL KILL US BOTH.
BUT AT LEAST YOU ALONE COULD LIVE.
I'M SORRY, INOSUKE.
I'M SORRY...
BAM
THUD

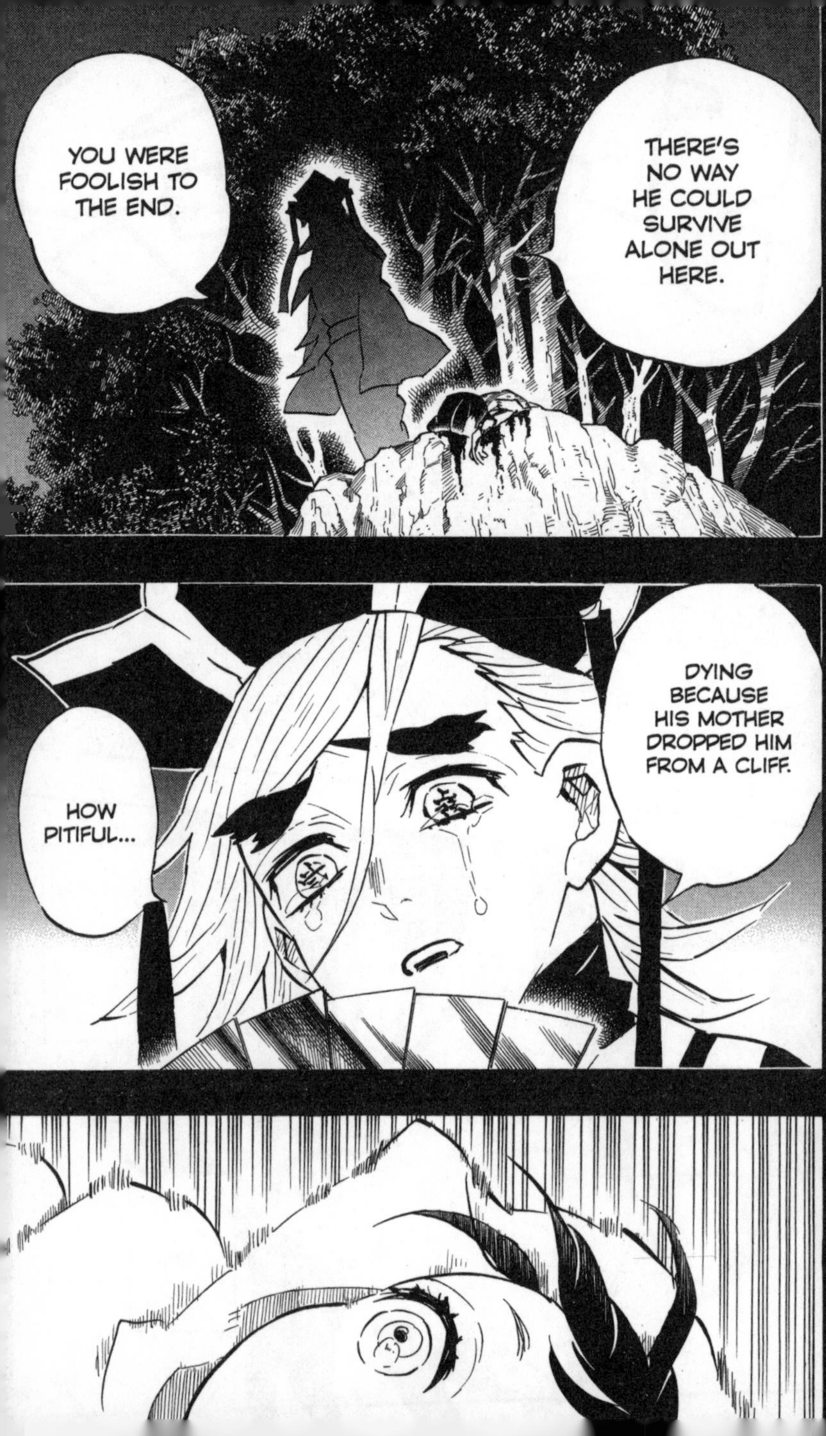
THERE'S NO WAY HE COULD SURVIVE ALONE OUT HERE.
YOU WERE FOOLISH TO THE END.
DYING BECAUSE HIS MOTHER DROPPED HIM FROM A CLIFF.
HOW PITIFUL...

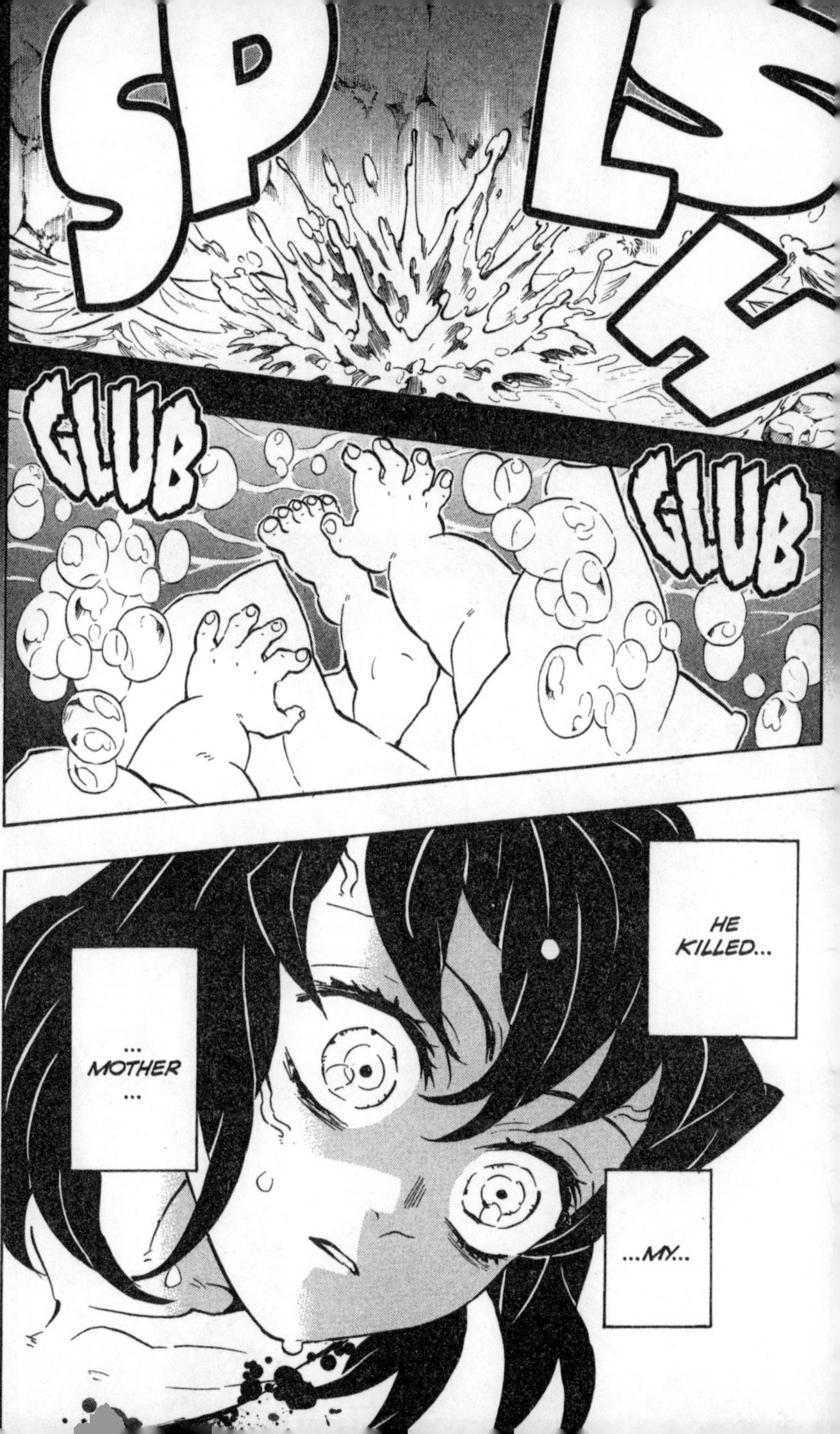
SPLASH
GLUB
GLUB
HE KILLED...
...MY...
...
MOTHER
...

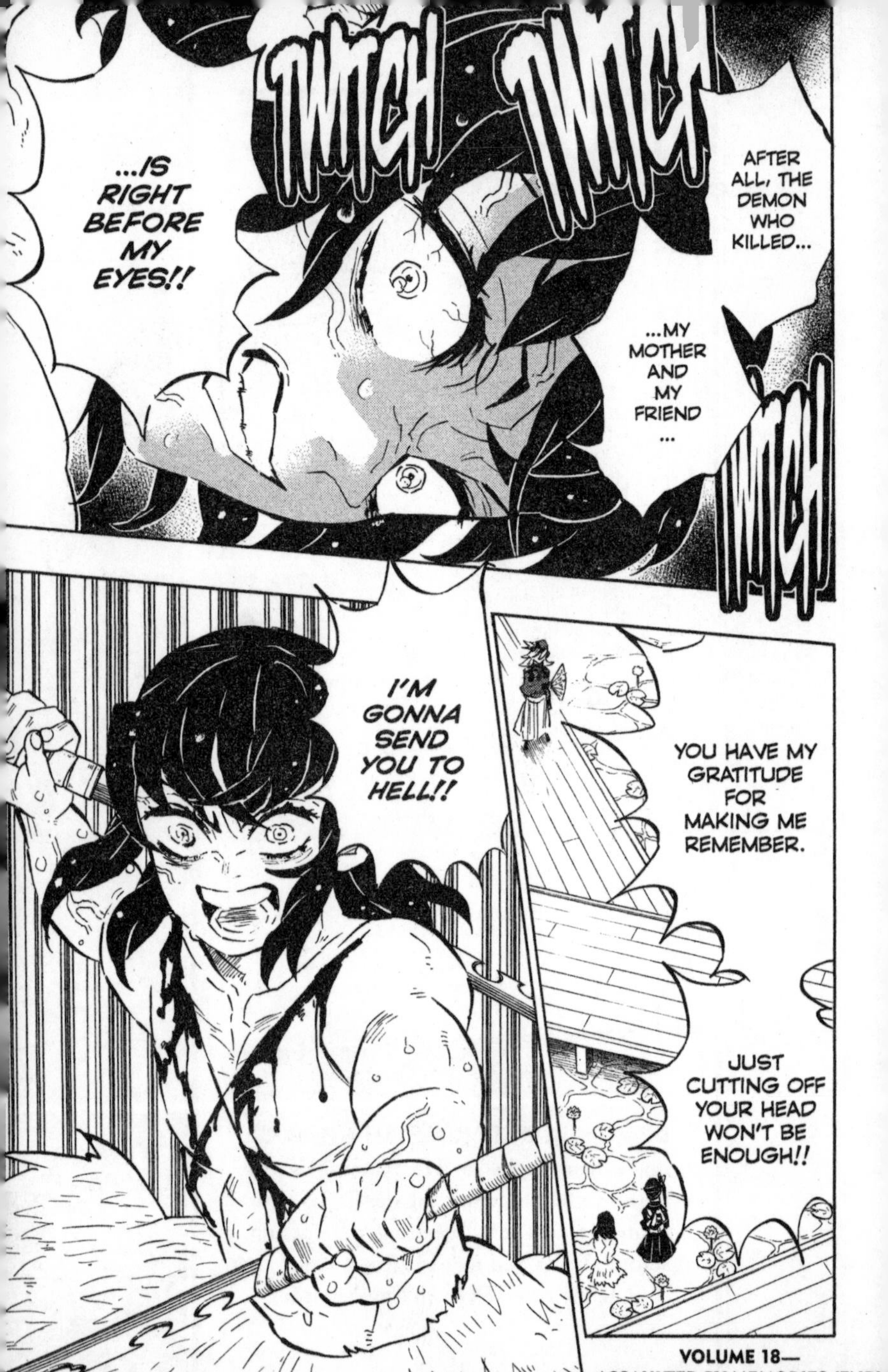
TWITCH
TWITCH
AFTER ALL, THE DEMON WHO KILLED...
...MY MOTHER AND MY FRIEND ...
TWITCH
...IS RIGHT BEFORE MY EYES!!
YOU HAVE MY GRATITUDE FOR MAKING ME REMEMBER.
JUST CUTTING OFF YOUR HEAD WON'T BE ENOUGH!!
I'M GONNA SEND YOU TO HELL!!

VOLUME 18—
ASSAULTED BY MEMORIES (END)

YOU'RE READING THE
WRONG WAY!

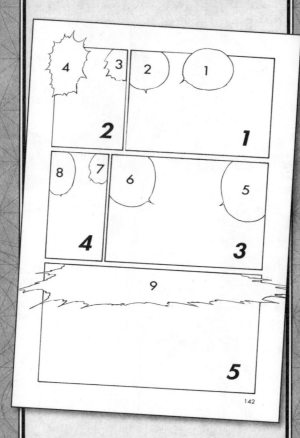

DEMON SLAYER: KIMETSU NO YAIBA reads from right to left, starting in the upper-right corner. Japanese is read from right to left, meaning that action, sound effects and word-balloon order are completely reversed from English order.

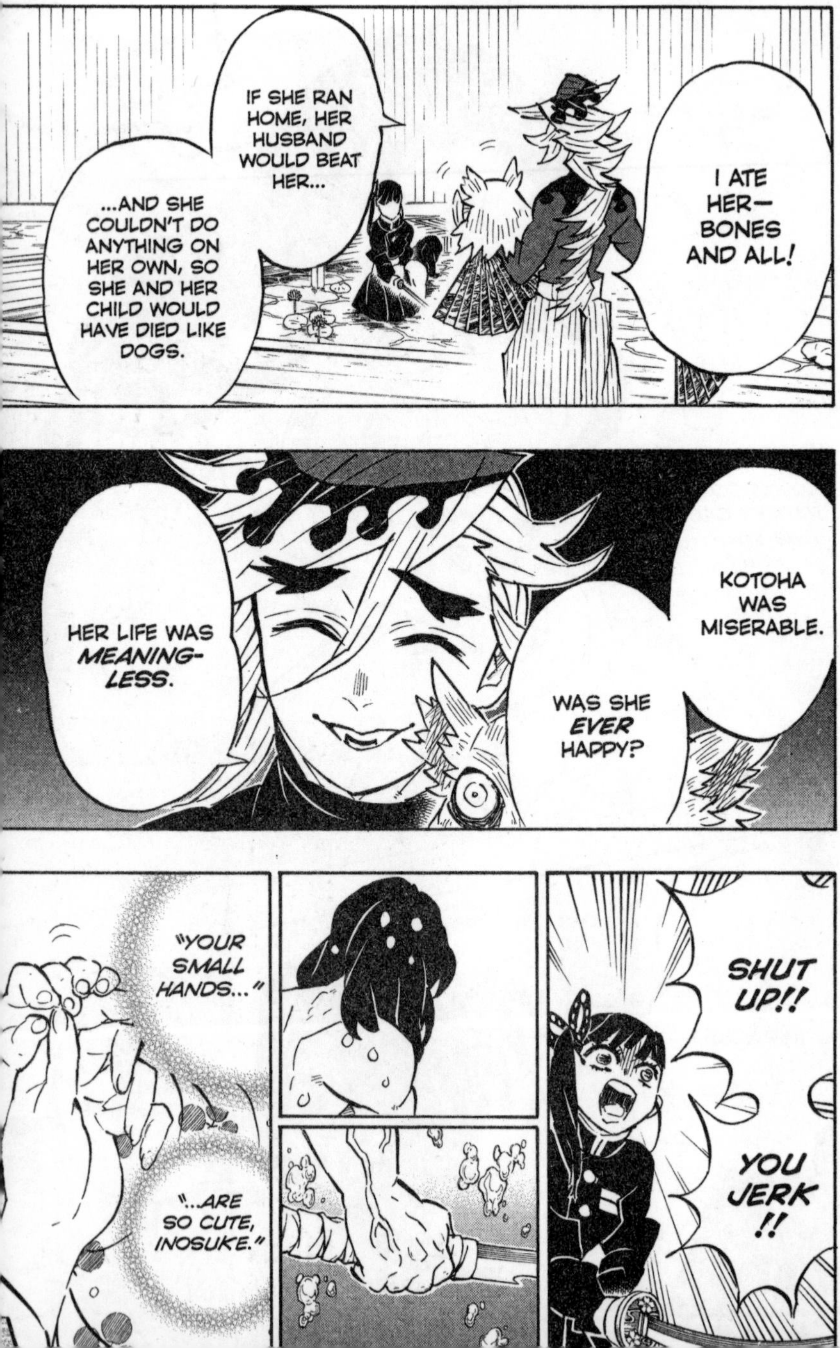
I ATE HER— BONES AND ALL!
IF SHE RAN HOME, HER HUSBAND WOULD BEAT HER...
...AND SHE COULDN'T DO ANYTHING ON HER OWN, SO SHE AND HER CHILD WOULD HAVE DIED LIKE DOGS.
KOTOHA WAS MISERABLE.
WAS SHE *EVER* HAPPY?
HER LIFE WAS *MEANING-LESS*.
SHUT UP!!
YOU JERK !!
"YOUR SMALL HANDS..."
"...ARE SO CUTE, INOSUKE."

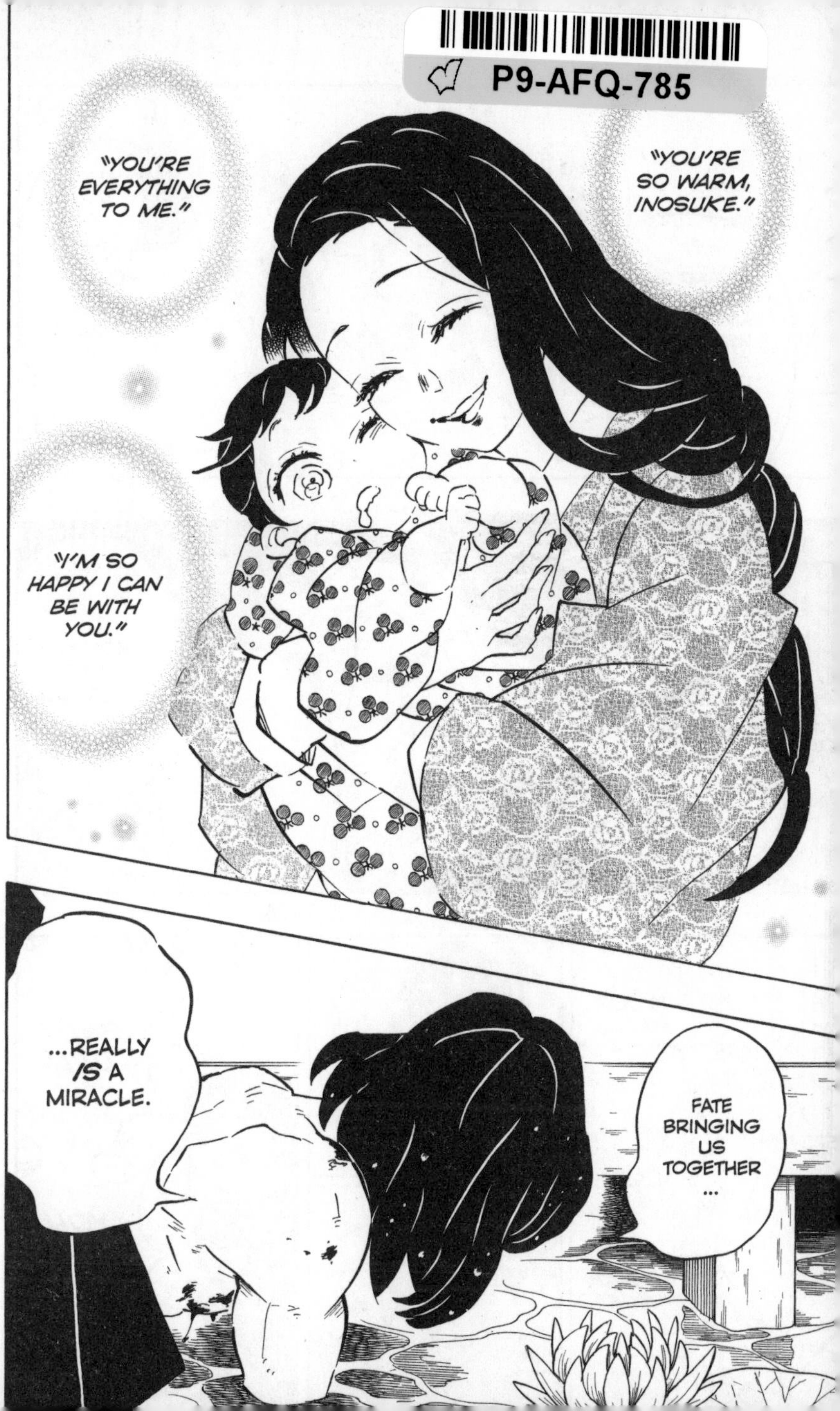
"YOU'RE SO WARM, INOSUKE."
"YOU'RE EVERYTHING TO ME."
"I'M SO HAPPY I CAN BE WITH YOU."
FATE BRINGING US TOGETHER ...
...REALLY *IS* A MIRACLE.